Capitalism and the Sea

Capitalism and the Sea

*The Maritime Factor in the
Making of the Modern World*

Liam Campling and Alejandro Colás

VERSO

London • New York

First published by Verso 2021
© Liam Campling and Alejandro Colás 2021

1 3 5 7 9 10 8 6 4 2

Verso
UK: 6 Meard Street, London W1F 0EG
US: 20 Jay Street, Suite 1010, Brooklyn, NY 11201
versobooks.com

Verso is the imprint of New Left Books

ISBN-13: 978-1-78478-523-9
ISBN-13: 978-1-78478-525-3 (UK EBK)
ISBN-13: 978-1-78478-526-0 (US EBK)

British Library Cataloguing in Publication Data
A catalogue record for this book is available from the British Library

Library of Congress Control Number
2020947418

Cover image: 'Frankfurt' by Mary Iverson, 2013,
maryiverson.com and @themaryiverson

Typeset in Sabon LT by Hewer Text UK Ltd, Edinburgh
Printed and bound by CPI Group (UK) Ltd, Croydon CR0 4YY

Liam dedicates this book to Mélodie Roulaud,
and to his mum and dad

Alex to Lalini

Contents

Contents

Figures

Tables

Acknowledgements

Some ten years ago, when we were both editors at the London-based journal *Historical Materialism*, one of us had the idea of dedicating a special issue of the journal to the relationship between capitalism and the sea. The special issue never came to light, but the sense that the project was worthwhile remained, and so in time we decided to embark together upon writing a book on the subject, combining our respective research interests in the political economy and the historical sociology of the sea. The voyage (we have failed in this text to steer clear of maritime punnery) took us to different places, both literally and figuratively, where friends and colleagues shared their valuable time and expertise to hear our argument and offer all manner of insights, comments, corrections and criticisms which we have done our best to incorporate in what follows. An informal reading group on the sea that met at Birkbeck College from time to time over the past few years has been invaluable in widening our intellectual and political horizons. We would therefore like to start by extending our gratitude to Stephanie Jones, Stewart Motha, Jonathan Stafford and David Styan for being consistently generous interlocutors in the free-flowing conversations on all sorts of maritime matters. Liam would also like to thank Jeremy Anderson, Kirsty Newsome, Adrian Smith and other members of a reading group on labour and logistics for wide-ranging and rich discussions; all of the members of the Historical Materialism and World Development Research Seminar; colleagues at the Centre on Labour and Global Production, Queen Mary University of London for the intellectual home;

Tony Lewis, Mike McCoy and, especially, Elizabeth Havice and Amanda Hamilton for many years of research collaboration on fisheries; and Steffen Fischer for research support.

The drafting of the book benefited immensely from the close reading of working chapters by Elena Baglioni, Kimberley Peters, Subir Sinha, Gagan Sood and (again) Stephanie Jones and David Styan, at a dedicated 'book lab' in 2018 hosted by Birkbeck's Politics Department. Prior to that, we had the opportunity to present some of the book's core claims at Queen Mary University of London, Birkbeck College, SOAS and the 2018 Historical Materialism Conference in London. Many thanks to all those who facilitated those occasions, and participated in the debate and discussion. Ben Richardson read much of the draft manuscript, casting a razor-sharp but thoroughly sympathetic eye over the text, which has improved it considerably. Jeremy Anderson (again), Gavin Capps, Satoshi Miyamura, Jonathan Pattenden, Clair Quentin and Theo Jennings each read a chapter and provided comments which shaped the book, but not its errors. Mike Berlin, James Dunkerley, Feyzi Ismail, Paolo Novak and Keith Nuttall are probably unaware of it, but have made us rethink various aspects of our own take on capitalism and the sea – to them we say thanks, too. Some of our initial ideas on the subject were first published as 'Capitalism and the Sea: Sovereignty, Territory and Appropriation', *Environment and Planning D*, Vol. 36, No. 4, August 2018. We are grateful to the editors of that journal and the anonymous reviewers of the paper, and also to Sebastian Budgen, who, together with two anonymous reviewers of the initial 2015 book proposal, gave us important guidance and followed the project through at Verso. Finally, thanks to John Gaunt for careful copy editing – remaining errors are our own.

Introduction

A Terraqueous Predicament

Global capitalism is a seaborne phenomenon. This simple fact gives us multiple reasons for thinking about the relationship between capitalism and the sea today. The global ocean still serves as a trade route, strategic space, fish bank and supply chain as it has since the advent of capitalism (and indeed long before then). Seabeds continue to be drilled for their fossil fuels and minerals, and coastlines developed for real estate and leisure. Container ports now act as regional hubs for the complex networks of global commerce, transferring commodities and generating value across different maritime-dependent sectors of the world economy ranging from shipbuilding to insurance, freight transport to cruises. The legacies of, and continuities in, seaborne slavery and bondage – as well as the modes of resistance and internationalism they engendered – remain central to emancipatory politics across the globe. Bioprospecting has extended capital's reach to the deepest underwater frontiers, while the offshore world accumulates, displays and recirculates the wealth, surplus and excess of the planet's super-rich populations and their often indistinguishable criminal associates. The toxic discharges of our carbon civilisation have for centuries now been absorbed by the oceans, expanding, warming and acidifying the blue-water part of the planet in ways that will bring unpredictable but irreversible consequences for the rest of the biosphere. These are all aspects of the complex interaction between capitalism and the sea that we address in this volume, showing how neither can be fully understood without the other.

I

The central concern animating the book is the creative destruction that accompanies the reproduction of a *social* system like capitalism in its interaction with a *natural* force like the sea. Ocean winds, currents, tides and weather patterns have combined with biochemical and geophysical characteristics like salinity, acidity, density and temperature, or natural features such as sandbanks, reefs, lagoons, inlets and shallows to produce specific risks, unique logistical difficulties and singular geographical obstacles in the way of capitalist accumulation. For all its power to subsume most of planetary life under the logic of commodity exchange, capitalism regularly confronts geophysical barriers to its own self-expansion, which in the case of the sea are especially challenging. This is largely because the high seas cannot be permanently occupied and settled as is the case on land, thus complicating capital's need to punctuate its constant circulation with the spatial fixes that secure surplus creation. By the same token, from its inception in the 'long' sixteenth century, capitalism has found in the sea a vital conduit for long-distance trade – including that in humans – and the place from which to embark on colonial ventures critical to its own existence. For capital, the sea thus presents both risks and opportunities. It has periodically acted as a site and source of competitive innovation and experimentation in finance, technology, insurance, labour regimes and spatial governance, as well as a major geophysical hurdle in the appropriation of nature through the enclosure and commodification of the sea. In turn, the expanded reproduction of capital has radically transformed the nature of the oceans, particularly since industrialisation. It has reshaped coastlines and reconfigured marine ecosystems through dredging, dumping, depletion and discharging. Together with global warming, the concentration of greenhouse gases in the oceans is drastically altering the biochemical attributes of the sea, and with it generating changes in marine geophysics manifest in ocean stratification, more frequent and more intense extreme-weather events, and coral bleaching, among other deleterious phenomena.

The starting point of this book is therefore the fundamental, but often overlooked, fact that the Earth's geographical separation into land and sea has significant consequences for capitalist development. Our terraqueous predicament – simply meaning 'consisting of land and water' – has from the beginning forced different land-based societies to reckon with the bountiful but potentially ferocious energy of the liquid vastness that covers seven-tenths of the planet – adapting, creating and transforming diverse coastal and marine spaces, institutions and cosmologies to human habitation and social reproduction.[1] But the historical specificity of capitalist social formations, with their inherent drive for the competitive accumulation of surplus value, has bestowed them with a special relationship with the oceans. The distinctive features of capitalism as a mode of production continuously seek to transcend the land–sea binary in an incessant quest for profit, thereby engendering new articulations of terraqueous territoriality – that is, uniquely capitalist alignments of sovereignty, exploitation and appropriation in the capture and coding of maritime spaces and resources. Although various human societies have through time engaged in different conceptions and practices of terraqueous territoriality, it is capitalism – particularly in its industrial form – which has intensified the relationship between land and sea, incorporating the oceans into the law of value, extending maritime commodity frontiers and attempting in the process to 'flatten' the geophysical division between solid ground and fluid water.[2]

While insisting that there are ineradicable material properties attached to land and sea, the chapters that follow also assume that they change in time and place. We are therefore necessarily addressing a socio-natural relation between the terrestrial and the marine which capital has sought to both channel and overcome in different spatio-temporal contexts. This is an interaction, moreover, shaped by both sociopolitical contestation and cooperation (involving state agencies, trade unions, companies and international organisations, among other bodies) over the parcelisation of the sea – but rarely under geographical conditions of their own choosing. Ours, then, is a contribution to the long-standing and mutually enriching exchange between historical materialism and political-economic geography in its widest acceptance (including the exploitation of fishers and seafarers, the appropriation of marine life and the ordering of maritime space).[3] It is organised around three broadly spatial phenomena (order, appropriation, offshore) and three mainly temporal processes (circulation, exploitation, logistics), although plainly this division is a matter of relative emphasis, rather than absolute contrast.

The book conceives of capitalism as a mode of production with its own distinctive logic of competitive production and accumulation of value through the appropriation of nature, which nonetheless finds diverse expression in concrete social formations across different geographical and historical contexts. Our principal objective is to offer an analytical framework through which to understand these various settings where capitalism interacts with the sea. Underlying this aim is an argument regarding the centrality of the 'maritime factor' in the origins and development of capitalism, while simultaneously making a case for the reciprocal impact of the law of value upon the saltwater world. At play here is the dual use of 'factor' as both a socio-natural force with its own material properties and effects (in our case, the sea), and the more specific etymology connected to the human figure of the commercial agent, or company representative posted to overseas 'factories' (trading ports). The remainder of this introduction identifies the theoretical commitments informing the rest of the book, in particular elaborating on our own understanding of the temporalities and spatialities that characterise the interface between capitalism and the oceans, as well as the vital experiences of those peoples living near the sea, from the sea and at sea during the modern period.

Temporalities

The much-quoted poem 'The Sea is History' by St Lucian Nobel laureate Derek Walcott has become a shorthand for the complex and overlapping conceptions of historical time that accompany modernity's relationship with the sea. From the perspective of many Americans and Caribbeans of African descent, the answer to the loaded question 'but where is your Renaissance?' is: 'Sir, it is locked in them sea-sands / out there past the reef's moiling shelf, where the men-o'-war floated down'.[4] Contrary to the common perception of the sea as a smooth horizon of opportunity which simply connects one market to another, merely acting as a surface in the realisation of masculinist reveries of adventure and enrichment, the ocean seabeds – not just of the Atlantic – can also be seen as the underwater resting place, both real and imagined, of lives sacrificed and destroyed at sea. 'Whenever a fleet of ships gave chase to slave ships', Martinican author Édouard Glissant says of the Middle Passage,

> it was easiest just to lighten the boat by throwing cargo overboard, weighing it down with balls and chains. These underwater signposts mark the course between the Gold Coast and the Leeward Islands. Navigating the green splendor of the sea – whether in melancholic transatlantic crossings or glorious regattas or traditional races of *yoles* and *gommiers* – still brings to mind ... these deeps, with their punctuation of scarcely corroded balls and chains ... the entire sea gently collapsing in the end into the pleasures of sand, make one vast beginning, but a beginning whose time is marked by these balls and chains gone green.[5]

For Elizabeth Deloughrey, one of the most articulate advocates of the 'tidalectics' involved in such trans-oceanic histories, 'the sea does not merely facilitate modernity, but is constituted by it.'[6] This is a strong claim, which we wish to both endorse and qualify here. The perception, conception and lived experience of

5

the sea have certainly been transformed by the economic, political, cultural and technological forces of modernity. Modernity, too, we shall be insisting, has been fundamentally moulded by the sea. Yet what is at stake in Deloughrey's statement is both the periodisation of this relationship between modernity and the oceans, and the recognition of multiple, overlapping and sometimes contradictory temporalities operating during this epoch. We place special emphasis upon capitalist development as setting the pace of this interaction between modernity and the sea: a historical specificity of capitalism which nonetheless also carries unsimultaneous temporalities, like those of the Middle Passage. Plainly the 'submarine unity' that Barbadian author Kamau Brathwaite identifies with the underwater connections across an archipelago of African diasporas also applies to other seagoing civilisations, both during and before the modern period.[7] Several centuries before the Roman Empire constructed its famed road network, the coastal peoples of Atlantic Europe had established a dense lattice of 'seaways' – the Gaelic *astar mara*, the Norse *veger*, or *hwael-weg* (the 'whale's way') in Old English – which linked today's northern Spain with England, France and Ireland, as well as the Atlantic and Baltic beyond.[8] Seafaring populations of the Pacific have, for centuries, developed intricate cosmologies that conceive of the waters surrounding them as a 'sea of islands', while the Norse and Icelandic sagas reflect a rich culture of maritime trade, skill, plunder, conquest and enslavement where the oceans become an active historical force.[9]

The enormity of the Atlantic slave trade was thus unprecedented not because of the underwater connections it spawned, but in its repurposing of the age-old institution of slavery to the requirements of capitalist accumulation. The slave trade integrated the merchandise of captive Africans into the emerging seaborne world market, thereby contributing to the process of capitalist development in Europe. The sea played a key role in this experience, acting both as the main conduit for human trafficking on an industrial scale, and as the site for the production of geographical distance necessary in the generation of profit through conveyance. Viewed from the depths of the Atlantic and the holds of the slave ships that criss-crossed it, there is therefore something historically peculiar about the modern ways of social reproduction at and through the sea. The capitalist mode of production – born on land, but from the beginning facing the oceans – has been the central driver of this special terraqueous relationship. Moreover, due to its uneven and protracted geohistorical development, capitalism has imbued this association with distinctive temporalities.

Consider the notion of 'value' when applied to the transatlantic slave trade. The bondspeople awaiting sale and transportation in the coastal barracoons and floating factories of West Africa found themselves at the confluence of two different, albeit compatible, logics of wealth creation: one based around practices of slave raiding, tribute, debt repayment and war booty; the other premised on the commercial trade in humans, inserted into a wider transnational commodity market. Both of these had long antecedents in Africa, Europe, the Americas and beyond, but by the beginning of the sixteenth century it was the latter expression of racialised profit making through 'civil slavery' that came to dominate human trafficking across the Atlantic. 'One might say,' Robin Blackburn suggests in an effort at specifying the modernity of Atlantic slavery, 'that many Roman slaves were sold because they had been captured, while many African slaves entering the Atlantic trade had been captured so they might be sold.'[10] European traders had created a new market in chattel slavery as they founded plantation colonies first in the Canaries, Madeira and Cape Verde, and thereafter in the Americas. But African captives had to be, in Stephanie E. Smallwood's phrase, *turned into* Atlantic commodities.[11] This required a multifaceted and extended process of deracination, classification, subjection and surveillance through both physical violence and confinement, as well as various methods of inducing 'social death'.[12]

7

Here, the ocean is not merely a barrier to circulation but a *place*, and the ship a site of social disciplining. It is unsurprising that such practices of subjection were principally conducted in the liminal zones of coastal forts, as the Atlantic Ocean became a real, not simply figurative, place where diverse African individuals were transformed into the generic racialised Negro labourer by the time of their New World landings. As Sowande' M. Mustakeem has argued,

> It is not enough to say that Africans were captured, transformed into commodities, shipped out of Africa, sold to interested buyers, and turned into slaves once moved into plantation. The human manufacturing process and, more importantly, the interior holds of merchant ships served as vital sites of power sailors used to dehumanize captives, enforce dependency, inflict pain, establish authority and prohibit any sense of control over one's own personal life.[13]

The Middle Passage thus produced both use- and exchange-value in that commodified bondspeople shipped from one coast were brutally primed for, and subsequently sold into, plantation labour for a profit on another shore. This surplus was, moreover, integrated into, and put to further profitable work within, complex circuits of capitalist finance, insurance, shipping and other marine-related industries along the Atlantic seaboards. The forced transportation of millions across the Atlantic Ocean involved the production of value through movement in that the human cargo of modern slave ships was transformed in space, arriving in places where they could be 'valued' and sold as property. The specific psycho-physical attributes of captive Africans – their gender, age, size, strength, health and temperament – formed the basis of property valuation:

> Every slave was viewed and valued for possessing a healthy, young-like, and reproductively capable disposition. Conversely,

any person perceived as unhealthy, old, or presumably barren in nature represented risky investments and thus extreme impediments in the process of securing future sales and satisfying customers.[14]

The profitable exchange was in *bodies*, not labour time. Simultaneously, the sailors charged with guarding, punishing and safely and efficiently transferring this human merchandise were among the first industrial workers to be paid a regular wage, which, notwithstanding the coercive aspects of sailors' lives, corresponded to a compensation for abstract labour time.[15]

These seemingly semantic or technical distinctions matter because they draw attention to the different, contradictory and often conflicting temporalities set in motion by modern seaborne trade. The transatlantic slaving ship encapsulated, as Paul Gilroy, Marcus Rediker, Ian Baucom and others have illustrated, both capitalist wage labour and ancient slavery, abstract exchange-value and concrete use-value, universal 'freedom' and racialised captivity.[16] The different social agents involved in the Middle Passage were subject both to the turnover time of an incipient capitalism (bondspeople insured, moreover, through the abstraction of human life as a 'general average'), and to what Orlando Patterson called 'natal alienation' (permanent separation of people from their kin) which permitted the enslavement of people *for life*.[17] The slave ship carried both an alienable, uniform time that found its way into a ledger sheet or a risk premium as a universal equivalent, and a notion of time embedded in particular, ancestral memories and cosmologies, whether these are lived or historically submerged, as in Glissant's 'scarcely corroded balls and chains'.

The chapters below on 'Circulation', 'Exploitation' and 'Logistics' are especially attentive to these contradictory temporalities, as they concern the role of the sea in the origins and periodisation of capitalism, as well as the place of distance and turnover time in the circulation of value (although Ernst Bloch's notion of the 'non-simultaneous' coexistence of conflicting historical phenomena also makes an appearance in the 'Offshore' chapter where the legacies and reinventions of overseas colonial outposts as offshore financial centres are explored). We try in the chapter on 'Circulation' to steer between the Charybdis of ahistorical formalisms that define capitalism merely on the basis of economic exploitation through free wage labour, and the Scylla of infinite regression whereby any and every historical instance of commodity exchange is classified as being capitalist. Our position can be summarised as follows: sometime in the course of the 'long' sixteenth century (1450–1650) a historically particular way of 'committing social labour to the transformation of nature' emerged,[18] first in the English countryside, and then gradually and unevenly extended overseas by latching on to pre-existing circuits of long-distance trade. This peculiar mode of production was grafted onto all sorts of labour regimes, forms of political rule and sociocultural institutions, but without ever forsaking its indispensable quality: the competitive accumulation of surplus value for the purpose of ceaselessly generating further value. It is this logic, we argue in the rest of the book, that gives shape to capitalist modernity as a historical epoch and condition. It is the imperative of value creation that produces the sea as a particular space of exploitation, appropriation and world ordering during the modern period. Such processes of creative destruction are, to be sure, prolonged, uneven and, in some instances, unsuccessful. In the chapters that follow we slice historical time into different periods, reflecting the diverse ways in which various technological innovations (e.g. the steamship), geopolitical changes (the rise of imperialist navalism), economic transformations (the foundation of chartered companies) or legal conventions (the freedom of the sea) appear, disappear and reappear at different junctures in the modern history of the oceans. Still, there remains an overarching assumption throughout, that the capitalist imperatives just identified find qualitatively different historical expression across three eras: that of commercial capitalism (from 1651 to 1849), that of industrial capitalism (from 1850 to 1973) and that of neoliberal capitalism (from 1974 to the present). In all this, the sea is indeed history, but one that is characterised by radical rupture as much as by enduring connections. Moreover, the pace at which change unfolds also varies both between historical periods and within different environments – the Earth's oceans or its cryosphere have changed more slowly than, say, our cities. By the same token, the conquest of the Americas or the Industrial Revolution arguably accelerated the transformation of nature, with global warming being the clearest instance of this. The geophysical properties of the deep-water world thus play an important role in defining what the balance is between change and continuity when thinking about capitalism and the sea, and so we turn now to the geographical determinants of this relationship.

Spatialities

Despite its etymological association with the term 'waste', the sea's 'vastness' has for many societies been a source of great riches. We have already mentioned the sophisticated world views and institutions of nautical cultures – both ancient and modern – that find in the oceans a crucial life force and cosmic power. The perceptions of scale that accompany the notion of 'vastness' also imply a historical variation in what constitutes distance, location, remoteness, marginality and periphery. The rise and global reproduction of capitalism have, however, given these geographical categories a distinctive quality by making them relative to processes of capital accumulation. In the specific case of the sea, the production of distance in the transatlantic slave trade considered earlier was premised on the generation of wealth through differential accumulation: 'buying cheap' on one coast and 'selling dear' in the other. The Atlantic Ocean acts here as a real geophysical and logistical barrier in forcible population transfers, yet also creates multiple profit-making opportunities for insurers, traders, bankers, ship- and slaveowners, manufacturers and shipbuilders, by turning distance into a market for risk, credit, manufacture, commodity exchange and transport. With the advance of industrial capitalism, the oceans became increasingly commodified – its living and inanimate resources appropriated, extracted and processed in the realisation of exchange-value, to the extent that fishing quotas or seabed exploration and bioprospecting are also being financialised. Yet, because the oceans retain some intrinsic bio- and geophysical properties that resist valorisation, capital has periodically been forced to experiment with, and attempt to enforce, new ways of exploiting at sea, and appropriating and ordering the oceans. We are thinking here principally of spatio-juridical forms such as exclusive economic zones (EEZs), or the open-registry 'flag-of-convenience' regime, although 'volumetric' conceptions of appropriation like the individual transferable quotas (ITQs) in fisheries also apply. At root, these exercises in capitalist valorisation of the sea raise some of the book's fundamental questions: where does authority lie on the high seas? What is nature's role in reproducing capital? Or who owns the fish?

The oceans have been used by humans mainly for energy, as a source of both protein and propulsion. Most obviously, winds, currents and tides have been harnessed for transport, while whales, walruses, seals, fish, crustaceans, molluscs and other shoreline flora and fauna – from seaweed to goose barnacles – were transformed into food, fertiliser and fuel. But the capitalist commodification of these 'free gifts of nature' has been far from straightforward, and in many instances much harder than on land. In the 'Appropriation' chapter, we concentrate on the case of capture fisheries, which, despite investment in technologies such as fish-aggregating devices, purse-seining and sonar detection, still cannot enclose highly migratory species like tuna that straddle different jurisdictions on the high seas. Unlike farmland or forests – and notwithstanding the notable exception of coastal aquaculture – the ocean's yield cannot be artificially 'improved' (although it can be depleted and restored), nor can most of its pelagic biomass be physically fenced in as private property (tuna ranching of high-value species for Japan's sashimi market is one of the few experiments that have proven profitable). Instead, capitalist appropriation has had to adapt – via mechanisms such as EEZ rent extraction or fishing quotas – to the natural properties of the value-in-motion that are highly migratory species. Capital, with the support of state and multilateral agencies, thus opens fresh marine commodity frontiers in an effort to capture and sell parcels of the oceans and their biomass. This is also true of the wind and wave energy that originally drove capitalist trade and transport during the age of sail, and which in our carbon-dependent era still significantly contributes to the commercial calculations of shipping companies and their underwriters (weather patterns, tidal currents and water depth continue to play a role in these computations). Even though shipping remains the most cost-effective means of long-distance transport in goods, there are also geophysical choke points – the world's major straits – that determine the routing of the global economy's principal shipping lanes. Regardless of liquid fantasies of seamless commodity flows across the oceans, friction at sea (involving storms, pirates, mechanical breakdowns) or ashore (inspections, industrial action, fuel costs) continues to characterise maritime freight transport.[19] Moreover, different seas behave through history and across changing seasons in different ways, following shifts not only in climate and weather, but also in salinity, temperature, density and depth. These are all geophysical phenomena that even the most technologically advanced submarines or container ships need to be aware of in order to effectively perform their tasks.

What this all adds up to is an argument about the distinctive materiality of the sea,[20] and its power to shape capitalist development. The unique qualities of the saltwater world just outlined have certainly served up exceptional opportunities for value creation, but they have also proved to be resistant to capitalist accumulation precisely for the same reasons: of course offshore hydrocarbons and minerals can be extracted at great depths, and water desalinated for more permanent human habitation at or by the sea, but the oceans (not unlike the exploitation of outer space) demand a high price for such subordination of natural forces to the further extension of commodity frontiers. A large part of such cost comes from sustaining a maritime order principally, though not exclusively, through the combination of public international law and naval forces. The closest the planet has (yet) come to a Third World War was during the 1962 Cuban missile crisis when the Soviets managed to deploy seaborne nuclear weapons some 100 miles from American territory. The US had for the better part of that century – and particularly so after 1945 – come to exercise global hegemony through its unassailable naval and commercial primacy over the high seas. The USSR, in contrast, emerged out of the Second World War as the far weaker superpower, but this imbalance with regard to Washington was further exacerbated by Moscow's lack of access to any significant naval bases outside the Eurasian land mass (certainly not until the African and Arab revolutions of the 1970s). The United Nations Convention on the Law of the Sea (UNCLOS), as we will see in the 'Order' and 'Appropriation' chapters, offered the Soviets and many of their allies greater leverage over their marine resources, mainly in the institution of the 200-nautical-mile EEZ.

Yet this regulation of the 'global commons' that is the sea beyond the twelve-nautical-mile territorial waters has largely benefited capitalist firms and economies (rather than, say, small or cooperative fisheries) insofar as the principle of freedom of the seas favoured those maritime nations of the North Atlantic seaboard that had, in previous centuries, created a necklace of overseas colonies connecting up their empires based on commercial capitalism. The geographical legacy of capitalist imperialism – both commercial and industrial – is also apparent in the London-centred offshore networks that link secrecy jurisdictions and financial centres of Caribbean and English Channel Crown dependencies to the former colonies of Singapore and Hong Kong. Here, once again, physical geography matters, since the naval basing, free navigation and access to financial services across time zones that underpinned capitalist development under British and now US hegemony are still reliant on strategic positioning. That distance is relative and space is produced are both givens; the questions are: in relation to what? And produced by whom? For what purpose and under what conditions? Our response is that the historical production of spaces such as Diego Garcia or the Cayman Islands as sites, respectively, of naval and financial power is relative to the ascendancy of British and later American imperialism. Their location is not merely incidental, nor is their geographic insularity. For all their 'topological' connection to wider imperial networks, Diego Garcia and the Caymans are also strategically situated in relation to the world's largest known oil reserves and within the American Eastern time zone; and their being islands facilitates claims to exceptional jurisdictional status so central to their value as distinct places.

Throughout the book, we emphasise how – in an amended adaptation of Andreas Malm's formulation – the material attributes of the sea have to be considered as being autonomous from, yet connected to, the logic of capital.[21] With Malm, we want to acknowledge the causal power inherent in natural forces (in our case, the sea and its biota) while all the time recognising that these are changed through human intervention. The terraqueous nature of the planet is ineluctable and socially significant, but the ways in which this is so will obviously vary according to the dominant forms of social reproduction within a given time and place. This is why our materialism is both historical and geographical. There is, once again, no disputing that a 'first', given, uncommodified nature retains many of its material properties even as it is transformed into a 'second' nature, produced for exchange-value – the Suez and Panama canals were for instance constructed upon natural isthmuses. As Neil Smith says of all social matter, 'though their form has been altered by human activity, they do not cease to be natural in the sense that they are somehow now immune from non-human forces and processes – gravity, physical pressure, chemical transformation, biological interaction'.[22] Our challenge instead lies in identifying the multiple tensions and contradictions that follow from such interactions, and in trying to offer some causal hierarchy when explaining the structured processes generated by the capitalist valorisation of nature. As we discuss in the 'Appropriation' chapter, the socio-natural variations in both international consumer tastes and the natural qualities of different tuna species determine the industrial capture techniques and processing in that sector. Similarly, the sea's natural attributes, we now know, are being actively transformed through industrial carbon emissions, but the consequences of this – beyond the quantifiable warming, expansion and acidification of the oceans – remain unpredictable, in large measure because of the complex interaction between biophysical/chemical and social processes. In this, too, there is a cost beyond that accounted through the neoliberal notion of 'negative externalities' in that, as indicated by the apparent consensus among climate scientists, increasing global warming beyond the extra 2°C threshold will, not least by shutting down certain forms of ocean circulation, lead to irreversible and catastrophic climate change.

In the rest of the book, then, we understand the global ocean in all its changing variety as part of what Jason W. Moore calls 'historical nature': a dialectical and therefore ever-changing, yet asymmetrical and stratified, relationship between nature and society (and indeed within society).[23] As recent geographical research variously informed by 'assemblage', 'New Materialist' or 'actor-network' theories has demonstrated, natural forces are not merely passive objects of human activity – ocean life and energy here being no exception.[24] Our analysis of capitalism and the sea indicates that, while all matter has potency, whether this is of social significance has a great deal to do with eminently human structures and agencies: ocean winds, tides and currents, as we have already noted, are governed by autonomous geophysical laws that certainly relate to biospheric dynamics and, of course, beyond to the Sun and Moon. But they have also been altered – radically so since the emergence of fossil capitalism – by human activity. Moreover, the social power of such awesome natural energy is by definition mediated through human practices and institutions of rule, knowledge, reproduction and exploitation which punctuate with critical turning points or lasting structures the otherwise 'pure process' of de-territorialisation and re-territorialisation. Contrary to Philip Steinberg and Kim Peters, we do not recognise marine place as being 'provisional and forever ... (re)produced',[25] but rather see specific sites of socio-natural reproduction (e.g. the EEZ or the open-registry fishing boat) as existing *because* fairly stable structures of rule, like private property rights or state jurisdiction, remain prevalent. The point, therefore, is not to dismiss the emergent powers and often unpredictable capacities of all matter, but rather to insist that these are enmeshed within enduring hierarchical relations where human agency – for good or ill – still claims the dominant role. Such ontological assumptions are especially important to our account because they help to justify the emphasis we place upon the metabolism between society and nature in the production of terraqueous territorialities. This will become particularly apparent in our discussion of 'Logistics' and also 'Appropriation', for it is here that even the most powerful social innovations pertaining to capitalism and the sea – from the galley ship to the shipping container, seafood canning to regional fisheries management organisations – are shown to be geographically conditioned by our terraqueous predicament, thus producing new spatial forms like EEZs or container ports and logistics hubs, precisely where land meets sea.

Lives

We cannot make proper sense of our dire global situation today, and the place of the sea in its unfolding, without considering the oceans as emphatically social spaces, where all manner of radical struggles and transformations have taken place in the past and continue today. The political implications and prospects of these changes will be discussed in the book's conclusions, but throughout the rest of the volume we are keen to illustrate how even (or especially) when it is presented as being hidden, distant and remote the sea is never void, nor indeed far from land. In its own way, every chapter of the book tries to honour Marcus Rediker's plea 'to see the world's seas and oceans as real places, where a great deal of history has been made, indeed is still being made', taking on board, moreover, that *maritime history is not simply the story of great, white, nation-loving men in the service of a small promontory of land off the Asian land mass, once called Christendom and eventually "Europe"*.[26] Whether it be the women tuna canners encountered in the 'Appropriation' chapter; or the South Asian seafarers who appear in 'Exploitation'; the poor, marginalised and oppressed of various nations and ethnic groups who were transported overseas to create the modern offshore world; or African and Asian merchants and mariners who introduced medieval Europeans to new seafaring techniques central to circulation, a book on capitalism and the sea cannot avoid class, gender, internationalism and racism, nor the complex and contradictory life stories that embody such experiences. If capital has historically approached the oceans as a site of both risk and opportunity, so have many groups and individuals who have under duress or voluntarily crossed the high seas. The motley crew of characters in Amitav Ghosh's riveting *Ibis* trilogy fictionalising British imperialism in South and East Asia during the mid-nineteenth century have one thing in common: whatever their social origins, gender, nationality, age or colour, the sea profoundly remade them in ways that would have been unthinkable had they remained on land.[27] The real-life stories of personal and collective sea change are reflected in the countless experiences similar to that of Dada Amir Haider Khan. Born in 1900 in Rawalpindi district (within today's Pakistan), he joined the British merchant navy at the age of fourteen, sailed to the USA where he was politicised by South Asian and Irish nationalists, thereafter became a member of the Communist Party and launched a lifelong career of radical militancy that saw him dispatched by the Comintern from New York to Moscow, and later Bombay and Lahore.[28] As we saw at the start of this Introduction, even for those for whom the sea is a submarine cemetery, it can be and has been powerfully invoked as a site of memory and resistance generative of other cultural and political resources for revolutionary emancipation.

This all said, we are intent throughout the book to avoid a blithe transnationalism that sometimes seeps into conceptions of the maritime world as a hybrid, indeterminate space of aleatory flows, chaotic cross-currents and horizontal networks. The sea has generally been a site of cruel confinement and exploitation central to the rise of modern imperialism and has witnessed the reinvention of the vilest practices of human oppression and degradation integral to these forms of rule. It has also become a key location in the occlusion of toxic waste, surplus wealth and destructive testing of nuclear weapons, among other 'externalities'. Ocean lives have been characterised by masculinist violence, racialised hierarchies and brutal exploitation of labour, only intermittently – albeit poignantly – fostering bonds of human solidarity and political mobilisation key to modern campaigns for justice and equality. We do not, therefore, wish to romanticise the sea, nor to hide the fact that, in analysing the origins and development of capitalism from a maritime perspective, we may inadvertently privilege some peoples' histories and

regions over those of others. Modern world history is inextrica-
bly tied to the Atlantic, but throughout the book we show how
all of the other oceans are central to this story, to the extent that
it becomes impossible to disassociate, say, the 'fall' of Britain's
thirteen American colonies in the Atlantic from the eastwards
pivot of the 'new' British empire after the Battle of Plassey
(1757), or the rise of American imperialism after 1898 from the
rivalry with an also emergent Japan over command of the
Pacific Ocean.

Equally, we recognise our prejudice toward maritime lives *at*
sea, rather than those lived *off* the sea but predominantly on
land (with some of the gender bias this also entails). Dockers,
wives and families, shipbuilders, rope makers, taverners, sex
workers, porters and the wider assortment of ocean-dependent
people living in the world's harbour communities do not figure
as prominently in our study as do seafarers. Yet we seek in the
'Circulation', 'Exploitation' and 'Logistics' chapters in particular to underscore the primacy of land-side infrastructures and
social networks in the reproduction of capitalism at sea. The
terraqueous predicament of the Introduction's subtitle refers to
a constant and generative interaction between land and sea
when it comes to reproducing maritime labour, capital and
value: the affective labour of (generally female) companions
left on land turns out to be vital in mitigating (overwhelmingly
male) desertion at sea;[29] onshore institutions of risk, credit,
regulation, construction, refuelling, maintenance and repair
are crucial to the smooth operation of offshore finance and
distant fisheries. The sea is a domain of capitalism as much as
it is of patriarchy, and insofar as our narrative sometimes
concentrates on the lives and travails of men, this is by way of
reflecting upon the material reality of a masculinised sphere,
not its political justification. We try in the Conclusion to identify possible avenues for future research on the relationship
between production and reproduction when thinking about
capitalism and the sea.

Agencies of the modern state, labour unions, maritime corporations, multilateral organisations, business groups and political movements will appear across the book as major protagonists in the mediation between capitalism and the sea. As we'll suggest in several chapters, the sea has been critical to modern class formation – be it of fishers, merchants, sailors or, as already mentioned, land-side stevedores, ship workers, bankers, truckers, slave dealers or cannery or plantation workers. The outcome of (geo)political struggles and socio-economic disputes over surplus, trade routes, access rights, quotas, subsidies, safety, pay or employment terms and conditions has varied considerably. Yet there is no question that at several key junctures (at the start of the seventeenth century in Europe, toward the end of the nineteenth century in America and East Asia, across the world since the 1970s) a distinctive 'maritime factor' has boosted capitalist development through a combination of technological or institutional innovation, imperial expansion, organised violence, state investment and multilateral cooperation. As we discuss in the 'Circulation' and then 'Order' chapters, it is difficult to understand the rise of English capitalism and state formation without taking into account the phenomenal role of overseas war, trade and plunder in this process, and the place of firms like Lloyds or Peninsular and Oriental (P&O) in facilitating it. Likewise, Japanese capitalism is inconceivable without factoring the maritime origins of *zaibatsu* like Mitsubishi or Mitsui. We draw on illustrative examples to make the case for our core argument that, in constantly seeking for fresh ways to valorise the oceans, capital produces new terraqueous forms of appropriation, exploitation and world ordering, sometimes in alignment, but generally in antagonism to both labour and nature.

There is no human agency without imagination, and so a final aspect of our understanding of capitalism and the sea relates to the fictions, projections and ideologies that have contributed to this romance – this commodity fetish – between value and the maritime world. When looking at the origins and evolution of the offshore world in the chapter on that subject, a utopian presence becomes evident in the relationship between capitalism and the sea. Islands, in particular, are valued among today's super-rich in ways not dissimilar to Renaissance utopias for their virgin, fertile, Edenic qualities, which, combined with remoteness, exclusivity and seclusion, distinguish them from land-lubbing plebeian society.[30] What tends to be occluded in such associations is the political act of secession that characterised the creation of More's Utopia, and which in the actual historical cases of say, Bermuda, Hong Kong or Singapore, involved conquest, forced labour and racial segregation before these island states were rebranded as offshore financial centres. Similarly, scholars of eighteenth-century English culture have noted the deep interconnections between the rise of the modern English novel and the development of a financial imagination among the general public during the decades after the founding of the Bank of England.[31] Early eighteenth-century authors like Daniel Defoe and Jonathan Swift combined their work as novelists with the art of 'projecting' and promoting financial enterprises like the ill-fated South Sea Company, aimed at generating credit for, and profit from, future returns on intangible, invisible investments.[32] More recently, among (neo)liberal seasteaders, the celebration of oceans as a horizon of possibility, where physical displacement leads to social mobility and personal development, is in large measure connected to the imagination of the sea as a placeless void that erases memory and identity, allowing enterprising individuals (generally white males) to embark on a life-changing journey of self-discovery.[33]

Such invocations of the sea and its islands as places of freedom and abundance are certainly products of a particular time and place. In the West, as Alain Corbin's erudite study suggests, the sea was mainly feared and reviled as a realm of chaos and destruction, but, coinciding with the ascent of Dutch maritime hegemony in the early seventeenth century, the sea and its shores started to be the subject of admiration:

> Two key images govern this national identity: the Dutch had tamed the fury of the oceans, and had successfully subjugated it to their mercantile aims ... The miraculous affluence of the shores reinforced the image of Holland as a country blessed by God. The fecundity of herrings rewarded the labour of the poor living along the coast, just as the prosperity of the fleets compensated the audacity of rich shipowners.[34]

Although by no means oblivious to the ideological power of maritime representations in the culture of capitalism – from J. M. W. Turner to Series 2 of *The Wire* – the chapters that follow only make passing reference to the sea in either popular or high culture.[35] Perhaps more controversially, we dedicate less attention than may have been desirable to the technical cultures – from cartography and oceanography, navigation to fishing techniques – attached to maritime lives. As will hopefully become apparent in the chapters that follow, with Henri Lefebvre we consider representations of space (e.g. nautical charts) to be dialectically intertwined with the spaces of representation (for instance, zonal organisations of the sea). In seeing capitalist development from and through the sea, a particular relationship with nature emerges – one characterised by moments of experimentation and innovation in the extension of the maritime commodity frontier, as well as episodes of retreat, where the particular properties of our terraqueous world force a momentary lull in the relentless accumulation of capital.

1

Circulation

The distinction between land and sea plays a fundamental but contradictory role in the origins of capitalism. Some world historians see maritime trade and the accompanying accumulation of wealth in coastal cities as the determining factor in the emergence of this revolutionary mode of production during the 'long' sixteenth century (1450–1650). This is the historical era that witnessed not just the circumnavigation of the globe, but also the consolidation of a world market with financial and commercial institutions which – in their use of words like 'flotation', 'liquidity', 'flows' and 'ventures' – invoke all the movement and risk of the sea. Marx's own famous statements on the primitive or previous accumulation of capital underline the place of overseas conquest, the Atlantic slave trade and commercial wars among Europe's naval powers in the 'rosy dawn of the era of capitalist production'.[1]

Yet in that very same Part VIII of *Capital*, Marx also identifies the separation of direct producers from their means of social subsistence, and the associated commodification of labour as the fundamental process that 'clears the way for the capitalist system'.[2] There, Marx asserts, 'The expropriation of the agricultural producer of the peasant from the soil is the basis of the whole process'. Commercial farmers, industrialists and their allies thus replace merchants as the chief protagonists in capitalist development by undermining the power of feudal landlords and medieval guilds, and delivering modern landed property, market societies and the accompanying 'free exploitation of man by man'.[3] Primitive accumulation appears to be less the outcome of an expanding maritime frontier than of agrarian class antagonism, and so the location of capitalism's birthplace migrates from port to country town, from coast to hinterland.

This tension between the role of accumulation, appropriation and exploitation on the one hand and trade, exchange and conveyance on the other in Marx's own understanding of capitalism's genesis plays itself out in one of the most fundamental relationships within this social system: that between production and circulation. Whereas the former is conventionally identified with the realm of value creation in the exploitation of labour, the latter is seen as a domain of value realisation in the form of profit upon sale of a commodity. Moreover, the sphere of circulation is characterised by the constant shape-shifting of capital in its diverse commodity, money and productive forms. Maritime trade has historically been linked to an assortment of credit, insurance and commercial institutions that propel commodity and money capital in particular across the globe. But it would be a mistake to make this an absolute and mechanical association – clearly the different circuits of capital operate on both land and sea and, more importantly, the complete capitalist circuit demands the smoothest possible coordination between production and circulation. Capital, in this sense, is amphibious.

This chapter aims to take seriously the complex integration between these moments in the circuit of capital and explores the different ways in which capitalism has from the beginning been conditioned by the peculiar natural-geographical properties of the sea. Although we will be referring to this influence as the 'maritime factor' in capitalist development, we seek to avoid presenting the sea as a force external to social relations on land. In line with the rest of this book, our focus is on those terraqueous spaces where land meets sea: ports, docks, ships, company houses and trading posts. Our intention, therefore, is to consider how the fundamentally temporal dynamics of a mode of production rooted on land have interacted through the elementary geophysical properties of the oceans, and vice versa. Rather than building an artificial (and unsustainable) opposition between firm land and fluid sea, between capitalism as a *social* formation and the ocean as purely *natural* agent, the chapter seeks instead to constantly probe the changing articulation between maritime circulation, mobility and exchange, and terrestrial accumulation, authority and production. In particular, we make a historical case for underscoring the maritime factor in the emergence of capitalism: while commercial exchange, seaborne trade and maritime labour regimes might not be necessary for capitalism to exist in theory, we argue that they were integral to the historical-geographical juncture of Western Europe at the end of 'the long sixteenth century'.

Recognising the variation in conceptions and uses of the sea in relation to the dominant form of social reproduction on land opens up the possibility of historicising the dynamic connections between maritime flows and terrestrial authority. Certainly, in the post-Columbian era 'all the seas of the world became one' (to paraphrase J. H. Parry) in the sense that navigators were fully conscious of the maritime interconnections between oceans.[4] It is also the case that the Earth's biosphere is teleconnected through complex and distinct inter-decadal relationships between water temperatures in the eastern tropical Pacific (El Niño/La Niña events), Eurasian snow cover, South Asian monsoons and subtropical and polar air masses.[5] But the world's oceans are also sharply differentiated by salinity, acidity, depth, temperature, precipitation and cloud cover, among other local or regional bio-geographical factors, and this naturally affects human interaction with the sea. Regularly overcast skies and low circumpolar latitudes complicated nighttime sailing by the stars for Northmen, while the pronounced salinity of the Red Sea, coupled with its 'maze of shallows', makes the Straits of Bab el Mandeb 'easier to enter, in terms of tidal current, than to leave'.[6]

These exceptional geophysical properties of the sea can also affect socio-economic and political relations on land and are in turn changed by the latter. For instance, several decades of far-flung Chinese expeditions across the high seas under the Muslim Admiral Zheng He famously came to an abrupt end in 1433, as the Ming dynasty turned the empire's attention toward China's north-west frontier, thereby effectively sealing the mainland from overseas trade and travel, both outgoing and incoming.[7] For its part, the Red Sea's characteristic wind and current patterns contributed toward what historians of the area have called the 'Jidda gap', where the Hijazi port marked an 'invisible yet palpable late seventeenth- and eighteenth century split' with 'the northern sector of the Red Sea ... controlled by Ottoman administrators and dominated by Cairene merchants while the southern sector opened up to Yemeni governance and Gujarati commercial preeminence'.[8] Like other emblematic maritime straits – the Dardanelles, Gibraltar, Hormuz or Malacca – the Bab el Mandeb continues, as we'll see in Chapter 3, to act as a strategic choke point in a regional commercial and geopolitical system fashioned by a changing combination of sociopolitical and geophysical forces. As Laleh Khalili's richly evocative account of shipping and Arabian capitalism shows, post-war oil extraction from the region's subsoil required its subsequent seaborne transportation. The reconfiguration was not just between hinterland and littoral, but also between land and sea in the very material sense that coastal sands dredged through complex processes of land reclamation literally found their way harbour-side in the shape of the cement used to construct roads, quays, buildings and other infrastructure.[9] Under specific histor-ical-geographical circumstances, then, the sea and its coastlines effectively become a productive force, simultaneously facilitat-ing generation of wealth through maritime traffic and exploita-tion, but also conditioning the development of relations of production on land.

In the rest of this chapter, a picture will hopefully emerge of capitalism as a mode of production deeply entangled in a web of maritime trade, risk and enterprise that has at key junctures of its evolution – particularly during the age of commercial capitalism, the Pax Britannica of 'free trade' imperialism, and the more recent neoliberal era – shaped the nature and dynamics of the system. We will be looking in the first section of the chapter at the historical sociology of the maritime factor in the birth of capitalism: the interaction through time between various commercial centres of the Mediterranean and the Atlantic and Indian Oceans in this process. From here, we proceed to consider the theoretical implications of this history for our understanding of distinct merchant, industrial and neoliberal forms of capitalism. This will require some discussion of contrasting definitions and interpretations of capitalism as a social system, in turn raising important questions about the periodisation of this mode of social reproduction, and its wider connections to environmental histories of the sea.

'Expediting of the affair of negoce': the maritime factor in capitalism

In a conventional definition, capitalism is associated with a list of social practices and institutions like market exchange, profit, competition, complex divisions of labour, wage contracts, banking, joint-stock companies and double-entry book keeping, all of which facilitate the accumulation of wealth. For the celebrated historian Fernand Braudel, 'capitalism has been *potentially* visible since the dawn of history' as many of its characteristic features just enumerated are latent in all civilisations, waiting to be released from the fetters of tradition or aristocratic privilege. 'Far in advance', Braudel declares, 'there were signs announcing the coming of capitalism: the rise of the towns and of trade, the increasing density of society, the spread of the use of money, labour market, the expansion of long-distance trade or to put it another way the international market.'[10] In this and similar accounts to be considered later in the chapter, capitalism is an outgrowth of the geographical concentration and socio-economic centralisation of international markets, aided and abetted by state authority: the quantitative accumulation of profit in towns reaches a tipping point, thereby triggering a qualitative capitalist transformation across the whole of any given society.

One of the chief drivers behind this concentration of wealth, aside from state formation, is the circulation of commodities, humans, ideas and technologies, principally, though not exclusively, by sea. Capital is value-in-motion, both in the abstract sense that it constantly shifts between commodity, productive and money forms, and through its more concrete embodiment in circulating goods, people and credit. The sea has been a protagonist in this transfer of actual and potential wealth either side of the early modern period, mainly because it offered a cheaper and faster means of transport, and also because it encouraged the institutional development and geographical convergence of banking, insurance, shipbuilding and related commercial infrastructure in seaports. In all this movement during the age of sail, ocean winds and surface currents gave the blue-water part of the planet a comparative advantage over continental land masses. These singular sources of marine energy (and their accompanying coastal ecology – natural harbours, tidal streams, seasonal weather, water temperature, reefs, shoals and so forth) have shaped patterns of commercial and civilisational exchange throughout history, but they acquired particular significance with the advent of capitalism as turnover time between production and consumption became central to economic activity. Even after coal and diesel replaced wind power as the engine of navigation, the ocean's 'free gifts' offered unique benefits and obstacles to capitalist circulation.

By way of illustration, it is useful to briefly consider some of the main urban sites of international exchange and accumulation during the medieval and early modern periods, such as coffee houses and bourses, dockyards and arsenals, warehouses and factories, which in turn draw attention to the institutions of capital circulation and accumulation – credit and insurance firms, stock exchanges and trading companies – that housed the fledgling world market.[11] To facilitate the exposition, we will follow the three moments in the capitalist circuit – commodity, money and productive capital – showing how the maritime factor played a signal role in each.

Networks of commodity exchange

The London Stock Exchange and Lloyd's are two iconic institutions of British commercial and maritime capitalism, as well as representing the City of London's continuing primacy as a centre of global finance and insurance. They both also had origins in coffee houses. The Royal Exchange was opened in 1569 as the City's main venue 'for the more facile expediting of the affair of negoce [commerce]'.[12] In the course of the seventeenth century, notoriously rowdy stockbrokers, merchants and jobbers were ejected from the Royal Exchange at Cornhill and took their business to the adjacent Exchange Alley, where Jonathan's and Lloyd's coffee houses eventually became the sites for the London Stock Exchange and Lloyd's Insurers respectively. These were places for the transfer of stocks, shares and market information, but they also hosted trade in commodities and, by the start of the eighteenth century, bills of exchange and foreign currency as well. They therefore incorporated the circulation of money, commodity and productive capital in a single fixed location, interlacing their City activity with wider trading networks, stretching to the Baltic, the Atlantic, the Mediterranean and beyond.

From a global perspective, however, London's ascendancy as a major economic hub was comparatively laggard. The City emerged in the course of the seventeenth century as an outgrowth, not the birthplace, of the 'commercial revolution' that had extended across Europe since the tenth century BCE, in large measure propelled by the intense economic activity across Africa, Asia and their connecting oceans.[13] Janet Abu-Lughod's absorbing study of a thirteenth-century world system featuring 'merchants and producers in an extensive (worldwide) if narrow network of exchange' reveals the powerful interconnections between various circuits of trade, language, religion and culture linking up the Mediterranean ports of Constantinople, Venice, Genoa and Alexandria, or Indian Ocean nodes such as Basra, Muscat, Mombasa, Aden and Calicut.[14] The London coffee houses were integrated into these commercial highways first and most obviously through the trade in coffee itself – a bean (or more accurately berry) of East African origin, cultivated in southern Arabia, processed and consumed across the Ottoman world and first served commercially as a drink in Christian Europe at Pasqua Rosée's London coffee house, founded in 1652.[15] A Greek national, Rosée had arrived in the English capital from his native Smyrna as a servant to Daniel Edwards, a freeman of the Drapers Company and member of the Company of Merchants of England Trading into the Levant Seas.[16] Tellingly, Europe's first public coffee stall was opened in a back street off Exchange Alley, chasing the business opportunities afforded by the cosmopolitan concentration of merchants, traders, seafarers and brokers in the area. The journey made by Rosée and his patron Daniel Edwards from Smyrna to Venice, and then via Livorno to the City of London, thus mirrored one of several maritime routes – trading not just in coffee, but also in spices, silk, precious metals and slaves – which linked the Indian Ocean to the North and Baltic Seas through the Mediterranean and Black Sea ports of Tunis, Tripoli, Alexandria, Acre, Famagusta Lataquiyah, Constantinople, Caffa, Ragusa, Venice and Genoa. These commercial circuits, which developed from the thirteenth century onwards, are richly represented in contemporaneous travellers' accounts, like those of Ibn Battuta or Marco Polo, as well as in more recent world histories by Andre Gunder Frank, Eric Wolf or Findlay and O'Rourke, among others.[17] What is perhaps most interesting for our purposes is the way merchants emerge from this experience as a major new social class, and the sea the principal surface for their wealth accumulation.

In essence, prior to the early modern era, trade was organised in one of two ways: as a local market where hinterland pastoralists and farmers (or, in coastal settlements, fishers) brought fresh produce and livestock to a town or fair, and urban artisans sold their wares for everyday use, or as a long-distance carrying trade in bulk goods for industry and food processing, and luxury commodities aimed at elite consumption. Among the latter, inland caravan or pilgrimage trails and commercial sea lanes served as the main transport routes. Both maritime and terrestrial traffic generated diasporic merchant communities, but it is arguably coastal entrepôts that acted as the key nodes in the differential accumulation whereby 'factors' or merchants now operating from a permanent urban base 'moved goods from areas of surplus production to deficit areas, and obtained a return for their service'.[18] Such profit making through arbitrage ('buying cheap and selling dear') was predicated on several institutional and practical technological innovations which proved simultaneously to be cause and consequence of an intensified maritime circulation during the long sixteenth century.

The joint-stock company is one such fundamental institution. Although first formally established through the English Muscovy Company chartered in 1555, many of the key features of the joint-stock company – shared risk, raising capital through stock shares and a unified management controlled by majority shareholders – are discernible in several medieval commercial practices. The institution of the *mahona* (from the Arabic *ma'una*, for mutual aid or assistance) led to the creation of corporate bodies with variants of that name in Genoa, Venice, Pisa and Florence which pooled capital in foreign (often colonial) ventures, and redistributed dividends among shareholders.[19] Similarly, the *commenda* contract which underwrote the commercial activity of Italian republics in the twelfth- and

33

thirteenth-century Mediterranean allowed one or several investors (*commendatores*) to either enter in partnership with, or instruct, a travelling agent (*tractator*) to trade merchandise overseas in return for an agreed share of the profit.

Specialists have disputed the historical origins and geographical spread of these legal instruments of trade, with some comparing the *commenda* to Jewish, Byzantine and Muslim equivalents (*'isqa, chreokoinonia* and *qirad* respectively) and suggesting possible inspiration across the three, while others insist on the formal differences between the latter and the *commenda*, as well as denying any causal connections in their evolution.[20] What seems undeniable is that by the fifteenth century, trading companies across the Mediterranean – whether predominantly state-sponsored (Venice) or mainly private (Genoa) – had institutionalised investment, risk and profit into shared maritime enterprises. The merchant diasporas generated by this overseas trade in turn extended their commercial tentacles across diverse and geographically dispersed populations, markets and polities which, in bringing into direct contact entrepreneurs, investors, captains and political agents, delivered the conditions and incentives for further market expansion.[21]

In the West, the best-known example of this was the venture that led to Christopher Columbus's 1492 Caribbean landfall. By the time of his expeditionary commission with the Spanish Catholic Monarchs, the Ligurian tractator had sailed widely across the eastern Atlantic seaboard – from Iceland to Elmina in present-day Ghana, via the Canaries and Madeira – initially as a sugar buyer for the Genoese merchant house Centurione, subsequently as an independent trader. Like other contemporary Christian and Muslim merchants, Columbus had a frontier-oriented world view that combined commercial drive, religious zeal and navigational skills honed through a prolonged immersion in the European trade circuits of the period. Yet these circuits, as we have seen, were further inserted into a lattice of intercontinental commodity exchange where the

Hanseatic *Kontor* of the Baltic was replicated in the Levantine *Founduk*, and beyond in the *Kothi* of the eastern Indian Ocean, all of them warehouses doubling up as lodgings for the universal figure of the commercial agent who intermediated between

Figure 1.1. 'Il Fondaco de' Tedeschi sopra il Canale Grande' (top) and 'Ashar Creek and the Whiteley Bridge, Basra, circa 1917' (bottom) Sources: British Museum (top) and Alamy (bottom).

markets and civilisations, be it the Western *factor* ('doer' or 'maker'), the Middle Eastern *wakil al-tujjar* ('delegate') or the South and South East Asian *bapari* ('factor') or *shahbandar* ('harbour master').[22] To this day, many trade-related words in English ('magazine', 'traffic', 'tariff') or in Romance languages (*aduana/douane* or *aval/avais*) derive from Arabic or Persian, reflecting their north and westward journey from the Indian Ocean to the Mediterranean Sea and beyond.

The geophysical properties of the ocean-space proved critical to the consolidation of such commercial circuits. In the case of the Atlantic and its seaboard, under the right seasonal conditions in the warmer months of the year, the northerly trade winds made plain sailing of the voyage from southern Iberia to the Canaries on a lateen or square-sail vessel. The challenge was beating the headwinds on the return leg, and the solution eventually became to 'sail around the wind':

> Sailors of the Mediterranean Atlantic pinned in the Canaries by the southward rush of air and water had to steer northwest into the open ocean and steadily sail farther and farther away from their last landfall, perhaps without gaining a centimetre toward home for many days, until they finally sailed far enough to tap the prevailing westerlies of the temperate zone.[23]

Out of this alignment with the prevailing winds and currents, Portuguese navigators forged the *volta* or 'circuit' which later made 'the gambles of Columbus, Da Gama, and Magellan acts of adventure, not acts of probable suicide'.[24]

In the Indian Ocean the famed monsoon winds structured pre-capitalist maritime circuits of trade, which for centuries prior to the rise of European empires had facilitated permanent connections between the Arabian and Persian coasts, the Indian subcontinent and the east African littoral.[25] The risk, speed and therefore profitability of voyages were principally dictated by the seasonal variation in winds and currents which, in their capacity to generate both hazardous tropical cyclones and powerful energy streams, necessarily affected the duration and reliability of crossings. One measure of this environmental influence on early modern Indian Ocean trade was the regulation of the merchants' accounting year through the *Naroj* (Iranian *Nayruz*) calendar which proved 'crucial in establishing dates for the settlement of debts throughout the annual trading season'.[26] Like their European counterparts at the time, seafarers of the Indian Ocean also developed cartographic techniques drawn from various traditions, such as the Gujarati *rahmani* (pilot's manual) written in both Gujarati and Arabic.[27] Across the Indian seaports, as in Europe and elsewhere, credit, insurance and shipbuilding networks emerged to service this expanding maritime frontier connecting Asia and Africa to each other and to the world beyond. The sea thus acted not just as a space that allowed faster and more intensive commercial transactions between distant lands and peoples, but also as a domain of innovation – pioneering and stimulating what Jason Moore calls novel 'technics of global appropriation' (the caravel, the seaman's astrolabe, the magnetic compass, maps and ship's cannon) as well as opening new markets in goods and human labour.[28] Society and nature were closely entangled in that process, thereby mediating the *longue durée* of biophysical systems to the more conjunctural seaborne trading patterns, reconciling the 'rhythms of the ocean's winds and currents' with new profit opportunities that emerged during the long sixteenth century.[29]

What became specific to early modern European commercial practices was the crystallisation of profit, proselytism and power in the shape of chartered trading companies. Venice and Genoa had already experimented in what Fernández-Armesto aptly labelled 'surrogate empire-building', in large measure fuelled by the later Crusades and geopolitical rivalry with the Ottomans and with other Italian republics.[30] The Columbian enterprise, itself spurred on by the closure of the Iberian frontier through Christian reconquest of the peninsula, pooled the political authority of an embryonic absolutism represented by the Catholic Monarchs with the commercial resources of Italian factors in Portugal and Andalusia opening a new frontier in the Americas.[31] Institutions like the Casa de la Contratación in Seville or the Portuguese Estado da India, which administered wealth extraction from the colonies, can thus be seen as the historical relayers between the late medieval Italian *colleganzas* or *societas* (trading syndicates or associations), and the early modern chartered trading companies of Protestant Europe. Although there was plainly a chronological overlap between these various bodies, the latter marked not just a geographical shift to Antwerp, Amsterdam and London as centres of global accumulation, but also a qualitative deepening in the financial, military and political structures that underpinned the rise of the Dutch and English (later British) mercantile empires.

The English and Dutch East Indian companies (EIC and Vereenigde Oost-Indische Compagnie, VOC, founded in 1600 and 1602 respectively) became the most powerful and enduring exemplars of European commercial capitalism in their symbiotic amalgamation of profit through overseas trade and domestic state formation.[32] These two joint-stock companies shared some common traits: they emerged out of a longer tradition of maritime exchange outlined above, balancing the class interests of merchants and nobility in the combined quest for geopolitical, territorial 'power' and commercial, economic 'plenty';[33] both were awarded a state-licensed monopoly over trade east of the Cape of Good Hope; both introduced limited liability and a legal separation between ownership and management; and they both offered smaller shareholders the possibility of investing stock in permanent, as opposed to one-off, long-distance business ventures. But the two companies also diverged in their form and evolution, not least through the pointed rivalry in the course of successive Anglo-Dutch wars. While the VOC was granted powers to wage war, make peace and sign treaties with foreign polities, effectively becoming the overseas branch of the newly established Dutch Republic, the EIC was for several decades after its birth treated at arm's length by the English Crown. Moreover, although the EIC was to play a critical role in British empire building during the eighteenth century, the VOC was, from the very beginning, intimately connected not just to Dutch colonial expansion, but also to the Netherlands' peculiar route to modern state formation. As we'll shortly see, this relative difference in the balance between the public–private partnership embodied in both the EIC and the VOC accounts in large measure for their distinctive trajectories as companies that variously integrated shipbuilding, shipowning, moneylending and asset management, as well as commodity trading and warmaking, into their multinational operations.

The EIC and the VOC were, to be sure, not the only agents of commodity circulation in the early modern period we have been focusing on. The Anglo-Dutch ascendancy of the time was facilitated by many other chartered corporations (their respective West India companies, the Company of the Royal Adventurers Trading into Africa, the Hudson Bay Company, plus the French and Danish variants, to name a few). These companies were, moreover, accompanied by a surge in piracy, privateering, smuggling, interloping and, above all, slave trading across various seas, all of which deepened the integration of the world market. The Eighty Years War (1568–1648) between Spain and the Netherlands became the centre of wider Mediterranean conflicts involving Habsburgs, Valois, Ottomans and Italian city states, which in turn rippled across the rest of the globe in wars of colonial conquest and European inter-imperial rivalry. One outcome of this general crisis was circulation of another sort: the displacement of people, whether forced or voluntary, which also contributed to the maritime reticulation of the early modern world. Refugee Huguenots, Jews and Walloons fleeing war and persecution across Catholic Europe took up residence in London and Amsterdam, swelling the existing expatriate communities trading from these cities.[34] The colonial settlement of the Americas for its part brought free and enslaved populations from different regions of the Old World into New World ports and their hinterlands, thus forging additional commercial hubs in that continent. With extensive population movement came the circulation of ideas and the accumulation not just of wealth, but also of knowledge. In the course of the long sixteenth century, maritime science in the form of navigational instruments, ship design, optics, cartography and cosmology, many of which had already been (re)introduced to Mediterranean Europe by Muslim traders, mariners and scholars in previous centuries, was transferred northwards to the new capitals of the world market either side of the English Channel.[35]

Calculations of risk, casualties of credit

In and around the London coffee houses of the seventeenth century there developed a public sphere which allowed merchants to congregate and discuss business news, assess commercial risk and lend or borrow money. The combination of intelligence, insurance and credit (often all under one roof) became a trademark of the emerging markets in London and Amsterdam during this period. In the course of those decades interpersonal or kinship-based expressions of financial trust were complemented by exchange mediated through impersonal contract and market pricing.[36] This, in turn, had the effect of valorising commercial data. Subscription-based public listings, price quotations and newsletters like the Dutch *Price Courants*, the London *Course of the Exchange* (produced by the Huguenot John Castaing) or *Lloyd's News*, informed investors wishing to put idle capital to work about new market opportunities. The London coffee houses which took such circulars also started charging cover and membership fees, thereby effectively becoming private members' clubs for the emerging merchant class and their associates. The influx of American money and the arrival of émigré communities with both social and physical capital, together with the growth of secondary markets in government securities, chartered company stock and foreign currencies, all contributed toward the creation of an international capital market based around London and Amsterdam.

This 'confluence of services' remarked upon by early frequenters of the Amsterdam Bourse was the product not just of spatial concentration but also of functional complementarity:[37] traders required a mathematical aptitude for bookkeeping, currency exchange and calculating interest rates as well as commercial acumen when dealing in commodity prices and shipping costs. 'A good merchant,' Perry Gauci emphasises, 'had to boast many of the attributes of a good financier.'[38] With the intensification of geopolitical rivalry among European powers in both the Old World and the New, the public authority of the state (be it the Crown or the States General) tapped into these capital circuits in order to finance war. Thus the Dutch and later English primacy during the 1600s was bookended with the creation of chartered trading companies and the Amsterdam Wissel (Exchange) bank in the first decade of that century, together with the founding of the Bank of England in 1694. The maritime factor in the shape of overseas trade played a critical role in interlocking these various forms of money capital into a single market in public debt, bank loans, insurance policies, bills of exchange and bullion transfers, among other financial instruments. These innovations in turn oiled the wheels of overseas commerce, accelerating the vast number of market transactions and effectively reducing the distance from one point of exchange to the next.

One of the earliest and perhaps most influential seaborne financial imports was the foreign bill of exchange, a form of deferred payment between merchants trading across distant locations and in different currencies.[39] Although introduced as a credit instrument in Northern Europe by Italian merchants, the practice had long antecedents in the Indian Ocean institution of the *suftaja*, and its variants, the *hawala* and the *sakk* (the latter often seen – wrongly, it appears – as the precursor to the modern 'cheque').[40] The crucial innovation in the early modern use of the bill of exchange lay in its increasingly limitless capacity to circulate across different markets – not just the one-off transaction between two merchants – and thereby acquire an abstract quality as a store of universal value.[41] By concentrating the trade in bills of exchange issued in separate marketplaces within a single location, a city like Amsterdam

> attracted a business in bills that exceeded by far the needs of its own trade. French, Spanish, Portuguese, and Italian cities could rarely provide direct exchange quotations for cities in northern and Baltic Europe, and vice versa. Merchants in these places bought bills on Amsterdam, where other bills on the intended destination could be acquired.[42]

To this important manifestation of an early modern 'financial revolution' we must add other forms of tradeable assets which were to characterise commercial capitalism. Equity in chartered companies has already been mentioned: in 1695, an estimated 150 English joint-stock companies quoted shares worth over £4 million – most of them issued by the large enterprises, including the newly founded Bank of England and the human-trafficking Royal Africa Company.[43] In the Netherlands the VOC had been launched a century before with a capitalisation of almost 6.5 million guilders, contributed by some 1,800 investors (only 200 of these accounting for 50 per cent of the value). In later decades, government bondholders 'awash with cash' reinvested millions of Dutch guilders in VOC bonds and 'in much riskier sectors, such as shipping, whaling, marine insurance, and acceptance credit'.[44] The gradual emergence of an interdependent cross-Atlantic economy from the seventeenth century was furthermore buttressed by a 'commissioning system' where agents were paid a fee as commercial intermediaries between American planters and Old World manufacturers, as well as supplying the former with 'a wide range of mercantile and quasi-banking services, including the provision of shipping, insurance, and eventually finance'.[45]

The London-based tobacco traders Perry & Lane represent a typical example of such maritime integration across the Atlantic world. Established as a partnership between Micaiah Perry and Thomas Lane in 1673, the company became by the early 1700s the largest importer of tobacco into London and Great Britain, making it 'in market terms the most important British firm trading to North America in those years'.[46] Micaiah Perry was the scion of a prominent merchant family who across several generations developed an international network connecting Exeter, Cadiz, Limerick and the Chesapeake Bay to the business's London headquarters. Through their powerful role in the Virginia tobacco trade, Perry & Lane also became major players in the Chesapeake market for slaves, credit and everyday commodities, acting as remitters of bills of exchange, small-scale people traffickers and wool and cloth importers, as well as agents for planter consignments in the Americas. In order to conduct such transatlantic business, Perry & Lane availed themselves of all the ocean-oriented infrastructure offered by the City of London, including account and discount facilities from the Bank of England, ownership of two Thameside quays and warehouses near Customs House and shares in several large ocean-going vessels.

A bespoke market in marine insurance underwrote such newfound liquidity issuing overwhelmingly from overseas trade and conquest.[47] The agentic attributes of the sea present in oceanic circulation of winds and currents (as well as in geophysical properties of coastal areas such as natural harbours, frozen waters and tidal patterns) have from the beginning conditioned human navigation, not least during the European 'discovery of the sea'.[48] Marine volatility acquired a particular force during this period as maritime hazards – including those posed by predatory pirates and enemy privateers – were factored into the early modern calculus of risk. The etymological connection between words like 'venture', 'adventure', 'chance' and 'fortune' was matched by their association with the dangers and opportunities offered by maritime enterprise. Interestingly, the analogy became a commonplace among observers of the time, including one contemporary critic of 'commercialism' (ironically named José Mercado – Joseph Market) who argued, 'Just as the ocean was perpetually brewing up storms that savaged ship and coast, the early modern market was seen as a theater of materialist appetites and unrestrained passion.'[49] This often gendered association of the sea with misfortune and unpredictability continued in future centuries (as we shall see in other parts of the book). But it was to be increasingly 'tamed', or at least mitigated, through markets, technology and political authority, as well as the growing confidence in positivist science and applied mathematics.

In a detailed study of the eighteenth-century Amsterdam marine-insurance market, Frank Spooner distinguishes between 'structural risks' and 'event uncertainties' which informed policies and premiums negotiated by merchants and insurance brokers.[50] The first incorporated perils of the sea (shipwreck, stranding, collision, predation, war and insurrection), technological improvements in shipbuilding and geopolitical considerations, including that surrounding jurisdiction over coastal waters and climatic differences between marketplaces. The second referred to the proverbial unforeseen circumstances ranging from extreme weather to declarations of war, from bankruptcies to protracted lawsuits. For Spooner, these 'changing realities of human ecology' combined with commercial considerations of profitability shaped by distance and time to produce a market for insurance premised on the '*formes informes* of events whether unstable or "chaotic" in themselves or composed of a few elements in mutual contradiction and disharmony'.[51] The sea – and coastal areas in particular – simultaneously acted as a threat to property and an opportunity to profit from risk, as an indispensable sphere of trade and a treacherous obstacle to efficient, fast and reliable movement. Such terraqueous interdependence encouraged innovation and integration across the burgeoning financial sector: 'As a market, Amsterdam was not necessarily perfect in the sense that it always cleared, but dealers were able to combine packages of credit, freight, and insurance which strengthened the opportunities for risk-aversion.'[52]

In London, too, the convergence of maritime traders, investors, shipowners and creditors generated the conditions for the further development of transnational marine insurance. The unique perils attached to seaborne trade could be more readily mitigated through the immediate availability in the City of transnational networks of commercial, political and navigational intelligence, as well as the financial–computational instruments used to underwrite such risk. A quantitative intensification of commercial activity in and around the London Exchange and its adjacent coffee houses eventually produced a qualitative shift in the course of the eighteenth century toward new, cheaper, more stable and diversified mechanisms of marine insurance involving premiums, secondary markets and probability-driven loss assessment.[53] Lives sacrificed at or through the sea raised distinctive challenges to the evolution of marine insurance in London and other English slaving cities.[54] Although seaborne human cargo had given rise to the notion of 'life insurance' in the course of the European Renaissance, the development of human trafficking on an industrial scale across the Atlantic posed the problem of calculating not just the insurance value of slaves as property (including the 'inherent vice' of death during transit), but also the risk of bondspeople rebelling as enslaved humans.[55] This tension between property and personhood temporarily resolved itself during the late eighteenth century in the figure of 'general average', summarised in John Weskett's authoritative 1783 insurance manual in these terms:

Ships and merchandizes from England to the coast of Africa, and at and from thence to our colonies in the West Indies, &c. are usually insured with the following clause policy, viz. 'Free from loss or average, by trading in boats, and also from *average* occasioned by *insurrection* of slaves, under *10 per cent.*[56]

English marine insurance thus came to interpret slave insurrection as a natural peril of the sea, while all the time calculating the threshold of compensation for such human acts of rebellion as being 'under 10 per cent' of the vessel's general average. The seemingly irresolvable tension that emerged here was between the naturalisation of enslaved Africans as commodities prone, like other goods, to 'despoilation' (and therefore uninsurable), and the valorisation of their human agency as potential rebels (insured under the 'excess clause' beyond 10 per cent of general average). In England, the insurance of bondspeople was abolished with the slave trade in 1807 (at least for captives transported on British vessels), but firms like Lloyd's and other marine-insurance businesses plainly profited in their origins from the calculus of death that accompanied the transatlantic slave trade. Legal notions of general average or inherent vice still in use today were, moreover, shaped by such responses to the peculiar risks and opportunities thrown up by the sea.

In sum, throughout the long sixteenth century and into the eighteenth, credit and insurance practices that had first reappeared in Europe through medieval traffic across the Mediterranean Sea gradually migrated towards the northern ports of Bruges, Antwerp, Amsterdam and London. In the Netherlands in particular, the techniques and institutions associated with the new 'rich trades' in sugar, tobacco, captives, dyestuffs, spices and silk were grafted onto long-established socio-economic infrastructure supporting bulk freightage in grain, timber, salt and herring along the North and Baltic Sea littorals. After successive punitive wars against its North Sea rival, culminating with the Anglo-Dutch dynastic 'merger' of 1688, London also benefited enormously from its triple status as financial capital, imperial entrepôt and seat of court and government.

This gradual but unequivocal transfer of socio-economic and geopolitical power to North West Europe was manifest in the 'embarrassment of riches' that came with it, and which proved to be so central to the cultural, architectural and demographic transformation of both London and Amsterdam during the seventeenth and eighteenth centuries.[57] But the staggering increase in accumulated wealth was also accompanied (and to a large degree facilitated) by the structural change in the relationship between finance, trade and government – mainly oriented toward profiting from or through the sea. The major chartered companies were the prime examples of this maritime mercantilism, as was the South Sea Company, which infamously crashed in 1720, and which we consider in greater detail when addressing the offshore phenomenon in Chapter 6.

Market integration through the sea

The focus thus far on merchants and their institutional vehicles for profit making should not obscure the place of production, and indeed class formation, in this process. The commodities traded, the ships insured and the bullion imported all had to be transported, manufactured, processed or extracted by workers. Moreover, at a time of constant mercantilist rivalry, any aspiring early modern empire required access to a permanently seaworthy fleet that could be manned, provisioned, armed and deployed in trade or combat both in nearby coastal waters and in far-flung theatres of war. This demanded not just an effective Admiralty and the corresponding naval force, but also an integrated infrastructure of weapons manufacture and procurement, shipbuilding, victualling, labour recruitment (including impressment) and vessel repair and maintenance on the home front. During its heyday, the Venetian Republic boasted a world-renowned Arsenal – a sixty-acre complex of shipyards and armouries directly employing 2,500 craftsmen and labourers ranging from shipwrights and rope makers to blacksmiths and sawyers.[58] The Netherlands, and subsequently Britain, both drew inspiration from the Serenissima, becoming the successive maritime hegemons of the period. At the height of their market domination in the second half of the seventeenth century, Dutch shipyards – the Amsterdam Admiralty's complex and the VOC's nearby plant being the largest ones – contracted hundreds, and in some cases over 1,000, workers within their walls, in total accounting for some 5 per cent of the country's industrial labour force.[59] Wharves in Amsterdam and Rotterdam came to specialise in repair and maintenance, while construction proper was centred in rural yards along the river Zaan.[60] The VOC naval shipyard was characteristic of many others in aggregating ropeyards, artisan workshops, tar refineries and – pioneering for its time – timber sawing mills all in a single location. The maritime sector during this period can thus be seen as a vanguard of developing capitalist social relations, beyond its role in enabling the circulation of capital through exchange. From 1600 onwards, the Dutch shipbuilding industry 'shifted from a medieval handicraft to something along the lines of modern factory organization': journeymen were hired on a fixed daily wage, negotiated between guilds and employers in a free labour market, and managed through a rationalised time discipline.[61] Calculations of the number of seagoing vessels produced annually in Dutch shipyards at the time vary, but few specialists would dispute Braudel's assertion: 'The real instrument of Dutch greatness was a fleet the equivalent of all the other European fleets put together.'[62]

Where the Dutch pioneered, the British followed – albeit using war, protectionism, and the Royal Navy to command the oceans. The English East India Company had in its early decades emulated the VOC by building its own ships at Deptford and Blackwall, with all the workforce and infrastructural implications this carried: dry docks, timber yards, warehouses, forge

48

smiths, as well as salting and brew houses operated by some 571 wage workers in 1618, directed by master shipwrights and their accompanying instrument makers, mariners and algorithmic experts.[63] The challenge of acquiring a market share in long-distance maritime trade across predatory waters and stormy seas was the driver of this phenomenal institutional investment in high-tonnage vessels known as 'East Indiamen', built in Britain and India. On the ground, the EIC's strategy of seaborne expansion thus resulted in the concentration of wage workers and highly skilled artisans labouring in enclosed shipyards which, according to Mike Berlin, witnessed 'the experimentation in the physical organization of the working environment in which attempts to enforce time discipline and productivity were inscribed in the architecture and physical layout of the environment'.[64]

Along with the Corn Laws, the Navigation Acts (1651 onwards) were among the more prominent of the legal totems of Britain's 'first' Atlantic-facing, seventeenth-century empire, initially designed to counter Dutch commercial dominance, including in England's coastal trade. Updated throughout that century, the essence of the Acts was 'to control the seas by targeting the ships that crossed them'.[65] Cromwell's 1651 Navigation Act blocked foreign vessels from trading with England's 'Lands, Islands, Plantations or Territories', boosting English maritime capitalism in requiring ships to be domestically owned and majority-crewed by nationals – 'the Master and Mariners are also for the most part of them'. This proved a boon to England's ports, which saw increased economic activity from the re-export of goods from Europe intended for England's colonies. The Act also banned the shipping of goods to England unless they were transported in ships 'onely from those of their said Growth, Production or Manufacture', thereby undermining Dutch and other foreign merchant capitalists trading goods procured from third countries.[66] Where England's commercial capitalists benefited, the practice of the law was less rigid – for example, a number of merchants sought and received dispensation from the Acts to use Dutch-built ships or accept goods as 'Dutch' that were procured from its hinterland, such as those transported down the Rhine.[67] Nonetheless, the Acts rapidly proved to be a mercantilist success story – English merchants trebled their cargo shipments between 1629 and 1686.[68]

This nascent industrial policy of the proto-capitalist state drew together Britain's growing colonial production and trade regime along 'national' lines – policies that would be reflected in post-Independence America, including the protection of national shipbuilding, maritime transport and landings. Protectionism was complemented by rising British dominance over transatlantic commerce (including trade in enslaved people) to produce a thriving shipping industry across many parts of coastal England by the turn of the eighteenth century.[69] Indeed, the 1677 Navigation Act 'specified the legal status of slaves as property'; this 'maritime standing of slaves as property also informed their legal status on land'.[70] Commercial–military logics combined in the maritime sector – shipbuilding was a new generative basis for accumulation, in turn providing the means for seaborne trade in the sphere of circulation as well as the military machines necessary to control and order that sphere.

In an expression of such thriving mercantilism, the Royal Navy expanded its own network of dry and wet docks beyond Chatham, Deptford and Woolwich to Portsmouth and Plymouth, dedicated in large part to refitting vessels seized in wartime privateering expeditions. The East India Company continued to build and repair its own ships at Blackwall, while private shipyards radiated out from London, Bristol and East Anglia to north-east ports of Whitby, Sunderland and Scarborough.[71] As in the Dutch case, the 'forward linkages' of the shipping industry gradually incorporated different manufacturing sectors into a network of local hubs like those where ancient woodlands and nearby iron manufacturers surrounding the Trent and Ouse valleys provided raw materials for the building of 'modest keels and coasters'.[72] In an oft-cited figure, up to a quarter of London's early eighteenth-century population was reliant in some way on international commerce for its livelihood.[73] Marcus Rediker's seminal study of maritime workers of the eighteenth-century Anglo-American Atlantic vividly conjures up everyday life in the English capital's 'Pool' between the Tower and London Bridge, where in 1702–1703 some 12,000 Londoners working in international trades exchanged and extracted goods, labour power, money and influence, as well as insults and personal belongings:

> Merchants bustled from ship to ship, pausing to watch with satisfaction as dock workers and seamen lowered the last bale of cargo into the vessel's full belly or to argue furiously with ship-builders over the costs or pace of slowly completed repairs. Captains and customs officials haggled, cursed, and winked at each other. Butchers . . . stocked the merchant craft with salt beef and pork . . . Slaves, servants and day laborers toiled under the sharp gaze of overseers, lifting from ship's hold to shore's warehouse the commodities of the world.[74]

Unlike the feudal commercialism of ports like Seville, Lisbon or indeed the merchant republics of Genoa and Venice, where the city acted as a 'collective seigneur',[75] with a corporate monopoly from which the rural hinterlands were excluded (or, in the case of the Italian city states, subordinated as sites of rent extraction), early modern Amsterdam and London became emporia in a wider ocean-facing, but domestically integrated, market. As we discuss in greater detail shortly, therein lay the distinctive character of Dutch and British merchant capitalism: its capacity to create commodity chains across the maritime-oriented markets and vertical integration within the seaward commercial sector.[76]

The Dutch herring buss is a notable example of a maritime commodity chain – the colonial factories operated by the chartered companies an instance of seaward vertical integration. In response to a decline in coastal stocks and competition from North and Baltic Sea rivals, the fishing communities of Zeeland and Holland turned to the open-sea 'great fishery', particularly in herring, from the year 1400 onwards.[77] Their main logistical challenge was to reconcile the perishability of quality herring with the requirement to spend longer at sea in order to reach more distant banks. This classic problem of turnover time – the narrowing of the distance between moments of production and exchange – was solved by gutting and salting the fish while at sea. Thus the herring buss became 'a veritable factory ship on which the herring were not only caught but processed on board'.[78] As a moving production plant, the herring buss slowed down the process of perishability and shortened the circulation time between deep-water extraction and coastal sale by bringing onto the seagoing vessel relations of production fixed on land. The invention in the 1590s of the *fluitschip* (flute or flyboat), a carrier with a high ratio of cargo to crew, accompanied by the political consolidation of the Dutch Republic and the economic infrastructure discussed above, allowed the Netherlands fishing industry to flourish during this period. Once again, though many of these institutional and technological innovations issued from the import and adaptation of overseas capital, credit instruments, ship design and skilled workforces, it was the consolidation of a domestic market linking up various stages in the commodity chain that facilitated this development. 'The combination of technical innovation with a high measure of integration of financing, production, and trade', De Vries and Ven der Woude suggest, 'plus the careful regulation of all aspects of the industry secured for the Dutch salted herring a monopoly position on western European markets for some two centuries after 1500'.[79]

Capitalism, circulation and production

The whirlwind tour we have just conducted of the commercial circuits that accompanied the 'rise of the West' shows that there was plenty of money, freight and human labour traded across continents in the early modern period. These various forms of wealth were exchanged, principally by sea, and mainly accumulated in (or at least distributed from) port cities. Profits derived from such transactions were, moreover, by the late seventeenth century increasingly reinvested in commercial infrastructures and mechanisms that encouraged unlimited capital accumulation. But is this capitalism? And does it matter?

Our answer to both questions is, unsurprisingly, affirmative – yet with some important qualifications. What this chapter has thus far described is a series of institutions characteristic of commercial capitalism – a period of European history lasting roughly from the fifteenth century to the early nineteenth, when commodity and money prevailed over productive capital. The result was a privileging of merchant's capital that, in Marx's words, 'is penned in the sphere of circulation, and since its function consists exclusively of promoting the exchange of commodities, it requires no other conditions for its existence ... outside those necessary for the simple circulation of commodities and money'.[80] This historical phase of capitalist development should be distinguished both from the feudal commercialism that it replaced, and from the industrial production which supplanted it (Marx's 'real' capitalist mode of production). In Eric Wolf's helpful summary, 'What we must be clear about is the analytical distinction between the employment of wealth in the pursuit of further wealth, and capitalism as a qualitatively different mode of committing social labour to the transformation of nature'.[81]

These distinctions matter because they play a very significant role in our own understanding of capitalism and the sea in the rest of the book, especially as it relates to claims we make about exploitation at sea, appropriation of marine resources, (inter-) state authority over the ocean, and the property relations that underpin all this. Since we conceive of capitalism as a set of historically specific social relations, and not merely a compilation of economic institutions as described above, the interplay between capitalism and the sea – between society and nature – in our account becomes fundamentally dynamic and dialectical. That is, it underlines the mutually constituted, yet constantly changing and causally uneven, interaction between land and sea in the reproduction of both capitalism and the oceans. Moreover, by placing special emphasis on the systematic integration between money, commodity and productive capital in the generation of value under capitalism, we also separate out in what follows the discussion of circulation and the sea in the *rise* of capitalism from their role in the *development* of capitalism. We thus identify the capitalist mode of production with unique 'laws of motion' that determine its interaction not just *with*, but also *through*, the sea.[82]

Because these definitional concerns are entangled in a whole bundle of knotty issues surrounding, inter alia, the relationship between abstract categories and historical experience in Marxist analysis, the historical transition(s) to capitalism and considerations about our collective metabolism with nature, the rest of this section is principally dedicated to untying, or at least loosening, those knots insofar as they facilitate our study of capitalism and the sea. We start with the place of maritime circulation in the conception of capitalism, both as a distinct historical epoch and as a mode of production with its own internal logic, offering a view from the sea (or, more accurately, from the ports and in the bays, where land meets sea). We then move on to identify how the development of capitalism has transformed social relations in and through the oceans, flagging there several ideas that resurface throughout the book regarding the sea as a frontier which pioneers new forms of capital accumulation and its accompanying class antagonisms.

Here again, the seas acquire a plural character as they too change through a differentiated incorporation into the capitalist laws of motion.

The commercialisation model and its critics

The story of Europe's rise in the long sixteenth century has at least two subplots that are relevant to our discussion. One concerns the role of mercantile circulation and overseas trade in the *genesis* of capitalism. The other relates to the place of transoceanic commerce and the world market in the subsequent *development* of capitalism as a self-expanding mode of production. Although these are clearly connected, they do necessarily represent distinct junctures in the history of capitalism: a foundational moment of primitive accumulation where capitalist social relations first become discernible, and a subsequent, more expansive process where capitalist reproduction becomes generalised, both geographically and socially (i.e. both across and within societies). Marx himself returned to this distinction in various formulations – as the difference between the 'formal' and 'real' subsumption of labour to capital; between capital's 'simple' and 'expanded' reproduction; or, more lyrically, in the affirmation that capitalist industry, rather than agriculture or ground rent, is the 'all-dominating economic power of bourgeois society ... the particular ether which determines the specific gravity of every being which has materialized within it'.[83] Since then, Marxist analysis has also grappled with these conceptual and historiographical issues in multiple ways: by identifying 'capitalistic sectors' within non-capitalist societies;[84] in distinguishing between a formally abstract 'mode of production' and a historically concrete 'social formation';[85] by exploring the 'articulation' of different modes of production;[86] or by separating essential 'relations of production' from phenomenal 'forms of exploitation'.[87] A distinction between capitalism and other modes of production has also been made according to

55

whether surplus is extracted mainly through a self-regulated market, or via extra-economic means of political, military or juridical coercion.[88] To complicate matters further, even among those Marxists who might, for instance, agree on the definition of capitalism as a set of social property relations characterised by competitive market dependence, there remains disagreement about how to identify 'competition' or to measure 'market dependence'.[89] We are therefore dealing with multipronged controversies between historical materialists (let alone their theoretical rivals) over not just the definition of capitalism, but also its historical development.

The sea comes into play here because, in several influential renditions, the advent of capitalism is implicitly (and occasionally explicitly) causally connected to the intensification of maritime trade. As we saw earlier, Braudel associates capitalism with a range of commercial, banking and manufacturing institutions that first emerged in the Southern European seaports and subsequently flourished in Antwerp, Amsterdam and London. His followers and successors have also defined capitalism as a global division of labour buttressed by unequal commodity exchange between core, peripheral and semi-peripheral regions. For Immanuel Wallerstein, the capitalist world system which took root in Europe during the long sixteenth century was at the centre of a series of global commodity chains that extracted surplus from peripheral 'coerced cash-crop labour' to then accumulate it in the capitalist core.[90] Giovanni Arrighi, for his part, identifies capitalism as one of two 'strategies of state formation' (the other being 'territorialism') where control over mobile capital, population and territory combine dialectically to produce a modern state system which originated in northern Italy:

The accumulation of capital from long-distance trade and high finance, the management of the balance of power, the commercialization of war, and the development of residential diplomacy

thus complemented one another and ... promoted an extraordinary concentration of wealth and power in the hands of the
oligarchies that ruled the northern Italian city-states.[91]

A critical factor in these conceptions of capitalism is capital's
political incorporation into the institutions of the modern
sovereign state. Again, Wallerstein insists that 'what was crucial
in this process [of world capitalist development] was the intru-
sion of force into the determination of price',[92] while Arrighi (in
turn referring to Braudel's dictum that 'capitalism only triumphs
when it becomes identified with the state') suggests that the
'really important transition that needs to be elucidated is not
that from feudalism to capitalism but from scattered to concentrated capitalist power ... the unique fusion of state and capital, which was nowhere more favourable for capitalism than in
Europe'.[93] It is no coincidence, then, that for these world-system
theorists it was the Italian maritime republics (particularly
Venice) and subsequently the Northern European seaborne
empires that represented the vanguard of a capitalist world
economy. Indeed, it is fair to say that, in their emphasis upon
the prevalence of money and upon commercial over productive
capital, especially as it becomes concentrated in coastal hubs,
what these authors are describing is commercial capitalism – a
historical category we consider interchangeable with 'merchant
capitalism', but distinct from the policy of 'mercantilism' usually
associated with mercantile empires.

This 'circulationist' understanding of capitalism was the
target of sustained criticism from so-called 'political Marxists',
thus labelled because of their claim that it was class struggle in
the English countryside, and not the 'unique fusion of state and
capital' in commercial seaports, that delivered the historical
emergence of this mode of production. Robert Brenner's ground-
breaking study of the agrarian origins of capitalism marked a
departure from the until-then mainstream views that it was
either demographic pressures or the commercialisation of

medieval Europe (or a mixture of both) which led to the histori-cal transition from feudalism to capitalism. Although Brenner readily acknowledges that the world market played a significant role in stimulating demand for manufactured goods and staples produced under capitalist social property relations, he also slams any notion that overseas trade and its accompanying global division of labour by themselves engendered capitalism:

> The original emergence of capitalist development is . . . incom-prehensible as a phenomenon of 'money', 'trade', 'the produc-tion of commodities' or of 'merchant capital'. The very signifi-cance of these forms depends on the class structure of production with which they are associated. They perform indispensable functions in production and reproduction under capitalist social-productive relations. On the other hand, by themselves, by their 'self-development' (the widening of commodity production alone) they cannot bring about the emergence of capitalist social-productive relations and a pattern of economic develop-ment in response to the demands of profitability on the market.[94]

His fellow political Marxist Ellen Meiksins Wood further elabo-rated on these themes from a more self-consciously comparative, historical-sociological perspective. In a characteristically trench-ant yet lucid and accessible study of the origin of capitalism, Wood makes a systematic distinction between capitalism as a histori-cally specific mode of surplus extraction on the one hand, and age-old, long-distance commercial activity on the other. Market exchange, overseas trade, profit making, wage labour and surplus product are present in most forms of society. But only under capi-talism is the vast majority of the population dependent on the market for its reproduction, is trade conducted competitively within integrated markets, is surplus reinvested in forces of production aimed at increasing labour productivity rather than in conquering more land or in conspicuous consumption of luxuries, or does commodified labour produce value and value in turn condition rates of profit. Wood enjoins us not to conflate trade with capitalism; profit with value; rivalry with competition; or, for that matter, the existence of market *opportunities* available in all commercial societies with the unique market *imperatives* that drive the capitalist 'laws of motion'.[95] Put differently, while most historical civilisations have involved societies with markets, only capitalism can be considered as a market society.[96]

The implication of these distinctions for our purposes is that the sea takes on a background role in the emergence and development of capitalism. Like Brenner, Ellen Wood has no problem in recognising that 'a great deal still needs to be said about how England's particular insertion into the European trading system determined the development of English capitalism'.[97] Yet she forcefully argues that, however complex and sophisticated, the commercial networks of medieval Europe were premised on profit generated by exploiting '[t]he fragmentation of markets, the distance between sites of production and sites of consumption, the separation of supply and demand'.[98] Rather than prefiguring capitalist development, the great commercial cities of Southern Europe (and by extension Asia and Africa) were enmeshed in the tributary social relations of their *terraferma* and *contado* hinterlands, and were still governed by 'extra-economic' regulation of exchange through monopolies, privileges and hereditary office.[99]

We now find ourselves at an analytical juncture where two contrasting conceptions of capitalism are on offer: one that underlines the distinctive combination of overseas trade and war in the birth and expansion of a Europe-centred capitalist world economy, the other which emphasises the commodification of social relations in the English countryside as the key to the emergence of a uniquely capitalist market in one country. Capital circulation characterises the first, the production of surplus value the second; merchants and maritime commerce are the protagonists in one, capitalist farmers and commodified agriculture in the other. Is it possible for both approaches to be right, at least in part?[100] Our view is that it is indeed possible and desirable to think of capitalist social relations as being born in the country-side but nurtured through international trade – to understand capitalism as a mode of production emerging out of feudal class antagonisms which subsequently developed by latching onto pre-existing money and commercial circuits of capital. Such a move is consistent with Marx's claim that although trade 'always has, to a greater or lesser degree, a solvent effect on the pre-existing organizations of production ... what new mode of production arises in the place of the old, does not depend on trade, but rather on the character of the old mode of production itself'.[101] We maintain that, as long as the distinction between certain abstract (but no less real) categories of capital and diverse spatio-temporal experiences of capitalism as a mode of production is respected, it is not just feasible and rewarding, but also imperative, to consider the interconnections between circulation and production in capitalist development.[102]

The first of these abstractions is the tripartite division of commodity, money and productive capital. As we have thus far seen, these are present in different societies across time and place – in coffee houses, *founduks*, factories and arsenals of Europe, Africa and Asia – but they acquire a particular character once it is surplus *value* that is produced through the exchange of abstract equivalents, including, crucially, labour power. Merchants' capital (including both commerce and credit) is not somehow 'external' to capitalist reproduction, but is one movement in the constant metamorphosis of capital. Jairus Banaji has made an especially powerful case for recognising the centrality of competition between merchants, vertical integration among trading companies, and the mobilisation of state-organised violence in the development of a distinctly commercial capitalism across different ocean-facing polities in Europe, Asia and Africa during the medieval period.[103] With Banaji, we wish to underline the integration between circulation and production, the way merchants often invested in manufacturing and vice versa, and how the sea facilitated these processes. Put

differently, the history of commercial capitalism saw the reconfiguration of relations of production in a diversity of places –
undermining neat divisions between Marx's abstract analytical
categories. Yet we do insist that the integration of circulation
and production acquired a generalised capitalist character in
the competitive accumulation of value only in the course of the
long sixteenth century, chiefly in North West Europe.

These abstract categories and their correspondingly challenging periodisation can be thought through in relation to concrete
historical experiences, for instance by conceiving of the EIC and
the VOC as quintessential forms of commercial capital, insofar
as they derived their immense profits by reducing the turnover
time between distant marketplaces (connecting, as Marx would
have it, 'the various spheres of production between which circulation mediates').[104] As the 'circulationist' account of capitalism
rightly indicates, state-sponsored violence, monopoly trade,
colonial conquest, maritime predation and resource plunder all
played a key role in facilitating this mediation between various
spheres of production, in effect creating new markets for capitalist reproduction. Commercial capitalism, moreover, reinforced
the process of modern state formation across Europe during the
long sixteenth century, and (all too literally) prepared the
ground, through the actual or near extermination of Amerindian
populations and the attendant environmental transformation of
the Americas, for the eventual development of capitalism in that
continent. Yet this moment of primitive accumulation through
overseas trade and conquest can only be seen as one side of the
process – that which created a world market in the circulation
of commodities. The other, almost simultaneous, episode of
primitive accumulation was under way in England as peasants
and other direct producers were dispossessed from their access
to communal lands and customary rights, and compelled into
accepting the 'double freedom' of the value-producing capitalist
market: relieved from their means of subsistence, and at liberty
to exchange their labour power for a wage.

We can thus posit a further distinction between the 'internal logic' of capitalism as a self-valorising social system and the unfolding of this logic in concrete societies. This allows for the recognition that the self-reproduction of capital encounters all sorts of obstacles and contradictions in actually existing societies, and that its development is thus conditioned by all manner of socio-economic, political and environmental forces, even if these are principally structured through class relations. The coexistence until the nineteenth century, for instance, of capitalism at home and slavery abroad under the British Empire must in large measure be explained with reference to the specific spatio-temporal circumstances and sociopolitical dynamics that linked up, but also differentiated, say, Caribbean sugar plantations and English refineries. The fact that Britain's West Indian colonies were acquired through inter-imperial warfare with its European rivals, who had already exterminated indigenous populations and pioneered plantation slavery, obviously gave social formations in that part of the world a specific class structure and political configuration, dominated by merchant adventurers, petty commodity producers and aristocratic planters. English refineries, on the other hand, were subject to the very different forms of exploitation and political rule that obtained in the metropole. Both societies were plainly integrated into a wider world market, but physical distance and jurisdictional separation allowed merchant capital to mediate between these two 'extreme' spheres of production in a process of differential accumulation. At the same time, as Sidney Mintz's classic treatise on the subject argued, the New World sugar plantations established forms of work discipline, divisions of labour and time-consciousness which were subsequently adopted in metropolitan factories.[105] From the long sixteenth century onwards, cash crops could thus be produced through different coercive, 'extra-economic' forms of exploitation; enter the world market as export commodities; and realise their value in the process of manufacture and sale at their capitalist destination or as a re-export. Once again, the role of merchant capital in this cycle is to facilitate and accelerate the realisation of surplus value – although the centrality of this role, its profitability, prevalence and extent, were, and continue to be, historically contingent.

Circulation and the maritime frontier

Looking at the origins and development of capitalism at the point where land meets sea, we have been suggesting, offers a unique vantage point from which to examine the combination of production and circulation in the self-expansion of capital. The sea has served as a privileged conduit in the transition between one part of the capitalist circuit and the next, or, put more prosaically, as a cost cutter in the process of linking up distant markets and creating new systems of production and their associated labour regimes. Maritime commerce, moreover, has also allowed for the concentration of, and subsequent integration between and within, different sectors of money, commodity and productive capital, especially in the coastal ports of modern seaborne empires. None of this is to suggest that the maritime factor in capitalist development is somehow morally or politically progressive, nor that the technical, institutional or productive advances made through the sea are irreversible. The reintroduction of chattel slavery in and through the Atlantic and Indian Oceans is a sorry testament to the first, while the decline of Dutch hegemony after the seventeenth century is a salutary reminder of the second. Similarly, maritime innovations like free trade zones or tax havens circulate money and commodities from landlocked states and inland centres. Location is not destiny.

Our claim, instead, is that the geophysical properties of land and sea have, in different combinations, strongly conditioned the extent and degree of integration between money, commodity and productive capital across various places and in different periods, in effect acting as ecological forces in the genesis and development of capitalism. Throughout this chapter we have used circulation simultaneously in a metaphorical and a practical sense, both as an abstracted moment in the metamorphosis of capital and as a concrete expression of movement of commodities and people. These transfers and transformations have furthermore been connected to the natural circuits of winds and currents, suggesting that such biophysical phenomena have to be incorporated into our understanding of circulation in relation to capitalism. The chief contribution of the oceans to the reproduction of capitalism lies in their acceleration and cheapening of turnover time. But to this we must add the production of value at sea through fisheries and whaling, and the 'freeing up' of money and productive capital by shortening the distance between each stage of the capital circuit and the next (again, both physically and figuratively).

The maritime frontier and its circulating environment offered seafaring peoples of the long sixteenth century an *opportunity* for commercial expansion and growth. How much of that market opportunity was converted into commercial dominance, let alone the wholesale capitalist transformation of society, varied significantly. While the Dutch Republic during the seventeenth century became the paradigmatic mercantile empire, with a central emporium in Amsterdam coordinating its networks of commodity exchange across the oceans, the Spanish–American Habsburg Empire remained institutionally wedded to its origins as a tributary social formation, principally concerned with extracting wealth from conquered lands and peoples. Spanish galleons were, of course, crucial for the repatriation of resources plundered overseas but, unlike their Dutch counterparts, they did not systematically reinvest the bullion extracted from the Americas in commercial or banking activity, but rather used it to fund archetypal tributary wars of imperial conquest. Put bluntly, a tributary empire like that of the Spanish used the sea as a medium to extend its terrestrial frontier; mercantile empires like the Dutch, on the other hand, used their territorial sovereignty to control lucrative sea lanes. The former extended to the Americas the practices of the Iberian raiding frontier, essentially extracting precious metals from subject populations; the latter, on the other hand, exploited commercial networks by facilitating and intensifying the maritime circulation of commodities from one marketplace to another.

Sociohistorical transformation, therefore, has combined with biophysical change to produce different terraqueous arrangements between society and nature across time and place. With Phil Steinberg, we identify merchant and industrial capitalism as two such 'ecological regimes', where our collective metabolism with nature generates idiosyncratic patterns of economic exploitation, spatial organisation, resource appropriation and technological innovation.[106] In the specific relation between land and sea, commercial capitalism exploited the oceans principally as a trade route – a surface that accelerates the circulation of expensive commodities, and channels access to distant markets. The advent of industrial capitalism from the late eighteenth century gave such mobility a fresh impetus as the sea itself became a site for the production of value (from industrial fishing to mineral extraction) and, through technologies like refrigeration or telegraphy, deepened the integration between the circuits of production, trade and credit.

To complicate matters further, the temporal rhythms involved in these changes, and the relative power of the 'social' and the 'natural' in their articulation, vary considerably, as Braudel and his fellow *Annalistes* have taught us. Yet out of these historically specific interactions between land and sea, there emerged peculiar modes of 'committing social labour to the transformation of nature'. Capitalism – in both its commercial and industrial forms – has harnessed the 'free gifts of nature' – wind power, water currents, fishing banks and coastlines – in distinctive forms and for different purposes to that of say, tributary polities of the Pacific, or the raiding societies of medieval Scandinavia. It has valorised both the surface of the sea (for transport) and its volume (for resources, including those beneath the seabed), thereby trying to impose on this fluid sphere some of the terrestrial structures of abstract space and value that make the sea knowable but also alienable (as we will see in Chapter 3).

In the same way as it is impossible to dissociate the history of capitalism from the blue-water part of our planet, the fate of our oceans has also been acutely affected by capitalist development. In the chapters that follow we explore various ways in which this is so with reference to, among other things, the appropriation of marine resources, the governance of the oceans, the effects of climate change on the saltwater world, and the unique forms of exploitation for those who labour at sea. Above all, however, we aim to demonstrate how capitalism has transformed the spatial relationship between land and sea in ways that has made them both increasingly interdependent and resolutely differentiated. The nodes of capitalist circulation discussed in this chapter – Lloyd's coffee house, the Amsterdam Bourse, the Blackwall shipyards, or Perry & Lane's Thameside quays – may physically have been port-side, but their very existence was predicated on the maritime frontier. As our story unfolds, the power of the zonal organisation of terraqueous spaces will become especially apparent as we consider exclusive economic zones or marine protection areas. This is also the case with the distinction between 'the sea' as a physical space representing seven-tenths of the world's surface; 'overseas' as those lands socio-economically and politically connected to, but geographically separated from, each other by the sea; and the more recent invention of the 'offshore', which refers to the exceptional juridical status of places (many 'overseas', most of them islands) linked to, but legally differentiated from, a metropolitan 'onshore'. Although they remain distinct expressions of our planet's terraqueous territoriality, circulation as we have conceived of it here also interconnects these three spaces in ways that are unique to the capitalist mode of production.

2

Order

Leaving aside the Panama and Suez Canals, a map of the world's busiest shipping lanes today looks very similar to one depicting the planet's major sea routes some 500 years ago. The Straits of Formosa, Malacca, Hormuz, Gibraltar and Magellan; the Gulfs of Aden and St Lawrence; the Bab al Mandab, the Bosphorus, the English Channel, the Danish Narrows and the Cape of Good Hope all currently continue to act as choke points of global maritime commerce in ways that have been in place since the early modern period, if not long before. Such historical-geographical continuity in transport networks tells a story about a particular type of order: an economic system premised on long-distance exchange of goods. It reminds us how the seaborne circulation of commodities explored in Chapter 1 is inscribed in capitalism's DNA. Yet such socio-economic patterns have always relied – indeed been embedded within – military, legal, diplomatic and technical infrastructures that underwrite the movement of products and people across the oceans.

This is a state of affairs usually associated with a world order where some coordination exists between, on the one hand, the socio-economic and legal–strategic practices and institutions sustaining commercial traffic and, on the other, resource appropriation at and through the sea. On a comprehensive understanding of 'order' as a substantive, not simply descriptive, condition of stability, where all manner of complex, constant and reciprocal international transactions can proceed reasonably safely and predictably, the term involves a dispensation of global power –sometimes known as hegemony – that allows the relatively smooth and unperturbed reproduction of dominant socio-economic and political structures. In the more conservative rendition of international relations theory, it refers to an enduring arrangement where sovereigns come to share a 'standard of civilisation' guided by certain common norms, values and rule-governed institutions that define an international society of states.[1] Of course, this ideal is rarely fully realised as the prevailing order is constantly challenged, resisted and occasionally overturned by all sorts of socio-economic and political forces. In the specific case of the global maritime order, we are dealing with a particular organisation of power that facilitates and legitimises the different uses of the sea – as an 'ecological service' and natural resource, a means of commercial transport and communication, and a site of military–diplomatic domination. Included in these governance structures are various maritime conventions and their corresponding multilateral agencies; the law of the sea, eventually codified in the United Nations Convention on the Law of the Sea (UNCLOS); the necklace of naval bases that permit superpowers and their allies to patrol coastal waters, wage war there and on the high seas, and conduct amphibious operations; diverse international agreements on the management and exploitation of marine resources; and the logistical infrastructure that facilitates all this pelagic activity.

Some of the agencies and institutions referred to here will be discussed at greater length in other chapters on appropriation and exploitation. Our chief focus in this chapter is on the military–juridical order supporting the sea as a location of capitalist reproduction in two senses: in a geopolitical guise securing trade flows and value-producing assets, and in the shape of the legal governance of the sea and its riches. These roughly correspond to the Western legal conceptions of *imperium* (sovereignty) and *dominium* (property) respectively, which to this day characterise the global maritime order. We trace the history of the law of the sea through to the largest enclosures in human history – the creation of exclusive economic zones (EEZs) which converted the natural resources within a given zone's waters, seabed and subsoil into a form of state property. This in turn connects to debates around the high seas as 'the common heritage of humankind', a 'global commons' or 'nobody's property'. Underlying these conceptions and organisations of the ocean space, we argue, is a specifically terraqueous territoriality that seeks to align sovereignty, territory and accumulation in ways that guarantee the smoothest maritime circulation of commodities and the most efficient valorisation of the sea.

We have already seen how, since its inception, the capitalist mode of production has encountered in the sea both a challenge and an opportunity for the generation and appropriation of value: on the one hand, a treacherous biophysical force that eludes control through settlement and occupation; on the other, an indispensable surface in the transfer of commodities. Far from representing a lawless frontier or a libertarian utopia, the oceans have over the past 500 years been the object of successive waves of legislation, regulation and management aimed in large measure at reproducing at sea the property relations that obtain on land. The tensions that emerge from this peculiar relationship between capitalism and the sea shed light on the distinctive ordering of our terraqueous planet, illuminating the juridico-military innovations such as zoning or naval 'pre-positioning' that have accompanied the global articulation of land and sea.

Towards the end of the chapter we take up recent experiments in multilateral counter-piracy as an instance of this attempt at resolving the contradiction between what legal scholar Carl Schmitt once labelled 'firm land and free sea'.[2] Maritime piracy challenges the existing world order in many other ways than simply disrupting the free flow of seaborne goods (damaging as this is): it probes the capacity of land-based sovereign power to enforce the law on the high seas, thus turning the ocean space into an experimental site for new forms of governance, management and surveillance that often wash back onto land. We also consider there the latest iteration of territorial disputes in the

South China Sea, where law, geopolitics and the transformation of nature have conspired to make the relationship between capitalism and the sea especially dangerous. The articulation of global strategy, law and order in and through the sea is therefore the main concern of the present chapter. While it will soon become apparent that there is no unmediated, mechanical connection between capitalism and naval strategy or the law of the sea, our contention is nonetheless that key doctrines, concepts and practices linked to the modern juridico-military ordering of the sea must be read through the prism of capitalist development over the past 500 years. Sir Walter Raleigh's late sixteenth-century maxim also holds true today: 'For whosoever commands the sea commands the trade; whosoever commands the trade of the world commands the riches of the world, and consequently the world itself'.[3]

A *nomos* of the sea

Despite its primordialism and occasional mystical flights, Schmitt's notion of planetary *nomos* is a useful starting point in our historical-geographical materialist account of capitalism and the sea in sustaining world orders. For central to Schmitt's thinking is the critical assumption that law, strategy and order are deeply enmeshed in modern world history. As Ken Booth astutely observed shortly after the completion of UNCLOS III in 1982, 'Both the law of the sea and naval strategy have their roots in and are concerned with the national interests of states in using the oceans in desired ways ... both law and war are continuations of politics by other means.'[4] This insight guides our own understanding of order at sea, since we associate the development and prevalence of certain naval strategies and legal norms with specific periods in the forging of a modern maritime order.

In a stylised and broadly chronological fashion, we can identify three such junctures. A first, foundational moment during the age of mercantile empires was characterised by the coexistence of piracy and privateering – sometimes in convergence, generally in conflict – with the Grotian principle of 'freedom of the seas' which subsequently defined the Pax Britannica. The late nineteenth century witnessed the turn to a geopolitical understanding of maritime strategy in the writings of Alfred Thayer Mahan and Sir Julian Corbett (and many of their followers in Europe, Japan and the US), as the sea became a privileged domain of mechanised warfare and inter-imperial rivalry among emerging capitalist nations. With the advent of the Cold War and the accompanying rise of the global South, a third phase in the development of the global maritime order crystallised around both the multilateral regimes governed through UNCLOS, the International Maritime Organisation, the International Seabed Authority or the Commission on the Limits of the Continental Shelf, and the ongoing naval competition between the two global superpowers. As we shall shortly see, there is considerable overlap between the doctrines, principles and norms governing each of these moments in the unfolding of the modern maritime order – the 'freedom of the seas' and its associated notion of 'innocent passage', for instance, remain today cherished principles of global governance. But there are equally significant ruptures in the history of this order (the prohibition and eradication of privateering is an obvious one), which are worth underlining by way of emphasising the messy, contradictory and therefore unstable combination of law, strategy and order in the global ocean.

Freedom of the seas

The conventional story of modern maritime law begins with the contrast between Dutchman Hugo Grotius's 1609 anonymous treatise *Mare Liberum* (Free Sea) and the English notable John Selden's 1618 riposte *Mare Clausum* (Closed Sea).[5] While the former advocated freedom of navigation across the world's oceans, arguing that 'all men are permitted to sail in the sea though leave be obtained of no prince',[6] the latter maintained 'that the Sea, by the Law of Nature or Nations is not common to all men, but capable of private Dominion or propertie as well as Land.'[7] Other eminent scholars – from the Iberians Vitoria and de Freitas to Grotius's own Dutch translator Cornelius van Bynkershoek and Scotsman William Welwood – often feature in these histories of the early stages of the modern law of the sea.[8] But it is really Grotius's claim that the oceans cannot be exclusively appropriated by any one nation which has proved to be the most controversial and, in retrospect, enduring.

Invoking both natural law and natural phenomena, the Scriptures and the ancients, Grotius insisted that, as an unoccupied realm central to the natural right of peoples to trade and communicate, 'those things which cannot be occupied or were never occupied can be proper to none ... no part of the sea can be accompted in the territory of any people'.[9] The counterclaims by John Selden, Welwood and de Freitas focused around fishing rights, defence of coastal waters and the possibility of exercising dominion over the sea. In Selden's view, the English Crown's reach stretched well beyond the three-mile cannon-shot limit for territorial waters, to include fishing grounds as far south as the Bay of Biscay, north to the Atlantic and east into the North Sea. For de Freitas, the high seas might not be subject to exclusive possession (*dominium*), but they could be parcelled out by great powers into distinct zones, in the way that the 1494 Treaty of Tordesillas split the Atlantic between Spain and Portugal. For Welwood, too, Grotius's insistence on the freedom of the seas went against the natural law of sovereign authority – including the right to control the passage of goods and peoples through territorial waters.[10]

Yet, as Phil Steinberg has convincingly shown, Grotius, de Freitas and Selden converge on the idea of stewardship of the sea: 'Claims to exclusive use or possession must be tempered because the ocean cannot be policed adequately and/or use of its non-exhaustible resources is guaranteed for all by natural law.'[11]

Their differences revolve around contrasting conceptions of the relationship between sovereignty and ownership, or *imperium* and *dominium*.[12] According to Grotius and the tradition of free-sea thinking he has since inspired, control and use of the sea are two different – if often complementary – exercises: territorial waters can and should be protected by sovereign authority, but the wider oceans must be open to free trade and navigation. From the Seldenian, closed-waters perspective, the oceans remain the geo-economic battleground of maritime powers and appropriation of the sea's resources is always conditioned by the capacity of one state or another to control those waters.

Rather than present Grotian and Seldenian views of the sea as stylised doctrinal opposites, it is perhaps more helpful to connect their claims directly to the geopolitical rivalry between the emerging mercantile empires of the early seventeenth century. Grotius's seminal pamphlet was, after all, hastily commissioned by the Dutch East India Company (VOC) to accompany the 1609 negotiations with the Spanish Monarchy leading to the Treaty of Antwerp, which in turn yielded the Twelve-Year Truce between the Habsburg Empire and the Dutch Republic. Its subtitle ('The Right Which Belongs to the Dutch to Take Part in the East Indian Trade') was refreshingly direct about the core aim of *Mare Liberum*: it was a legal justification for the participation of the new republic and its commercial wing, the VOC, as equals in the lucrative world market that had been forged by Iberian imperialism after 1492.[13] Fundamentally, Grotius's case in a later-discovered treatise, *A Commentary on the Law of Prize and Booty*, amounted to a retrospective vindication of the Dutch right to self-defence and reprisal when seeking to freely trade and navigate across the world's oceans.[14] By attempting to enforce a commercial monopoly with the East Asian spice islands and exercise jurisdiction (*imperium*) over maritime access to these markets, the Portuguese – so Grotius reasoned – had violated the Dutch right to their share of property (*dominium*) accumulated through the sea, and so the capture of the 1603

Portuguese carrack *Santa Catarina* off the coast of the Malay peninsula was justified as an act of self-defence. A key and innovative element of the case presented in the *Commentary* was the recognition of Johor as a 'sovereign principality' whose ruler 'clearly possessed the authority necessary to conduct a public war'.[15] The Kingdom of Johor had forged an alliance (however informal) with the VOC captain Jacob van Heemskerk and, in Grotius's account, had been invited by the sultan to protect the kingdom from Portuguese aggression. Moreover, the presence of the sultan's brother, Raja Bongsu, on Dutch privateer Van Heemskerk's flagship *De Witte Leeuw* ('the white lion') during the course of the battle that ended with the seizure of the *Santa Catarina* further confirmed self-preservation as the just cause behind the attack. Through this sequencing of the argument, Grotius established one of the main doctrinal and strategic pillars of open-sea thinking: the combination of territorial sovereignty with freedom of trade and navigation. As we saw in the 'Circulation' chapter, agents of merchant capitalism like the VOC crystallised the symbiotic relationship between domestic state formation and profit through overseas trade – except that abroad the former was supplemented by means of alliances with independent, if not always equal, polities.[16] Freedom of trade and navigation have thus from their inception been buttressed by the military–juridical authority of states and their diplomatic interaction.

The centrality of merchant capitalism in the Grotian doctrine of the freedom of the seas becomes readily apparent when considering how the principles of *Mare Liberum* were subsequently deployed in the Anglo-Dutch rivalry during the course of the seventeenth century, eventually resolved in England's favour through the 1688 dynastic merger which sealed the Glorious Revolution. On the diplomatic front, Grotius himself represented Dutch commercial interests in East Asia at the Colonial and Maritime conferences of London and The Hague in 1613 and 1615 respectively,[17] where *Mare Liberum* was cited by English jurists defending their own East India Company's rights to trade freely in those markets: the seas might be shared, but markets could not be.

This eminently mercantilist logic, where profit is extracted through power, also conditioned the Anglo-Dutch wars of 1652–54, 1665–67 and 1672–74, which 'more than any others fought by the British in the past four centuries', Paul Kennedy unequivocally asserts, 'were trade wars'.[18] Without reference to commercial capitalism and the geopolitical rivalry between mercantile empires, it is difficult to fully understand some of the key strategic and operational features of these and other pivotal naval battles between European powers during the seventeenth century – privateering, the *guerre de course* (commercial war/raiding), the professionalisation of navies, the battleship and overseas naval bases. As an English rhyme of 1663 would have it, 'Make wars with Dutchmen, Peace with Spain. / Then we shall have money and trade again'.[19]

Put simply, England entered the world stage as a global maritime power through its seventeenth-century antagonism with the Dutch, and by the turn of the nineteenth century had emerged as Great Britain, ruling the proverbial waves, after its defeat of the French during the Seven Years War (1756–1763), and then the Revolutionary and Napoleonic Wars. Across these two centuries of naval confrontation, European maritime powers experimented with new strategies and innovative tactics which were to characterise Western naval warfare during most of the age of sail. Unlike the sixteenth- and seventeenth-century Mediterranean, blighted by war and corsairing, the largely peaceful Baltic waters had allowed the Dutch to dominate the carrying trade in that sea through the use of unarmed and therefore light, fast and reliable vessels. Convoys were deployed in the protection of Dutch ships against both pirates and rival privateers in the Mediterranean and overseas, and in the course of the seventeenth century the Netherlands developed a battleship fleet to meet the growing English threat to their own maritime trade.[20]

The first of the Anglo-Dutch wars was precipitated by the 1651 Navigation Acts granting English shipping a monopoly of trade in and out of the island. This in effect launched a half-century-long campaign to throttle Netherlands trade by blockading the English Channel and disrupting Dutch control over access to the East Indies. Thus was born the 'line of battle' as a naval tactic, and the 'ship of the line' as the large, heavy gunship that could deliver victory at sea through overwhelming firepower. 'In essence', Andrew Lambert has argued, 'the Dutch wanted to use the sea, the English to control it, and deny it to others.'[21] In order to do so, however, the naval line of battle had to be held by a disciplined crew, drilled in the efficient use of heavy artillery at sea and directed by professional officers. The new tactical advantage thus required wider strategic and infrastructural support which, in the event, only the public–private partnership of an effective state and an integrated market were able to provide: 'Victuals, stores and, most important, trained seamen were vital to keep these vessels at sea.'[22] Equally significant was the fact that 'ships were close to the dockyards, which in turn were close to the forests or the waterways by which timber came for construction and repair. These yards had access to the pine forests and Baltic trade routes that brought the vital naval stores of pitch, deal and hemp.'[23]

The gradual professionalisation of the Royal Navy in the course of the long eighteenth century (1689–1815) accompanied the consolidation of the British fiscal–military state, connecting the 'sinews of power' between domestic state formation, overseas trade and naval warfare. In addition to the principal administrative bodies – the Admiralty, the Naval Board, the Ordnance Board, the Victualling Board and the Navy Office – which managed the Royal Navy's budgets, shipyards, personnel, command and repair facilities and procurement agencies, the expansion of Britain's naval infrastructure abroad was also financed through the credit mechanisms introduced by the 'financial revolution' at home, and the Bank of England itself.

'By the beginning of the eighteenth century', Harding suggests, 'Britain was almost unique in being able to concentrate its military expenditure upon its navy and have a large enough pool of seamen, skilled labour and maritime industries to absorb significant losses of warships and seamen.'[24] This sociopolitical complex was buttressed further by the acquisition of a global network of naval bases – from the capture of Jamaica's Port Royal in 1655 to the cession of Malta in 1814 – which not only gave Britain unprecedented access to key sea lanes and markets, but crucially offered strategic repair, logistics and refuelling stations across its expanding empire.

One rich paradox in this maritime contribution to British state formation and empire building is the critical role played in this process by quintessentially non-state (and generally anti-state) actors like pirates and their licensed counterparts, privateers. As we have already seen in earlier chapters, seaborne plunder and predation by state-sponsored pirates like Sir Francis Drake and Sir Walter Raleigh were integral to the development of the early modern English government and economy. By the beginning of the eighteenth century, the west Atlantic in particular became a focal point for the Royal Navy's counter-piracy campaigns. Deemed to be enemies of all humankind (*hostes humani generis*), pirates served as a foil for the incipient principle of universal jurisdiction, and the Royal Navy its main enforcer. Though piracy is a practice as old and ubiquitous as war and commerce, the intensification of the inter-imperial rivalry in the Atlantic between France, Spain, Britain and the Netherlands combined with domestic pressures to end lawlessness at sea to produce an especially violent and repressive clamp-down on Atlantic piracy in the decades after the 1713 Peace of Utrecht.[25]

Tensions persisted in both theory and practice between the suppression of piracy and its part in sustaining the local trade and contraband networks of the Caribbean and American Atlantic seaboard, and between the vilification of pirates and the constant recycling of manpower and repurposing of vessels from illegal piracy to licensed privateering. Thus Britain's ambition to 'award universal jurisdiction to English courts over maritime crimes and seizures committed anywhere' through the figure of the pirate in fact delivered a much more variegated, overlapping and plural legal geography which Lauren Benton has convincingly shown produced an 'interimperial sea space that could not be owned but could be dominated'.[26]

The absence of a uniform and codified maritime international law at this time is hardly surprising given the strategic importance of trans-oceanic waterways in the unfolding antagonism between mercantile empires during the eighteenth century. Each imperial power imposed its own rules wherever it could, and applied the naval strategy that best suited its interests. Having launched a formidable programme of battle fleet investment in the late 1600s under Colbert, France continued to rely on the privateer-led *guerre de course* as the main weapon against its Anglo-Dutch adversaries. The Dutch Republic proved too weak by the start of the eighteenth century to successfully repel this strategy, but the British navy complemented the existing mechanism of convoys escorting commercial vessels with a system of small, cruising squadrons stationed along main thoroughfares of the English Channel, the Western Approaches, the West Indies and the Mediterranean, all tasked with warding off commerce raiders.[27] The counterpart to the *guerre de course* was the blockade. As Andrew Lambert notes, this had two naval expressions: a commercial blockade 'intended to cut the economic lifeline of a maritime nation', and a military blockade which 'denied the enemy navy opportunities to go to sea'.[28] Each had different objectives and methods – the former was more offensive in its ambition to stifle economic activity on land by controlling maritime traffic through close patrolling of multiple harbours by dispersed fleets of small cruisers; the latter was a more defensive posture imposed by larger battle fleets over the opponent's major naval bases, and aimed at preventing enemy ships from leaving port.

After 1713, and well into the twentieth century, the Royal Navy used both instruments in various combinations and in different settings. But importantly, it did so on a global scale, challenging its Continental rivals abroad, off the coasts of America, Africa and Asia. The centrality of Britain's overseas naval bases in its defeat of France during the Seven Years War came to represent the triumph of this offshore balancing strategy which England had been honing since the 1651 Navigation Acts. A 'blue-water policy' which secured territorial sovereignty by controlling the English Channel and the North Sea maximised the role of trade and shipping in the British economy through its overseas colonies, and minimised the costs (both economic and political) associated with a standing army by eschewing prolonged land campaigns and encouraging instead tactical alliances with Continental powers and mercenaries. 'The English grand strategy', Daniel Baugh famously suggested of this long eighteenth century, 'was essentially defensive in Europe (and European waters) and aggressive overseas. Overseas aggressiveness was aimed at enlarging the maritime and commercial base of England's naval power while at the same time reducing that of actual or potential enemies. Success in war could be achieved only by economic pressure.'[29]

The globalisation of navalism

The world order born out of the 1814–15 Vienna settlement consolidated Britain's blue-water policy into the famed Pax Britannica. While 'total control of all seas by the British navy made it irrelevant whether any territory was under the British flag or not', Eric Hobsbawm said of this period, 'In Europe British interests merely required no power to be too strong.'[30] Revolutionary wars at home and naval defeat abroad had severely debilitated Britain's fiercest contemporary imperial challenger, France, and significantly strengthened the triangulation of colonies, trade and navy that proved so central to launching Britain's industrial revolution. Anti-slavery replaced counter-piracy as the Royal Navy's universal mission to enforce freedom on the high seas, while the principle of global free trade gained ground in the course of the 1830s and 1840s, eventually leading to the repeal of the Corn Laws in 1846 and the Navigation Acts in 1849 – two emblematic pieces of mercantilist legislation. This did not stop the Royal Navy from exercising gunboat diplomacy to keep China open for trade in opium, nor from imposing British hegemony over the Aegean Sea (prompted by the 1850 *Don Pacifico* incident in Greece). The absolute preponderance of the Royal Navy (in 1859 the British fleet had ninety-five 'ships of the line' against France's fifty-one) and Britain's merchant navy (see Chapter 5), allied with London's continued centrality as the commercial–financial–maritime capital of the global economy during the bulk of the Victorian era, left no remaining power in a position to dominate the world's oceans.[31] Other emerging capitalist nations were at this time immersed in either revolutionary upheaval (France), civil wars (the USA) or both (much of Latin America). Large chunks of Africa, Asia and the Middle East were experiencing the opening shots of European capitalist colonisation, while Germany and Japan were only beginning the processes of national unification and state-led capitalist development that would turn them into major economic and military contenders by the end of that century.

It was in this context that the Pax Britannica harnessed the freedom of the seas for its own benefit as the world's leading (some might argue, only) industrial nation from 1815 to 1870. The Royal Navy upheld the Grotian conception of the high seas as nobody's property, since it was only Britain that was in a position to fully exploit the oceanic commons. Perhaps the most revealing codification of these principles was the otherwise obscure 1856 Declaration of Paris which committed its first seven signatories (France, Britain, Russia, Prussia, Austria, Sardinia-Piedmont and Turkey) to abolishing privateering and permitting the transport of 'Enemy Goods' by 'Neutral Flags'. As Jan Martin Lemnitzer's painstaking study suggests, the Paris Declaration was the outcome of complex international diplomatic negotiations and domestic party-political rivalry which essentially pitted the Royal Navy's historical privilege to search and seize enemy property carried on neutral vessels against the demand of competing maritime powers like France and Russia that the principle of 'free ships, free goods' should prevail.[32] Lemnitzer suggests that the accord was one of several early multilateral arrangements that provided a set of 'house rules' guiding the conduct of maritime affairs among the members of 'international society'. It formed part of an emerging body of positivist public international law, in turn reflecting a new consensus on the norms shaping international maritime trade and naval conflict, including the delegitimisation of privateering as a practice of statecraft. The core principle here was that free trade should continue even during times of war among third parties – to 'establish the immunity of private property from capture at sea'.[33] In many important respects, the 1856 Paris Declaration thus mirrors the transition after the Napoleonic Wars from a world dominated by the mercantilist generation of wealth through plunder and predation to the capitalist circulation of value through trade in industrial goods.[34]

The gradual and uneven shift from commercial to industrial capitalism was further represented in the increasing valorisation of the sea's depth and bottom, not just its surface. Technological advances brought by the Industrial Revolution introduced the steamship, refrigeration, canning, ironclad vessels and undersea telegraphic cables, which in turn allowed the intensification of distant-water fishing and whaling, the extensive acceleration of travel and communication, the spread of commercial networks and the mass migration of peoples across oceans (see Chapters 4 and 5). The latter part of the nineteenth century in particular witnessed a celebration of the sea by liberal internationalists who experienced it as a site of cosmopolitan mobility, international cooperation and scientific research. The ocean's seabed begat one of the world's first universal international organisations – the International Telegraphic Union, founded in 1865 – while some of the pioneering international trade unions first organised around maritime-related occupations (see Chapter 3). What today is known as 'global governance' had its early origins in European and world conferences dealing with riverine navigation (1861, 1863 and 1866), marine signalling (1864) and the 'neutralisation of submarine cables' (1882).[35]

This incipient multilateral institutionalism was complemented by the internationalism of empire. Steamships might have outpaced sailing vessels, but they had shorter range and required more frequent refuelling, so Britain added to its existing portfolio of colonial outposts in Singapore (1819), the Falkland Islands (1833), Aden (1839) and Hong Kong (1841), and in later decades Fiji, Mauritius, Seychelles, Diego Garcia, Samoa, Cyprus and Port Said, among others, as key coaling stations of empire. Importantly, many of these naval bases and commercial ports constructed dry dock facilities essential for the cleaning, maintenance and repair of both commercial liners and warships.[36] This global maritime network was literally connected through the laying of trans-oceanic submarine cables which by the 1890s made London the hub of a vast communications web radiating out to its west in the Americas and – via Alexandria, Aden, Bombay, Colombo and Singapore – to Hong Kong and Australia in its east and south-east.[37] The 'dual-use' capacity of such infrastructure was fully in evidence in the development of shipping lines like the iconic Peninsular & Oriental (P&O) Company, which started out as a mail service connecting the British mainland to its Mediterranean colonies and in later decades evolved into the main carrier of settlers, narcotics, colonial troops and imperial administrators across the length and breadth of empire.

Free traders and their allies thus had good reason to associate the oceans with peace, progress and prosperity. Through maritime trade, communication, cooperation and migration, the seas had – at least during the middle decades of the nineteenth century – acted as conduit for the creation of a British-ruled, market-driven world order they so treasured. The problem was that, by the turn of the twentieth century, industrial warfare had also led to underwater and seabed militarisation through the use of submarines, torpedoes and mines. Moreover, the technological advances of the Industrial Revolution were also transforming land, most notably via the expansion of railways. Newly industrialising states like Japan, Germany, France and the USA began to challenge the Pax Britannica, and the sea was the site chosen to do so. The German Kaiserliche Marine was founded in 1871 shortly after national unification. The Imperial Japanese Navy, Nippon Kaigun, followed closely in the early 1870s, while the US launched its 'new' navy in 1882, during the period following postbellum Reconstruction Era. All three navies were administered by reorganised and expanded government departments, with their own general staff and budgetary appropriations, and supported by their respective naval academies in Tokyo, Kiel and Annapolis. All three countries embarked on ambitious shipbuilding programmes from the 1880s, which by the early 1900s overturned Britain's absolute dominance in terms of battleship fleet size, and with it Viscount Castlereagh's post-1815 policy of ensuring that the Royal Navy's strength was always greater than that of its two closest rivals combined.[38] In France, too, naval rearmament after the Crimean War – represented by the launch in 1858 of the first seaborne iron-hulled warship, the *Gloire* – was accompanied by the brief but influential *jeune école* strategy which advocated the use of commerce raiding principally through the dispersed deployment of torpedo boats, destroyers and submarines against enemy warships and their merchant navy.

The result was the rise of a 'new navalism' which delivered not just a naval arms race in the run-up to the First World War, but also the jingoistic championing of imperial rivalry at sea and through the sea. Notable statesmen of the time like Theodore 'Teddy' Roosevelt, or Kaiser Wilhelm II and his Grand Admiral Alfred von Tirpitz, invested their respective navies with an explicitly imperial mandate, as did the Japanese ruling class.[39] Naval campaigns like the Spanish–American War of 1898, decisive battles like that which brought an end to the 1905 Russo-Japanese War at the Tsushima Strait, or shows of naval prowess such as Kaiser Wilhelm II's landing in Tangiers during the first Moroccan crisis of 1905, all reinforced the association of navy with empire. The 'new' imperialism of the late nineteenth and early twentieth centuries cannot, therefore, be properly understood without incorporating the command of the sea as its chief instrument. No doubt the railways and other land-based communications contributed to the process of European, Japanese and American colonial expansion, but they were strategically subordinated to the maritime connections which integrated subject populations and their resources into the global economy. Even the entangled geopolitical alliances of the period, most notably the Triple Entente between France, Britain and Russia, and the parallel Anglo-Japanese alliance, reflected this new distribution of naval capabilities.

The alignment between strategy, law and world order during the Pax Britannica was never smooth and mechanical. Like all hegemonies, ruling ideas and ideas of rule were contested, both intellectually and politically.[40] The prevalence of 'navalist' over 'continentalist' conceptions of strategy during Britain's period of 'splendid isolation' was hardly absolute or definitive, as there were always influential voices and interests advocating investment in the army and highlighting the amphibious nature of military power, especially under conditions of mechanised warfare.[41] It is therefore important to underline how the 'new navalism' of the age of empire (1870–1914) was informed and

84

promoted by leading strategic thinkers of the time. Foremost among these was the American Alfred Thayer Mahan, who, through his 1890 book *The Influence of Sea Power upon History*, popularised the geopolitical principle that the open seas acted as 'a great highway; or better, perhaps . . . a wide common, over which men may pass in all directions', and thus strategic dominance would reside with that nation able to secure '[t]he possession of that overbearing power on the sea which drives the enemy's flag from it, or allows it to appear only as a fugitive; and which, by controlling the great common, closes the highways by which commerce moves to and from the enemy's shores'.[42] In effect, for Mahan, as for Raleigh 300 years before, this meant depriving the adversary of access to maritime trade routes. It could involve commerce raiding and the close commercial blockade of enemy ports, but with trade networks so widely dispersed across the globe, military command of the sea would above all be exercised 'by prolonged control of the strategic centres of commerce'.[43] What this amounted to was an argument for US acquisition of overseas naval bases and the development of an American blue-water fleet capable of concentrating naval power for decisive battle on the high seas and in distant war theatres.

Much as Grotius had done for Dutch hegemony at the start of the seventeenth century, Mahan targeted his ideas at the end of the nineteenth century to a broad audience with the aim of advancing American imperialism. After compiling his lectures at the Naval War College (where he was appointed as faculty in 1885) into *The Influence of Sea Power*, Mahan proceeded to publicise his work extensively, acting as one of several leading American navalists – another being the later president Theodore Roosevelt – who 'called for the [new] navy to fulfil the nation's expansionist destiny, and by the 1890s agreed that it required a blue-water navy – a battle-oriented fleet of fighting ships'.[44] Leaning – in more respects than one – on an open door, Mahan and his fellow navalists found support in the recently appointed

Secretary of the Navy Benjamin F. Tracy, who in 1891 author-ised the commission of close to a dozen new warships. By the turn of the twentieth century, the US Navy was reported to have the world's second-largest metal-hulled battle fleet and increased its naval personnel fivefold since the rise of the 'new' navy in the early 1880s to 44,500 enlisted men by 1908.[45] Having acquired Puerto Rico, Wake Island, Guam, the Philippines and – indi-rectly – Cuba and Hawaii in the *annus mirabilis* of 1898, Teddy Roosevelt recognised the new state of Panama in 1904, across which an eighty-kilometre canal was opened a decade later, linking the Atlantic and Pacific oceans and reducing by almost two-thirds the sea route from New York to San Francisco.

If the Indian Ocean had been the main fulcrum of Dutch maritime ascendancy during the early seventeenth century, and the Atlantic that of the Royal Navy during the long eighteenth century, the Pacific Ocean proved to be the geographical pivot of the American century. Mahan and his navalist colleagues explicitly identified Pacific islands as strategic staging posts in the US's blue-water policy. The Monroe and Open Door Doctrines were combined with a virulently anti-Japanese preju-dice to justify the Pacific turn in US grand strategy at the start of the new century. In 1910, asked by the Naval War College to comment on their existing war plans, Mahan's advice was to 'cover the Pacific coast against landing, and at the same time protect our other interests in the Pacific – the Open Door, the Philippines, Hawaii – Pearl Harbour should receive the devel-opment now contemplated, and Guam should be constituted a kind of Gibraltar'.[46] Unsurprisingly, perhaps, Mahan's ideas proved especially influential among Japanese naval strategists who, having first translated *The Influence of Sea Power* in 1896, soon adapted many of his principles to East Asian conditions in the form of Sato Tetsutaro's 'navy-first' ideology or Kato Kanji's 'blue-water' navalism.[47] By 1910, the Imperial Japanese Navy had fulfilled its critical role in Japan's annexation of the Ryukyu islands, Taiwan (Formosa) and Korea.

The decade before the First World War thus witnessed an international re-emergence and recognition of the sea as a site of great-power rivalry. Britain's naval mastery, and the imperialism of free trade it supported, were being challenged by a plurality of new maritime actors, transformations in technology and the accompanying naval arms race. Law and strategy sought to address this alteration in the global balance of power, albeit through conflicting emphases on neutrality, arbitration and the regulation of contraband on the one hand, and naval arms agreements, wartime 'right to capture' and denial of access on the other. The differences between liberal internationalist calls for the legal regulation of world affairs and the nationalist advocates of inter-imperial competition were therefore played out in discussions over the governance of the seas. Immunity of private property at sea became a focal point of disagreement both domestically and at successive conferences in The Hague (1899 and 1907) and London (1908), where Mahan and, later, British naval strategist Julian Corbett, urged their respective governments to reverse the principle of 'free ships, free goods' in favour of a right to seize neutral ships supplying enemy countries.[48]

In the event, the main substantive agreements emerging from these diplomatic initiatives were over the definition of blockades and contraband, as well as the German idea of an international prize court. The notion that maritime powers might restrict their control of the sea was, however, never in contention – international maritime law was at the time plainly subordinated to national state interests, and the dominant naval strategic doctrines reflected this rejection of a multilateral stewardship of the sea. As Corbett had argued in *Some Principles of Maritime Strategy*, 'The object of naval warfare must therefore always be directly or indirectly either to secure the command of the sea or to prevent the enemy from securing it'.[49] This defensive posture, often sharply contrasted with Mahan's bluewater imperialism, underscored the role of naval power in denying access to communication, interdicting commerce and facilitating amphibious operations on land.[50] Yet for all their differences, both Mahan and Corbett put their strategic thinking at the service of a world order where either Americans or the British exercised the command of the sea.

Command of the commons

When Saddam Hussein invaded Kuwait in August 1990, the USA's immediate response was the deployment of several 'forward defense' naval task forces to the eastern Mediterranean and the Strait of Hormuz, the latter departing from its Western Indian Ocean base in Diego Garcia to join an eight-ship battle fleet already in place at the mouth of the Persian Gulf.[51] Operation Desert Storm subsequently proved to be a show of overwhelming air power, though much of it launched from naval aircraft carriers and sea-launched surface-to-air missiles. One critical contribution to the war effort was the US Navy's Maritime Prepositioning Ships (MPS) programme: 'the largest, fastest strategic sealift in history, with more than 240 ships carrying more than 18.3 billion pounds of equipment and supplies to sustain the forces of Desert Shield/Storm'.[52] A by-product of the Carter Doctrine's commitment to secure oil flows through the Persian Gulf, the US Military Sealift Command's Prepositioning Program called for 'the prepositioning of equipment and supplies to permit a rapid response to a crisis around the world with firepower, tactical mobility, and sustainability'.[53] With the 'fall' of Iran in 1979, and limited access to military facilities in Saudi Arabia and other Arab Gulf allies, the US looked to its seaborne assets as a source of logistical support. Today, a total of fourteen American MPSs float across the world's oceans providing at least thirty days' worth of services and equipment for any US-led combined- and joint-force operations in most global war theatres. This phenomenal logistical exercise requires access to multiple naval bases across the planet, thus raising critical questions about the place of the oceans, sea power and the law of the sea in upholding world orders during and after the Cold War.

Broadly speaking, three main factors shaped the global maritime order after the Second World War: decolonisation, oil and nuclear capabilities. The USA emerged from global conflict after 1945 as a superpower with military installations of varying sizes in all continents, and a homeland that – unlike the other belligerents – had escaped the destructive ravages of war (notwithstanding the enormous human loss). The 1941 Lend–Lease Bill formalised an agreement sealed the previous year transferring to the US air and naval basing rights on British territories in Newfoundland, Bermuda, British Guiana and several Caribbean islands on a ninety-nine-year lease.[54] Over the following years, Washington gained a foothold in Iceland, Ascension Island and the Azores, and signed an Agreement on the Defence of Greenland which by the end of the war had yielded seventeen US bases on the world's largest island.[55] In the course of the war, the USA added further air and naval bases across the Mediterranean littoral following Operation Torch in North Africa and the Sicily landings, while in the Pacific theatre Americans acquired staging posts in the Marianas, Marshall, Bonin and Caroline islands, as well as occupying Okinawa and recovering Guam. The proclamation of the Truman Doctrine in 1947, the founding of NATO in 1949 and the outbreak of the Korean War a year later marked both the beginning of the Cold War and the consolidation of Washington's wartime planning for 'a worldwide network of bases after the war'.[56]

With over 30,000 installations spread across 2,000 base sites in around 100 countries,[57] the USA was, until the early 1960s, able to contain communism within the Eurasian land mass, mainly through its command of the sea. Its signal contribution to the American war effort, or, more precisely, the integrated land–air–sea operations it facilitated, gave the US Navy a strategic centrality it has since retained. During the Second World

War, James Kraska suggests, 'Expeditionary art was advanced through execution of inter-service, and often multinational, operations from the sea – the predecessor to today's joint and combined coalition efforts'.[58] Indeed, the Second World War and the early decades of the 'first' Cold War helped to entrench the trope of the USA as the first among equals of a democratic, maritime trading confederation in the image of ancient Athens, in contrast to the militaristic tyranny of the continental Spartan empire.

There was, however, from the beginning a real challenge to the Pax Americana in reconciling the exercise of hegemony while espousing decolonisation. Roosevelt entered the world war to defeat Axis imperialism, and the 1941 Atlantic Charter (appropriately presented aboard a ship moored at the US naval base of Argentia in Newfoundland) promised a post-war order committed to seeing 'sovereign rights and self-government restored to those who have been forcibly deprived of them'.[59] Almost a decade later, President Truman adopted the recommendations made in the NSC-68 report favouring a 'rapid build-up of political, economic, and military strength' against the USSR, aimed at 'conduct[ing] offensive operations to destroy vital elements of the Soviet war-making capacity'.[60] For the remainder of the Cold War (and arguably beyond), US strategists struggled to combine Roosevelt's Wilsonian internationalism with Truman's 'forward defense', to conjugate the freedoms promised in the Atlantic Charter with America's strategic primacy outlined in NSC-68.

The 'leasehold empire' formula was one response to this tension. It involved various agreements on basing rights with post-war allies and protectorates: the 1949 Petersberg Agreement with West Germany, the Washington Treaty, the 1951 Treaty of Mutual Cooperation and Security with Japan, and a similar agreement with the Philippines that year, as well as the 1953 Treaty of Mutual Defence with the Republic of Korea. Under this arrangement, the US sustained a hegemonic

world order through a strategy of open doors and closed frontiers – that is, by shoring up the formal territorial sovereignty of
its allies and clients so that they could integrate into a US-led
capitalist order, in exchange for American access to military
facilities inside their jurisdictions.[61] The US thus emerged as a
post-war empire that ruled *through* rather than *over* other
nominally equal polities.[62] This came with the risk that radical
social forces in independent states would take political sovereignty into their own hands, and pursue alternative paths of
socio-economic development and diplomatic alignment. The
early 1950s witnessed some attempts to do so outside the
communist Eurasian heartlands – in Mosaddeq's Iran, Arbenz's
Guatemala, Nasser's Egypt. But it was in the course of the 1960s
and 1970s that, inspired by Cuba, Vietnam and Algeria, decolonisation adopted a revolutionary character across Washington's
spheres of influence in South and South East Asia, Africa and
the Americas. Moreover, this period of revolution and anti-
colonial insurgency – in Vietnam, Malaya, Kenya, Yemen, Iraq,
and later Ethiopia, Central America, Mozambique, Angola and
Iran – further weakened France and Britain's lingering imperial
reach, particularly in the greater Middle East.

With the strategy of Eurasian containment compromised and
its junior partners in Paris and London in terminal decline, the
USA had one more strategic domain to exploit: the command of
the commons. Among the pledges made in the Atlantic Charter
was that of a post-war peace that 'should enable all men [*sic*] to
traverse the high seas and oceans without hindrance'.[63] Together
with airspace and outer space, the world's oceans have represented for American strategists a global commons 'that belong
to no one state and that provide access to much of the globe'.[64]
Yet, as in the past, the *mare liberum* principle often clashed with
geopolitical and economic interests of many states during and
after the Second World War. Shortly after the outbreak of war
in September 1939, North and South American republics met in
Panama to declare a 'neutrality zone' stretching 300 to 500

nautical miles into adjacent waters, which they resolved to keep 'free from the commission of any hostile act by any non-American belligerent nation'.[65] Six years later, as the war came to a close, President Truman issued two proclamations – one on the 'Natural Resources of the Subsoil and the Seabed of the Continental Shelf', the other on 'Coastal Fisheries in Certain Areas of the High Seas' – which opened a protracted period of post-war negotiations over ocean governance, culminating in the third UN Convention on the Law of the Sea (UNCLOS III), signed in 1982.[66]

In the first Truman Declaration, the US government made clear that it regarded 'the natural resources of the subsoil and sea bed of the continental shelf beneath the high seas but contiguous to the coasts of the United States as appertaining to the United States, subject to its jurisdiction and control.'[67] The first offshore oil well had been sunk in 1937 and technological developments during the post-war decades allowed an increasing number of coastal states and specialist companies to extract hydrocarbons and minerals from the seabed beyond the three-mile territorial waters, as well as develop sizeable distant-water fishing fleets (see Chapter 4). Spurred on by both the American resource enclosure of its continental shelf and the reaffirmation of national sovereignty in the aftermath of the Second World War, coastal Latin American states proclaimed in the early 1950s their exclusive right to exploit resources within 200 nautical miles of the high seas adjacent to territorial waters. This became the immediate precedent in customary law for the idea of an exclusive economic zone (EEZ) later codified in UNCLOS III. It also reopened questions about the dominion or appropriation of the seas explored elsewhere in this chapter and this book, and their relation to the sovereign jurisdiction of states. By the 1970s, in the context of a revitalised Third World call for a New International Economic Order, the United Nations and its specialised agencies became the locus of debate and negotiation over ocean governance. Malta's ambassador to the UN, Arvid Pardo, had introduced in 1967 the idea that the world's oceanic seabeds should be declared 'common heritage of mankind' (CHM), and management and appropriation of its mineral resources be administered by the UN with a mandate to redistribute the extracted wealth equitably among member states. This, in turn, informed many of the multilateral discussions which by 1982 delivered an International Seabed Authority tasked with regulating deep-sea mining in the Area (Figure 2.1), administering seabed resources and ensuring the environmental protection of the CHM.[68]

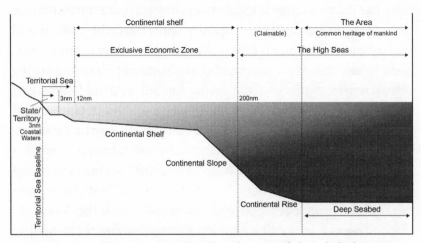

Figure 2.1. The post-war legal ordering of the global ocean
Source: Drawn by Ed Olivier.

Although the US has to date not ratified UNCLOS III, it has nonetheless recognised the convention as customary law and in 1983 declared its own coastal 200-nautical-mile EEZ. For all its opposition to the CHM ideals, Washington's principal concern with regard to the territorialisation of the sea has historically been the guarantee of free transit through the world's principal choke points and 'innocent passage' through territorial waters. This was reinforced under UNCLOS, thereby also reaffirming the separation of the political (sovereign powers) from the economic (property rights) enshrined in the EEZ, which in turn neatly conveys a capitalist logic where the sea is functionally exploited as a resource, rather than politically occupied as a territory. Though by no means a mechanical reflection of US interests (as Chapter 5, 'Appropriation', shows, the UNCLOS negotiations were deeply political and contested), the combination of Grotian principles of freedom of navigation in the high seas with Seldenian notions of exclusive rights of appropriation in near coastal waters did converge with Washington's post-war ambition to command the commons.[69]

The recognition of America's 'long range world-wide need for new sources of petroleum and other minerals' was explicit in the first Truman Declaration.[70] Ever since Churchill's decision as first admiral in 1914 to power Royal Navy steamships with oil rather than coal, the 'command of the commons' became closely connected to crude geology. As oil-fuelled automobility across industrial economies and militaries became widespread, Washington's principal post-war strategic aim was to secure the circulation of commodities, energy and capital across the 'free world'. Direct colonial rule had been delegitimised as a means for doing so, and thus control over access to the global commons became the principal mechanism guaranteeing these flows. The difficulty, once again, was that known oil reserves were concentrated within states bordering the Persian Gulf, where the US had the lightest post-war military and diplomatic footprint. Until the late 1950s, the greater Middle East remained within the Franco-British sphere of influence, and Washington only had permanent operational access to one naval base in Bahrain, resulting from an informal agreement with Britain in 1948.

It was against this backdrop that the Defense Department established a Long-Range Objectives Group in 1955 tasked with 'planning the Navy's long-term technological, weapons, and strategic needs'.[71] The group (known to the Navy as Op-93) eventually delivered a report to the US Joint Chiefs of Staff on 'The Strategic Island Concept', identifying dozens of potential sites across various oceans where US installations might be established with minimal political friction. Stu Barber, the Pentagon brains behind Op-93, had concluded in one of his early memoranda that the US was particularly vulnerable in the Indian Ocean region:

> access via Suez, and undisputed access via Singapore or through the Indies may be denied, as may air communications other than via Australia or Central Africa. Access to anchorages and airfields may be denied or limited north of the equator, as the product of anti-colonialist feelings or Soviet pressure.[72]

This is how the remote, sparsely populated, yet strategically positioned, and, crucially, British-governed, overseas territory of Diego Garcia became, from the first framework agreement of 1966 to the present, an 'unsinkable aircraft carrier' and refuelling base for American B-52 bombers and surveillance aircraft, as well as home to some 900 service personnel, one of the world's four GPS stations, up to two dozen prepositioning (or sealift) ships, and facilities ready to support a carrier task group as in the 1991 Gulf War.[73]

If Diego Garcia is a quintessential product of a post-war American maritime order which, through command of the commons and indirect imperialism, married the Atlantic Charter's freedom of the seas with the Truman Doctrine's 'forward strategy' encircling communist Eurasia, then the island of Tinian in the Marianas – where the planes carrying the atomic bombs dropped on Hiroshima and Nagasaki took off – came to represent the power of the sea in a nuclear age. As with Tinian, and its better-known southern neighbour Guam, the US developed naval bases during the post-war period in remote islands across the various oceans in support of its nuclear-powered and nuclear-armed fleet of ships and submarines. Such islands and their surrounding waters also became attractive nuclear testing sites for all atomic powers from the 1960s, as local inhabitants could be more easily displaced and distanced from the populated mainland enhanced secrecy, and masked the socio-environmental consequences of such experimentation.

The Cold War witnessed submarines in particular acquiring a pronounced strategic role for purposes of both deterrence and intelligence gathering. The US built its first nuclear-powered ballistic missile submarine (SSBN) in 1958, and within the space of eight years had added a further forty-one SSBNs to its fleet.[74] The Soviet Union followed suit, amassing by the early 1970s an SSBN force comparable to that of its Western rival. One result of this was the development of 'second-strike' capability as mobile and undetected SSBNs might survive a first nuclear attack and then be used to launch 'second-strike' missiles. The 'second-strike system', the great strategic scholar Philip Windsor averred, 'provided the greatest possible incentive not to attack at all. Insofar as any system of nuclear deterrence can be said to be safe, this was it'.[75] Thus as the sea became nuclearised during the Cold War, the two major superpowers invested heavily in their seaborne nuclear capabilities (up to one-third of US$2 trillion spent by the US on nuclear forces, according to some experts), respectively deploying them to contain the USSR and control the transatlantic sea lines of communication in the case of the West, and in that of the Soviets acting as 'bastions' in the wartime denial of enemy access to the Norwegian Sea and the North East Pacific approaches to the USSR.[76]

Stocks and flows: piracy and disputed sovereignty in the contemporary maritime order

For the international security analyst Barry Posen,

> Command means that the United States gets vastly more military use out of the sea, space, and air than do others; that it can credibly threaten to deny their use to others; and that others would lose a military contest for the commons if they attempted to deny them to the United States.[77]

This seems an accurate description of the contemporary, US-led post-Cold War world order. It certainly conveys the emphasis placed in this chapter upon the powerful combination of law and strategy in upholding a maritime order tailored to the reproduction of global markets. Having moved beyond an era of mercantilist inter-imperial rivalry, the global economy is today fundamentally reliant on the smooth circulation of value across the planet, much of it by sea. This does not, however, mean that the oceans have become a surface of frictionless, unencumbered transit. The counter-piracy campaigns in the Western Indian Ocean in the early twenty-first century, and the recurring territorial disputes in the South China Sea, are a testament to the continuing challenges of ordering the sea, and the unique forms of terraqueous spatialities that capitalist states and firms create in doing so.

After virtually disappearing as a social practice during the twentieth century, incidences of maritime piracy (criminal acts of violence, detention, rape, robbery or depredation committed for private ends by the crew or the passengers of a private ship on the high seas) resurfaced off the coast of Somalia during the first decade of the twenty-first century, reaching an annual peak in 2011 of almost 180 piratical attacks – mainly involving holding seafarers to ransom – in the Western Indian Ocean region.[78] In August of that same year, a group of maritime industry organisations, including the International Chamber of Shipping and the International Transport Workers' Federation, issued the fourth version of guidelines entitled 'Best Management Practices for Protection against Somalia Based Piracy' (BMP4).[79] The document produces an explicit territorialisation of a High Risk Area in the Gulf of Aden, defined as 'an area bounded by Suez and the Strait of Hormuz to the North, 10°S and 78°E'. This particular area is one of several zones in the North and Western Indian Ocean (the Internationally Recommended Transit Corridor and the Extended Risk Area are two others mapped in Figure 2.2) which for the past decade have been delimited, monitored and patrolled by a combination of diverse state and private organisations – from the UK Maritime Operations office in Dubai, to the Maritime Security Centre, Horn of Africa, 'an initiative established by EU NAVFOR with close co-operation from industry'.[80] Such exercises have adopted some of the core characteristics of transnational governance – multilateralism, 'hybrid' (military–civilian) mandates and public–private partnerships. One faithful reflection of this was the redefinition in December 2015 of the High Risk Area by a private international shipping association, the Baltic and International Maritime Council.

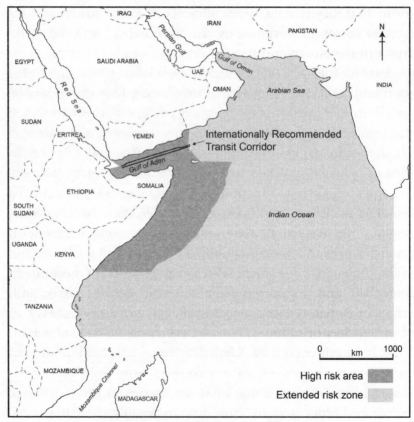

Figure 2.2. Maritime zoning of the
risk of Somali-based piracy

The UN's 2008 Security Council Resolution 1816, the first of several such resolutions on Somali piracy, occasioned the establishment of the EU NAVFOR, ostensibly to protect World Food Programme (WFP) and African Union Mission in Somalia (AMISOM) vessels from piratical attacks in both Somali and international waters. This humanitarian mandate was, however, from the beginning informed by a wider commercial concern, clearly (if somewhat surreptitiously) stated in the International Maritime Organisation's Resolution A.1002 (25) adopted in November 2007, which called on the UN to recognise 'the strategic importance of the navigational routes along the coast of Somalia for regional and global seaborne trade and the need to ensure that they remain safe at all times'.[81] There is therefore no mystery surrounding the motivation behind this (re)territorialisation of the North and Western Indian Ocean: as the reach of the Extended Risk Zone indicates, even if its origins lie in the WFP and AMISOM humanitarian effort in Somalia, counter-piracy in the Gulf of Aden has plainly become a policing and governance exercise aimed at securing the maritime circulation of commodity capital through that strategic region.

Much of this analysis is uncontroversial, but the distinctive terraqueousness of these counter-piracy initiatives is perhaps less obvious. For a start, because most piratical attacks at their height in the five years after 2008 took place outside territorial waters, it proved almost impossible to patrol the whole extent of the designated risk areas. Instead the latter were monitored, controlled and supported from strategic coastal bases and offices in Dubai, Djibouti or Seychelles (the operational HQ of Maritime Security Centre, Horn of Africa, is further inland, in faraway Northwood, Herefordshire, England!). The contemporary attempt at policing the flowing sea from fixed land thus generated new imperial geographies as counter-piracy campaigns recolonised older imperial outposts and recharged these locations with the mission of rendering the unruly seas stable and secure. Moreover, for all their high-tech attempts at delimiting

the sea as authorities try to do on land, the distinctive geophysical features of the ocean remain stubbornly resistant to governance regimes seeking to guarantee a 24/7, 365-days-a-year
passage through perilous waters like those of the Gulf of Aden.
Transit through the Internationally Recommended Corridor
was statistically safest at nighttime, while the 'Best Management
Practices for Protection against Somalia Based Piracy' recognised that seasonal weather conditions can significantly affect
the patterns of pirate activity.[82] Finally, and perhaps most
importantly, the efforts at territorialising sections of the ocean
through counter-piracy regimes have created new valorisations
of risk that bind land and sea in peculiar ways. The incidence of
piracy increases the risk and therefore the costs – labour, insurance, fuel – of transit across the Gulf of Aden. The mapping of
high-risk areas has since had direct implications for the terms
and conditions of seafarers working on vessels in those areas:
the International Bargaining Forum, the union–employer negotiating body for the maritime industry, has in the past agreed to
a series of bonuses, compensation packages and rights to refuse
sailing within those designated areas. Similarly, on some calculations, the excess costs of insurance premiums resulting from
Lloyds Market Association declaring the Gulf of Aden a 'war
risk area' in 2008 amounted to anything between US$460
million and US$3.2 billion a year.[83]

None of these phenomena – remote control and command,
the 'friction' of weather patterns, the increased premiums in
high-risk zones – are necessarily unique to the high seas. But
they are distinctive as the scale and fluidity of the ocean space
precludes the traditional terrestrial response to such predica-
ments: effective occupation. Multilateral governance initiatives
like those off the coast of Somalia that try to make the sea safe
for commodity circulation have to battle with the challenge of
enforcing the monopoly over the means of violence within
designated high-risk areas that are in constant motion. The
attempts at transcending the sea–land divide through the

delimitation and pacification of maritime zones in fact generates new spatial configurations which in many respects rein-
force that very duality (while acknowledging their interconnection): counter-piracy, as explored in the twenty-first century
Western Indian Ocean, takes on a multilateral character at sea,
but regional states and their onshore coastal facilities acquire a
critical geopolitical role; the supposedly free seas become
increasingly regulated by land-based regimes of risk – insurance
premiums, special employment terms and conditions, corporate
security-proofing.

States and firms have in the past few decades struggled to
give greater definition to this legal ambiguity through the (re)
regulation of maritime space. In the case of contemporary
piracy, as we have seen, a combination of multilateral counter-
piracy initiatives and the invocation of universal jurisdiction
resulted in attempts at territorialising the sea, thereby securing
safe and uninterrupted passage of commercial traffic through
the Gulf of Aden. The experiments in global governance have,
however, come across geophysical obstacles in the flowing sea
and in forms of land-based territoriality (essentially sovereign
control) which create distinctive problems for those seeking to
police the seas – most obviously, how to process suspected
pirates captured on the high seas. The result has in most cases
been a reconfiguration of the relationship between sovereignty,
territoriality and accumulation that renders piratical waters like
those off the coast of Somalia terraqueous zones: both delimited and patrolled, yet also associated with high risk and lawlessness. Responses to contemporary piracy, then, illustrate the
tensions and contradictions in creating a world order that (in
Schmitt's sense) aligns order and orientation by securing the
seaborne circulation of commodities through land-based
systems of sovereign rule.

Contemporary piracy is significant principally because it challenges the capitalist world order by delaying, threatening and
thereby increasing the cost of transit through some of the key

maritime choke points in the global economy. Piracy also presses on an Achilles heel of the capitalist world order, namely ambiguous jurisdiction on the high seas. On the one hand, piracy is clearly an outlawed practice in public international law, yet on the other, even the most powerful states – America, China, EU members and Russia – constantly run into juridical complications in combating maritime piracy. Washington and other Western capitals signed bilateral conventions with Kenya and Seychelles to avoid processing alleged pirates through their own domestic legal systems, instead outsourcing the task to courts in Mombasa, while China and Russia have been forced to deploy counter-piracy forces in the Western Indian Ocean in defence of their own cargo fleets. Contemporary piracy has thus turned parts of the ocean space into a laboratory for new multilateral forms of governance and force that are largely absent on land. The experience of Somali piracy in particular has driven home the point that the high seas and unpoliced EEZs act as the dump site (both literally and figuratively) of land-side crises and pathologies – be they so-called collapsed states or the illegal disposal of toxic waste. The ocean world appears in these cases as the space of exception, where the laws and powers of the sovereign state are seemingly suspended in order to address the peculiar challenges of sea-borne violence and illegal practices – a phenomenon we will return to in Chapter 6 on the offshore world. To that extent, the sea presents itself to the dominant powers as a disorderly geopolitical sphere in dire need of regulation, policing and management so that the ceaseless and unimpeded flow of commodities across the planet can be guaranteed.

The regulation of such flows, however, relies on the 'stock' of territorial power, mainly represented in the military capabilities and juridical reach of states. The continuing geopolitical tension over the disputed sovereignty of the South China Sea neatly combines questions of freedom of navigation, naval basing, maritime strategy and the geophysical determinants of world order we have been exploring in this chapter.[84] It speaks to the difficulties for a capitalist world order of reconciling access to and control over the oceans – of enforcing a maritime commons while upholding state sovereignty over the sea and its resources. Seven jurisdictions (Vietnam, Indonesia, Brunei Darussalam, the People's Republic of China, the Philippines, Malaysia and Taiwan) currently have competing claims over the sovereignty of hundreds of islands, reefs, rocks, sandbanks, shoals and their surrounding waters in the South China Sea. The principal motivations behind these claims involve economics, ideology and politics: access to fishing banks, gas and oil reserves, mineral deposits; nationalist calls for territorial integrity; and strategic considerations relating to both national interest and energy security. The fundamental geo-economic feature of these disputes is that the South China Sea remains an indispensable gateway for East Asia's commodity exports and its energy imports. China alone ships in 82 per cent of its oil needs via the Malacca Straits, and close to 40 per cent of global sea trade (some 40,000 vessels a year) passes through the South China Sea. The sea's hydrocarbon reserves are comparable to those of Mexico – 11 billion barrels of oil, and 190 trillion cubic feet of natural gas, both of considerable value, particularly for resource-poor yet growing economies like those of Vietnam or the Philippines. As more of the region's countries develop advanced capitalist economies, distant-water fishing fleets acquire greater importance (not least through remittances from seafarers), while shipbuilding and related maritime industries do so too.[85]

Yet these commercial imperatives also have a geopolitical dimension since effective occupation of islands, and declaration of an EEZ in adjacent waters, open up the possibility of challenging, or at least interfering in, the freedoms of navigation and overflight. This is what happened in March 2009, when an American spy ship chartered by Danish conglomerate Maersk, the USNS *Impeccable*, was forcibly diverted by Chinese aeroplanes and ships while monitoring waters seventy-five miles south of Hainan Island, where up to twenty nuclear submarines are docked at the Yulin naval base. Washington and Beijing subsequently traded accusations of harassment and violation of international law. The Chinese claimed that USNS *Impeccable* was breaching UNCLOS articles that outlaw 'scientific marine research' in a foreign EEZ without the coastal state's authority. The United States (despite not having ratified UNCLOS) insisted that all sea beyond the twelve-nautical-mile territorial waters is open to unimpeded movement by military vessels.[86] At stake in these legal–diplomatic exchanges is the US Navy's capacity to patrol the South China Sea and defend its allies across the bulk of Asia; in other words, to sustain its hegemonic power in that region and globally. 'Part of the strategy of China', maritime security analyst James Kaska has suggested, 'is to repeatedly suggest that there are important unresolved legal issues pertaining to the EEZ that should be "clarified."'[87] Aware of the centrality of freedom of navigation to this organisation of world order, Beijing has developed a series of strategic and tactical concepts aimed at denying US access to the Western Pacific and South China. Dubbed 'the assassin's mace' (*shashoujian*), the strategy's main objective is thwarting a US military intervention in support of an independent Taiwan, and its principal means involve the combination of cyberwarfare and semi-ballistic 'antiship' missiles such as the DF-21D that can disable American military assets within China's 'second island chain', stretching from Japan to Indonesia.[88]

Much has been made in recent years of China's rise as a naval power, with its *zouchuqu* ('Going Global') policy and sovereign designs over all of the South China Sea inside the historical nine-dash, or U-shaped, line exemplifying this hegemonic ambition.[89] Yet at the time of writing, the People's Liberation Army Navy (PLAN) has one overseas base recently constructed in Djibouti (in contrast to America's military presence in over 150 states), only brought a second aircraft carrier into service in April 2017 (compared to the US's eleven currently on active duty), and has seventy-eight principal combatant ships (relative to the US's 290), most of them lacking a blue-water capability. The PRC is, in David Shambaugh's apt phrase, a 'partial power', with a strong investment in its own coastal defence and maritime sphere of influence within the Western Pacific, but with a very limited naval projection beyond that region.[90] Like other powerful states and economies, China aims to secure its sea lines of communication (including, as we briefly saw earlier, against Indian Ocean piracy) and has – together with twelve other non-Arctic nations – been granted observer status on the Arctic Council, given its commercial interest in the northern and north-west passages to and from the Atlantic. But most of this international maritime presence is conducted with respect to the law of the sea, and generally through multilateral governance structures. Even the 'maritime silk road' element of Xi Jingpin's much-discussed Belt and Road Initiative might more properly be seen as a fundamentally geo-economic exercise in exploiting the so-called 'blue economy', guaranteeing smooth maritime trade and exporting the country's surplus capital in the form of overseas infrastructure, rather than a frontal strategy aimed at undermining the existing multilateral order.[91]

It is with these facts in mind that the ongoing disputes in the South China Sea might be seen as a contemporary instance of a more enduring tension between capitalism and the sea when it comes to reconciling property and sovereignty, circulation and accumulation, *dominium* and *imperium*. When the Chinese state, like other countries in the region, engages in vast (and environmentally toxic) land reclamation projects in the South China Sea, it is not only building military infrastructures and surveillance facilities, righting historical wrongs, or preparing the ground for maritime resource extraction. It is also producing a new alignment between law, strategy and order where the relationship between firm land and free sea becomes essential. In a world dominated by the production of capitalist value, every legitimate profit-seeking enterprise has an interest in trade flowing across the planet (even those who benefit from hoarding, destroying or blocking require the circulation of wealth to resume at some stage). The sea, we know, is a privileged site for such circulation, and indeed resource extraction. But like any extractive space, it also needs regulation, delimitation and policing – that is, an order. The contemporary exercises in counter-piracy off the coast of Somalia and sovereign appropriation in the South China Sea, we have argued in this chapter, reflect a broader history – protracted, uneven and conflictive, to be sure – whereby law, strategy and order are mobilised to secure the reproduction of capitalist value at, through and near the sea.

3

Exploitation

In Joseph Conrad's 1917 novella *The Shadow-Line*, a green captain faced with a disease-stricken crew and the need to meet shipping contracts feels the full psychological pressure of keeping on time:

> The word 'Delay' entered the secret chamber of my brain, resounded there like a tolling bell which maddens the ear, affected all my senses, took on a black colouring, a bitter taste, a deadly meaning . . . The men ailed. And thus time was not only money, but life as well.[1]

At the same time that Conrad was himself working his way up the ranks of the merchant navy, a royal commission launched in 1885 investigating the loss of life at sea on British-registered ships found that seafaring was the most deadly job in that country.[2] It determined that a flurry of legislation on vessel safety in the mid-1870s 'had little or no effect' because of the reluctance of regulators to risk litigation by shipowners for their losses. While recognising the ever-present danger of harsh weather while at sea, the commission identified avoidable causes of death as 'the pressure of the demand for quick passages' and 'an insufficient number of hands on the watches'. Where shipowners were insured and 'ships were lost with all hands . . . [owners] were considerable gainers from the loss'.[3] Put differently, through their intensification of the rate of exploitation of crew, British shipowners were responsible for the deaths of thousands, and in fact profited from this macabre reckoning.

Oceanic seafarers and distant-water fishing crews experience unique conditions of work. Evenings and weekends are spent in a confined and hierarchical workplace where '[w]atch after watch, day by day, week after week, and month after month, sailors carry out ... tasks while eating, sleeping and living aboard worksites in motion'.[4] Crew are squeezed by the drive to maximise productivity for minimum cost in a contracted shipping time on the 'structured space' of the ship, where they reproduce daily routines for several months alongside their bosses.[5] While crew and officers are literally in the same boat, they are by no means equal. Captains have long been thought of as individual sovereigns on the ship: that 'hierarchical State in miniature'.[6] Representatives of capital and state, the captain's rule could not be opposed, unless crew were willing to face the charge of mutiny. Seafaring ships, we contend, are exceptional spaces of exploitation. But the changing nature of onboard labour regimes through time and place is fundamentally the product of varying social, not technological, relations. As Heide Gerstenberger argues, 'it is not the technical frame of the "ship" which determines the extent of authority and hierarchy aboard' but capitalist social relations and 'economic and managerial strategies'.[7]

Set in the Sea of Okhotsk, Kobayashi Takiji's 1929 novel *The Crab Cannery Ship* illustrates the brutality of working life at sea. One of Kobayashi's protagonists – a fisherman – responds to the fears of a fellow crew member that they'll be killed by the captain if they resist their intensifying exploitation. He exclaims,

> That's just a trick. Do you get it? They know that if they kill us, they're the ones who lose out. Their goal – their real goal – is to make us work like the devil, tie us to the tree, squeeze us till we squeak, and make loads of profits from us. That's what they're putting us through every day ... Our bodies are being killed just like mulberry leaves are gobbled up by silkworms.[8]

Contemporaneous critics derided Kobayashi's novel as clumsy communist propaganda. (Kobayashi himself was tortured to death in 1933 by the Tokkō police – a force charged with supressing subversives).[9] But his tale was generalisable beyond the militarised capitalism of interwar Japan. For example, the use of corporal punishment as a disciplinary mechanism in maritime labour regimes was only made illegal in 1915 in the USA.[10] In 2015 slavery and murder at sea were uncovered on Thai fishing boats and slave-like conditions found on New Zealand-flagged vessels; both cases were initially hidden from public view beneath the glisten of cheap seafood.[11] Despite this exposure, unfree labour practices on fishing boats remain widespread.

Behind the headlines, people labouring at sea in the early twenty-first century remain crucial to keeping capitalism global. Their work makes possible the fragmentation of production and labour arbitrage across the planet, integrating food production and manufacturing through tenuous supply chains which are now monitored in real time by capitalist managers, as expounded in Chapter 5, 'Logistics'. As with Conrad's crew and captain, capital's drive against the clock saturates this work with a 'deadly meaning'. One hundred and thirty years after the royal commission on deaths at sea on British ships the rate of fatal accidents had declined very substantially, but seafaring remained the most dangerous occupation in Britain.[12] Work at sea is lethal not simply as a 'direct consequence of a struggle with the elements', but as 'a product of the business practices prevalent in the industry, which frequently cause the management of risks to seafarers to be a secondary consideration to the pursuit of profit'.[13] What is specific to the calculus of exploitation, risk and labour time at sea? How has the 'maritime factor' identified in this book's Introduction shaped the labour regimes on ocean-going vessels? Have the working lives of those toiling at sea changed since the inception of commercial capitalism?

This chapter addresses these and related questions empirically, theoretically and conceptually. The empirical focus is on the capitalist exploitation of seafarers and fishing crew, its dynamics and institutional contexts. The two occupations are commonly separated in the trade union movement and in international labour law. The 1920 International Labour Conference on seafarers set out 'persons employed on fishing boats' as constituting 'a distinct class' because they can be owner-operators or have 'a special interest in the enterprise', such as the share system.[14] Almost a century on, fishing crew were similarly excluded from the 2006 Maritime Labour Convention.[15] Crew working on ships are archetypal maritime workers and we look to labour regimes in the merchant navy to think through the varied forms and conditions of capitalist exploitation at sea. This focus does not imply homogeneity among such workers.[16] When considering exploitation at sea we draw on selective snapshots in historical time, outlining similarities and differences in maritime labour regimes across two periods – the merchant navy under the 'second' British Empire (roughly 1793–1914) and global seafaring in the neoliberal era of the late twentieth and early twenty-first centuries. Contemporary maritime labour regimes contain a degree of path dependency which needs to be explained in connection with their past, but the dialectical relationship between capital and labour also means that these regimes are never entirely stable and are always in motion.

Exploitation on ships is understood theoretically as the production of surplus value in the movement of commodity capital around the world (e.g. the merchant navy) and in the appropriation of nature at sea (e.g. fishing). We use exploitation in the technical Marxist sense as the extraction of surplus value by capital from labour power, i.e. a worker's time that is not paid for and which produces surplus value for a capitalist. Under conditions of 'normal' competitive accumulation, vessel owners seek to maximise the rate of exploitation of the living labour animating the dead labour embodied in the fixed capital of the ship.[17] This gets directly at the fundamental antagonism in capitalist social relations of production between the asset-owning ruling class and the labouring classes who must sell their labour power to survive. Antagonistic class relations are always dialectically articulated with other sources of social domination and subordination, and are not the sole orientation of political struggle;[18] as we shall see, this is as much so at sea as it is on land. Further, not all labour is based on wages per se, since historical capitalism works, as Jairus Banaji shows us, 'through a multiplicity of forms of exploitation *based on* wage-labour',[19] which can be mediated in various ways, including diverse management regimes, the household and/or debt relations.[20] Put slightly differently, we find it useful to distinguish between capital as a process of surplus value extraction – 'exploitation' – and historical, living–breathing, eating–shitting *capitalism*, i.e. the diverse forms that exploitation takes in the world of work.[21] Yet, in a very real sense, the ship can be seen as a factory engaged in the production of movement of commodities by capitals-in-competition, each of which is seeking to exploit labour in doing so, including by investing in technologies to competitively intensify this rate of exploitation ('relative surplus value') as discussed below and in Chapters 4 and 5.

In a narrow sense, seafaring is a predominantly male occupation – notwithstanding the incorporation of women into the liner workforce in the course of the twentieth century – and maritime labour regimes are strongly masculinised. In a broader sense life on ships depends on life on land where the labour of social reproduction is historically and disproportionately provided by women. Evidently, rates of exploitation and their varied forms in historical capitalism cannot be understood in the absence of unpaid human labour, not least – but not limited to – the social reproduction of human beings. Nonetheless, even during the age of sail, women were regularly on board ships when in port and the wives of warrant and junior officers regularly went to sea and worked on the ship. Women would also disguise themselves as men to work as crew and, more rarely, as marines. It is for this reason that unless describing formal titles, we choose to use non-gendered words such as 'crew', 'sailor' or 'seafarer'.[22]

Capitalist shipping is the production and sale of movement – the ability to transform a commodity in space – and has been historically fundamental to the completion of capitalist circuits on a global scale, as we have already suggested and examine more fully in Chapter 5.[23] There is, however, an important tension between the assumption that the exploitation of labour *presupposes* the system and the following historical account in that labour regimes on Britain's merchant navy in the 1600s and 1700s existed when 'the system as a whole' was only *incipient*. Indeed, as established in Chapters 1 and 2, maritime circulation and order went hand in hand with the transition to global capitalism, and a period of primitive accumulation was a fundamental ingredient for this *emerging* totality. As we shall see, this much is apparent from the early maritime labour regime under Pax Britannica, which depended on direct recruitment through violence, force and deception, and indirectly through processes like land enclosures.

Conceptually, we adopt and develop labour regime analysis to study and compare forms of capitalist exploitation and its regulation on ships in different times, spaces and oceanic regions. The labour regime is an intermediate category that tries to bridge the essential relations of capital-as-process and the ever-greater levels of concreteness of historical capitalism.[24] Labour regime analysis is thus not concerned solely with the labour process (obviously crucial though this is in a ship at sea), but is also about recognising the range of social relations at various scales that shape (and are shaped by) labour processes, such as articulations with local and national political economies, state regulation and private ordering of particular sectors or industries, and specific histories and cultures of labour organising and resistance. For example, as is discussed below, crew agencies are a central plank of the contemporary maritime labour regime. Crew subcontracting allows employers to bypass labour law and avoid direct negotiation with workers, and in doing so crew agencies are 'rewarded' with a portion of surplus value taken from seafarers. In this and in many other ways, one labour regime is always in dynamic interaction with other labour regimes.[25]

But 'where' are maritime labour regimes? Where do their analytical boundaries stop and start? Seafarers' working lives, and sometimes deaths, are subject to considerable jurisdictional ambivalence and often overlap. When at sea, *the ship* as a place combines the labour process and daily reproduction of seafarers – their lifeworld – and constitutes the immediate spatial extent of the labour regime.[26] Yet it is not the regime's limit. Methods of labour recruitment are based on land and their terms seep into employment relations at sea, such as the distinction between crew organised in strong onshore unions and those precariously employed by crew agencies. Similarly, regulatory power over working lives at sea tends to be mediated by the flag state: it is likely to be of significance on a Scandinavian-flagged ship that moves between 'advanced' maritime states, but it can also matter very little if the ship is flagged to an open registry (flag of convenience) designed solely to reap rent from sovereignty. In comparing the diverse social relations involved in maritime employment across time and space through the lens of a labour regime, we identify some of the overarching themes relating to seafaring work.

The story of capitalist exploitation at sea is one of commercial and then industrial capital capturing surplus value through particularly globalised combinations of freedom and coercion, confinement and mobility, opportunity and inequality, integration and hierarchy. It is characterised by distinctive forms of organisation and resistance aboard, and specific socio-economic and political relations ashore (involving the state, intermediary agents and labour organisations). In all this, the global ocean acts as a natural force that pushes maritime capital to develop new ways of recruiting and disciplining an international workforce, while reinventing novel forms of racialisation, coercion and regulation. The rest of this chapter compares labour regimes on ships at sea in the era of the British Empire with those of the post-war, especially neoliberal, era, thereby fleshing out how the peculiar dialectic of capital and labour at sea – and its associated transformations wrought by imperial wars abroad and legal–political changes at home – has produced unique expressions of both exploitation and solidarity.

Maritime labour regimes under the Pax Britannica

By the late nineteenth century, Britain accounted for between 40 and 50 per cent in tonnage of the world's merchant navy, propelled by a world-leading productivity (or rate of exploitation) of its maritime workforce.[27] The sheer scale of this influence and global reach shaped profoundly the competitive conditions of other merchant fleets. A disciplined, reliable, and skilled yet economical multinational crew of wage earners tending to the most technologically advanced ships under a London-centred administrative network with legal–diplomatic and commercial–infrastructural backing in all corners of the world became the dominant form of maritime labour regime, the standard bearer and model to emulate. In order to realise and reproduce this ideal type, the British merchant navy (the Royal Navy in different ways) had during its nineteenth-century heyday to reconcile often contradictory requirements: nationalist protectionism with a reliance on foreign labour, nominally free contracts with the brutal imposition of order on board, strict turnover schedules under changing and testing environmental conditions. Out of such efforts emerged a labour regime particularly oriented to the challenges of recruiting, retaining and managing a multinational workforce on a 'worksite in motion'. Mobility, containment, segmentation and isolation thus became the hallmarks of ocean-going labour. Seafarers to this day share many of these features with migrant miners, truckers, construction workers, domestic employees and others, but no land-based worker (bar the possible exception of long-distance road hauliers) lives and produces value in the same confined space while constantly moving between places and jurisdictions. These unique characteristics, we shall now see, accompanied exploitation at sea across different periods as the 'maritime factor' gave the labour regime on ships a very particular inflection.

Globalising capital and cosmopolitan labour

'The deep-sea proletariat' was among the largest and most prominent workforce in the era of commercial capitalism, and continued to be crucial to industrial Britain's control over the world's largest merchant navy and its international commercial networks. As mentioned in Chapter 1, the mercantilism of the Navigation Acts from 1651 onwards was a major boost to maritime capitalism in Britain and included the requirement that captains and the majority of crew were nationals. Merchant mariners were Britain's third labour force in 1721 (approximately 20,500 people) following agricultural and textile workers. And this excludes those employed in other areas of maritime logistics such as shipbuilding, harbour and warehouse workers. In the 1720s London was the world's largest port, serving as base to more seafarers than all other British ports combined.[28] With Britain's growing global hegemony, the number of merchant seafarers rose to 49,000 in 1770 and to 174,500 in 1820.[29] The imprint of this maritime activity was felt inland in the suburban spread of port town populations in Bristol, Cardiff, Glasgow, Liverpool, Plymouth and Portsmouth.

The average seafarer on late eighteenth-century British merchant ships worked at sea for fifteen to twenty years. A workforce 'freed' by the torrent of private and parliamentary enclosures, some joined as children as young as five, and almost all had started by the age of twelve. Given the gruelling nature of the work most left by their early thirties.[30] Without formal training, crew ('ratings' in modern parlance) were classified – and thus paid – according to the amount of time they had previously spent at sea, along with an eye to their skill and knowledge. Using the gendered language of the time, a landsman could be considered an ordinary seaman after spending a year at sea, and a total of two years was necessary to become an able seaman. The working day was (and often still is) organised around the watch – normally four hours on and off, seven days a week (although some more benevolent captains introduced three watches to allow for a night's uninterrupted sleep every three days).[31] Crew would generally specialise in handling particular sections of the sails. The cooperative social relationships of this labour process under conditions of disciplinary management of a captain and senior and petty officers made seafarers the first 'collective labourers':[32] assigned to a strict technical division of labour, yet requiring fast and precise coordination across ratings. 'Seamen during the Age of Sail', Jeffrey Bolster reminds us, 'constantly interpreted orders, anticipated problems, and used their knowledge of ropework, steering, and shiphandling to execute the captain's or mate's plan'.[33]

The acceleration of exploitation of crew was a major structuring dynamic in the development of the capitalist merchant navy. For commercial capital, an indicator of productivity is the number of crew per gross ton of ship; that is, the volume of commodities moved per worker. The early Dutch commercial capitalists in the 1500s were leading innovators. They designed different ships to carry specific commodities, eventually settling on convoys of *fluits:* slow-moving 'floating boxes', with smaller sails requiring reduced crews and without armaments, which mean that they were reliant on accompanying warships and the Dutch state. These same merchants spread risk among themselves by splitting vessel investments into shares.[34] For British ships, labour productivity increased from around eight tons per crew member in 1686 to ten tons in 1736, reaching up to fifteen tons by 1766. These East Indiamen were the largest merchant ships in the world; they were not built for speed but to carry as much cargo as possible, and unlike the *fluits* had double gun decks to ward off pirates and privateers.[35] Ships suffer a high level of depreciation caused by the eroding power of brine, wind and waves, and thus need regular maintenance and repair.[36] Thousands of East Indiamen were built in world-leading shipyards in Surat, India, generally at the same price as in North West Europe, but being made of teak they could last for up to forty years at sea, compared to fourteen years at most for a European equivalent.[37] The relative technological dynamism of shipbuilding investment by Europe's commercial capitalists is indicated in the average labour productivity per ton of commodities carried by the Northern European merchant fleet, which averaged three times greater than the Southern European equivalent through 1672–1803.[38] The British and Dutch merchant navies globalised the logic of commercial capitalism – driven by competition between capitals to maximise profitability from the exploitation of seafaring labour;[39] the Southern European fleet was, by contrast, a throwback to an era of late feudal Iberian plunder.[40]

In order to sustain this extraordinary commercial success into the nineteenth century, Britain (and indeed its rivals) had to address several structural challenges thrown up by capitalist production of movement at sea. One was the perennial labour shortage that affected Britain's merchant navy in particular, generated through a combination of the mismatch between the country's regulatory requirement under the Navigation Acts for the majority of a ship's crew to be from Britain and its colonies; the available labour supply at any given time; the voracious demands of its global empire; the diversion of manpower to the

Royal Navy during times of war; and the understandable reluctance of landlubbers to engage in dangerous, highly regimented, poorly paid work at sea for extended periods of time. Second, and partly in response to this latter reality, exploitation of labour on ships posed specific problems of discipline and resistance, involving everything from mutiny to desertion, insubordination to corporal punishment. Finally, the necessarily cross-jurisdictional nature of global maritime commerce raised complex questions of rights, rules and regulations for private firms, the state and, in different ways, the wider public and organised labour. Diverse strategies were adopted in all three of these areas during the long period of British dominance of the world economy, but they were all directed at upholding the capitalist labour regime at sea that underwrote this hegemony.

The internationalisation of Britain's mercantile workforce was one response to labour shortages, although this only developed into a concerted and successful strategy after the 1849 repeal of the Navigation Acts, and the subsequent rise of competing merchant fleets in the late nineteenth century. Prior to the nineteenth-century consolidation of the nation-state and the institutionalisation of citizenship, the ocean-going workforce was genuinely cosmopolitan in its mongrel, polyglot, syncretic and rootless character, and only acquired a degree of permanence in certain emblematic maritime quarters of the world's largest ports. Peter Linebaugh's classic history of London's popular classes in the eighteenth century highlights the multinational diversity of seafarers drawn to the capital – often from colonial territories – by the prospects of maritime and related employment, and makes the case that their lives on the terraqueous Thames made London cosmopolitan.[41] The imperial circuits of commercial capitalism, as we saw in Chapter 1, produced new 'motley crews' of trans-oceanic workers along the Atlantic seaboards – many of whom, like the famous abolitionist Olaudah Equiano, were former bondspeople. Across the Indian Ocean and South China Sea, too, European merchant ships tapped into long-standing networks of multicultural mariners who populated the great ports of that region – from Mombasa to Bombay, Aden to Surat, Singapore to Kolkata. However, England's Navigation Acts meant that East Indiamen built in India were generally barred from British ports and instead concentrated on the trade with China.[42]

Employment at sea often opened opportunities for social and geographical mobility and autonomy in a world increasingly stratified by race and class. During the age of sail, many Asian, African, Caribbean and African American crew members displayed longer experience and closer knowledge of the seas they crossed than their superiors within the ships they sailed. In the aftermath of the late eighteenth-century Atlantic revolutions, almost one in every five American seafarers was black. The transition from bonded to wage labour on American ships at the turn of the nineteenth century, W. Jeffrey Bolster contends, offered men of colour better prospects:

> As waged workers rather than bound ones, sailors and would-be sailors were among a constantly changing pool of applicants for available berths. This allowed free black men (or those claiming to be free) to come aboard ships on a similar footing with transient and inexperienced white workers.[43]

The cruellest expression of this perverse and contradictory predicament was lived by black freemen working on slave ships, and indeed black Yankee sailors trading in the ante-bellum South, carrying as they did the double burden of their own everyday discrimination while contributing, however indirectly and reluctantly, to sustaining the continued enslavement of fellow African Americans. Such experiences generated novel forms of black consciousness and solidarity across the eastern American seaboard and beyond which, revealingly, prompted further repressive legislation like South Carolina's 1822 'Act for the Better Regulation and Government of Free Negros and

Persons of Color', which stipulated that any black crew member of a ship docking in any of the state's ports 'be confined in jail until said vessel shall clear out and depart from this State'.[44]

The ambivalence and ambiguity attached to the promises of freedom at sea are well reflected in the multiple identities that mariners of colour in particular adopted to avoid discriminatory classification – from Anglicised names to 'racial passing', sailors were generally reluctant to officially disclose their origins and instead often self-identified with urban centres or 'mixed and shifting spatial identities'.[45] Although complicated by the lack of formal citizenship papers such as passports and the then considerably more porous nature of 'nationality', it is possible to trace the internationalisation of maritime labour markets using records of crew from ships captured for profit by naval or privateer vessels ('prizes').[46] These sources indicate that at the end of the eighteenth century Denmark, France and Spain were particularly parochial, engaging largely national crews and often legislating to limit the employment of foreigners (in the Spanish case, through successive 'General Ordinances against Corsairing [Privateering]' from the early seventeenth century).[47] Both the city state of Venice and Portugal used slaves, prisoners of war and convicts alongside free labour; and Sweden crewed its small merchant fleet with a system of conscripted labour from agrarian communities in coastal regions.[48]

Locating the origins of 'Asian' crew in the maritime labour market of commercial capitalism is more difficult because of the relative lack of interest in and ignorance of the European assessors of prizes. A sample of prize records shows that the 'muscles of empire'[49] came from the east, south and west coasts of India, including Bengal, Kochi, Kolkata, Pondicherry and Surat, as well as from China and Java.[50] Seafarers from South Asia were generally undifferentiated by the British as 'lascars', despite wide cultural and geographical differences among them.[51] Importantly, records from the late seventeenth century and the early eighteenth indicate that there were only minor differences in wages paid to European and South Asian crew.[52] Van Rossum et al. argue that the positive experience of Dutch merchants with Asian crew in intra-Asian ('country') trade encouraged their increased employment in European shipping. Holland's maritime labour regime was, for a time, Europe's most cosmopolitan in character. Rapid capitalist development created a general labour shortage, and the share of foreigners in Dutch maritime employment doubled from around 15 per cent of the total in 1607 to over 30 per cent in 1694, before peaking at over 50 per cent of 60,000 in the maritime workforce in 1785. Mirroring the decline of the Dutch Republic, absolute maritime employment dropped to around 25,000 by 1850, when only around 13 per cent of whom were foreigners.[53] Despite this rapid peak in maritime employment, the Dutch state did not sponsor forced labour, except during times of war. In parallel, British sailors in the mid-nineteenth century were paid up to nine times more than Asian crew working on the same British ships.[54] This early experiment with labour arbitrage through multinational workforces intensified in the late nineteenth century and became generalised in the late twentieth century, as we explore below. In the meantime, British hegemony and the growth of nationalism through the nineteenth century more broadly saw nationality emerge as a dominant factor in shaping maritime labour regimes, with important exceptions for crew from colonial possessions – mainly from South Asia.[55] The British state was central to this process.

The saltwater cosmopolitanism that accompanied the rise of commercial capitalism gradually gave way after the Napoleonic Wars to an increasingly protectionist organisation of labour markets, where 'nationals' took precedence over 'foreigners'. In Britain, the latter constituted only about 10 per cent of the merchant and naval workforce in 1811–1813, the largest component of which were Irish, driven to maritime employment by poverty at home.[56] The Navigation Acts shaped intimately the nature of the labour regime on British ships, legislating that the majority of crews be nationals and for a complete ban on 'foreigners' working on ships in the coastal (or cabotage) trade. The Acts were, in part, designed to limit South Asian seafarers working in the Atlantic, despite being in demand for return voyages on East India Company ships. White British seafarers were often complicit in the nationalistic rejection of 'foreign' crew, as well as in the reproduction of racism and categories of race.[57] In arguing against the flogging of the 'true British seaman' from the 1790s onwards, they implied that non-white crew and bondspeople were categories of people who *should* be subject to corporal punishment. Following public revelations in 1814 of South Asian seafarers being flogged in the London barracks of the East India Company, the British state sidestepped the problem of the coexistence of 'metropolitan freedom and imperial disciplinary practices' by restricting the arrival of 'Asiatic' and African sailors through the requirement of a bond of up to 100 pounds per person as a guarantee against return to their home country.[58] This ignored the fact that seafarers often did not have a home – one account of sailors arriving in London in the 1880s found that one-third reported as much.[59]

Another significant aspect of Britain's maritime labour regime – impressment – had important international effects, including as a grievance contributing to the American Revolution and to the War of 1812 between Britain and the United States as well as to a hardening of notions of nationality and citizenship. The colonialists thought that the 'America Act' of 1708 gave them immunity from impressment, while the British Admiralty saw things differently and persisted with the policy.[60] Legal challenge and popular opposition meant that this faded as an onshore practice in the colony by the 1760s. But British captains continued impressing crew on US ships at sea, adding more grist to the mill of the American Revolution. The imperious British state justified its actions under the doctrine of 'indefeasible nationality' – that British citizens could never expatriate themselves. Yet, in parallel the shortage of seafarers saw Britain hypocritically reduce the period of naturalisation for *foreign* seafarers to two years.[61] Even after 1776, British captains would board US ships and identify deserters absconding from national service on the basis of their accents alone.

The War of 1812 was popularly pitched in the United States as one fought for 'free trade and sailors' rights'.[62] But in reality it represented a conflict between two mercantilist powers about their respective national jurisdiction over citizens and citizenship, and its implications for the supply of seafarers and concomitant maritime (and thus national) security. As Leon Fink points out, the flag was treated with greater propriety than were people – as if a 'nation' could be morally affronted. The United States' Seamen's Bill in 1813 sought to deflate bilateral tension by legislating that only US citizens could work on US-flagged ships and that foreign seafarers must have a passport even to travel as passengers. In this way the bill papered over US naval weakness in the face of superior British seapower by 'eliminating any rationale for stopping and pressing U.S.-flagged ships at sea'.[63] This maritime motivation for the deepening bureaucracy of citizenship was only practised briefly as neither the merchant navy nor the US Navy were able to recruit enough nationals as crew. Combined with the deeper commercial interdependence of the two national political economies and the sudden exigency of reduced 'manpower' in the American Civil War, Congress quickly repealed restrictions on crew nationality except for officers.

The combination of this crisis in labour supply, increasing competition among newly emerging industrialised powers and their merchant navies, and the consolidation of steampower in shipping, precipitated the (re)turn to recruitment of colonial seafarers in the decades either side of the First World War. The 1849 repeal of the Navigation Acts signalled the 'liberalisation' of overseas trade, and with it the opportunity for shipping capital to radically reduce labour costs by recruiting from the colonies. Non-European crew became commonplace on board cargo ships on imperial routes, and remained the majority in the country trade along the littorals of the Indian Ocean and beyond. By 1891, over 22 per cent of crews employed on British ships were non-British and 24,000 (10 per cent) were South Asian.[64] The trend continued into the first half of the twentieth century: 'lascars' accounted for 26 per cent and other non-British crew around 5 per cent of all seafarers employed on British ships by 1938.[65]

One reason behind the heightened demand for labour when docking in Asia was the loss of British personnel after the southbound leg of journeys from the metropole. Trans-oceanic voyages between Asia and Europe tended to have particularly high death rates among crew. 'Between 1830 and 1900', Jonathan Hyslop has indicated, 'one out of every five British mariners died at sea – perhaps a quarter of them from drowning, and the rest from the effects of disease, exposure or malnutrition'.[66] Shipmasters tried to compensate for this by over-recruiting on outward journeys. From 1781, the Dutch VOC progressively employed more Asian sailors on trips to Europe. European ships involved in intra-Asian trade relied predominantly on diverse non-European crews – perhaps reflecting mixed crewing practices on Asian merchant ships before the arrival of capitalism. Prize papers show only 11 to 15 per cent European crews on Dutch, French and Portuguese ships plying the country trade between 1744 and 1810.[67] Similarly, deaths at sea on Atlantic trips meant that additional crew were sometimes needed. As Rediker documents, crew could command vastly increased wages on under-crewed return voyages from the Caribbean, having earlier jumped ship there.[68]

But the principal incentive to hiring overseas labour on European ships was cost. As had remained the case since the mid-nineteenth century, South Asian seafarers' wages were the lowest, at one-sixth of British ratings' wages in 1919, and their employment conditions the worst. The 'lascar articles' setting out the terms of engagement allowed employers to restrict freedom of movement, including the denial of shore leave; their provisions were of the poorest quality and their working hours the longest (in fact, in contrast to British crew, their working conditions were not formally regulated).[69] Unsurprisingly, British shipowning capital took full advantage of this heightened rate of exploitation with its cost-cutting pay and detrimental terms and conditions, and by the 1920s employed over 50,000 South Asian seafarers, constituting around a quarter of all ratings on the British merchant fleet – even into the 1960s.[70] The British state stuttered in its attempt to regulate the growth of South Asian hands on the muster rolls of British ships, with some legislation in the early 1800s banning their employment westward of the Cape Colony.[71] But shipowners worked around this and successfully countered further attempts at regulation, either of their ability to employ Indian Ocean seafarers or of any improvements in the conditions of their work. As Ravi Ahuja shows, the British state and shipping capital set out the contours of a racist hierarchy in the maritime labour market which 'intensified and consolidated into a defining and permanent structural property'.[72]

Once again, it is important to underline that the incorporation of 'lascar' labour into the British merchant fleet was a complex and contradictory process. Many seized the opportunity of waged employment aboard metropolitan ships, and long-standing recruitment practices – epitomised by the *ghat sarang*, literally 'harbour/wharf headman' or more loosely 'intermediary/agent' – insuring that locals were by no means passive subjects to the interaction.[73] *Ghat sarangs* had supplied European vessels with Indian labour since the fifteenth century, offering a cheap and reliable solution to manpower needs characterised by the depletion of European crew on outward voyages mentioned earlier, and the urgency of hiring during the relatively short ocean-bound sailing periods dictated by the seasonal monsoons.[74] Once on deck, 'lascar' crews (or, to use the more neutral self-description, *khlassies* – sailors) were directly managed by a ship *sarang* and their *tindal* assistants (or boatswain mate). Thus, from the very beginning, a pattern of intermediated recruitment on land and devolved authority at sea emerged when managing South Asian crews which reproduced the familiar 'indirect' rule of empire via 'native' chiefs and headmen. Such arrangements varied from one contract to the next, with simultaneous tugs of war between company, brokers, intermediaries, seafarers and state authorities (both local and metropolitan) delivering different forms of engagement, ranging from indentured labour to 'family allotments' (whereby shipowners made monthly payments to families of absent seafarers through a port-based registrar).[75] Indeed, the latter system – however uneven its implementation – sheds light on the multi-layered conflicts over land-side social support and reproductive labour involved in guaranteeing the constant supply of sailors at sea.

'Small shipowners', Gopal Balachandran says of the mid-nineteenth-century situation in Kolkata, 'had little interest in the longer term reproduction of labour, and were content with a cheap labour market dominated by boarding-house keepers and brokers who profited from its constant churn . . . of single, unattached male workers'.[76] Yet several decades of reliance on an itinerant, unskilled, low-waged and volatile labour market risked replacing quality for quantity, undermining regular supply with cost cutting. By the turn of the twentieth century, Balachandran continues,

> Shipowners attempted to reconcile cheapness with reliable supply through engineering the circular movement of small/ medium peasants and owner-cultivators between their rural homes and jobs at sea. Such labour was cheap because the cost of reproducing it was externalized to low productivity agriculture.[77]

Figure 3.1. Lascars on board the *Dunera* (1910)
Source: National Maritime Museum.

Thus the role of the ship's *sarang* was reinvented at the turn of the twentieth century as a figure of 'traditional' or 'native' authority mediating between the minority of white commanders aboard, and the majority of South Asian sailors from an otherwise geographically and ethnically diverse provenance.

The spread of steam-powered shipping toward the end of the nineteenth century had an enormous impact on the labour process at sea. The 'muscle of empire' was gradually concentrated in the stokehole or engine room rather than on deck (although steamships continued to rely on wind power during longer voyages).[78] Occupations and individuals alien to the mariner's world became central to maritime transport: stokers (known as 'firemen' in the merchant navy), trimmers (coal cutters and transporters) and their engineer supervisors replaced sailors and, with the advent of passenger liners, additional crew (again, generally with little or no experience at sea, and now including some women) were assigned to a 'steward's department' dedicated to victualling, cooking, service and cleaning. However fragmented, the 'collective labourer' of the sailing ship was slowly but surely transformed into an equally hierarchical, yet more rigidly compartmentalised, and in many respects deskilled, workforce aboard the steamship. Race and nationality became the vectors of this rearticulation of the on-board division of labour:

> Not surprisingly, Britons nearly monopolised the higher ranks in all three departments [engineer, sailor and steward]. The luxury liners of the North Atlantic carried largely British and Irish crew, at all three departments and all positions. On less prestigious North Atlantic vessels, and in other oceans, northern Europeans served mainly as sailors. Yemeni Arabs who enlisted in Aden usually worked in the stokeholes, as did Somalis and many men from southern Europe.[79]

Figure 3.2. Photograph of the crew of *Cawdor* (1884)
including four African lascar crew members
Source: National Maritime Museum.

Racial differences among crew were naturalised, ascribing certain stereotyped attributes to specific ethnic groups – Blacks and Asians could withstand better the heat of furnaces, British sailors were routinely drunk and disorderly, South Asian sailors were subservient to the 'traditional' authority of the *sarang* – when justifying the static and unequal division of labour (and distribution of pay and working conditions) afloat.

Discipline and punish: 'the special circumstances of a ship at sea'

The modern dialectic between liberty and oppression was experienced in unique ways by those dependent on the maritime world. Mention has already been made of the vicious coexistence on eighteenth-century ships of chattel slavery and free waged labour. Similarly, work on ships presented many people with a chance to undergo a sea change – escape social and geographical bonds of land to enter the confined and hierarchical space of ships only to then chase fresh, autonomous futures, sometimes by literally 'jumping ship' and restarting a new life on foreign soil. The freedom of the seas has, however, always been accompanied by distinctive uses of force, violence and domination, which has given exploitation in merchant fleets a markedly militarised character. The modern ship has been a worksite characterised by the exception – it is a space ruled by its own laws, governed by the captain's absolute authority, where corporal punishment, physical abuse and social distinction are ruthlessly imposed, and where death, disease and injury are statistically more probable. Once ashore, the generalised reluctance to go to sea has occasioned the coercive practices of impressment, crimping and indenture. It is often hard to disentangle cause and effect when it comes to accounting for this maritime exceptionalism, but it seems indisputable that labour regimes at sea have been acutely affected by the peculiar dynamics of discipline on ships.

As we have thus far seen, recruiting sufficient seafarers in the British Empire's age of sail was often difficult – especially during periods of war – as ships were labour-intensive, requiring a wide combination of skills and experience, including sailors, carpenters, caulkers and gunners. Given the choice, seafarers preferred work on British merchant vessels over the Royal Navy. Wages in the Royal Navy were regulated by Parliament and stood frozen between 1653 and 1797.[80] In contrast, there was considerable wage fluctuation for merchant sailors: from a monthly peak in the 1690s of fifty-five shillings they dropped to thirty shillings in the 1720s. In response to a buoyant labour market, the state under the reign of George II introduced a temporary wage cap of thirty-five shillings per month, and it was not until 1748 that the wage returned to fifty-five shillings.[81] Despite these attempts at wage repression by the British state, a shortage of skilled seafarers meant that by the early 1790s merchant mariners working the North Sea coal trade made between five and nine pounds a month, while sailors in the Royal Navy earned only eighteen to twenty-four shillings. On top of this, state coffers were often overstretched in war, producing long delays in wage payments that were already irregular and often deliberately deferred by captains to pre-empt desertion or drunken binges once onshore. Even the lure of a 'prize' vessel taken by force from the fleet of other nations offered little recompense for a sailor. The distribution of loot favoured heavily the officer class, and payments were delayed and also often only available to collect in London – rather an inconvenience for a sailor based in Liverpool.[82]

Poor wages could be supplemented by the right of merchant mariners to a portion of a common freight tonnage – their 'privilege' – made available for the transport of the crew's own speculative cargo. At 5 per cent of the chartered tonnage in the seventeenth century and a set tonnage in the late eighteenth to be shared among the crew, this privilege could be worth as much as three to ten times the monetary value of an individual sailor's wage.[83] In this way, seafarers took a share in the success of the voyage and bought into the speculative, self-expansive logic of moving commodity capital around the world.[84] So while there can be no doubt that sailors were part of the transatlantic multiracial multitude of men and women rebelling against Atlantic capitalism, as depicted in the seminal *The Many-Headed Hydra* (including the democratic 'hydrarchy from below' of pirates united in their hatred of captains, capitalists and the state[85]), they were also subject to class compromise in the smooth running of cargo.

These labour recruitment strategies in the British navies were both a response to, and a product of, the brutality of work and life at sea. In 1811 the Royal Navy lost around 19 per cent of its available workforce to injury, desertion and death. Disease was the biggest killer, no doubt propagated by the close quarters of living conditions – only 35 centimetres was allocated per width of hammock.[86] During various periods between 1755 and 1812 when Britain was at war, desertion from the Royal Navy ranged between 7 and 14 per cent of deployed seafarers.[87] The increased length of trans-oceanic voyages by the merchant fleet from the eighteenth century, when carrying the commodities of the first capitalist empire, meant that more crew members died – naturally and otherwise – or jumped ship en route. But within the general rate of desertion there was wide variation among individual ships, reflecting the highly particularised nature of labour regimes on ships as shaped by individual captains (e.g. some captains sought to discipline crews by restricting shore leave).

Low wages and poor working conditions contributed to often harsh methods of labour control – methods that were justified by 'the special circumstances of a ship at sea'.[88] The pre- and early capitalist North Atlantic culture of maritime labour is widely considered as being less hierarchical,[89] and has even been characterised by some as based on 'collective decision-making'.[90] Either way, this was overturned by the British state in the 1749 and 1757 Naval Articles of War, which acted as the system of law administered on Royal Navy vessels. The Articles formally instituted despotic hierarchy in the captain and militarised the workplace. Any opposition while at sea was considered mutiny, whether in actual acts, the mere utterance of 'any words of sedition or mutiny', or even behaviour seen as showing 'contempt to his superior officer'. Further, a seafarer should not even 'presume to quarrel with any of his superior officers', since doing so risked court martial and the certainty that they 'shall suffer death'. All other crimes not specified in the Articles 'shall be punished by the [unspecified] laws and customs . . . used at sea'.[91] For capital punishments, the captain and his officers acted as judge and jury. In other words, the

Articles permitted British captains considerable leeway to summarily administer punishments of crew, which they did, liberally. In the mid-1700s, between 7 and 9 per cent of a typical ship's crew would have received twelve lashes or more. Punishments were administered publicly and were sometimes even set to music.[92]

Although the Articles did not formally extend beyond the Royal Navy, merchant sailors were in no way immune to similar forms of arbitrary violence. There is some controversy among maritime historians about the extent and intensity of such punishment, not least since, as one judicious summary indicates, 'Everything connected with discipline at sea was shrouded in vagueness and subject to different interpretations by captains, sailors and judges. No one doubted, however,' Peter Earle adds, 'that the "master has authority over all the mariners on board ... and it is their duty to obey his commands in all lawful matters relating to the navigation of the ship and the preservation of good order'.[93] In the absence of a single, codified body of law, most seamen on British ships were until the end of the nineteenth century subject to a haphazard combination of Continental ordinances, 'customs of the sea' and Admiralty law.[94] Yet as Jeffrey Bolster indicates, during the age of sail, 'Admiralty law denied to seamen the rights and protection afforded most landbound Englishmen, and later white Americans. Fostering a tractable labor supply through strict obedience, Admiralty law put mariners under the authority of individuals with recourse to corporal punishment.'[95]

The martial dimension of maritime labour regimes (partly reflected in the language of 'officer', 'petty officer', 'watch', 'duty' or 'station') was perhaps in proportion to the vulnerability of the profits of the collectivity of shipowners, cargo and insurance firms, as well as the vulnerability of capitalist circuits to disruption more broadly, should seafarers resist their exploitation and strike the topsail. On a micro level the captain was the embodiment of the state on board, reflecting his own (and at this time it was always *his*) and his officers' isolation among a social class of maritime workers. The disciplinary power given to captains was also indicative of the deep interdependence of 'public' and 'private' interest, with the merchant navy providing essential logistical services to the British army and navy. The class bases of a ship's management would have been only too apparent to its crew. N. A. M. Rogers identifies the French Revolution as the turning point of growing class consciousness on British ships, including of an increasingly bourgeois officer class.[96] Around 90 per cent of commissioned officers in the Royal Navy's officer corps came from parents in peerage, landed gentry and the professions in the period 1793 and 1849.[97] Hierarchy on merchant navy vessels tended to be looser and open to those of working-class origins. Nonetheless, the class lens of British naval officers produced a derogatory view of crew – often seeing them as dangerous, unruly and lazy drunkards, which perhaps served to vindicate their ever more frequent administration of perverted punishments. This comes through in the scribblings of a 'Commander in the Royal Navy' in 1827, who, in seeking to justify the institution of impressment, painted the British sailor as 'spoiled by idleness and indulgence'. He is 'naturally capricious, he has his sullen moods and sulky fits – in which he must sometimes be indulged – always watching him as a child, he must still be governed as [a] man'.[98] Brutal techniques of 'governance' such as flogging were defended by the officer class; although, of course, they themselves were not subject to such punishments, these being reserved for the mass of common crew.

In this context, labour recruitment to Britain's navies could be a challenge to capital and state. Debt peonage – whereby wage earnings were advanced by the 'master' to recruit sailors – was a common device to source seafarers in the metropole, as it was through *ghat sarangs* in the Indian Ocean. Payments were often made to crimps who had entrapped sailors in debt, including that incurred in port taverns, which would provide accommodation, food and drink on credit.[99] In a further culture of trickery and deceit, when paying off these advances, while at sea further deductions to wages were made for alcohol and tobacco consumed on board, as well as even for damages to cargo incurred by its movement. When British capital was the world leader in the transatlantic slave economy, captains worked African women and men on the very ships that were transporting them to their ongoing bondage. The principal task appears to have been preparing food and cleaning the ship, with 'payment' taking the form of extra food, alcohol or tobacco for personal consumption. At times, African men pumped out the ship to avoid capsize, worked the sails (especially when the crew were ill), and even fought off privateers.[100] A 'trickle' of crew in the Royal Navy also came from the recruitment of petty offenders – 'freed' on condition of their enlisting.[101] But by far the bulk were trapped by the press gang.

The spectrum of labour unfreedom in 'the first capitalist nation' is starkly apparent in the British practice of impressment. Low, stagnant wages and hard, isolated and often deadly work saw the British state depend on the Impress Service as a major supplier of labouring bodies to the Royal Navy, justified on the grounds of national defence. Morriss shows that between 1775 and 1783, over 113,900 men were 'procured', initially centred on London and the major port towns, but as sailors moved progressively further inland to avoid them the press gangs soon followed.[102] Press gangs received formal guidance from municipal authorities and Parliament to target the dispossessed, propertyless and unemployed. When this proved insufficient to meet Britain's martial demand, 1795 Quota Acts set out numbers to be plucked from cities and counties. And even though merchant mariners were issued formal protections from impressment to ensure that the military machine was properly supplied with provisions, these were often overturned out of desperation for able bodies on ships. Impressment always peaked in periods of war. Between

1810 and 1812, around 40 per cent of the 72,000 recruits were pressed.[103] The practice dropped off after the Napoleonic Wars – except for convicted smugglers – because the British state mimicked France and phased in a professional 'standing' navy and a system of naval reserves from among its world-leading merchant navy.

Other forms of naval recruitment centred on children. A 1704 Act gave parish officials the right to offer up children to work for captains for free for up to nine years, and the philan-thropic Marine Society was set up in 1756 by a merchant 'to establish a trained crew of recruits' from the mass of 'orphans and boys from poor backgrounds'.[104] The Marine Society 'took destitute boys off the streets of London, gave them clothes and some basic education and sent them to sea either in merchant ships or in the navy'.[105] Given the very high rates of injury, mortality and child abuse at sea, of the tens of thousands of men and boys dispatched by the Marine Society, it is hard to imagine that many were thankful for the charity meted out to them.

Radical resistance, liberal reform

Clearly, the British state and its capitalists were no strangers to violent strategies of labour deployment – slavery, indenture, colonial labour regimes – but by the eighteenth century an ideo-logical and institutional apparatus propping up the myth of free labour was extended through liberal thought and the statute books, most notably with the 1807 Abolition Act. Not so for maritime workers: for a few years, press-ganged seafarers worked the ships that policed the African coast for slaver vessels. But this irony was not to last.

The sheer volume of goods circulating through Britain's ports gave maritime workers considerable structural power. Where they were able to self-organise and withdraw labour power, they could cut off the commercial capillaries of empire. Seafarers' strikes were thus felt well beyond the claustrophobic confines of the workplace, and because of the mobile nature of their labour, were prone to make connections with other workers, most notably dockers and stevedores, and in the age of steam, train workers and coal miners.[106]

The press gang was among 'the most hated of the institutions of Old England' and a principal target in numerous political uprisings and direct actions.[107] During the Gordon Riots in June 1780, over twenty crimping houses were targeted, alongside prisons and debtors' houses, and impressed sailors, debtors and petty criminals were freed.[108] Members of Parliament opportunistically mirrored the popular mood and launched an inquiry in 1787 into the process and role of impressment in the American War of Independence, finding that 180 died at the hands of the press gangs.[109] Dockworkers in London and Kent organised themselves to successfully scare off press gangs in 1790 and 1801 respectively; and sailors on barges transporting coal down the Tyne and Wear went on strike in 1803 and 1811 against impressment.[110]

Even after the era of impressment, maritime labour regimes retained unrestrained violence as part of their disciplinary repertoire and so resistance took varied forms.[111] Mutiny was perhaps the ultimate expression of this, with as many as one in ten sailors experiencing mutiny, although the term encompasses a multitude of actions and motivations: from opposition to low pay and despotic captains through to politically motivated acts with links to rebellions onshore, such as the Irish Rebellion of 1798, and rebellion on slave ships.[112]

The first recorded maritime trade unions in Britain appeared in 1825, again among the coastal sailors carrying coal from the Tyne and the Wear, spurred by the success of their resistance to impressment.[113] Labour organising in Britain's other main ports of London and Liverpool started hesitantly in the early 1850s, largely fading from view under the pressure of the British state's disciplining of seafarers with the 1850 Mercantile Maritime Act, and the difficulties of organising the broad church of maritime labour with its internal divisions of ideology, race, skill, and type of contract.[114] Nonetheless, the 1851 seafarer's strike in response to the 1850 Act was sufficiently effective 'to paralyse the east coast ports [and] provoke the Admiralty into despatching warships to the Tyne and Wear'.[115] Despite military repression, the North East of England was once again a place of radical, experimental resistance, this time the Chartist leadership of merchant seafarers joined with that of the coal miners – recognising the social power of their combination as the two leading (and materially intertwined) industries of the region. The Miners' and Seamen's United Association only lasted for a couple of years before collapsing under internal and external tensions, but it was an early example of an attempt at 'general' unionism, which is usually dated from the 1880s.

The first sustained maritime unions were established in Britain during the 1870s. For seafarers, the drive to unionisation had its long-term origins in eighteenth-century collective organisation to improve wages,[116] and in the short term in refusals to work on death ships, which had led to the imprisonment of over 1,600 sailors between 1870 and 1872 alone.[117] Maritime workers had engaged in industrial action in all of the major English ports between 1879 and 1881 as part of the incipient 'new unionism'. The following decade witnessed a wave of strikes in ports across Europe and the white settler colonies, of which maritime labour historian Frank Broeze identifies as 'particularly bitter' the actions in London, Liverpool, Glasgow and St Nazaire in 1889; Hamburg and the ports of eastern Australia and New Zealand in 1890; Hull and Nantes in 1893; the canal port of Manchester in 1895 (one year after its opening); and Antwerp, Rotterdam and Hamburg in 1896.[118]

By the late 1880s mass unionism had taken full hold in Britain's maritime industries and the first *national* seafarers' union was established in 1887 – what would become the

National Union of Seamen. Soon after, in 1896, the International Transport Workers' Federation (ITF) was founded in London, initially grouping maritime and other transport workers from Australia, Belgium, Britain, Denmark, France, Germany, Holland, Italy, Norway, Russia, Sweden, Spain and the USA.[119] The ITF was organised on the basis that 'sectional disputes are useless' as 'employers in all the European countries immediately join up forces, and use their combinations to provide blacklegs and pour them by the thousands into the ports affected.' It proposed a transnational strike action for higher wages across the maritime ports of its members and threatened employers with 'a colossal industrious war'.[120] The ITF was then an internationalist innovation by maritime workers' organisations, in part necessitated by the highly internationalised nature of the maritime logistics industry (see Chapter 5).

Seafarer militancy often sparked and permanently peppered the wider working-class and anti-colonial movements of the late Victorian era and in the lead-up to the First World War. Along with miners, the group of workers most likely to strike in this period were seafarers and dockers.[121] For example, between 1911 and 1912, maritime workers in every port in Britain were 'at one time or another . . . on strike and violence was at its greatest'.[122] The country's port cities would play an important cultural and political role in the rise of the Independent Labour Party (affiliated with and then eventually merged into the UK's Labour Party). Solidarity among seafarers, dockers and stevedores proved to be a winning strategy. When maritime workers combined to lock down the seaward sinews of international commodity trade, the circuit of industrial capital was interrupted and capitalist accumulation was quickly threatened with stagnation, especially in maritime states such as Britain and export-dependent economies such as Australia and New Zealand. Maritime workers in Australia and Britain recognised that they constituted 'a linkage of labour rather than capital ... in an industry where pressure could be applied at both ends of the crucial lines of communication within the empire'.[123]

But these advances did not last. Pragmatism among union leaders, capitalist association and bourgeois reform help to explain why. After a burst of militancy, the leaders of Britain's maritime unions took the view that their members' jobs were dependent upon the commercial health of the Imperial Commonwealth's networks of ports and shipping. Set in the context of European inter-imperialist rivalry and manufacturing competition with Germany, Japan and the United States, Britain's ability to integrate its empire and extract colonial surplus was threatened by upstart maritime workers. In parallel, several maritime union leaders in Britain, Australia and New Zealand would use the power that came from their institutional role to advance their personal political careers.[124] For example, J. Havelock Wilson, the founder and lifelong president of the National Union of Seamen, became a long-standing Member of Parliament for the Liberal Party. Wilson stood charged with a litany of evidence by the Seafarer's Minority Movement as a 'faithful flunkey of the British shipowners', the starkest of which being that the NUS was the only major union not to join the General Strike.[125]

Militant maritime labour was matched by capitalist association. For example, the successes of the London dock strike of 1889 and the associated maritime strikes of 1890 in Australia and New Zealand were the result of building militant place-based solidarities and trans-oceanic organisation, but also an outcome of conflict, confusion and competition among maritime capitals. Bosses had been wrong-footed. But increasingly concentrated shipping firms learned from these mistakes and established industry associations. The most important of these was the Shipping Federation set up in 1890 by the major London-based shipping companies – including P&O, British

India, Orient Line and the New Zealand Shipping Co. It was formed first and foremost as 'a fighting machine to counter the strike weapon, and it made no secret of the fact'.[126] The Shipping Federation worked through the 1890s to undermine, crush or bypass future strikes and solidarity or secondary actions.[127] And as might be expected, the state and local police forces could be counted on to support capital in breaking strikes. This type of countervailing strategy is mirrored today in the alliances harnessed in the Pacific Maritime Association on the US West Coast, where liner, port and buyer firms cooperate to undermine organised labour.[128]

Maritime labour struggles in Britain and the United States were paralleled by top-down, middle-class activism, in part spurred by popular depictions of the brutality of working life at sea in literature and popular media.[129] This contributed to a series of reforms of seafarers' working conditions, targeted mainly at mitigating some of the worst excesses of risk and depravities of the maritime labour regime. One example of this was legislation introducing the 'Plimsoll line' – or international load line – on a ship's hull which indicates the loading limit, depending on temperature and water type, in order to ensure buoyancy. But these efforts did little to address systemic exploitation. As one liberal commentator put it,

> Save when the indignant Plimsoll cursed the opulent gentlemen of a lethargic House of Commons into a spasmodic effort, the country did nothing for the men who brought its daily food and its monstrous riches ... Like some millions of his fellow-creatures on shore, [the seafarer] was the chattel of limited liability companies, whose shareholders took no sort of interest in anything whatsoever except dividends.[130]

We have seen how the institutions of the eighteenth- and nineteenth-century British maritime labour regime were both products of and responses to the peculiarities of work and life in the 'structured space' of the ship. The risk of disease and injury was high and intensified by the drives to maximise space for cargo and speed up turnover. Wages were delayed to reduce the risk of desertion, but in doing so further dulled the allure of an already difficult job. Subsequent increases in impressment brought new evils to an already inhumane labour regime. Inter-state conflict over maritime labour between Britain and the United States contributed to hardening notions of nationality through the nineteenth century, while race and racism – including of the British state – shaped the contours of maritime working lives, undermining class solidarity among crew. By the early twentieth century, mass radical resistance by maritime labour in Britain and its white settler colonies was being moderated by the reformist pragmatism of the leadership of seafarers' unions. This combination of contradictory political cultures and the ambitions of organised labour, allied to a flurry of liberal internationalist legal reforms, set out some of the central contours of maritime labour regimes in the late twentieth century, and beyond.

Maritime labour regimes in the neoliberal era

Maritime labour regimes in the first capitalist empire undulated between relative cosmopolitanism in the eighteenth century and deepening nationalist and racist inflections through the nineteenth and early twentieth centuries. At the same time, these labour regimes moved from being characterised by violent labour recruitment and control that was consistent with a period of primitive accumulation when the contours of capitalist competition and labour markets were still shaky, to being more formalised, bureaucratised, shaped by worker self-organisation, and eventually regulated internationally. Maritime logistics in the eighteenth century encountered possible interruptions as a result of labour shortages, war and political unrest, while throughout the nineteenth century and into the twentieth it was self-organised labour that produced vulnerabilities, albeit ones that were only intermittently activated

because of the combination of reformist tendencies in bureaucratic union hierarchies and the difficulties of organising at sea.
Several path dependencies can be traced from these tendencies
into the maritime labour regimes of the late twentieth and early
twenty-first centuries. We start our survey of the contemporary
period by setting out elements of continuity and change in conditions of work. We then move to re-examine the new institutional
terrain of the flag of convenience (FOC) as a capitalist response to
the growing power of organised maritime labour (first introduced
in Chapter 2), the changes that this brought in for maritime labour
markets, and responses to these emergent dynamics by labour
organisations and international labour regulation.

Changing conditions of work

Despite massive technological change since the era of Britain's
dominance of the maritime labour regime, the risks of seafaring
remain high compared to most other occupations. Between
2000 and 2005, a daily average of '18 ships collided, grounded,
sank, caught fire or exploded'.[131] The modern seafarer works
for an average of eleven hours per day, seven days a week. A
voyage may be as short as a few weeks or as long as two months.
A typical merchant seafarer works on anything between forty
and fifty ships through a standard career, each under different
employment contracts, in a life that 'swings pendulum-like
between spells at sea and stays on land'.[132] Seafaring remains a
male-dominated occupation – the ITF estimates that women
seafarers make up around 2 per cent of the world total, mainly
in the cruise and ferry sectors. This intensity of work, social
isolation and regimentation of life at sea contribute to explaining why the socio-psychological traits of contemporary seafarers are often compared to those of prisoners, and are the focus
of specialised study.[133]

Crew working on fishing boats are often more intensively
exploited than seafarers. Fishers work under a great diversity of

conditions, wage forms and lengths of time, and are more likely to die at work than seafarers. But the data for fishers are even scantier and less systemised. Reliable statistics on deaths and injuries on fishing boats do not exist because most countries fail to systematically report them, which is partly a symptom of open vessel registries or 'flags of convenience'.[134] In contrast to factories, fields and mines, fishing circumscribes physically the labour process to floating platforms of production that can transcend legal jurisdictions in various ways (e.g. legally through FOCs and/or geographically following the fish between EEZs and the legal grey zone of the high seas). This makes one of the world's most dangerous jobs also among the most poorly regulated, in both policy and practice.

Social hierarchy on the cargo ships of contemporary capitalism has its origins in militarised naval organisation dating back to well before the emergence of this mode of production. Nonetheless, as we have seen the shifting technical and social divisions of labour on cargo ships from the eighteenth century to the nineteenth and the reconfiguring of their social and political contexts were reflected in the sharpening of class divisions between officers and ratings.[135] These social divisions have been reinforced into the twenty-first century. The training of cadet merchant seafarers in Eastern Europe and the Philippines is militaristic in tone and tempo – early morning drills and the saluting of staff are commonplace; preparing trainees with a taste of the 'rigid rules of conduct, relatively defined work routines, clear lines of authority and major imbalances in the distribution of power' when working in the merchant marine.[136]

Rank mediates class dynamics of exploitation. The interests of capital are represented and reproduced by the managerial role of senior officers (captain, chief officer, first and second engineers) in their relationships with the ratings, such as in ensuring competitive turnover times. Social relations of exploitation and subordination are mediated directly by junior officers – who have a more operational role – and petty officers (bosun, chief cook) who all supervise ratings. Officers tend to be formally educated at technical college or university, and while ratings may have spent some time in training,[137] their employment position is shaped principally by experience, much as it was in previous centuries. All crew rely on habituation to move up the ranks, reflected in the universal issue of discharge books which record time and tasks at sea, acting as a formal record of employer appraisal and disciplining.[138]

Social stratification is physically reflected in ship design, with ratings' accommodation normally located on lower decks and that of officers, especially senior ones, on higher decks. Ratings are much more likely to share cabins and toilet facilities than officers.[139] This is another historical throwback, including to the hierarchical organisation of the ship in the Royal Navy, where officers stood on the quarterdeck and crew worked on the forecastle, and were not to approach the quarterdeck without officerial assent. Most modern ship design reproduces this social organisation of life-space, and the pressures of tight competition among shipowners to maximise labour productivity per tonne of commodities shifted on schedule means that space is further segmented and squeezed.[140] Crew accommodation is often smaller in the twenty-first century than it was the 1970s.[141]

Racialised divisions of labour and working conditions continue to articulate with class divisions on ships in the twenty-first century, reflecting and refracting the relationships between 'lascar' and white British crew in the nineteenth century – the major difference being that the labour market is now, in principle, properly internationalised with ranks open to all nationalities. Yet seafarers from the global South are still usually employed as ratings, while officers tend to be recruited from the 'traditional' or 'embedded' maritime states, with the latter not only being better paid but enjoying shorter voyages. If an officer is recruited from the global South, they will normally receive a far lower salary than the equivalent from an OECD country.[142]

In many respects, the captain remains sovereign on the 'structured space' of the ship in the twenty-first century – that 'hierarchical state in miniature' mentioned earlier. They are still responsible for the vessel, its crew and its cargo, and have various legal rights in order to ensure their safe passage. Moreover, as the direct representative of the shipping company, captains can make snap decisions with a distinct commercial edge.[143] However, debt-fuelled vessel construction undermined the status of owner-operators from around 1973 onwards. And as we shall see in Chapter 5, cheap, modern communications mean that captains are beholden to the daily orders of onshore managers from liner firms, ship management companies and charterers, who in turn are acting on behalf of the increasingly financialised logics of transnational capital focused upon shareholder value and private equity.[144]

Just as in the early commercial capitalism plied by British and Dutch merchant vessels, technological change in merchant shipping today is characterised by the ability to employ fewer crew to move greater volumes of commodity capital across the global ocean. The intensification of the rate of exploitation of crew has seen average pay decline; fewer crew employed on the average cargo ship, from forty to fifty per ship in the 1960s to twenty to thirty by the 1990s, despite massive increases in the average ship's carrying capacity; and speed-up of turnover time in port through the mechanisation of (off)loading and by reducing seafarers' shore leave. In this way, not only is the quantity of a seafarer's leisure time reduced, but their socio-psychological embeddedness in the ship is intensified. Seafarers are increasingly prisoners of maritime logistics networks as ports move away from urban centres. In combination, these strategies save money and time for capital, while accentuating fatigue and stress and decreasing well-being for crew.[145]

Transnational capital/multinational labour

Five strategies characterise shipping capital's competition for profit in the late twentieth and early twenty-first centuries: investment in ever-larger vessels that need fewer crew per tonne of cargo, state subsidies, corporate concentration and centralisation, buying flags of convenience to increase post-tax profits and reduce the costs of compliance with labour and other laws, and precariously employing seafarers from lower-income ('labour supply') countries. We explore the last two strategies further here – how capital has sought to enhance its own transnationality (incompletely) while fragmenting labour across multiple countries. The first three strategies – technological change, state subsidies and corporate concentration – are the focus of Chapter 5.

Open registries or flags of convenience (FOCs) use state sovereignty to create new spaces of accumulation that cut costs and bypass the legal resources available to organised labour. By 2014, the owners of well over 70 per cent by deadweight tonnage of the world fleet chose to use flags other than that of their own 'nation'.[146] To tell the history of the open vessel registry is to trace an incremental but very deliberate series of capitalist strategies to avoid business tax and to bypass or undermine previous political victories by organised labour as enshrined in national legislation. The legal innovation of the modern flag of convenience originated in practice in Panama in the 1920s. Designed to short-circuit US law on prohibition and workers' rights, Panama gave illicit and legal US enterprises alike the ability to register vessels under its flag in return for a small fee. The global stagflation of the 1970s and the frantic hunt for improved profitability among shipowners intensified this process of 'flagging out'.[147] These capitalists are essentially 'choosing the laws that apply to them',[148] not unlike secrecy jurisdictions for money capital but with the crucial difference of directly incorporating living and breathing human beings. The flag of convenience allows for the downgrading of extensive (and costly) legal regimes regulating work and life on ships. It also gives shipping capital the ability to employ crew from anywhere – creating perhaps the only genuinely global labour market from what used to be distinctly national ones.[149]

Fiscally squeezed post-colonial countries such as Liberia, the Marshall Islands and Vanuatu joined Panama as leading post-war FOC states. In using their newfound sovereignty as a going concern, these governments captured rents from vessel registration powers as a form of state property. But the process of flag registration is often outsourced by FOC states; the majority of these 'private flags' are administered by private companies in the United States.[150] The ease and cheapness of private flags means that very small sums of money are all that is needed to short-circuit long histories of maritime labour struggle. To register for the Vanuatu flag, for example, a shipowner or management company must pay US$0.35 per net tonne of a ship, and then an annual fee of US$0.25 per net ton.[151] As Leon Fink neatly puts it in *Sweatshops at Sea*, for maritime workers flags of convenience are 'a stunningly unique economic phenomenon. In one sweep of a pen … an entire ship's labour force could be transferred overnight to the jurisdiction and sovereignty of a new national "master"'.[152] But these small sums add up for small states. Vanuatu captured around US$10 million in revenue from flagging in 2013, which was almost 10 per cent of the country's tax revenue.[153]

By way of stymying the slow decline of market share in and influence over shipping, 'traditional' maritime states such as the UK and Norway set up parallel second (international) registries in the 1980s.[154] To attract business, they peeled back national regulatory requirements, especially with regard to crewing requirements and working conditions and taxation. Some international registries, such as Denmark and Norway, kept a degree of regulatory flesh on the bone, while others, such as France and Germany, are much closer to the original FOC states and are classified by the International Transport Workers' Federation as FOCs.[155] In short, there are important jurisdiction-specific differences among flags.[156] Elizabeth DeSombre's study of international regulation of FOC vessels found a degree of convergence on environmental and safety standards (on paper at least), sparked in part by the demands of the maritime insurance industry. But this was not the case for labour standards, which have diverged considerably.[157] There are profound differences in labour regimes between, for example, Swedish-owned cargo ships traversing the Atlantic between the EU and North America, and Taiwanese-owned longliners using an FOC that are fishing on the high seas. And contrary to DeSombre's optimistic conclusions based on the counting of laws on the statute books, the patchy available evidence on the *practice* of safety standards suggests that bigger, faster ships operating with fewer crew can increase the risk of injury.[158] Some evidence suggests that crew working on ships that use an FOC are more likely to die at sea due to the flagging out of substandard ships, and/or that 'lower cost but less competent crews have been employed, perhaps to bypass more rigorous safety standards'.[159] Indeed, serious gaps in the reporting of deaths and severe injuries at sea by some FOC registries may even 'serve a market function' by attracting vessel owners or managers to register there.[160]

Ship management companies were major early users of FOCs. They emerged in the 1960s to manage vessels on behalf of integrated oil corporations when they began to outsource vessel operations. Management companies proliferated with the 'great shipping crisis' from the late 1970s to 1985 (see Chapter 5) as banks and other financiers suddenly found that they owned ships as collateral against unpaid loans and turned to outside operators to turn a profit from the asset.[161] Given ongoing overcapacity in shipping, profit margins were tight and management companies scrambled to reduce costs, including the squeezing of crew. This gave a second boost to the FOC and 'second registries', which meant that by the 1990s 'flagging out' was ubiquitous in international shipping. While latecomers to the practice, Japanese shipowners are a prominent and representative example, but also one that illustrates the combined historical peculiarities of national regulation, maritime logistics and labour regimes as they shape each other over time.

Japanese seafarers had been major beneficiaries of the postwar national compromise between capital and (male) labour: they were guaranteed lifetime employment, and fully paid shore leave was factored into a ship's operational costs. But when wage costs per trip rose five times between 1965 and 1975, Japan's highly concentrated deep-sea merchant fleet (then controlled by six firms) deployed a variety of organisational, legal and financial arrangements to 'de-Japanese' crew requirements. One technique, 'chartering back', saw Japanese capital sell (generally older) ships to entities based in FOC states – predominantly Panama and Liberia – and then charter them using crew from developing countries. The more sophisticated mechanisms of 'tie-in ships' saw Japanese firms arrange for interests based in a foreign jurisdiction (usually Hong Kong) to build ships in Japan which they would then charter for long periods.[162] The 'maru-ship', in contrast, keeps the vessel flagged in Japan – necessary for fishing vessels to benefit from domestic offloading and domestic and foreign fisheries access arrangements – but the Japanese owner leases the boat to a foreign entity, who then crews the vessel, and the owner then re-charters it.[163]

Nowhere was the process of 'flagging out' automatic or frictionless. The employment of foreign crew on Japanese-owned boats, for example, was slowed down by interventions from the All Japan Seamen's Union as well as the government, which was concerned both about unemployed Japanese seafarers and about the implications for accepting foreign workers on land.[164] However, the 1985 Plaza Accord, which saw the US and Japan agree to depreciate the dollar to the yen, was the death knell of Japan's national registry. By 1995, the majority of

Japanese-owned merchant ships were controlled by ship management companies in Japan (60 per cent) and overseas (35 per cent), allowing capital to dollarise its administrative costs and introduce a step of remove from crew recruitment and vessel maintenance and repair.[165] The implications for capital of crew costs are huge: in 1995 there was a forty-one-times national difference between the highest-paid (Japanese) and lowest-paid (Bangladeshi) seafarer of equivalent rank.[166]

The emergence of a transnational shipping fleet in the 1980s was paralleled by new possibilities in the employment of multi-national crews.[167] For shipowners and operators, intensifying the rate of exploitation of crew is a central accumulation strategy, not least given that variable capital (wages) can amount to up to 42 per cent of the total operating costs of a bulk carrier.[168] Maritime 'manpower' studies by shipowners' associations estimate that there was in 2015 a global 'supply' of around 774,000 officers and 873,500 ratings, which represents a small shortage of officers compared to 'demand' and a 'surplus' of 119,000 ratings.[169] The 'surplus' of ratings and shifts in gas oil price have been used by employers as justification for the suppression of seafarers' wages since 2009, but this does not explain the fact that average actual monthly salaries for seafarers fell by a quarter between 2009 and 1992.[170] This *is* explained by the dynamics of competitive accumulation among shipping capital and ship management companies who are well aware that labour power is the *sole* source of variable capital – a 'variable cost', in their terms. The peculiarities of the occupation – its long-term extreme mobility and highly deregulated nature in an FOC world – mean that the labour market for seafarers is probably the most open one in the world, which allows capital to keep 'labor costs as low as possible, playing on the differences between national living standards'.[171]

Questions of social differentiation beyond rank are ominously absent in the employers' mode of dehumanising 'manpower' accounting; in the context of the global maritime labour market, people are seemingly effortlessly allocated – 'slotted in' – to capital's needs. While the employers' lens is seemingly post-national, the realities of the labour market are deeply embedded in particular places – largely Asia and, since 1990, Eastern Europe and the former Soviet Union. Recruitment of ratings from 'labour supply' countries tends to be shaped primarily by low wages, alongside the prerequisite minimum qualifications, but also shared language. The top five 'labour supply' countries for ratings in 2015 were the Philippines, China, Indonesia, Russia and Ukraine. There is considerable discrimination among nationalities, especially in the employment of captains and senior officers, where the nineteenth-century deepening of racialised maritime divisions of labour remain manifest.[172] By divorcing the prior direct connection between seafarers and particular employers and specific workplaces/ships, capital ensured that seafarers circulated the sale of their labour power between ships through a series of casual contracts, heightening their precarity and undermining the potential for workplace solidarity. And where seafarers have sought to organise themselves, crew agencies engaged in the nefarious practice of negative listing of labour activists – even where seafarers simply complain about wages or working conditions.[173]

Multinational crews offer employers a number of advantages. First, employment conditions may change in the labour supply country and employing crew from a single country could expose shipowners to the risk of legislative reform in labour supply countries, which encourages operators to hire crew from a range of nationalities at different wages and with different working conditions.[174] Second, in industrial fisheries, contracting a certain number or percentage of crew from a country may be necessary to gaining a particular flag or access to a fishery. For example, in the Western Indian Ocean the EU industrial fishing fleet has to employ at least two Malagasy and two Seychellois crew as a condition of fisheries access arrangements with these countries, which are necessary to the commercial viability of tuna fisheries (i.e. the ability to follow the fish).[175] Third, whether by design or as unintended consequence, the employment of crew from different countries at different rates of pay can act in practice as a disciplinary mechanism, making crew easier to manage by fragmenting the potential for social solidarity.

The close working environment of a ship provides the conditions for the potential fostering of solidarity among crew, including across ranks, which can be countered by pitting different nationalities of crew against each other. For example, the European distant-water tuna fleet employs French or Spanish captains and senior officers, but the rest of the crew are variously from West and East Africa – mainly from Senegal, Ivory Coast, Ghana, Madagascar, and Seychelles, and to a lesser extent from Kenya and Tanzania. Crew employed on this fleet are always a combination of nationalities, which is part a condition of access agreements, part the (post-)colonial history of European boats moving through diverse African waters (see Chapter 4), and part disciplinary strategy of divide and rule, with the crew from countries on the Eastern Tropical Atlantic tending to be paid more than double those from countries on the Western Indian Ocean.[176] Japan's distant-water fishing fleet uses a similar hierarchy of race and region in shaping its labour recruitment. On its boats in the Western Central Pacific Ocean, mainland Japanese crew are paid the highest, followed by Okinawans and South Koreans, and then South East Asians and Pacific islanders.[177] Even though multinational recruitment practices create recognised difficulties for captains and officers in the management of labour, such as the need to navigate different languages and cultures of work, differences among crew simultaneously undermine the potential organisational power of labour, despite their intense socio-spatial proximity.[178] This is nothing new for crew working on ships. Consider the opinion of a 1921 International Labour Office report:

Unlike workers in many other fields, seamen must often do their work in several countries, in each of which it may be necessary for them to know something of the law as to their relations with their employers and their fellows. Even when not in other countries, much of the seamen's work must be done on the world's highway, far removed from the usual reach of public authorities. Moreover, on the ships of most countries the seamen are frequently of many nationalities. It is not unusual that the seamen on a ship neither speak the language of the ship's country, nor understand its laws.[179]

As in other industries, the leadership of national fishers' trade unions can reflect lines of perceived 'national' interest, which is all the more contradictory in an industry where capital is so close to being transnational in its mobility.[180]

Yet if shipowners are able to recruit globally, why is it that a country like the Philippines supplies a disproportionately large share of the global workforce of seafarers? A large part of the answer can be found in three interconnected issues to do with the state regulation and private ordering of maritime labour regimes. First, as already noted, FOCs and international registries broke the – historically always unstable – connection between ship ownership, its registered flag and (often) national regulatory requirements on crew composition. Second, in the mid-1970s Ferdinand E. Marcos's regime rolled out a national 'development' strategy of labour exports with the aim of countering high domestic unemployment and capturing foreign remittances. The Philippine state provided training schools for domestic, care and construction workers and seafarers – occupational paths that are largely highly gendered.[181] This provided a steady supply of qualified ratings and junior officers to the increasingly transnational capitalist organisation of the merchant navy. According to official statistics, the number of Philippine seafarers grew from around 52,000 in 1986 to over 240,000 in 2015.[182] Overseas Philippine workers are required by the Philippine state to remit 80 per cent of earnings to a national bank account. Remittances from seafarers as a share of all Philippine workers overseas in 2002 were around 31 per cent of a total US$6.4 billion.[183] Third, the state established crew agencies to actively promote the movement of seafarers to pick up ships by the voyage, thereby countering the build-up of workplace solidarity over time and reducing the prospects for wage and other gains by labour.

Today's seafarers are typically recruited by crewing agencies. Agents 'procure' workers, check training and medical compliance, and facilitate travel to and from port at either end of a journey. Employment contracts are most often on a 'per-voyage' basis and ratings rarely stay with the same ship or company.[184] Combined with the regular use of mixed-nationality crews who have different trade union links (if any) and the disciplinary mechanism of appraisal on discharge books, these employment practices seriously erode the possibility of developing and sustaining bottom-up relations of solidarity among ratings. The relatively fluid, global nature of the labour market and the sheer number of qualified crew means that labour organisers can be easily replaced.

Much like the eighteenth-century crimpers, crew agencies directly exploit ratings by offering unfair terms in the advancement of wages, living costs and/or transport, and by charging direct and indirect fees to access jobs.[185] For example, agents can take advantage of the inter-jurisdictional complexities of work at sea to extract value, such as in Madagascar, where a crew agency recruiting seafarers was found to have cheated seafarers out of salary by citing artificially low foreign exchange rates from US dollars to Malagasy ariary. The national maritime trade union, Sygmma, successfully challenged the agency in the Malagasy courts.[186] Depending on the type of fishery, fishing crew can be more closely tied to a specific vessel compared to seafarers. The intensity of the labour process when actively engaged in fishing demands a skilled and highly cooperative working relationship, and so captains seek to retain crew, incentivised through catch shares. Nonetheless, crew do move between boats and agents play a central role in this process. Agents claim to crew that they represent their interests, such as in discussing higher salaries and better working conditions with boat owners, but they will rarely push matters with them 'because they're our bosses'.[187]

In general then, while an important source of employment for crew from the global South, 'the out-sourcing of labour supply . . . has had a manifestly negative impact upon the terms and conditions of employment for seafarers and has further distanced them from employers facilitating neglect of welfare, of health and safety, and even in some circumstances of training and competence.'[188] This is despite wide-ranging labour regulation at the international level.

Reform and reaction in international labour regulation

As we saw in the opening of this chapter, fishers and seafarers started and ended the twentieth century working in the world's most dangerous occupations. Both fall easily between the cracks of regulatory jurisdiction: flag state, port state, vessel owner, crew agency, national waters, high seas. In addition to this jurisdictional complexity, the genuinely international character of large segments of maritime industries and intense competition among capitals has meant that it has long been recognised that 'improvements in the labor standards on the ships of a single country were very difficult to obtain unless similar changes were made on those of other countries'.[189] This set of complexities explains why seafaring was a major focus of the work of the International Labour Organisation (ILO) from its inception and has more occupation-specific regulation at the ILO than any other job. From 1919, the ILO passed over thirty-six conventions and twenty-six recommendations on the specific industrial relations and working conditions of seafarers,[190] most of which were harmonised in the 2006 Maritime Labour Convention discussed below. But this was not the outcome of reformist altruism in the inter-state system. The genesis of this early twentieth-century social regulation – and of the very institution of the ILO itself – was the wider context of radical, revolutionary and anti-colonial politics from the early nineteenth century onwards. And it was seafarers themselves who put their concerns on the ILO's agenda, compelling representatives of capital and states to take the matter seriously (if far from completely) in tripartite maritime conferences.

We have noted how seafarers were often in the initial vanguard of the strikes that sparked the unfolding of wider labour movements in Australia, Britain and New Zealand in the late 1800s. But they were rarely able to sustain them. Seafarers' unions were often smaller, with fewer resources, and seafarers harder to organise, because of the locationally transitory nature of their work. At the same time, the spectre of 'foreign' crew was used to threaten jobs, and maritime union leadership often appeared more willing to acquiesce to employers while the more militant rank and file were at sea.[191] Until the 1970s maritime trade unions in Western Europe and its white settler offshoots were embedded in national shipping industries owned and controlled largely by European capital.[192]

Maritime labour organisation in Britain and the white settler colonies was often racially framed and even explicitly racist, and pitched in politically reactionary terms. In the United States, membership of the International Organization of Masters, Mates, and Pilots of America was restricted to 'any white person of good moral character, in sound health, and a firm believer in God', and a 1949 constitutional amendment of the National Maritime Union barred membership to those with Communist links.[193] In Britain, the National Union of Seamen (NUS) supported a 1935 government subsidy to tramp shipping that was available only to ships with British crews, excluding Indian and other colonial subjects. The NUS (and the government) quickly had to backtrack because shipowners could not find enough British seafarers and its rank-and-file members, including many sailors born outside Britain, were opposed to the policy.[194]

Reactionary 'white unionism' was counterpointed with the harnessing by black seafarers of the internationalist potential of their working lives. While black seafarers were actively discriminated against by white unionism and the British state, they used their mobility to link up struggles in Africa, the Caribbean and Europe, which was 'integral to the production and reproduction of . . . Communist inflected black internationalisms',[195] including the formation of the Colonial Seamen's Association in 1936 and the coordination of strikes in British West Africa during the Second World War.[196] Internationalist struggles were brought back to Britain in the form of the Seamen's Minority Movement within the left trade union movement. '[S]haped by the multi-ethnic cultures of seafarers organizing in port cities such as Cardiff, London, Liverpool and South Shields',[197] this movement is suggestive of the cosmopolitanism of seafarers based in eighteenth-century London. But seafarers' unions in and of the global South are just as prone to reformism and nationalism as those in the North. For example, the main Philippine Seafarers' Union is generally very poorly organised on the ship floor. Instead they tend to prioritise the promotion of Philippine 'competitiveness' in the global labour market as opposed to pursuing improved working conditions and pay.[198]

Yet, despite the advantages of transnationality available to shipping capital and the constraints on organising labour on board ships, it is organised labour, not states, that has thwarted the anti-regulatory tide of open registries. Because of the consistently casual nature of their employment on a per-voyage basis, seafarers can be typified as 'a highly exploited workforce with limited "muscle" in terms of industrial relations with their employers'.[199] Nonetheless, the ITF represents up to a half of the combined global total of 1.6 million seafarers (officers and ratings) either through affiliated trade unions or on ships covered by ITF agreements.[200] National and transnational labour organisation and class struggle have ensured that the FOC is not an automatic or smooth strategy for capitalist accumulation. It was contested most prominently by the strategic countervailing power deployed in the ITF's FOC campaign, initiated in 1948.[201]

The political dimension of the ITF's FOC campaign – to bring an end to ships with no 'genuine link' to the flag state – has clearly failed, at least so far,[202] whereas the industrial dimension – to represent seafarers working on FOC ships – is arguably the most materially successful of any of the global union federations' transnational bargaining campaigns.[203] It really took off when huge numbers of seafarers from the former Soviet bloc joined ITF-affiliated unions and FOC ships with ITF agreements grew from less than 8 per cent in 1990 to over 30 per cent in 2000.[204] Crucial to the success was the ITF's shifting of the FOC debate from 'one of protection of union jobs in rich countries to one of establishing global collective bargaining structures for the benefit of all working seafarers'.[205] This was made possible through the solidarity of dock workers who refuse to offload FOC ships without ITF agreements and who in turn gain from the same agreements committing shipowners or operators to not allow crew to engage in 'non-seafarers work' (i.e. any type of cargo handling services).[206] As we saw earlier in this chapter, the structural power of solidarity among workers in the maritime logistics chain had been identified by the ITF when it was founded in 1896.

ITF agreements are monitored by a transnational network of over 130 ship inspectors based in multiple ports in 54 countries. They made an annual average of 9,500 inspections in 2016–2018, of which almost 70 per cent identified problems, ranging from breach of contract or international standards to owed wages and successfully claimed back pay of almost US$100 million in these three years.[207] In these ways, calling into an ITF port can erode a ship operator's bottom line and, if they refuse to comply, an inspector can initiate a ship boycott. Despite these impressive gains, it must be remembered that ITF agreements are only with particular ships and for particular periods – 2000 was a particularly 'good year';[208] secondary action (i.e. port worker solidarity with FOC crew) is allowed in only very few countries since the ongoing neoliberal assault on organised labour; relatedly, 'traditional' dock workers – ITF's 'industrial muscle' – are on the decline both in terms of their absolute number with increased automation and in terms of their relative power. The latter has been worsened due to important divisions between rival dockers' unions, as represented by the creation of the more militant, shop-floor driven International Dockworkers' Council in the late 1990s.[209]

What is specific about attempts to codify responses to forms of exploitation at sea? The iterative complexity of multiple ILO regulations on seafaring led to calls for its harmonisation and consolidated in the 2006 Maritime Labour Convention (MLC), in force since 2013 – a process pushed by the ITF. The MLC is thus the culmination of ever-increasing layers of regulation of work at sea through the twentieth century, and even if the usual tension between the statute books and enforcement (policy and practice) is exemplified in this sector, the convention is a useful prism through which to explore the peculiarities of maritime labour regimes.[210]

The MLC recognises that seafaring is a distinct type of work and that there is a need to bring it into the 'norm' of social regulation. Four distinct elements of work at sea are highlighted in the MLC. While each is itself unexceptional, often having close parallels in other types of work on land, we argue that in combination they add up to a significant 'maritime factor' and a distinct labour regime. First, in maritime industries, capital is physically highly mobile between and *outside* jurisdictions. While the capital–labour relation can be seen to be in literal motion between jurisdictions in several industries, such as trucking and trains, seafarers share only with aviation workers the experience of working for considerable periods in areas outside national jurisdiction. Second, unlike aviation workers, seafarers live constantly at work for several weeks at a time (several months for many fishing boat crew), and because the ship is a 'structured space',[211] it is necessary to specify the contours of the 'working day'. In living for long periods of time *within* their place of work, like au pairs and other domestic workers, seafarers are more easily subject to the bleeding of work into leisure time and the intensified exploitation that this entails. Third, and connected, the MLC regulates multiple dimensions of working conditions and social provisioning, including healthcare, repatriation, social security, paid annual leave, the basic content of employment contracts, recruitment and placement practices, safety training, etc.[212] Again, this is not so different from the regulation of some forms of work on land and in particular countries, but it is unusual in that the sector is so intensively and extensively patrimonial, arguably making a qualitative difference that reflects the peculiarity of the place of work (and of life). Finally, the MLC seeks to improve the ability to trace ship ownership, which continues to be notoriously difficult, especially when legal liability becomes an issue, such as with accidents at sea.

The advantages of transnationality to capital are nothing new,[213] although, as we saw earlier in relation to the FOC, arguably it was innovated as a strategy of *industrial capital* in shipping. Anonymous ownership one or several steps removed from direct legal responsibility for employment relations and working conditions contributes to the difficulty of identifying *whom* crew can engage with in a labour dispute (to strike is a difficult option while at sea), and is compounded by the problem of *where* a dispute might be heard (the question of the jurisdiction of courts). Abandonment most starkly illustrates this tension; shipowners sometimes prefer to abandon a debt-laden vessel in a distant port without paying wages and other costs. An ILO database of reported abandonments of vessels has recorded 367 cases since it was set up in 2004.[214] Again, while there are similar issues facing labour in other forms of work, the jurisdictional dimension introduces layers of legal ambiguity and political complexity that are hard to find elsewhere.

The maritime labour regime

In the structured space of the ship as a place of work and life, maritime labour regimes can be shaped by workers as well as by the personalities and practices of captains; the technical specifications of the workspace, such as a ship's design; and the broader institutions that simultaneously connect multiple places of work, such as (non-)regulation by flag states. A labour regime is something more sociologically complicated and dialectical than simple notions of 'cheap labour'. Similarly, an ocean-going ship is not simply a vessel of exchange; it is also a site of work and production. Workers shape labour regimes through past class antagonisms and their compromises, which may become codified in national and international law and forms of private ordering; in local historical cultures of labour organising of greater or weaker militancy; and in contemporaneous struggles, whether in the form of direct resistance, indirect resilience or reworking.[215]

We have argued that the maritime labour regimes sketched in this chapter constitute a critical attribute of the terraqueous relationship between capitalism and the sea. The risk, opportunity and profitability associated with forms of exploitation at sea are accompanied by distinct forms of labour recruitment, management, discipline and organisation. Maritime labour regimes are overdetermined by the articulation of industry segment, flag and its associated regulation, private ordering, social relations of class and race, and a formalised hierarchy of rank, from the captain through the first engineer down. The distinctively militaristic hangover of rank on ships can define a workplace, from the profound (the risking of life, limb and, most commonly, digits) to the seemingly banal (the policing of access to email).

162

Even in the twenty-first century, the 'captain is king'.[216] Maritime labour regimes have, moreover, pioneered a form of 'offshoring' through the labour arbitrage that in many respects is locked into an industry that realised surplus value through movement from one locale and jurisdiction to another. Many of the labour contracting and management practices essential to exploitation at sea have found their way onshore – for instance in the hiring of migrant agency workers for mega-infrastructure projects. The 'open registry' illustrates how fishers and seafarers are never far off land when they're at sea: they carry with them many of the characteristics of a land-based labour process associated with, say, mining: ethnic segmentation of the workforce, strict labour discipline, repetitive physical jobs, combination of workplace and lifeworld in a single confined space. Similarly, the liminal qualities of seafaring workers – the fact that they straddle rural hinterlands of supply and cosmopolitan ports of demand, that to this day they often speak various languages or patois and have to negotiate multiple national legal systems – signal a continuity with the South Asian sailors of previous centuries, which also tells a deep story of the role of the sea in the construction of the modern world. These are all outcomes, we have argued, of a distinctive maritime factor to the development of capitalism, where the imperative to create value while at sea necessarily produces novel, if generally thoroughly deleterious, social practices and institutions.

4

Appropriation

The appropriation of marine life sustains human bodies, state revenue and capitalist accumulation in a variety of ways. The capture of marine fish, shellfish and mammals provides vital protein and nutrients – constituting around 17 per cent of all available animal protein globally in 2015. Fish consumption per capita has more than doubled since the 1960s: from nine kilogrammes in 1961 to 20.2 kilogrammes in 2015, which excludes fish destined for non-food uses.[1] Fish and fish products are a highly traded commodity internationally. Trade data do not distinguish between wild-caught and aquaculture; nonetheless, fish exports from developing countries generate a higher monetary export value than coffee, bananas, cocoa, tea, sugar and tobacco *combined*.[2] Around 120 million people are directly dependent on the *commercial* capture-fisheries industry and the post-harvest sector. All of this is driven by the law of value and the capitalist compulsion to 'accumulate or die'.[3] Corporate managers and the asset-owning class reap the profits extracted from the circuit of capital based on this 'free gift' of marine life. For example, the combined annual net profit of four of the largest multinational corporations involved predominantly in the canned tuna industry *alone* averaged annually US$366.5 million between 2006 and 2016.[4] More broadly, the world's 150 largest seafood companies accounted for around $120 billion in sales in 2018 – a number that combines marine capture, inland capture and aquaculture.[5]

The expansion of profit-driven extraction has caused an increase in the fraction of fish populations that are fished at biologically unsustainable levels from 10 per cent in 1974 to 33 per cent in 2015. While the share of aquaculture in global fish consumption has grown rapidly since the 1980s – overtaking wild-caught fish available for direct human consumption for the first time in 2013 – marine-capture fisheries provide a major input to animal and aquaculture feed.[6] Enormous volumes of wild populations of small species such as anchovies, herrings, sardines and 'trash fish' are caught to produce fishmeal and fish oil to feed commercial aquaculture species such as salmon and shrimp. The 'fish-in–fish-out' ratio produces an 'inherent contradiction' in that 'industries must amplify their exploitation of marine biomass to feed farmed fish'.[7]

Together with other key marine and coastal resources (minerals and hydrocarbons, wind and wave energy, recreational spaces), fish thus constitute one of the main 'free gifts' of nature which capitalist firms and states have through the centuries sought to valorise. In thinking about nature-at-sea we unequivocally reject social theory that attempts to collapse the human and the non-human. As Marx made clear, labour *and* nature are the source of all material wealth: 'the material substratum' is 'furnished by nature without human intervention' and when people engage in the process of production they 'can only proceed as nature does', i.e. we can only *reorder* matter.[8] Conventionally – and in contrast to other modes of production – capitalist appropriation requires the commodification of things, turning the use-value of something quite specific into a universally transferable exchange-value. On land and in coastal waters, this has involved enclosure of commons, dispossession of direct producers, and the accompanying legal–bureaucratic infrastructure that guarantees property rights within a particular territory through government, courts, law enforcement agencies and so forth. At sea, however, property rights have historically been much harder to define and enforce: outside territorial waters, the ocean (its surface, depths, seabed and subsoil) was until recently 'nobody's property'; a realm of free navigation and unfettered appropriation for those with the means to do so.

Much of this is to do with the biological and geophysical qualities of marine life that we have been emphasising through the book so far, which make an appearance here principally in the form of unique species' characteristics. Despite common parlance informed by terrestrial bias, oceanic fish populations are not 'stocks' to be 'harvested' – they were never 'sown' or planted. State power and market pressures also figure prominently in our account of how capitalist development has produced some historically unprecedented ways of appropriating nature, of extending the 'commodity frontier' at and through the sea. In its quest to commodify the oceans, capital has encountered successive barriers that have delivered spatio-juridical innovations in the extraction of rent from exclusive economic zones, experiments in governance through regional fisheries management organisations and individual transferable quotas (ITQs), as well as technological advances aimed at increasing productivity in the appropriation of marine life. Multilateral regulation, international rivalry, sectoral competition and consolidation, and socio-political contestation involving unions, NGOs, consumer advocacy groups, regulatory bodies and industry associations have thus all played a part in creating successive 'pelagic empires' characterised by specific legal infrastructures, subsidy regimes, labour processes, marine technologies and epistemic communities.[9] Our starting point in this chapter is to address a seemingly banal question: how does a wild, indomitable and majestic fish like say, the bluefin tuna, end up as a global commodity? How can property rights be established over life in the seven-tenths of the planet that is in constant liquid motion? Responding to questions of these sorts reveals how our social metabolism with nature is conditioned – however asymmetrically – both by dominant patterns of production and consumption, and by the intrinsic qualities of marine life. Jason W. Moore's notion of 'ecological surplus', defined as that share of 'unpaid work/energy . . . appropriated in service to commodity production', plays a significant role in our account as it underlines how this surplus is accrued mainly 'through geographical expansion, and is most effective when empires and states do the hard work of imposing order – cultural, scientific, juridical and the rest – on new spaces'.[10] We thus pay special attention to the distinctive political institutions, spatial forms and legal frameworks that facilitate market forces appropriating nature for exchange. We first consider commodity chains in marine life, and then proceed in the second part of the chapter to examine the complex combination of geopolitics and geo-economics that extends (and indeed depletes) the commodity frontiers in the saltwater part of our terraqueous world.

Commodity chains in marine life

When salmon or tuna enter a cannery, the animal's biomass already constitutes a commodity. But before they are caught, they are wild animals. So-called 'natural resources' are not innate, they *become*. What is considered to be of 'value' in one historical culture or mode of production may be more or less so in another. But just as humans determine natural resources by discovering and inventing new use- and exchange-values by appropriating and commodifying nature, so too do natural resources shape and determine the limits and potential of the production process.[11] Thus the extraction and consumption of marine life acquire distinctive characteristics under capitalism. Although small-scale and household artisanal fishing still account for the bulk of global employment in the marine fisheries,[12] it is industrial deep-water fisheries wholly subsumed by capital that dominate in terms of capture volume. Industrial fisheries are capital-intensive, proletarianised, often vertically integrated and, importantly for our purposes, organised purely for the transformation of nature into exchange-value.

Commodifying the sea has therefore been an eminently social process, subject as much to varying regimes of accumulation as it has to political efforts in establishing property rights on the oceans.

Take, for example, the contrast between tuna meat and whale oil. The canning of fish has only ever existed *within* generalised commodity production – it does not have a romanticised past. But whaling does. It is whaling where we encounter the most iconic images of Man and Machine battling biological and geophysical nature – whales and waves. Popularised in visceral tales told in folklore, 1851's *Moby-Dick* and the 2015 Hollywood blockbuster *In the Heart of the Sea*, there is, of course, nothing romantic about using the rendered ooze of dead cetacean to light cities at night. By the nineteenth century, both these marine resources had been subject to capitalist appropriation. And yet their radically divergent historical trajectories as commodities indicate the importance of historicising cultures of consumption: canned tuna is ubiquitous today, while whale oil is a thing of the past. To get at the historical dynamism of commodity chains based on the appropriation of marine life we explore the interplay of social relations and biophysical features in two distinct tuna fisheries – one focused on the production of a wage good and the other on an item of bourgeois consumption.

Fish that feed workers

Whaling and tuna processing are quite clearly about the merging of labour and nature. A tuna cannery is an abattoir. Frozen bodies are piled into metal bins for gradual defrosting before being cooked in giant ovens, then hand-cut – most often by women – and 'cleaned' (i.e. flakes of dark meat picked off).[13] Dark flesh is channelled into canned food for pets or, in the global South, local human markets, as Western cultures of consumption have learned to like light meat in their salads and sandwiches (in the US a favoured flesh is 'white meat' – albacore tuna). The cleaned 'loins' are then packed into cans to be sealed and cooked again, this time in retort ovens (large sausage-shaped machines that simultaneously heat and pressurise). Depending on the sophistication of the factory, varying shapes and sizes of cans are labelled, embossed and packed for export according to national market segment and product differentiation. The production line for French *thon au naturel* is distinct as the large, defrosted, shimmering albacore or yellowfin are hung whole from a hook where they are expertly butchered into bright red cuts before being cooked, only once, in the can.

The canning of seafood originated in the 1800s as a military technology in the context of European war. The process was invented in response to a 12,000 franc *encouragement* by Napoleon for new methods of preserving food given the trade blockades cutting off prior supplies of slave-plantation-produced cane sugar, then widely used for the preservation of food.[14] The official report recommending Nicholas Appert's invention noted the implications for international commerce, both in terms of the export of French products and for the import of preserved food from other countries.[15] Like so many other capitalist technologies, canned food was born in war but was a basis for future accumulation. It allowed the organic matter of ecological surplus appropriated in one part of the world to be preserved, stored and then consumed in another. The world's first commercial food cannery or 'preservatory' was set up in London in 1813, benefiting from Britain's (then) leading industrial base, including in domestic tinplate production and national military contracts.

Always already a commodity geared to international exchange, the canning of fish created new industrial working classes and coastal landscapes in Western Europe and North America. Canning allowed preservation of large catches during high fishing seasons without the significant adulteration of flavour and texture that came with earlier methods of preservation such as salting, smoking, drying or pickling. Apart from its clear use-value, canning enhanced exchange-value because of the higher quality and increased durability of canned fish compared to earlier preservation methods, in effect giving capital greater control over commodity circulation time. Sardine canneries were established in Nantes and Brittany on the West Coast of France in the 1820s, and by 1880 the latter region alone produced nearly 50 million cans.[16] Canned sardines were exported from France to supply miners in the mid-nineteenth-century gold rushes in white settler colonies in the USA and Australia.[17] The American Civil War further spurred demand for canned food in the US to supply Union and Confederate soldiers – a habituated taste that was brought back to households and communities.

Seaward-facing capital in North America built canning plants along coasts and estuaries through the 1800s, creating new regional economies. In the US, factories canning lobster and salmon were established in Baltimore and Boston in the late 1810s and, fifty years later, canneries were perched on the mouths of the great West Coast rivers such as the Colombia. Here, Pacific salmon were unceremoniously plucked from the river by mechanical wheels as they returned to spawn after two years of living in the ocean.[18] The entire lengths of the Pacific coast of North America and the Atlantic coast of Canada were dotted with canning factories, creating a new proletariat 'to feed the British working classes'.[19] This commodification of marine life contributed to the destruction both of 'indigenous foodways' where 'salmon runs fed densely settled communities' preserved in the form of jerky, and of 'cultural traditions that both revered the fish and regulated its catch'.[20] In parallel, salmon packing shaped intimately new articulations of social relations of race, gender and class. Because fish perishes so swiftly without refrigeration, and the density of salmon runs is not predictable within a season or from year to year, cannery owners created highly precarious and segmented labour regimes. On Canada's Pacific coast in the late nineteenth century, for example, indigenous migrant men caught salmon while women cleaned and canned the fish, but intercontinental migrants from China began to be favoured by cannery managers because they were seen as being more subordinate. A subsequent wave of Japanese migrant fishers entered the fishery – bitterly opposed by white settler fishers – and brought 'picture brides' from Japan who began working in canneries.[21] These regional economies of seafood commodity production thus generated divisions of labour that reflected and refracted social relations of class, patriarchy and racism. But, as will be explored later, this is only part of the story: industrial fisheries were formed and reproduced in a context of imperialism, where state-subsidised boat owners sought to accumulate super-profits based on (temporarily) high ecological surpluses.

The dynamics of competitive accumulation saw the rapid cheapening of canned fish by the turn of the twentieth century – by then it was a working-class staple. The massification of salmon extraction and destruction of spawning grounds through agriculture, hydropower, logging and mining rapidly depleted the initial ecological surplus. The North American Pacific salmon industry had to seek out and develop new commodity frontiers – most notably in Alaska, which by 1916 supplied three-quarters of the world's canned salmon.[22] Another strategy was to appropriate new species altogether. The United States' first tuna cannery produced 35,000 cans in its first full year of operation in 1903; in a Californian factory in the twenty-first century this number of cans is produced in only two hours.[23] Around 215 tuna canneries are dotted across the planet today, collectively using approximately 3 million tons of fish per year.[24] That this processing capacity is for one product of one type of fish alone makes clear that the daily hunt for oceanic life involves the extraction of mind-boggling volumes of fish.

To grasp the dynamics of accumulation based on the appropriation of marine life requires an understanding of the latter's biological and geophysical specificities.[25] Taken as a whole, tuna fisheries are among the largest in volume and monetary value of the other major marine fisheries since 1950, such as anchovies, pollock, small pelagics (herring and mackerel), cod, cephalopods (squid and octopus) and shrimps.[26] Tuna species have a large spawning potential and very rapid growth in their juvenile phase, both of which enable potentially high levels of reproduction – subject, primarily, to the extent and intensity of human extraction as well as wider regional and global environmental changes, including anthropogenic ones such as intensified ocean acidification and warming. The growth rate leading to spawning age varies significantly among species of tuna. Different ages of sexual maturity and spawning duration make each species more or less vulnerable to intensive fishing methods. Depending upon the species targeted, this imposes a relative limitation on the absolute extent and intensity of levels of fishing effort. For example, southern bluefin tuna reach maturity at eleven to twelve years and their spawning duration peaks in a five-month period, whereas skipjack reach spawning age on an all-year basis at 1.5 years. Their rapid generation of biomass has allowed skipjack tuna populations to withstand long-term, mass commodity production (albeit within limits). In contrast, slow-growing, long-living species such as Atlantic and southern bluefin tuna are far less resilient to human predation than skipjack.[27]

Skipjack and yellowfin tuna are the main species used for canning and both are caught using purse-seiners – boats that are able to catch a whole school of the fish in one set of the net. Purse-seining took off in the mid-1960s to supply burgeoning demand for canned tuna in North America and Western Europe.[28] Highly capital-intensive (one boat costs upwards of US$30 million), modern purse-seiners use a skiff to tow a net with a circumference of up to two kilometres around a school of fish. Once encircled, the bottom of the net is then tightened like a purse string to concentrate the fish. The catch is normally too heavy to haul directly aboard, so it is either scooped aboard using pan nets or pumped on to the vessel using seawater.[29] Once on deck the fish is transferred to freezers in the hull – by conveyor belts in modern vessels – and sorted by species and size along the way. The freezers use seawater mixed with a high concentration of salt (brine). This allows a temperature of around −18°C without block freezing the brine as this would result in complications and delays both in storing future catch and in offloading. Such processes create several negative effects on fish quality.[30] They lead to severe distress and/or death by suffocation for a large proportion of the fish (like sharks, tuna gill systems preclude breathing without swimming). The flesh of tuna killed slowly under stress undergoes chemical change – known as 'burning' – degrading the quality of the meat. Further, the fish are crushed against the side of the net or against each other, especially those in the lower levels of the net, which results in bruising of the flesh. Storage in brine at sea for months on end results in salt seeping into the flesh of the tuna, further diminishing its quality and raising the sodium content of the final canned meat. The combination of these damaging effects on meat quality means that purse-seine-caught tuna is generally only consumed as canned product. In other words, the design and technology of industrial purse-seining is locked into producing for the global commodity chain in canned tuna; its raw material production rarely contributes to other use-values.

It is in the context of this high-volume, low-quality but highly standardised industry that multinational firms like Heinz, Mitsubishi and Lehman Brothers took an interest in the sector and began buying big brands and their processing capacity – most often in highly concentrated markets where the rich pickings of oligopsonistic brand rents were ripe for collection. Other big players in the industry at the turn of this century started out in the 1970s and 1980s as highly specialised, low-profit processors packing to contract for big tuna brands and

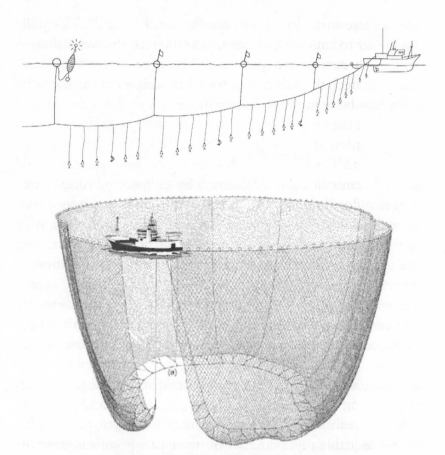

Figure 4.1. Industrial fishing technologies:
longlining (top) and purse-seining (bottom)
Source: FAO, top illustration redrawn by Ed Olivier.

supermarkets, like Thai Union. Now the largest canned tuna firm in the world, Thai Union bought major brands in Europe and the USA such as Chicken of the Sea, John West and Petit Navire.[31] When it tried to buy another leading North American brand (Bumble Bee) for US$1.5 billion from a private equity firm in 2015, Thai Union had to withdraw under the spotlight of a massive price-fixing scandal involving the main three brands in the USA, a market where big capital already competes through product degradation, including the use of ever-smaller cans and production of low-quality 'tuna soup'.[32] The dull compulsion of market competition further up the chain sharpens the pressure on the owners of fishing boats to catch more fish more cheaply, pushing boats into new commodity frontiers and intensifying the exploitation of crew.

One of life's little luxuries

In stark contrast to the humble can of tuna – bruised and burned in the net, soaked in brine, and cooked twice – the fresh, raw, fatty flesh of bluefin tuna can command astronomical prices. The vast variety and volume of marine life for sale every day at Tokyo's Tsukiji market is an optic onto the combination of forces, relations and processes that are engaged in the systematic appropriation of ocean life. Since the last quarter of the twentieth century, Japan has consumed a dizzying diversity of seafood – almost 500 species of seafood are available at Tsukiji on a daily basis – and generally at extremely high prices in relative terms. Tsukiji is a central node in the global seafood industry – 'the fish market at the center of the world'.[33] It is a reminder of the country's imperial history – where, as we shall see below, fishing boats acted in practice, if not necessarily in intent, as the advance party of empire. Since the 1960s, boat owners and traders dotted around the world have sought to sell here, reflecting Japan's high purchasing power and pole position in the post-war international division of labour. This scramble for market share has been exacerbated by the decline of Japan's national fishing fleet, itself an outcome of an ageing and deskilled domestic labour market. A generation ago much of the seafood consumed in Japan would have been caught by Japanese boats with Japanese crew, but these fleets are in decline and skippers, chief engineers and fish masters on Japan's fishing fleet are older Japanese men commanding crew drawn from Indonesia and other 'labour supply' countries (see Chapter 3).[34] The boom of the 1980s and the strong yen, especially post–Plaza Accord (1985), saw the extension and expansion of airfreight links to Japan, allowing for year-round supply of imported sashimi-grade seafood. Fresh tuna imports more than tripled from 17,000 million tons in 1985 to a peak of around 56,000 million tons in 1992.[35] But this bonanza was not sustained. Japan's per capita seafood supply dropped considerably from a peak of seventy-one kilogrammes per annum in the mid-1990s to forty-eight kilogrammes in 2013 (for comparison, US annual per capita supplies peaked in 2006 at twenty-four kilogrammes).[36] Japan's quantity of consumption disguises perceived qualities as indicated by price. For example, of the US$6.2 billion global tuna market, Japan's consumption consisted of 20 per cent in volume but 55 per cent in value, which can explained by the higher price of sashimi.[37]

Contemporary patterns of seafood consumption in Japan do not, therefore, reflect, as is often implied, deep-rooted cultural traditions. For example, *ō-toro* sashimi – the sought-after fatty flesh from the belly of tuna, especially bluefin – is perceived by many (and paid for accordingly) as a luxurious Japanese delicacy. But before the Second World War, *ō-toro* bluefin tuna was seen as low-quality because the lack of refrigeration meant that the fat would deteriorate quickly. It was fed to cats.[38] The rise of *ō-toro* can be traced to 'slick promotion by central wholesale market middlemen in the 1960s' and the commercialisation of airfreight which allowed chilled fish to be auctioned fresh in Tokyo only days after being caught thousands of miles away.[39] In the twenty-first century, a parallel market segment uses ultra-low temperature (ULT) freezers at −60°C which keep the flesh in virtual stasis, thereby allowing big trading companies, led by Mitsubishi, to shape the market by holding inventory in ULT warehouses.[40]

Industrial longline tuna fishing was developed by Japanese capitalists in 1914, but this was a coastal fishery and catch volumes were tiny compared to levels after the Second World War.[41] Even post-war, most of Japan's longline catch was used for canning for export because onboard freezing capacity (at −20 °C) meant that the flesh was brown and thus unsuitable for sashimi. It was not until the mid-1960s and the development of onboard freezing capacity at −40 °C (hitting −55 °C by 1969) that Japan's longliners shifted fishing effort from export-oriented canning species (yellowfin and albacore) to high-value sashimi species (bluefin and bigeye) for Japan's new rich.[42]

Bigger tunas are able to survive – and hunt – in deeper waters. The industrial longline technique uses fishing lines of up to 120 nautical miles with *thousands* of baited hooks. The use of weights and floats allows the crew to target depths up to around 300 metres, which is in the upper layer of the mesopelagic – or twilight – zone.[43] Tunas have highly streamlined body shapes and physiological adaptations to their habitats, allowing them to sustain high-speed swimming and efficient thermoregulation. This countercurrent heat exchange system permits quick movement between surface (warmer) and deeper (colder) waters within and, for the larger species of tuna, below the epipelagic zone (200 metres from the surface). Different species of tuna thermoregulate to varying degrees, with implications for 'catchability'. Most tuna fishing techniques use surface gear, such as purse-seining, limiting extraction to when tuna feed in the upper levels of the epipelagic zone. Longline gear is the exception. It is used to target larger tuna species which – because of their insulating layer of fat – are able to survive at deeper levels in the ocean. And it is precisely this fat content (*toro*) that makes the fish so desirable for consumption as sashimi – it melts in the mouth, a sensation that the use of avocado in 'California roll' sushi seeks to mimic.

The manipulative art of marketing bluefin tuna continues every January when Japan's top sashimi restaurants bid at Tsukiji to buy the biggest and best-quality fresh-chilled bluefin of the new year, giving them free advertising in the national press. These fish often sell for over one million US dollars and every year gullible journalists in the West dutifully write stories

178

on the conspicuous consumption and seeming rapaciousness of the Japanese appetite for seafood without recognising the annual marketing coup that this purchase provides to the restaurateur.[44] Outside these showy moments, the 'traditional' Tsukiji market is in relative decline, albeit not as a destination spot for tourists. Despite consumers in Japan tending to buy groceries in smaller quantities than those in the USA, Britain or France, for example, the market power of supermarkets has similarly increased and Japanese households now buy just under 70 per cent of their seafood from supermarkets.[45] Buyers in Japan's supermarket and restaurant chain conglomerates now cut out market intermediaries and buy from 'the big four' trading companies, including a Mitsubishi subsidiary, which account for around 70 per cent of Japan's traded volume of frozen sashimi tuna. These firms are able to buy a boat's entire catch and process the fish in-house ready for retail.[46] The articulation of changing cultures of consumption, capitals in competition and growing corporate centralisation and control in retail and trading have changed the conditions for accumulation in the Japan-centred tuna sashimi commodity chain, leaving behind 'traditional' marketing systems as an artefact of the twentieth century, and putting further pressure on boats to catch harder, further and faster, and to do it for less.

Theorising marine appropriation: or why there are not plenty more fish in the sea

We have illustrated how the capitalist appropriation of marine life is mediated not only by commodity chains and the abstract labour time they rely on, but also by the very concrete natural properties of fish with varying reproductive and migratory patterns. In transforming ocean biomass into a commodity, capital has to organise our collective metabolism with nature in ways that allow conflicting commercial circuits and biological rhythms – consumer demand and spawning duration, turnover time and feeding cycles – to align as efficiently as possible in the realisation of profit. We have seen how different technologies and types of fishing gear are used to catch similar, sometimes identical, species for differentiated markets (e.g. longline for tuna sashimi and purse seine for canned tuna), and also how the biophysical characteristics of wild fish species determine the ways in which humans try to capture them. With fish being active participants in the process of appropriation, there are also implications for the reproduction of the animals themselves.

From its inception, fisheries science was beholden to late Victorian capitalist logics of limiting 'waste' and maximising 'efficiency'. It has long been held that the infamous claim by 'Darwin's bulldog', Thomas Huxley, that 'the most important sea fisheries, such as the cod fishery, the herring fishery, and the mackerel fishery, are inexhaustible', was grounded in chutzpah and ignorance.[47] But recent research indicates that he simply disregarded testimony from fishers, industry and government officials about the negative effects of industrialised methods on marine fish populations, instead advancing his career, laissez-faire ideology and class bias. Damningly, Huxley's arguments influenced fisheries science and management into the twentieth century, which, rather than examining the effects of capitalist appropriation on fish populations, focused on 'modernizing the industry', oblivious to 'unstated political and economic preconceptions', and endorsing 'hegemonic capitalist practices that privatized sea resources and diminished independent fishers' political power'.[48] In 1948, for example, a leading fisheries scientist employed by the US government stated that tuna 'offer the greatest possibilities for the development of valuable commercial fisheries' and proposed a programme of fisheries science 'to assist in the development of profitable fisheries'.[49] Here the 'Gospel of Efficiency' developed in German scientific forestry management was transplanted to the oceans, where scientists saw 'marine spaces as robust and resilient, and they informed efforts to transform ocean spaces into static management areas with artificial borders'.[50] Approaches to fisheries management and science are increasingly interdisciplinary, combining ecosystems and historical perspectives, but these remain marginal in mainstream policy and the field continues to fail to question its underpinning ideological assumptions of economically 'rational' extraction.[51]

Plenty has been written about the global fisheries crisis. The trends are stark. Over 90 per cent of commercially targeted marine fish species are at (60 per cent) or beyond (33 per cent) biologically 'sustainable' limits of catch.[52] There are, of course, huge variations across species and regions, and some overfished populations are now being 'rebuilt' by limiting extraction. But even these dramatic headline figures mask deeper, more contradictory dynamics – humans are catching fewer of the larger, commercial species. Capitalist accumulation in fisheries is eroding the 'free gift' upon which it depends. This partly explains why the total volume of marine biomass extracted from the global ocean has remained stagnant since the 1990s. The appropriation of species for mass commodity markets is at the higher trophic level of the marine food pyramid (i.e. predators feeding on smaller fish, and so on), which is highly inefficient from the perspective of the total food energy produced in the ocean.[53]

More often than not the marine fisheries crisis is framed simplistically as a 'tragedy of the commons'.[54] The argument that private property is the solution to the problem of unregulated fishing is the underlying ideology of most academic writing and policy making on capture fisheries. This iteration of the natural-rights school of property rights recognises that private ownership may produce inequality, but contrasts this with the absence of property rights, which it claims produces economic inefficiencies and species decline – 'Injustice is preferable to total ruin'.[55] The polemic that 'open access' is ubiquitous and the driver of decline in fisheries systems has been firmly rebutted by showing that historical property relations in fisheries have been designed as 'strong', 'weak', 'private' or 'open-access' according to the interests of the social class doing the defining.[56] Despite most marine fisheries today being regulated under the sovereign rights of states in exclusive economic zones (EEZs), the ideology of private property continues to shape dominant thinking on fisheries governance.[57] More sophisticated approaches focus on the industrial overcapacity of fishing fleets, thereby identifying the role of competing states and their 'home' firms as active agents in the problem.[58] Yet this is often undermined by accompanying technical solutions that seek to reduce the number of boats and the fishing effort that they engage in, which generally downplay, decontextualise or simply ignore the historical dynamics of the industrialisation of fisheries, including state–capital relations, uneven development and the unequal inter-state system. With Stefano Longo, Rebecca Clausen and Brett Clark, we insist that marine fisheries decline is far better understood as the 'tragedy of the commodity'.[59] For example, *whose* boats should be reduced in number? How to regulate the technology and techniques that allow capital to catch more with fewer boats ('fishing power')? How to understand the relationship between fishing boats (capitalists) and resource owners (state landed property)? And what happens when there are no new commodity frontiers?

Two accumulation strategies present themselves to capital when dealing with the ecological limit or decline of commercial marine fisheries: intensification of extraction using new technologies that open previously untapped frontiers of appropriation, or 'solving' the problem by taking fish out of the wild and growing, reproducing and killing them under intensive conditions of aquaculture. But even here the sea returns to land as oceanic species of salmon, for example, require a proportion of their nutritional intake to come from fish protein, so that farmed fish are often fed wild fish.[60]

Capitalism is reproduced through nature-at-sea in distinctive and sometimes startling ways. Jason W. Moore's theorisation of commodity frontiers as central to the reproduction of capitalism is a useful optic for thinking about oceanic fisheries. Historical capitalism is necessarily reproduced through new commodity frontiers organised around the appropriation of nature through the labour process. Firms are driven to open new commodity frontiers because of the enhanced possibilities for accumulation when entering zones of minimal (or zero) prior appropriation of nature.[61] And this is one of Moore's crucial points: appropriation in new commodity frontiers is greater than in existing zones of commodification, allowing for the competitive increase in relative surplus value through productivity gains. This 'commodity-*widening* strategy' based on *extensive* development offers the possibility of the appropriation of a high ecological surplus by firms.[62] Over time, the initially high ecological surplus deteriorates into 'mature' frontier conditions. The typical responses by capital to these conditions are to search for a new frontier in a different place, or intensify appropriation in an existing frontier through enhanced 'capitalization and socio-technical innovation'.[63] This 'commodity-*deepening*' strategy generates a new frontier based on *intensive* development. This is why commodity frontiers are historically zones of innovation, including, in the examples above, capital-intensive fishing gear to maximise extraction, and cutting-edge freezing technology to extend periods spent fishing at sea and the transport of raw materials.

The state and an unequal international system are integral to the production and reproduction of commodity frontiers.[64] As we go on to show, for the better part of the twentieth century, the globalisation of industrial oceanic fisheries was driven from the dominant capitalist countries in North America, Western Europe and East Asia, countries that were never solely terrestrial powers, but which projected their power on, in and through the oceans. The myth and hypocrisy of free trade is easily laid bare in relation to national fishing industries which continue to be protected by governments in the global North and South. For a variety of reasons, fisheries punch politically well above their economic weight. Even after the multilateral liberalisation of the Uruguay Round and the formation of the WTO, fish processing industries deemed sensitive to global competition remain protected by steep import tariffs in the EU, the USA, Japan and South Korea, while *annual* fisheries subsidies to keep boats at sea fishing harder, faster and further hover around US$20 billion (65 per cent of which is provided by developed countries to national fleets).[65]

All of today's distant-water fishing nations started out with national production systems based on the extraction of fish from coastal waters and adjacent seas.[66] The widening of commodity frontiers over time was propelled by various factors: growing proletarianisation, morphing cultures of consumption, the drive for super-profits available in ecological surplus, and the depletion of fish populations. But while capital is willing to reap the 'free gift' of marine fish populations, it is far less disposed to take the risk of locating potential fisheries.[67] Here, then, as with other realms of natural resource extraction, the state plays a central role not only in reproducing commodity frontiers in creating and enforcing (or not) international fisheries law, but also in 'discovering', delineating and managing fisheries and their environmental conditions of extraction through oceanographic and marine fisheries research and development. Borrowing from William Tsutsui, we can speak here of pelagic imperialism – a process whereby powerful states directly or indirectly provide economic and geopolitical support for their fishing capital to expand into distant waters.

The ocean-based appropriation of nature can be distinguished from that on land because – for most of the history of capitalism – there was an absence of property rights beyond territorial waters. This in turn has meant that the class relation involved in modern landed property at sea is also different: in the absence of exclusive monopoly over parcels of high seas, rent extraction has necessarily taken on peculiar forms. The doctrine of freedom of the seas explored earlier in the book included the idea that fish were 'nobody's property' and thus up for grabs by whomever could catch them. (In this sense oceanic fisheries were not, legally, a 'commons' under capitalism). Freedom of the seas meant that territories yielding profit-through-nature were created and reproduced by pelagic imperialism, unencumbered by landed property. This was a free gift to capital in a double sense: as 'first' or 'received' nature and as an ecological surplus – with their promise of super-profits – extracted without payment of a portion of surplus value to landed property. But this does not imply that *access* to oceanic fish and the creation of particular 'fisheries' merely means following natural resources wherever they happen to appear. State power and capitalist commodification, assisted by scientific research and development, *produce* these territories of fishing profit – locating, delimiting, regulating and therefore giving shape to these places in the sea.[68]

One good illustration of this exercise in engineering property rights at sea is the individual transferable quotas (ITQs), a regime of resource allocation pioneered by public authorities in New Zealand, Chile, Norway and Iceland in the 1980s (and today adopted by some 150 fisheries) whereby a species-specific and government-defined 'total allowable catch' or TAC for a given fisheries is divided into volumetric (i.e. weight-based) quota shares which are then distributed to a variety of fishing concerns, following a diverse set of technical–scientific and political–bureaucratic criteria that ostensibly have sustainability and efficiency at their root.[69] The challenges of imposing a rigid market rationality that allows the buying, selling or leasing of biomass quotas to domains that have hitherto been 'nobody's property' were played out in political and cultural disputes which mobilise class, ethnicity, custom and history in the determination of seemingly neutral quota management systems (QMSs). Thus, in Iceland, the early application of ITQs witnessed the clash between boat owners' preference for *catch* quotas (which rewarded the fixed capital in boats and gear) versus fishermen's claim that *effort* should guide the allocation of quotas since it was expertise and labour power (i.e. variable capital) that determined the size of catch.[70] In New Zealand, too, comparable wrangles surfaced between customary Maori conceptions of access to fisheries and the market-based, neoliberal QMSs – although, interestingly, the possibility of rent extraction accompanying ITQs has allowed for a sophisticated articulation of customary practice and market logic.[71] For our purposes, the most significant aspect of the ITQ system is that it 'create[d] a market for access – where one did not exist before . . . Thus, ITQs are a form of both privatization and marketization',[72] as Becky Mansfield puts it so well. The application of property relations in the oceans has been deeply contested, and indeed transformed, according to a particular socio-historical and political–geographical balance of forces.

It is in this context that we use the category of appropriation in a second, narrower sense connected to the class relation of modern landed property – Marx's 'third class' alongside capital and labour. By virtue of monopoly ownership of some portion of the earth, landed property is able to appropriate ground rent as a portion of the future surplus value that is expected to be produced. This is a redistributive relationship and not *itself* productive of surplus value.[73] But *if* (a) a fishery (or a portion of land) naturally has more biomass (more productivity) than a comparable fishery or (b) there is investment in making a fishery (or portion of land) *more* productive (e.g. by installing fish-aggregating devices), then when either is worked by labour there will be an increase in relative surplus value.[74] As on land, modern landed property may seek to capture ground rent from capital accumulating through the sea – it may do so through the use or threat of violence and/or the law. But this takes different forms in different spatio-temporal contexts depending on the

degree of access to the appropriation of oceanic fish populations. Sovereignty at sea is a negotiated process, and the exclusion of access to oceanic fisheries is often bitterly contested.[75]

The moment of capitalist appropriation of nature through
labour is necessarily a spatio-temporal process. Moore's theorisation of the commodity frontier helps us now to activate this
moment, which we explore through a potted history of marine
enclosure that encompasses food systems, war and imperialism,
and class antagonisms/cooperation in the sector, told through
the eyes of a fish, so to speak. Here the state re-enters the fray
as a constitutive agent in the (re)production of commodity frontiers. The rest of this chapter explores these historical dynamics
of pelagic imperialism and its eventual contestation by coastal
states in the global South.

Pelagic imperialism

The appropriation of marine life before steam and oil

The hunt for fish and marine mammals has shaped imperial
rivalries and geographies of colonialism across the globe.
Capitalist appropriation of these animals did not start with
steam. Mass extraction of life from the sea for a profit was
carried out with brutal 'efficiency' with sail.[76] Longer-living,
slower-reproducing species such as seals and walruses, by virtue
of living in dense colonies, are prone to low-tech slaughter.
While these and other mammal populations such as whales
offered a rich ecological surplus to capital, this was only ever
temporary. In the early 1600s the Muscovy Company – the first
joint-stock company to be chartered in England – had funded
unsuccessful voyages to find a north-west passage, which nonetheless turned a profit though the hunt for walrus and the boil-
ing down of their blubber.[77] Seal and walrus killing was intensified by those seeking to sell to skin traders in China – a booming
market from the 1790s – as well as a substitute for whale oil.[78]

Herds were rapidly depleted as the fishery worked its way through secluded locations where vulnerable pinnipeds had previously hidden, eliminating a herd of 25,000 walruses in Svalbard on the border of the Arctic Ocean, and decimating seal colonies on networks of islands off the tip of Latin America, the South Indian Ocean and the edges of the Antarctic (or Southern) Ocean.[79]

The history of whaling is not dissimilar. Darwin's 1835 visit to the Galapagos Islands might be imagined as an exploration of an unknown place, but when the HMS *Beagle* arrived the area 'was overrun with American whalers'.[80] Whaling is an ancient fishery traceable to Neolithic cave paintings in Korea, but, like sealing, under capitalism the hunt for whales changed profoundly, quantitatively and qualitatively. Whales' bodies were the raw material for a new energy regime that lit the streets, industries and homes of the growing urban populations of Western Europe and its settler colonies from the late seventeenth century onwards. Dutch and English commercial capitalists built ships and recruited crew – initially using experienced Basque labour – which they sent to catch whales around the island of Svalbard. Driven by the whale oil market for energy and soap, the Muscovy Company pioneered speculation on Arctic whaling in the 1610s and sought to exclude competition from the fishery. Its fleet of whalers was accompanied by a twenty-two-gun ship which boarded competing Basque, Dutch and French vessels, confiscating their catch.[81] This attempt to assert *dominium* over the fishery was met by Dutch whalers organising themselves into a chartered trading company that was allocated a monopoly on Arctic whale hunting by the States General of the Netherlands. It armed its fleet and was escorted by States General warships. A temporary stand-off ensued, but the Dutch doctrine of *mare liberum* discussed in Chapter 2 won out. By the 1720s, over 2,000 Dutch whalers set sail, with an average profit rate of 12–13 per cent, and Amsterdam led the European market for whale oil until the 1780s, all of which existed through the ecological surplus of the Arctic Ocean's biomass.[82]

Across the Atlantic, whaling off the New England seaboard from the 1690s was among this colonial territory's first industries, marking the 'beginning of early American industrialization'.[83] It quickly grew from a near-shore fishery to an offshore one in the 1710s, based on the famed Nantucket Island, and after 1740 long-distance deep-sea voyages lasting several months became commonplace. By the 1820s New Bedford had superseded Nantucket, boasting more whaling vessels than the rest of the world's fleets combined in the 1850s, which was also when new technologies such as the exploding harpoon made the kill more efficient.[84] The growing demand for artificial lighting had pushed whaling harder, faster and further. What each of these fisheries had in common in their distinct drives to produce for the world market in whale oil was the constant opening of fresh commodity frontiers in new places, and capturing new species as the more valued ones became commercially less viable to catch.[85] With the decline of whale oil as a source of fuel at the end of the nineteenth century, distant-water fisheries took on the role of extending the maritime commodity frontier.

War, food and imperialism, 1880s–1940s

The story told here centres on Japan as the world's largest industrial fishing nation until the Second World War. Total marine fisheries production in 1936 is estimated at around 17 million tons, with 3.6 million tons landed by Japan, 2 million by the USA and 1.7 million by Korea (then a Japanese colony), followed by the USSR, Norway and Britain.[86] In the absence of claims to property rights over marine fish in all but coastal waters, the Meiji Restoration created new oceanic territories of profit.[87] These were formed, protected and legitimated by an imperialist and modernising logic that mimicked and morphed the practices of Western European 'great powers'. The early industrialisation of Japan's fishing industry was motivated by several factors: exporting 'surplus' population from fishing villages, earning export revenue from manufactures in the context of a trade deficit, supplying domestic food demand, and bypassing the 1922 International Conference on Naval Limitation (Washington Naval Conference) with a distant-water fishing fleet that could act as a naval reserve.[88] In 1939, Japan's fishing industry was valued at around ¥778 million (US$202 million), supporting directly and indirectly over 30 per cent of the population, and providing a major source of foreign exchange. Marine product exports such as canned seafood and whale oil (e.g. for manufacture in Europe into margarine and soap) were worth ¥175 million. In terms of monetary export value, this was behind only raw silk, cotton fabrics and apparel, much of which required imported raw materials.[89] Crucially, as recognised by an apologist of empire in 1940, the 'fish cost practically nothing.'[90]

Pulled by the competition for profit and pushed by the state, Japanese fishing fleets bloated the boundaries of Japan's imperial sphere of influence. Inspired by Germany's Listian industrial policy, the Japanese state supported the expansion of fishing capital into new commodity frontiers such as with the 1897 Fisheries Promotion Act. This was one part of Japan's broader imperialist drive for food, raw materials and export revenue to feed the hands, machines and social reproduction of industrial capitalism. Between 1905 and 1915 Japan began export-oriented production of canned king crab, salmon, tuna and sardines. Markets included the USA, Britain, France, Russia and China, and production volumes grew continuously until the late 1930s.[91] Voluminous commodity production required seeking out new commodity frontiers. Research ships undertaking oceanographic and ichthyological surveys acted as the advance party of capital and the imperial state.[92] Contemporaneous evidence suggested that overfishing in Japan's coastal fisheries drove this geographical expansion.[93] For example, overfishing saw canned crab exports drop in 1919, driving the creation of a new commodity frontier to the north of Japan using factory ships, often in contested Russian waters.[94]

The extent of Japan's northern fisheries oscillated with the simmering inter-imperial rivalry with Russia – gaining the southern half of Sakhalin island, for example, as part of the Treaty of Portsmouth that settled the 1905 war. Sakhalin's icy coastal waters were home to herring, salmon and trout, which in turn attracted up to 20,000 Japanese fishers over the next ten years.[95] In later decades, offshore fishing by Japanese factory ships just outside the three-mile limit of Russian waters allowed the imperial navy to test the resolve of the Soviet Union; as richly portrayed in Takiji's proletarian novel *The Crab Cannery Ship*, where the Japanese Navy escorted fishing boats owned by giant *zaibatsu* (holding companies) into the Sea of Okhotsk.[96] When the Soviet Union began to develop its own fleet to extract from the same salmon fishery targeted by the Japanese, the Japanese government responded in 1919 by 'encouraging' the merger of a number of small fishing enterprises into one giant private entity – Nichiro Gyogyo.[97] Part of the government's logic was to 'facilitate a cut in the labor force and alleviate the lamentable practice of competing for laborers'.[98] It sought also to mitigate conflict with the USSR by reducing the risk of multiple, uncoordinated operators and to maximise production efficiencies, which Nichiro Gyogyo did with its system of large mothership vessels supported by fleets of small fishing boats. By the late 1930s, Nichiro Gyogyo monopolised Japanese production of canned salmon and trout in Soviet waters, processed either on its factory ships or in land-based canning facilities.[99] This was a big business. The salmon extracted from Soviet waters in 1938 was valued at almost ¥19 million when canned, most of which was exported.

South of Japan, state-sponsored experimental fishing trips were quickly followed by the creation of fishing bases in colonial South East Asia in the 1910s, initially to supply burgeoning local markets created by mines, plantations and growing cities.[100] Japanese imperialism produced new commodity frontiers in South East Asian seas – based on the appropriation of marine life and exploitation of Japanese and local workers. This investment was welcomed at the time by the British and Dutch as it allowed for colonialism on the cheap. But by the late 1930s new fishing technology allowed Japanese firms to land fish caught in South East Asian waters in Japan and its colony Taiwan.[101]

Taiwan was a crucial part of Japan's pelagic empire. During its fifty years of Japanese rule between 1895 and 1945, Kaohsiung, in the south of the island, became the centre of colonial Taiwan's industrial fishing fleet. Tuna longlining was the most important fishing industry in colonial Kaohsiung, accounting for 80 per cent of motorised vessels based in the port. In the late 1930s, 81 per cent of colonial Taiwan's tuna longline catch was by boats based in Kaohsiung.[102] Tuna was transported by train and truck for consumption in Taipei and shipped by steamer to be sold in Tokyo's fish markets. Korea played a similar role in the Greater Co-prosperity Sphere, with fish caught off its coast being transported to Japan.[103] At this time, these were largely offshore fisheries and it was only during the mid-1960s that South Korea and Taiwan's distant-water tuna fishing fleets were developed. Nonetheless, Japan benefited from the rich ecological surpluses of the coastal fisheries of its East Asian colonies.[104]

Even further south, Japan had been gifted colonies in Micronesia by the Treaty of Versailles – the South Pacific Mandate – and by the 1930s it had developed bases for fishing operations in other Pacific islands, employing around 7,600 Japanese fishers.[105] Many of these people were from the Miyako Islands – close to Taiwan and annexed by Japan in 1897, which was considered an outback of the already peripheral Okinawa prefecture.[106] Japan's tropical distant-water fisheries spread across the equatorial region of the Western Pacific Ocean throughout South East Asia, including in the Celebes, Java, South China and Sulu Seas.

The diversity of oceanic conditions encountered by Japanese fishing capital required sophisticated technology and boats, pushing extraction outwards to waters little fished in the past. This process was accompanied by, and further expanded with, the development of state-funded fisheries science. Understanding the seasonal relationship between oceanic temperature and currents allows for high volumes of catch when a particular species of fish is caught in a thermal barrier, 'impounded' in a pocket of warm waters between cold ones.[107] After the Second World War, researchers associated with the Natural Resources Section of the Headquarters of the Supreme Commander for the Allied Powers made such forms of knowledge readily available for American capital as it pushed into new commodity frontiers.

The scientific know-how and technological changes that defined post-war capitalist fisheries were already showing their ruthless extractive potential by the 1930s, allowing for both increased volume of catch from existing fisheries, and the opening of previously untouched ecological strata.[108] As noted, the Japanese government financed the mechanisation of its national fishing fleet from the early 1900s but because of the relatively low cost of labour power, Japanese boats tended to be more labour-intensive by ton of fish caught than the American equivalent.[109]

While it is a less significant case, it is instructive to explore parallel dynamics of pelagic imperialism in the West. Spain's national fisheries production system showed several similarities with Japan's. It became Europe's largest distant-water fishing nation by the 1970s, a trajectory that can be traced to the 1920s. Spain's fishing fleet experienced a boom period after the First World War, expanding from the Bay of Biscay and the Mediterranean into new commodity frontiers off the Canary Islands and Morocco. In the 1930s the majority of the Spanish fishing fleet was industrial, with around 50 per cent of the fleet powered by steam engines, 20 per cent by diesel motors, and the remainder by sail.[110] But at the same time, rising operating costs, falling prices and lack of capital, combined with the Spanish Civil War, all led to a series of bankruptcies in the sector. This was a period of 'low returns and scant possibilities of capital accumulation'.[111]

After the Civil War, Franco's fascist state identified fisheries as a major source of import-substituting animal protein and provided low-cost, long-term credit facilities to develop the sector, although this support did not bear fruit until after the Second World War.[112] Franco's regime also placed strategic value on the role of armed fishing boats during the Civil War and, in its planning for potential war with Britain, posited distant-water vessels to target submarines. In the second half of the 1940s, Spanish-built distant-water vessels began to target cod in fisheries off of Ireland and, later, Newfoundland. Franco's fixation with autarky and the consequent reduction in cod imports meant that it supported large-scale cod fishing firms over smaller, coastal fishers.[113] This had deleterious results which only became fully apparent after the Second World War: both the Irish and Newfoundland cod populations experienced partial collapse in the 1950s and mid-1970s respectively. The Newfoundland fishery recovered after the mid-1970s when Canada banned foreign fishing boats, only to collapse entirely in 1992 when the fishery was one-third of 1 per cent of its estimated pre-capitalist biomass.[114] Indeed, as we shall see, this combination of new technologies and modernising scientific techniques, struggles over fisheries access and state property and marine resource decline would characterise the post-war era.

The globalisation of industrial fisheries under the American pelagic empire, 1950s–1970s

Until the mid-twentieth century, the extraction of marine life by industrial fishing capital was justified under the doctrine of the free seas. But we have seen how the politics of access to oceanic fisheries was far from being 'free'. Imperialist states mediated the creation and reproduction of commodity frontiers in distinct (and often competing) national production systems. This began to unravel in the 1950s and collapsed in the 1970s, so that by the 1980s the question of who owned the fish had a very different answer. The protracted and conflict-ridden shift from an interwar inter-imperial rivalry over the *creation of* new marine commodity frontiers to a post-war US-led regime of *access to* these new spaces of appropriation was mediated through the contradictory universalisation of national fishing rights. In line with the post-war American hegemonic rule *through* rather than *over* sovereign states, until the 1980s Washington oversaw a pelagic empire that pursued simultaneously the appropriation of marine life by national fleets and the maintenance of inno-cent passage and freedom of the seas. However, contrary to the hub-and-spokes imperialism that rendered states like Taiwan and South Korea military clients, inter-state rivalry among pelagic empires came to characterise post-war fisheries. The valuable biomass swimming across the oceans became the target of a 'Seldenian' notion of the seas as a domain for national appropriation.

The US state played a central role in facilitating access by American fishing capital into new commodity frontiers – a move that had become all the more important given the asser-tiveness of many Latin American states over the control of fish in 'their' waters. With Japan's distant-water fishing fleet annihi-lated by war and the MacArthur Line temporarily blocking its redeployment, the US tuna fleet began to pour into Japan's former sphere of influence. Just like Japan in the first half of the twentieth century, the US state sponsored experimental fishing trips, 'testing' the fishing grounds already extensively surveyed by the Japanese. The US used overseas territories like American Samoa and Puerto Rico as pelagic bases, propping them up with a combination of government aid, subsidies and procurement contracts, as well as import tariff protections.[115] From the early 1950s onwards, big US canned tuna brands established processing plants in American Samoa, creating a lucrative and growing local demand for American-caught tuna based on this new commodity frontier. Crucially, the US government's design of rules of origin meant that canneries in US overseas territories were locked into buying fish from the US-flagged fleet.

The globalisation of industrial oceanic fisheries after the Second World War was built around *national* fishing fleets from Japan, the United States, France and Spain, among others, supplying domestically owned processors – sometimes vertically integrated, other times not. As we'll see presently, despite their territorial dispersion across different spheres of relative geo-economic influence, these 'national' production systems were connected by fishing–processing–market linkages and locked in by a range of mechanisms such as geopolitical reach, aid and investment, as well as trade and industrial policies. As late as the early 1990s, for instance, the general manager of a French seafood multinational considered the canneries in francophone West Africa to be fully integrated with the *French* production system.[116]

The 1950s was a period of rapid development in industrial fisheries, sparked by military technology developed during the war and closely supported by 'home' states and scientific establishments. While diesel-powered fishing boats were commonplace from the early 1900s, it was not until after the Second World War that they were constructed using steel hulls rather than wood, allowing safer and longer-distance fishing trips.[117] Larger boats were also installed with mechanical refrigeration and freezing systems – overcoming the prior constraint of limited organic durability and the concomitant need to salt fish at sea. This was a capital-intensive industry. A new American tuna vessel cost up to US$500,000 in the early 1950s and was estimated to be 'the most expensive commercial fishing craft in the world'.[118] The ever-deepening technological sophistication of fishing methods, combined with growing knowledge of tuna biology through fisheries science, has made oceanic fish more vulnerable to extraction.[119]

From the 1970s onwards and especially into the 1980s, distinctly national systems of appropriation and fish production began to be destabilised in the context of a wave of mergers and acquisitions and the industrialisation of parts of East and South East Asia, in the new international division of labour. While these production systems had never been truly 'national' given their dependence on the extraction of fish from distant waters, their logic as national projects was further complicated by the interpenetration of capital in fish processing and branding,[120] the rise of new industrial fishing fleets (e.g. South Korea and Taiwan), and the emergence of contract processors dependent on fish supply from their own regional waters (e.g. Indonesia and the Philippines) or from around the world (e.g. Thailand) which were established through a combination of foreign investment and host state subsidies to supply big retail and branded capital in Western Europe and North America.

In the 1970s, Japanese trading companies (*sōgō shōsha*) financed South Korean and Taiwanese fishing companies, which also received substantial support from their respective 'developmental states'. These new industrial fleets targeted oceanic fisheries and were tied to the *sōgō shōsha* through fixed supply contracts and/or loans repaid in fish, assuring a diversified source of raw material for their Japanese clients. While this practice declined in significance with the boom in global industrial fishing capacity by the early 1980s onwards, it provided the finance and marketing networks necessary to making South Korea and Taiwan leading industrial fishing nations, competing directly with the Americans and Japanese.[121] Taiwan's fishing industry, for example, is heavily reliant on distant-water activities, which constitute over 50 per cent of the country's marine-capture production. While its distant-water fleet started out in the Pacific Ocean, by the 1980s it had become active across the global ocean.[122]

With relatively small volumes of domestic consumption and minor export-oriented fish processing, these new East Asian industrial fleets supplied raw material via freezer reefer vessels to emerging non-branded processors in South East Asia supplying American and European brands and retailers. This divorced the prior geographical embeddedness of processing in states close to fisheries, producing a world market for fish raw material among competing processors, and cheapening fish product prices.[123]

The dynamics of appropriation were now reconfigured with a larger number of boats competing to supply a greater diversity of processors, shifting the balance of ecological exchange, and undermining the cost-competitiveness of processors in several countries in the global North. The national fisheries production systems of the 1950s and 1960s interacted directly and indirectly. In some cases, they were so eroded by foreign competition and cross-penetration of capital through the 1980s that it is no longer useful to consider them 'national' by this time, even in the limited sense of the word used here. For example, in 1982 there were twelve canneries based on the US mainland and by 1986 there was only one.[124] But important counter-tendencies remained, such as Spain's huge seafood processing industry, still (largely) owned by Spanish families through the 2010s, which continues to receive state protection from world market competition via import tariffs and public subsidies.[125]

The post-war Pax Americana, then, saw major shifts in the system of oceanic appropriation, facilitating the paradoxical globalisation of 'national' fishery systems, and the development of new industrial fishing fleets in East Asia and processing factories in the global South. Yet a distinctly imperialist logic remained, albeit in mutated form. In an attempt to counter the (re)incursion of Japanese fishing capital into 'its' waters, the United States unintentionally sparked the eventual internationalisation of a peculiar and contradictory property regime in the form of the exclusive economic zone (EEZ) and the sovereign rights to marine life it guaranteed. Fisheries dovetailed with broader geopolitical concerns around American naval and maritime supremacy over the emerging world order. Japan's early twentieth-century pelagic imperialism was emulated by the USA after the Second World War, but now supported by pseudoscientific claims around maximum sustainable yield (MSY). The US push into the Western Pacific in the 1980s brought US hypocrisy to a head in a moment of South–South cooperation by tiny Pacific island states using the property relations associated with the EEZ.

After the Second World War the United States was faced with a conundrum. How to block the fishing capital of rapidly reindustrialising Japan from returning to fish for salmon off the US West Coast on the one hand, while simultaneously supporting the expansion of the US tuna fleet into new commodity frontiers in the Pacific Ocean on the other hand? The 'tuna question' was, of course, about fisheries commodity production – as the US Secretary of the Interior stated in 1947: 'Tuna is a magic word in any community or country which looks to the sea for food and profits.'[126] But it was also about oceanic geopolitics: tuna populations happened to mirror the US sphere of influence off the Pacific coast of Latin America and, crucially, in the Central Pacific Ocean where the US Navy was unveiling a plan for a series of post-war bases.

Two distinct segments of American fishing capital with contradictory interests drove US international fisheries policy, and would in turn shape the contours of the Law of the Sea negotiations from the 1950s onwards. On one end was the sizable salmon canning industry, established in the 1800s along the Pacific coast of North America. It wanted to stop Japanese boats catching salmon before they could return to their spawning grounds. This was driven not by a conservationist logic but by the aim of ensuring availability of raw material for American industry. On the other end was the US tuna industry. Tuna are a highly migratory species in the sense that the populations swim great distances, traversing human-drawn borders in the oceans. San Diego's tuna canneries started out in 1903 by catching fish relatively close to the USA, but by the 1930s American tuna boats based in San Diego were catching as far as the Galapagos Islands.[127] This industry was so intensive that by the early 1940s the US fleet appeared to have overfished the bait used to attract the tuna.[128] The ocean-going US fishing fleet was decimated during the war, and post-war demand for highly profitable convenience foods in light of growing labour costs drove a government programme of subsidies and state-sponsored science oriented towards an expansive, extractivist logic.[129] Buoyed by state supports, the fishing industry was rapidly rebuilt and in need of new fishing grounds.

The US state's solution to the conundrum was to simultaneously protect 'its' salmon populations and support the expansion of the American tuna industry into new commodity frontiers. The tools developed to advance this strategy continue to shape global ocean governance to this day. In 1945, President Truman famously and unilaterally proclaimed US sovereignty over the continental shelf, motivated by control over access to oil and other mineral resources in the seabed and, in a linguistic hangover of terrestrial thinking, the 'subsoil'.[130] The proclamation made a point of maintaining that the waters above the shelf would retain their legal character as high seas.[131] An unintended consequence of Truman's proclamation was a flurry of declarations from 1947 onwards of 200-nautical-mile EEZs and corresponding jurisdiction over continental shelves by a number of Latin American states. These included Argentina, Chile, Ecuador,

Mexico and Peru, which were directly motivated by keeping American fishing capital away from fish in 'their' waters.[132]

Less well known is that, on the same day, Truman also unilaterally proclaimed the United States' right to establish fishery 'conservation zones' in the high seas contiguous to the US coasts,[133] what might be called the 'other' Truman Proclamation. This specified that where a fishery was 'developed' by *Americans* it could be universally managed by the US state in the interests of 'conservation', allowing for the exclusion of non-American fishing boats. If a fishery had historically been targeted by fishers from another nation then a system of joint management could be established.

But how to specify where and when 'conservation' is needed? This all came together with a 'scientific' concept, which was actually more a contradictory product of economic nationalism and free market ideology than having any original basis in fisheries *science*. MSY is the idea that a maximum volume of a species of marine life can be taken from the ocean on an ongoing basis, year after year. The approach posited that fishing could be sustained at high levels into perpetuity. It became a part of American foreign and domestic policy in 1949 when the State Department formally adopted it as the goal of American fisheries policy.[134] MSY quickly also became the cornerstone of international fisheries law and management practice from the 1950s onwards and remained the dominant measure in use through the 2010s. A sophisticated scientific apparatus for MSY now exists,[135] but it did not when the concept was first devised in the early 1950s. Even so, the heart of the measure is a Victorian notion of 'waste' as a 'legitimating precondition of capitalist modernization',[136] whereby, if an ecological surplus is not 'fully utilized' before its natural mortality, then it has been wasted. MSY was implemented as a tool to avoid restrictions on fishing unless there was scientific proof that stocks were overfished – proofs that were (then) hard to ascertain. MSY thus provided a basis for the US fleet to expand into waters across the Pacific, despite political objections from coastal states and analytical critique from scientists on the weakness of MSY as applied to fisheries.[137] But even with contemporary technologies, many fisheries suffer from partial and delayed reporting and as such biomass would have to fall below MSY before scientists could confidently identify this fall.[138] In short, the US restricted fishing on 'its' salmon, but made ownership of tuna 'nobody's property', at least until it was extracted by fishing capital. The concept of MSY and its regulation changed the *conditions* of fisheries *access* – it was deployed as a contradictory mechanism of inclusion and exclusion in the ocean. This regime would serve the US distant-water fishing fleet industry well until the 1980s.

The politics of property relations in the sea, 1980s–2010s

Until the 1970s, access to oceanic fisheries was governed by the interaction of inter-imperial rivalry, collusion and compromise; the threat and use of force; and spheres of relative influence. Oceanic commodity frontiers are moments of imperialism – even in a post-war epoch when capitalist imperialism in the 'classic' sense of direct, formal control over territory had apparently ended.[139] As we have seen, the oceans provided a unique space for these rivalries to continue, albeit in augmented form. Spheres of maritime influence were informally established by distant-water fishing fleets from the US, Japan and France for the appropriation of marine life as raw material for factories producing commodities for markets at home and abroad. By expanding into new commodity frontiers where the class relation of landed property was absent, these fleets were the vanguard in the formation of 'territories of profit'.

Emboldened by the unintended consequences of the first Truman Proclamation, and the world-historical context of the 1970s, coastal states directly challenged this form of oceanic territorialisation. But the materiality of marine fisheries – hunting an animal that moves seasonally, often across various jurisdictions – complicated this challenge. Highly migratory species such as tuna and swordfish swim across areas covering millions of square kilometres, thus posing an additional problem for those seeking to assign social property relations to biomass that pays no attention to human borders imagined in the oceans.

The fragmentation of national systems of seafood production was paralleled by the growing assertiveness of coastal states in projects of national developmentalism. Post-colonial states sought to use 'national' marine resources as a basis for industrialising fishing fleets, creating onshore employment and earning foreign exchange. In parallel, many more capitals-in-competition were chasing oceanic fish populations harder, faster and further. Long-standing rivalries between Japan and the US were playing out once again in the Pacific Ocean. Japan's distant-water fleet had dominated Western Pacific oceanic fisheries until the 1970s, when it was met by a westward-moving US fishing fleet seeking a new commodity frontier, to escape from increasingly conflictual relations with coastal states on the Eastern Tropical Pacific, and to reduce dolphin bycatch, which does not aggregate with tuna in the Western Pacific. In this context and in anticipation of the emerging regime of state property over the oceans with the advent of EEZs, Japanese multinationals began to establish joint ventures with Pacific island governments in the 1970s, most notably in Fiji and the Solomon Islands.[140]

By the mid-1970s, the EEZ had been accepted in customary international law. In the greatest single enclosure in human history, states gained sovereign rights over access to marine resources, including the seabed and subsoil, in up to 200 nautical miles of ocean from their coastlines. In 1982, the EEZ was codified in public international law via the United Nations Convention on the Law of the Sea (UNCLOS). EEZs today cover 35 per cent of the total area of the seas, and contain around 90 per cent of the world's marine fish populations.[141] In short, while fish are in its waters, they are owned by the coastal state. But who benefited from this enclosure?

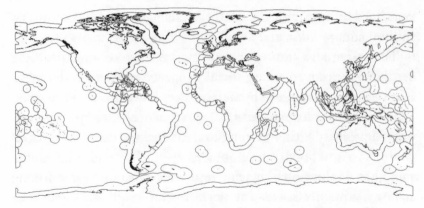

Figure 4.2. World map of exclusive economic zones
Source: Flanders Marine Institute.

One interpretation of UNCLOS is that it was a 'resource grab' by the former colonial powers, allowing them to 'dominate enormous stretches' of the global ocean.[142] A handful of countries laid claim to huge new areas of oceanic jurisdiction created by UNCLOS. Countries with small coastlines (e.g. in West Africa) and, of course, the landlocked states were the obvious losers.[143] Britain, France and the USA were among the major beneficiaries because of their control over a large number of overseas territories (the 'confetti of empire'); the geographical location of these islands (which they mostly are) delivers large oceanic territories. The USA enjoys sovereign rights across overseas EEZs (including Alaska and Hawaii) that cover 80 per cent more oceanic surface area than the forty-eight contiguous states in North America. In relative terms, France dwarfs the USA, given that the EEZs claimed by its overseas countries and territories (OCTs) are thirty times greater in surface area than mainland France.[144] Likewise, the UK has rights over 6 million square kilometres of ocean surrounding its overseas territories (many former slave plantations), which is eight times the area of the EEZ around the islands of Britain and the north of Ireland.[145] Combined with the white settler colonies of Australia, Canada and New Zealand, these six countries today control over one-third of the world's total surface area of EEZs of 137 million square kilometres.

The imperialist 'resource grab' perspective on the UNCLOS settlement on sovereign rights over marine and seabed resources is of especial pertinence to China given its relatively very small EEZ on a per capita basis. The skewed outcome certainly contributes to China's contemporary contested claims over parts of the East and South China Seas. But it does not account for the fact that Japan and the USA and other distant-water fishing nations explicitly *rejected* the creation of sovereign rights over those fisheries that their 'national' capital once accessed as a 'free gift' in both of the senses outlined above: as 'received' nature and as an ecological surplus extracted without payment of ground rent. Japan, for example, argued that access rights to migratory species should be determined by customary use, not an abstract juridico-political enclosure.[146] The neo-colonial 'resource grab' argument also misses the point that the EEZ was consciously negotiated by leading post-colonial states in the world-historical moment of Third Worldist calls for a New International Economic Order.[147] Coastal developing countries asserted their sovereign right over *any* fish while it is in their 200-nautical-mile EEZ. It was widely argued at the time that UNCLOS could serve as an institutional mechanism to coordinate a substantial redistribution of resources from distant-water fishing nations to the global South.[148] The UNCLOS agreement resulted in an uneasy compromise to 'solve' these contradictory positions. Coastal states were allocated sovereign rights over the exploration, extraction and management of all living resources 200 nautical miles from their coasts. The EEZ acts as a form of state landed property, allowing governments to capture ground rent as a portion of the future surplus value extracted by fishing capital.[149] In this context, the EEZ was pitched as one part of a multifaceted challenge to the history of European domination of the world economy and one moment among many of a series of nationalisations of privately controlled natural resources.

Despite this new international legal regime of state landed property, inter-imperialist rivalries continued to jostle for access to old and new commodity frontiers on behalf of their 'national' capitals, albeit under augmented institutional conditions of accumulation. Boat owners now had to pay to access the fish populations that they had previously 'freely' extracted, but oceanic fisheries continued to be dominated by capital from industrialised countries. In 1976 the (then) EEC member states pooled and transferred sovereignty to the European Commission for 'foreign policy in the fisheries sector' and established the first EEC access agreement in 1977, which was with the US, followed in 1979 by an agreement with Senegal,[150] thereby reproducing France's 'national' production system noted earlier, but now at the macro-regional scale of the EEC. These were the first in a long series of access agreements where European fishing capital continues to be subsidised directly by the EU in the twenty-first century, and, in turn, where coastal state revenue from access payments remains well below the estimated monetary value of the ecological surplus being extracted.[151] In parallel, Japan and Korea negotiated the first of a global network of formal fisheries agreements on the management of fishing boats and payments for their access to coastal state EEZs.[152] Unlike the EU, East Asian fisheries access agreements tend to be signed by industry associations (groups of boat owners) or even individual companies, but during negotiations a senior representative of that fleet's government is normally also in the room – implicitly or explicitly dangling aid payments and other sources of geopolitical–economic power as sweetener or stick.[153]

But the US protested *any* state's sovereign rights to tuna in EEZs. Emboldened by US laws supporting pelagic imperialism established in response to Latin American oceanic property claims in the late 1940s and the 1950s, American vessels continued to fish in Pacific island countries' EEZs without paying for access.[154] In its blunt rejection of state property over tuna, the US used its geopolitical, diplomatic and geo-economic power to contest coastal states' efforts to regulate US boats' fishing. In particular, the US refused to accept that highly migratory species could be state property and it encouraged its distant-water fleet to fish in coastal state waters with impunity. At the time, cash-strapped newly independent Pacific Island countries were looking to ground rent from tuna access as vital government revenue. In response to what it saw as the illegal capture of its resources, in the mid-1980s the Solomon Islands apprehended US vessels fishing without paying rent. But this did little to deter the fleet because the US government reimbursed all of the expenses incurred by what it saw as the 'illegal' seizures of US vessels. Further, the price of this penalty was subtracted from foreign aid that would have otherwise gone to the coastal state. To paraphrase Marx, between equal rights, power decides.

Yet it was precisely the bipolar power politics of the Cold War that the Pacific islands would leverage. The island nation of Kiribati began negotiating a fisheries access deal with the USSR and the United States *jumped*. Rather than allow the Soviet Union a foothold in the Central Pacific the US set up a multilateral fisheries access agreement with all fourteen independent Pacific island countries, that for a long time was among the most comparatively lucrative of tuna access deals.[155] With a population of just 60,000 people, Kiribati brinkmanship had transformed the United States' recognition of property relations in the oceans.[156]

South–South maritime cooperation in the context of 1970s Third Worldism and stagflation was a response to pelagic imperialism. While the negotiated institution of the EEZ disrupted the old oceanic order of appropriation, it did so only in part. As we have seen, the confetti of empire meant that UNCLOS gave former colonial powers sovereign rights over giant swathes of ocean, while others – China especially – lost out. Similarly, Japan benefits from a huge EEZ by virtue of the chain of islands running south of Tokyo to Taiwan. The terms of UNCLOS reflected the compromise of the era, such as the 'use it or lose it' clause. Article 62 of UNCLOS requires a coastal state to ensure 'optimum utilization' of 'surplus' fish, albeit subject to conservation measures; if not, distant-water fishing nations can (and do) claim a right of access.

The institutionalisation of the EEZ cannot be characterised simply as a moment of 'accumulation by dispossession'. This category, while widely used, offers only a half-truth. As Gavin Capps points out, dispossession provides the necessary conditions for the next moment in the movement of landed property – *appropriation*, which, given the class-relational politics of contestation of modern landed property, is never complete.[157] This, then, provides for the possibility of the movement to *elimination* – where state property over access to a fishery may be provided rent-free or at reduced rent to certain fishing capitals in the context of global competition. The USA offers this in the form of 'collective privatisation' of access, Namibia through the localisation of ownership, and Papua New Guinea in the creation of onshore jobs.[158] This type of 'Ricardian reform' seeks to eliminate the rent drain on profits to capitalist accumulation based on access to natural resources.[159]

Rethinking rent capture as the manifestation of a broader set of struggles over surplus value introduces a more complex understanding of the socio-natural relations at stake in EEZs. It forces reflection on the EEZ as a sovereign mechanism for extracting ground rent, where the coastal state assumes the 'class function' of modern landed property because, as with private property over landed resources, access rights to fish, or exploration and extractive concessions, are 'separated from capital: it is merely the jural form and social location of ownership that has changed'.[160] Furthermore, the forms of surplus appropriation adopted by sovereign states on land and capitalist firms at sea are strongly conditioned by the socio-natural cycles and oceanographic forces in and of the global ocean.

In seeking to maximise the capture of surplus value through the relation of state landed property, coastal states have come close to occupying the ocean. Contemporary techniques of fisheries surveillance can track in real time the movement of boats into EEZs and ascertain whether or not they are likely to be fishing. The threat of force (imprisonment), disruptions to the circuit of capital (e.g. denial of access to markets by fish caught by 'pirate' vessels), or making accumulation strategies less likely to be profitable (e.g. fines and confiscation and sinking of boats) are all used by states to reproduce this class function and the struggle over maximising the portion of surplus value it is able to capture.

But what of those states excluded from UNCLOS? China has a relatively small EEZ, tiny on a per capita basis. This is a direct legacy of its lack of a maritime empire in the twentieth century.[161] To address this gap in the twenty-first century, Beijing is seeking to transform China 'into a powerful distant-water fishing nation'.[162] Indeed, China has been the world's largest fishing nation in terms of volume of fish caught since the 1990s.[163] One estimate of the average annual monetary value of this catch in the 2000s was around US$ 10 billion and its average reported catch volume in 2014–2016 was around 19 per cent of the world total, equal to that of the next-largest three countries/regions *combined* (Indonesia, the EU and the USA).[164] The expansion of fishing capital into distant waters is designed to take pressure off fish populations in China's own EEZ. To this end, the 13th Five-Year Plan (2016–2020) continued to place considerable emphasis on the development of high seas fishing and the processing of fish caught outside its national waters.[165]

State subsidies are central to understanding this expansion. In the context of the global fisheries crisis, through the late 1990s and into the 2010s a coalition of states led by New Zealand and the United States sought to use the World Trade Organisation to establish a specific set of rules to ban certain subsidies to marine-capture fisheries. This was even established as a United Nations Sustainable Development Goal in 2015. The justification is that subsidies support the profitability of capital to overfish where it would otherwise relocate or divest, since fewer fish equate to lower profits.[166] The dominant role of state-owned enterprises in China's distant-water fishing fleet has rubbed roughly against the neoliberal sensibilities of the US state. And by the late 2010s it was clear that China was the principal target of these proposed WTO rules,[167] despite the fact that subsidy payments as a share of revenue from the ongoing fishing bonanza on the high seas by the 'traditional' fishing nations of France, Japan, South Korea, Spain, Taiwan and the USA are between two and four times greater than China's.[168]

But the appropriation of marine life for commodity production is not the sole logic of China's strategy. The marine fishing industry provides work for its shipyards and logistics industries, and raw materials to domestic fish factories as they expand to become world-leading sites of accumulation. It is also a component of China 'Going Out' – a dual strategy of supporting 'national champions' to compete on the world market and to procure natural resources – since the 10th Five-Year Plan (2001–2005), and a drive to uphold (contested) 'national maritime rights and interests, strengthening China's status and influence within relevant international territories', and thereby extend its geopolitical–economic reach (see Chapter 2).[169] Part and parcel of China's growing power as a fishing nation is its rising influence over global fisheries regulation. The deputy head of China's Fisheries Management Bureau pointed out that the size of China's fishing fleet, market and exports means that it is overtaking the role previously assumed by hitherto dominant fishing nations such as Japan and Spain.[170] In these ways, China's contemporary strategy to appropriate marine life to a large extent mirrors the pelagic imperialism of the Western powers. When fisheries became industrialised, fishing capital was most highly concentrated in Japan, the United States and Western Europe. Like China today, state and capital were embroiled in the appropriation of life from the global ocean.

The sea, the state and capital

We began this chapter with the dual question of who owns marine life and how fish become a commodity. Our responses demonstrate the centrality of geo-economics (establishing a legal framework in the capitalist appropriation of marine life) and geopolitics (extending commodity frontiers through the promotion and subsidy of national fishing fleets) when answering these vexed questions. Yet added to this is the protagonism of the marine biomass itself when shaping the ways in which geopolitics and geo-economics combine in given spatial and historical contexts. By focusing on distant-water fisheries involving highly migratory species, the constraints nature places in the way of capitalist appropriation became especially apparent. These obstacles have found solutions (however contingent) in the shape of technological innovations, market differentiation, sectorial restructuring and major (inter-)state interventions. From the outset, industrial capitalism sought to apply to the extraction of marine resources the same logics of competition, productivity and profit that obtain on land. This produced new regimes of accumulation characterised by commodity chains which simultaneously formed new working classes onshore in processing plants and afloat distant-water fleets, providing these and other workers with cheap protein in the form of canned seafood. With the development of new consumer cultures in the post-war years, many fisheries have been forced to radically adapt their techniques and investment strategies, prompting fresh rounds of corporate mergers and acquisitions.

Above all, however, the quest for new maritime commodity frontiers has led to the codified parcelisation of large parts of our saltwater world. Maximum sustainable yield and the EEZ, we have seen, were conceived principally as zones of property rights (and therefore rent appropriation) rather than as areas of sovereign jurisdiction (and thus of law enforcement), thereby generating novel forms of territoriality and management at sea.

At the same time, the high seas remain a 'stateless' space, but paradoxically only in existence because of the relations between states. As well as providing raw material for accumulation, marine fisheries allow distant-water fishing nations to extend their reach into the waters of other states – acting as a kind of commercial–diplomatic tentacle from which other relations are articulated. Contrary to the wider tendency of US hegemony and inter-imperial collaboration, oceanic fisheries were the subject of inter-imperial rivalries – and still are as the contemporary state-sponsored expansion of China's maritime fisheries makes very clear. The human transformation of nature at sea has thus combined biophysical properties of marine life and the social forces of states and markets to produce new and distinctive terraqueous spaces where geopolitical power and private property is both reaffirmed and contested.

5

Logistics

The value of logistics: the annihilation of time by sea?

Ocean transport is 'the main body of the infrastructure of the world economy'.[1] Maritime trade accounts for over 80 per cent of the world's volume of merchandise trade. This drops in monetary value terms, partly because airfreight is used to transport smaller, expensive cargo. But estimates of seaborne trade still range from 55 per cent to over two-thirds of the total monetary value of merchandise trade. Worldwide, an estimated 3,000 ports load and offload this diverse mass of cargo from merchant ships in a daily routine, but, as we shall see, only a small number of ports dominate.[2] These are the hubs – and potential choke points – of transhipment and import in the world's leading macro-economic regions: North America, East Asia and Western Europe – the 'global triad'. These maritime hubs connect, in developmentally highly uneven and politically unequal terms, the rest of the world, the bulk of humanity, which is in turn so very crucial to the material existence and reproduction of the 'triad' regions, not least through the maritime movement of raw materials, intermediate goods, machinery and finished goods.

As we argued in the opening chapter of the book, circulation is the lifeblood of global capitalism, and the oceans act as its arteries. It is through the sea that we most clearly witness the interplay between circulation in the circuit of capital and the physical movement (circulation) of commodities. They are interrelated, but not the same; both are shaped by, and shape, time and space, but in different ways. As Marx famously put it in the *Grundrisse*,

> The more production comes to rest on exchange value, hence on exchange, the more important do the physical conditions of exchange – the means of communication and transport – become for the costs of circulation. Capital by its nature drives beyond every spatial barrier. Thus the creation of the physical conditions of exchange – of the means of communication and transport – the annihilation of space by time – becomes an extraordinary necessity for it.

He goes on,

> while capital must on one side strive to tear down every spatial barrier to intercourse, i.e. to exchange, and conquer the whole earth for its market, it strives on the other side to annihilate this space with time, i.e. to reduce to a minimum the time spent in motion from one place to another. The more developed the capital, therefore, the more extensive the market over which it circulates, which forms the spatial orbit of its circulation, the more does it strive simultaneously for an even greater extension of the market and for greater annihilation of space by time.[3]

This is why blockages and obstructions in the metamorphoses of value – the delay in the sale of commodities for money – are so inimical to the reproduction of capital.[4] While smoothness may be the preferred texture of the world economy, maritime logistics is a site of multiple forms of friction in the circuit of capital caused by wide-ranging factors including strikes and labour disputes, political conflict and wars, adverse weather (and now climate change), poor infrastructure and bureaucratic 'red tape'. At the same time, the uninterrupted movement of capital, its seamless transfer from money to commodity form and back, are the guarantors of profitability. As Chapter 1 showed, the world's seas have played a critical role in this process, acting as surfaces for the circulation and realisation of value.

Shipping is subject to the general dynamics of capitalist competition, and its particular effects and expressions are played out in the contingent relationships between speed, reliability and costs, which are in turn shaped by types of cargo, ships and/or routes. Here there is a qualitative contrast to be made with past experiences in coordinating the oceanic transport of commodities, most notably the Atlantic slave trade. Whereas the latter unquestionably involved 'complex, even diabolical, logistical technologies, supported by finance, insurance, law, and of course state and extra-state violence',[5] one of the distinctive features of a specifically industrial capitalist logistics – namely the commercial decoupling of cargo ownership from the transport of commodities, and indeed shipbuilding (the separation between traders, shippers and shipbuilders) – had not yet been generalised during the eighteenth-century heyday of commercial capitalism.

As this chapter continuously underlines, states play a decisive role in competitive accumulation within maritime logistics, and the uneven geographies of the global ocean mean that the annihilation of time by sea can only ever be incomplete – oceanic movement is far from 'smooth' or 'flat'. A central component in this bitter struggle of capitals-in-competition is the tendency towards concentration and centralisation. On the one hand, concentration involves the self-expansion of individual enterprises through the reinvestment of profits (accumulation) and their attempt to realise more surplus, while, without state support, smaller enterprises crumble in the face of competition. On the other hand, centralisation proper entails the more antagonistic process of mergers and acquisitions – of 'expropriation of capitalist by capitalist' – as facilitated by the limited liability of owners and the corporate form.[6] Thus capitalism 'intensifies and accelerates' the scale of accumulation and 'extends and speeds up' technological change as it reduces prior demand for labour in particular industries.[7] The global shipping industry has, since the latter part of the nineteenth century, been at the forefront of these dynamics, adopting and developing new sources of energy (first coal, then oil); coordinating money, commercial and productive capital through finance, shipping and shipbuilding; and reshaping the socio-economic geographies of the planet in the space of decades by building new port infrastructures and opening new waterways (the Suez and Panama canals are, of course, the most emblematic) in the competitive race for more intensive accumulation.

But what might make perfect sense from the perspective of an individual enterprise, such as building a larger fleet of bigger boats, can contribute to causing industry-wide crisis through downward pressure on freight rates. Indeed, while an ever-smaller number of multinational corporations control more of the world economy and capture a greater share of surplus value[8] – a dominant tendency in both late nineteenth- and early twenty-first-century merchant shipping – it must also be remembered that competitive *countertendencies* remain, as new technologies are unleashed, states intervene and crises unfold.[9] As explored below, the advantages of late capitalist development allowed emerging maritime powers to bypass Britain's initial technological lead, including through sector-specific supports such as mail subsidies, and in the shift from coal to diesel. Another aspect where maritime logistics prove to be central is the role of capitalist strategies of relative centralisation and dispersal in separating workers across firms and national jurisdictions – developing networks of macroregional and global production, and reducing the ability of workers to combine and contest capitalist control.[10]

The 'merchant shipping industry' – the production of human and non-human mobility, profiting through transport – in fact comprises several industries, albeit with important interactions between them. Qualitative differences matter, such as among types of cargo and ships, associated business strategies, different degrees of articulation with states, and the myriad other contexts within which maritime industries exist and, in turn, shape the global economy. All of which, of course, changes over time, in ways that make it impossible to speak of 'capitalist shipping' in the singular. For example, contrary to assumptions in much writing on logistics, speed-up is a relative, not an absolute, commercial concern across segments of merchant shipping. In the twenty-first century, a faster turnover time is crucial for some cargos – especially smaller, more expensive ones – but less so for bulk freight where cost trumps speed, therefore making a slower voyage, burning less 'bunker fuel' (fuel or gas oils), the priority. Ships regularly 'slow-steam' at speeds below their design capacity to keep the costs of distanciated supply chains viable.

Shipping is a global and globalising industry in the sense that it is simultaneously a conduit and enabler of the production of new spaces for capital accumulation. The sector shifts enormous tonnages of raw material from natural resource industries, and articulates regional production networks based around complex and fine-tuned divisions of labour. As such, the business of shipping is tied intimately to the 'health' of the world market in the form of the physical trade in goods.[11] The shipping *industry* deals in the movement of tonnage and volume.[12] It is the cheapening, relative speed and most of all, we argue, *regularity* and *reliability* of ocean-going sea freight that allows for the fragmentation of global production – spatially expanding capitalist circuits and strategies for capital accumulation; pitting firm against firm, worker against worker; transforming labour regimes in ever-more-outward-facing ways; and opening and stabilising new commodity frontiers.[13] Maritime logistics, then, is intrinsic to capitalist *planning*. The deductive mainstream economic assumption is that shipping is derived from the growing demand in international trade – comparative advantage in action.[14] But, as we hope to show throughout this chapter, such thinking simplifies a complex history of capitalist competition and state power in the development of maritime logistics and, in turn, its role as a 'catalyst' for global production through the cheapening of transport costs.[15] From our perspective, maritime logistics is fundamentally the art of coordinating the pace and rhythm of overseas commodity exchange, including the synchronisation of labour, (inter-)state authority and the physical geography of the oceans in the maximisation of profitability and market share, as well as managing the tendencies and countertendencies associated with the sector's successive bouts of concentration, centralisation, crisis and fragmentation. The oceans help this exercise in capitalist planning by offering a fast, cheap and increasingly reliable global commercial freeway. But they also hinder it by encouraging cost cutting, tight margins and just-in-time market volatility across the supply chain.

Logistics industries demonstrate that the spheres of production and circulation are closely intertwined. In providing the use-value of commodity transfer from sellers to buyers (or between entities within a multinational corporation) and thereby enabling the realisation of value through the sale of commodities, 'the *production process itself*' inherent to transportation also generates value through the exploitation of the labour power necessary to this movement (e.g. crew, dockers, warehouse workers) and through their animation of 'the value carried over from the means of transport'.[16] The production of physical circulation in shipping entails the selling of movement – the ability to transform a commodity in space. The main theme of this chapter focuses on the dynamics of shipping enterprises as capitals-in-competition, and the strategies deployed in this competitive struggle.[17] We highlight the interface between maritime dimensions of the geopolitical economy (e.g. colonialism, state power, subsidies), technological and organisational change in shipping, crises, mergers and acquisitions and shipping cartels in the unfolding story of maritime logistics from the 1860s to the 2010s and its articulations with global circuits of production and exchange.

Maritime logistics under the *Pax Britannica*, 1860s–1930s

Contemporary thinking on the dynamics of logistics tends to be characterised by narrowness and presentism, in large measure due to a (justifiable) fascination with the phenomenon of containerisation and its socio-technical role in cementing the new international division of labour and its accompanying social relations. 'Narrow' because, as we shall see, the role of maritime logistics in the contemporary configuration and organisation of global production is broader than the container ship. 'Presentist' because the contemporary 'logistical moment' is not quite as singularly revolutionary as is often suggested. There are two intertwined aspects to this last point: shipping as a discrete industry, and its part in a logistical system designed to maximise the accumulation of capital on a global scale.

Making money from maritime movement is nothing new. What is peculiar to maritime *logistics* is the emergence of the specialised business of steam shipping from the 1860s onwards, the associated transformation of terraqueous spaces such as ports, marine telegram cable networks, and their combined role in revolutionising capitalist *planning*. As we will continually emphasise, it is only the extensive mechanisation of ship propulsion that permitted this new era of planning of global production. The high cost of steamships meant that marine transport was increasingly divorced from merchant capital – 'a revolution in ownership'[18] – and became a capitalist sector in (and for) itself: selling the ability to move masses of commodities to other capitalists, or the transport of fee-paying people.[19] In the latter part of the nineteenth century, the merchant navy became physically connected to riverine, rail and canal transport, which were all informationally integrated (in principle if not always in practice) through the telegram and, by the 1920s, wireless radio. Capitalist circuits were reconfigured by this combination of socio-technological forces as localities, regions and national

economies became ever more deeply entangled in the choreo-
graphy of markets – sometimes synchronised, other times
drunkenly flailing, but always unforgivingly focused on extracting profit and increasing market share.

Although maritime logistics emerged as a specialised function and as a discrete industry with steamships, it was the
particular conjuncture of social relations associated with
European industrialisation and the 'new' capitalist imperialism
of the late nineteenth century that propelled this organisational
and technological change. Much thinking on the co-evolution
of transport and industrialisation focuses on railways, but these
mainly fostered economic integration *within* countries while
steamships encouraged integration *between* them, albeit in
highly asymmetrical ways.[20] Over a startlingly short period of
time, volumes of sea cargo increased from 20 million tons in
1840 to 137 million in 1887, and they were being moved over
far longer distances.[21] To cope with and profit from this shift,
maritime transport underwent a momentous transformation,
changing the face of the shipping industry with regard to the
ways in which it is organised and by whom, and its integration
into (and generation of) networks of global production.

Given the power of 'logistics' in US military planning,[22] it is
possible to miss, or at least downplay, the centrality of maritime
logistics to nineteenth-century colonial production and trade
regimes when explaining the development of this capitalist
technology. Britain's military machine did not refer to the
administration, integration and coordination of supply lines as
'logistics', but that is what it was.[23] We do not address in this
chapter the integral role of the Royal Navy, its interpenetration
with the commercial world of maritime logistics and its role in
(re)producing industrial capitalism and the world market, but
the navy and the British state more broadly are always present
in this era (see Chapter 2).[24] The repeal of the Navigation Acts
in 1849 mirrored the wider push to 'free' trade by the British
state and manufacturing capital, conventionally associated with

the 1846 abolition of the Corn Laws. But as with the Corn Laws, the conditions leading to the exposure of British maritime transport to international competition were already being paved by the collapse of the Dutch East India Company, the disintegration of the Spanish Empire and the end of the East India Company's monopoly in 1833. This was followed by the emergence of a network of private shipping firms, as well as the accompanying web of reciprocal treaties between Britain and other states from 1815, which opened up shipping competition in non-colonial trade from British ports.[25]

In this context, the origins of 'seamless' logistics lie not in containerisation per se but in the interpenetration of 'national' capitals and inter-firm alliances linking colonial and non-colonial shipping and port complexes *for* acceleration and reliability in the transfer of commodity capital and *against* organised labour. For example, the success of the 1889 London dock strike and the associated maritime strikes of 1890 in Australia and New Zealand noted briefly in Chapter 3 were in part a result of conflict, competition and confusion among maritime capitals wrong-footed by transnational labour solidarity. But vessel owners and port authorities quickly learned from their failure in Australia and New Zealand, establishing inter-capitalist alliances aimed at crushing or bypassing strikers and solidarity or secondary actions. This dialectic of capital–labour relations is mirrored today in the Pacific Maritime Association on the US West Coast, where liner, port and cargo-owning firms collude to negotiate with organised labour on the one hand, but on the other it is a historic victory of solidarity for organised labour in achieving a high-paying, coast-wide labour contract.[26]

Steam, steel and cable

We trace the origins of maritime logistics to Britain's coastal coal trade from the north of England to London in the second half of the nineteenth century. The operations and ship design of these early steam colliers are most clearly paralleled in today's bulk carriers.[27] But the commercial and organisational logic – if not the architecture of the vessels – is reflected in other types of contemporary merchant shipping. As we saw in Chapter 1 when addressing the centrality of shipping to the Dutch golden age, capitalist shipping can be back-dated to the seventeenth century. The Dutch *fluitschip* was designed to run with smaller crews as a lower-cost hauler of bulk commodities (timber, grain, fish, salt, coal) and was generally unarmed. In the seventeenth century, Dutch capital controlled as much as three-quarters of the tonnage of Europe's merchant fleet and at its peak built 2,000 ships a year, albeit mostly for export.[28] In the eighteenth century, Dutch shipowners still generally had a stake in the commodity being shifted. Further, like all sailships, the *fluitschip* was subject to the vagaries of the winds, which undermined the ability to plan industrial production around the intercontinental movement of commodities.

The increasing reliability and speed of steam-powered engines, screw propulsion and large iron hulls from the 1860s, together with the commercial deployment of the compound engine from the 1880s, allowed shipping 'liners' to offer a scheduled freight service, facilitated by (and contributing to the development of) the emerging bureaucratic corporation, all without the owners having a stake in the cargo. Linked to this, colliers specialised entirely in moving a particular commodity (like much of today's 'bulk' fleet), were immediately highly productive in terms of the tonnage shifted (initially double that of a sailing collier), and quickly proved profitable, notwithstanding the cost of coal compared to the 'free gift' of wind power. Crucially, investments were made onshore to speed up turnover time in port, including the construction of elevators for (un)loading.[29] This terraqueous infrastructure was designed to accelerate processing at both 'nodes' (ship and dock) in an integrated system with the intention (although not necessarily the realisation) of extracting a greater rate of profit on ever heavier capital investment. Along with the availability of coal as cheap energy, these factors combined to intensify the rate of exploitation of crew vis-à-vis competing capitals (e.g. sail colliers).[30] The coastal coal fleet provided for a huge increase in coal shipped to London, from around 400,000 tons in the late seventeenth century to over 9 million tons by 1910, and steam colliers were able to carry a threefold increase per load, contributing to a falling unit cost of freight rates.[31] Moreover, the *reliability* of supply reduced storage costs because high ground rent in London placed (and places) a premium on local inventory. The role of the colliers in energy supply chains may even be seen as an early and primitive form of just-in-time production in the sense of reducing the volume and cost of companies' coal inventories such as the London gas companies and other industrial users.[32]

Despite the rapid advance in turnaround time and vessel profitability of steam colliers plying Britain's coastal waters, it took time for *deep-sea* steam shipping to become profitable. Sailing ships operated – and competed – alongside steamships until the early twentieth century. Rapid technological changes – from paddlewheel to screw propulsion, and wood to iron hulls – spurred on by competition and the opening of new markets meant that the original steamships were quickly outmoded and lost profitability, requiring costly hull maintenance given the physical force of steaming against winds and tides, as well as erosion by brine.[33] Moreover, coal was both expensive and not always available along routes like those connecting Europe, Australia and the East Indies, thus requiring ships to carry their own fuel and thereby limiting both their distance and productivity in shifting cargo.[34] This remained the case until networks of coaling stations and new coal mines were established in the colonial territories in a British-led trans-oceanic race of dispossession, appropriation and ordering by '[a]gents of the imperial machine'.[35]

By 1870, steamships accounted for three-quarters of ship construction in Britain, while the merchant fleet registered in those isles accounted for 43 per cent of the tonnage of world shipping – four times that of the USA, five times that of France and six times that of Germany and Italy. Britain's maritime hegemony peaked at the turn of the twentieth century at just over 50 per cent of the world merchant fleet – 'a figure never before or after touched'.[36] While the world merchant fleet's gross registered tonnage doubled between 1870 and 1910 from 16.7 million to 34.6 million tons,[37] Britain consistently controlled over 40 per cent of the volume. In a reminder of the terraqueous nature of capitalism, Britain's lead in steamship technology produced new industrial landscapes and labour regimes as it became the 'shipbuilder for the world'.[38] Further, as steamships became bigger, faster and more capitalised, owners were increasingly exposed to the costs of stoppage when they came into port.[39] Speeding up turnover time in port was (and remains) a major commercial concern as liners sell regular and reliable movement. All of which demanded modifications to ports in order to accommodate ships with wider and deeper hulls. Port authorities responding sluggishly to these changes would see ships turn to competing hubs, as illustrated in the laggard growth of Amsterdam and Rotterdam compared to other European ports between 1840 and 1870.[40] In this layered light, the provision of maritime logistics appears critical to Britain's evolution as a capitalist power at the time, with the additional twist that central to this process was the *production* of a technology like the steamship to facilitate *circulation* of commodities.

A crucial dimension in the emergence of Britain's maritime logistics industry was the creation of an intercontinental telegraph network from the 1850s onwards. Deep-sea cabling could, in principle, follow a more direct (if not straight) route between places, and offered a degree of relative security compared to overland telegraph wires given the risks of accidental damage and sabotage by anti-colonial movements. Yet oceanic geographies encompassed two major technical challenges to a marine cable network. First, running signals along submerged wires posed a problem given that the ocean is highly conductive and diffuses signals. Second, cable laying needs to proceed at sufficient depth to avoid damage by dragging anchors or fishing nets or by oceanic oscillations. The solution to the insulation problem came in the form of gutta-percha, a latex gum extracted from trees in colonial Malaya, used as a natural thermoplastic.[41] In parallel, Isambard Brunel's ungainly giant the *Great Eastern* – a commercial flop in its original design to ferry passengers between Britain and Australia – was repurposed to address the second problem, carrying and laying huge reels of cable, generally along the routes of shipping lines.[42] As with the liner industry, a cocktail of public subsidies and private profits underpinned the submarine telegraph system, and Britain's maritime world order was once again both built and sustained through its state-sponsored system of colonial production and trade.

Running cables across the floor of the global ocean highlighted the intimate relationship between transport and communication in creating new 'territories of profit'.[43] The new technology transformed capital's ability to plan global (then largely colonial) systems of raw material extraction and distribution, and introduced the possibility of contemporary 'supply chain capitalism'.[44] Buyers of raw materials and sellers of commodities were no longer dependent on ships' captains or supercargos to convey their orders, and thus integrated maritime logistics was born. This once again foregrounds the relationship between maritime logistics, financial power and information and communications networks explored in Chapter 1. By 1903, around 10,000 messages were sent along the submarine North Atlantic connection and the businesses operating the twelve transatlantic cables were among the world's largest multinationals.[45] Britain's giant cable companies owned the great majority of telegram cabling networks, both marine and overland, and continued to do so until the First World War, by which time the system also criss-crossed the Pacific Ocean. The 'vast intercontinental network of telegraphic communications centred mainly on London',[46] consolidating control of trade and finance in the city, including in ocean-facing industries such as commodity trades, marine insurance and shipping markets such as the Baltic Exchange, which was set up to pool what at the time were very expensive telegram communication costs as a centralised market to fix cargo, especially in the tramp fleet.

Tramp ships were an integral but less well-known part of the merchant shipping industry, yet they were no less important in the development of maritime logistics. Tramp shipping was based on a different underlying business strategy to liners. The former either tended to be smaller enterprises moving commodities between locations not served by liner companies, or they would steam on main routes where they were able to compete directly by undercutting liners' freight prices.[47] This opportunist responsiveness to market dynamics meant that trampers often did not have a fixed route. Smaller carrying capacity and lower costs per ship meant that tramp ships were often chartered by cargo owners, and even at times used as mobile warehouses – a form of at-sea inventory, where bulky raw materials are stored while in motion.[48] Their coexistence with liners in the nexus of maritime logistics is underlined by trampers even being chartered by liners in order to boost freight capacity to fulfil cargo contracts. As we explore further below, the distinction between liners and trampers is a commercially important one, and has significant implications for differential dynamics of competitive accumulation in merchant shipping. While trampers survived, their business models were reshaped by the growing use of the telegram and, especially from the early twentieth century, by the development of far cheaper wireless technology which eroded the 'autocratic power' of captains or supercargos over the commercial aspects of command of tramp ships. Henceforth, the high risks involved in steamship ownership, much higher than in any other capitalist enterprise bar the railways, 'could be reduced considerably by permanent surveillance'.[49]

The logistics of imperialism

Yet the role of capitalist maritime technologies – steamships and marine cables – and of port-side organisation does not *explain* Britain's dominance of international maritime logistics networks from the 1860s to the First World War. The fleet of British-registered steam vessels had a number of distinct advantages that underpinned and reproduced the interplay of its commercial primacy and industrial scale.[50] Most of all the merchant navy had a virtual monopoly on trade within the world's largest empire. In 1913, Britain's ships carried 90 per cent of trade between the metropole and its empire, 80 per cent of trade between territories within the empire, and 50 per cent of these territories' trade with places outside British dominion and imperium.[51] The fleet transferred a significant chunk of the food and raw materials fuelling Britain's labouring bodies and mass industrial production, as well as its (often lighter and less voluminous) exports, including ships (see below). Despite the repeal of the Navigation Acts and the opening of Britain's international sea transport to competition, its merchant navy still carried 50 per cent of the UK's direct (non-colonial) foreign trade in 1913. Britain also dominated the long-distance export of coal. With coal a ballast cargo, Britain's coal mines provided shipowners with tonnage for their outward trips, supplying bunkering stations and railways the world over, thereby enhancing the possibility of profitable runs. This also highlights, once again, the terraqueousness of maritime logistics: Britain's merchant navy had profound and varied land-side economic and political connections. In a ceaseless chase for profits under domestic and international conditions of competitive accumulation in shipping, the merchant navy was able to build bigger, better ships and compete in areas less directly tied to Britain's state and industrial power. For example, again in 1913, vessels flying the red ensign shifted around 25 per cent of the cargos traded among foreign countries.[52]

Greater predictability in marine logistics changed the politics of accumulation for shipowners – they now offered a service whose profitability was far more financially vulnerable to friction and stoppages generated by workers or others, especially in port. Unlike the age of sail, where cheaper ships and high risks contributed to the fragmentation of ownership, the age of steam demanded huge capital investment by liner companies (and, as discussed presently, state subsidies), which further eroded the ties between owners and crew. Gone were the days when crew had a stake – or 'privilege' – in the productivity of the vessel's turnover in the form of a share of freight tonnage. While this prior incentive was always disguised wage labour, the form of exploitation on steam vessels was *explicitly* organised around a regular payment for labour time, and so other forms of social division, differentiation and domination – including those of race and nationality explored in Chapter 3 – now articulated with, and often muddied, the class dynamics at play.

Britain's late nineteenth-century shipping magnates were often from humble backgrounds, but many – like Sir Charles Cayzer (1843–1916), or Donald Currie (1825–1909), both key players among the UK colonial steam liner operators – advanced to prominent political positions as Conservative and Liberal Party donors, or as Members of Parliament, manoeuvring opportunistically between support for free trade and fixing cargo and passenger rates, as well as vigorously pursuing anti-trade-union policies.[53] Liner owners could only accumulate if ships *moved* according to fixed schedules – they could not hoard this commodity to protect against slowdowns or stoppages – and given the relatively high value and/or perishability of their cargos compared to those of tramp shipping, they were (and are) extremely sensitive to strikes by crew and port workers. This also played out in inter-firm competition: the large London-based shipowners such as the British India Steam Navigation Company, the Peninsular and Oriental Steam Navigation Company (P&O) and the Orient Line opportunistically used the aftermath of the 1889 London

dock strike to force defeated dock companies to adapt managerial changes which, 'for the first time, gave the shipowners considerable power in the handling of cargoes'.[54] In parallel, while the
giant liner companies competed among themselves, as noted in
Chapter 3, like 'enemy brothers' they formed the Shipping
Federation in 1890 as 'a fighting machine' to counter the increasing power of seafarers' unions.[55]

The logistical dimensions of the liner industry contrasted
with sail, where movement was less regimented by clock time.
During the age of sail, 'the patterning of social time in the
seaport [and on ships] follows upon the rhythms of the sea; and
this appears to be natural and comprehensible to fishermen or
seamen: the compulsion is nature's own'.[56] Reflecting on the
transition from sail to steam, the report of a 1920 International
Labour Conference highlighted two elements central to the
'speed, frequency and regularity' of steam liners: the revolution
in navigation facilitated by steam power, and the emergence of
giant, highly capitalised limited companies.[57] To this day, shipping remains a heavily capital-intensive sector, deeply integrated
into money, capital and equity markets, despite (or perhaps
because of) volatile revenue streams, mobile assets and opaque
financial structures.[58] From the beginning, steam liners drew on
public investors to raise capital, and with the 1862 Limited
Liabilities Act, this became the dominant source of finance.
During the 'first globalisation' of the decades either side of the
belle époque, fierce competition over emerging markets and the
accompanying technological innovations placed great financial
pressures on shipping companies. Focusing on the specific case
of P&O, Freda Harcourt notes how switching from paddle to
screw propulsion forced company directors to complement
lucrative mail contracts and shareholder investment with other
financial instruments like debentures (long-term securities).[59]

This is one of several instances during the era of the 'New
Imperialism' where logistics came to encompass not just adopting
new energy sources, but conjugating these with the imperatives of

productivity, competition, market share and, of course, access to public procurement. Put bluntly, it is never just new technologies in themselves, but the form of their deployment by organisations, that transforms society. The liner companies were multi-divisional, transnational bureaucratic organisations. This was not just because of the scale of investment in steamships (enormous though this was), but also due to the need to coordinate the movement of countless items of 'break-bulk' (general) cargo from one location to the next. The labour required to stuff and strip (load and unpack) each piece of cargo, combined with its bureaucratic handling, could constitute up to a quarter of the total shipping costs, and absorb up to two-thirds of liners' time in port.[60]

Britain's big liner companies, such as P&O, the Cunard Steamship Company (or Cunard Line) and the British India and Orient Line were, in Freda Harcourt's phrase, the 'flagships of imperialism'.[61] Public subsidies were as important to the development of Britain's liner companies as they were to the rise of its competitors. Mail contracts were among the key mechanisms for the state-led promotion of national shipping industries among the imperial powers, and from the 1830s onwards they 'enabled British shipyards and shipping companies to establish a lead which was not surpassed for a century'.[62] The Cunard Line and P&O were major beneficiaries and the first recipients of British Admiralty funding for an ever-expanding maritime postal network. Aside from supporting British capital invested in maritime logistics, the private provision of regular and reliable postal communications was an essential technology to the world's first capitalist hegemon. Mail and other subsidies, including troop transfers, continued to flow when the liners consolidated their monopoly power through the 1870s and into the 1910s, when seven corporations controlled around 50 per cent of British shipping – accounting, once again, for over 40 per cent of the world's merchant tonnage. The terraqueous interactions of this global dominance were no more apparent than in Britain's shipyards. In 1911, Britain built almost 70 per cent of the world's ocean-going vessels, distantly trailed by its Continental industrial rivals Germany (10.5 per cent) and France (3.5 per cent).[63] The age of steam put an end to the days when Indian shipyards built among the biggest and best merchant ships in the world – the East Indiamen – as they had in the eighteenth century (see Chapter 3). Indeed, the Indian shipbuilding and shipping industries were decimated by Britain's state-subsidised lead in steam shipping, including in coastal trades. Indian shipping capitalists were also actively excluded from the 'conference' system of shipping cartels – a process marked by imperialist and racist motivations.[64]

Centralisation of liner shipping allowed for high levels of oligopolistic leverage by liner firms. This was a function of their ability to control capacity – and, as we shall see later, is in sharp contrast to the dynamics of competition in the twenty-first-century shipping industry. This leverage was especially prominent in highly capitalised and specialised shipping segments, such as the 'conference' between Furness Withy and Royal Mail in their contracts for the shipment of refrigerated meat on mail or passenger liners which squeezed packers in Argentina.[65] More generally, from the 1870s, the eastbound transatlantic movement of live cattle from America to Europe was dominated by only four large liner firms. Cattle shippers needed annual or longer-term contracts to secure regularity in this specialised seaborne transport, which only liners with multiple ships could provide. Further, cattle are relatively light and need ventilation and so could only be carried on upper decks, which gave liners the advantage of selling lower hold space and available buoyancy in the same ships to carry bulk trades such as grain and heavy ores.[66] The legacy of the combination of capitalist investment in steam-based maritime logistics and its geographical concentration in a small number of places to serve colonial production and trade regimes contributed to reproducing dominance by the imperialist world, accelerating 'the economic divergence that is observed between the richest countries and the rest of the world in the second half of the nineteenth century'.[67] Put plainly, steam shipping exacerbated the geographical unevenness and socio-economic inequality inherent to capitalist imperialism and development.

Capitalist competition and liner shipping

The centralisation of British shipping capital was in part a response to increasing competition from major steam liner companies from other emerging economies. With considerable state support,[68] companies from Western Europe and Japan began to set up competing services – often using British-built ships – spanning their own (growing) empires and wider commercial–industrial networks. The North Atlantic was a major competitive arena, accounting for between 73 and 82 per cent of world tonnage in 1850–1900, a period during which the German share almost doubled.[69] For example, the German company Hamburg-America Line (Hapag) was set up in 1847 and by 1900 was working with a capital of almost 140 million marks (around £7 million).[70]

Initially, submarine telegraphic networks replicated the concentration of trade along the transatlantic Europe–America route; in this way '[s]ubmarine cable companies followed imperial logic only as far as it was profitable'. But from the 1890s, imperialist states and corporations 'began to lay submarine cables either to open up new markets, particularly in Asia and Latin America, or to use telegraphs for military, imperial, or strategic control'.[71] This infrastructure in the benthic zone was intertwined with that of the liner industry on oceanic surfaces. As part of its Listian policy of promoting heavy industries (e.g. chemical and steel production) to counter Britain's dominance, the German state pursued an aggressive policy of maritime expansion, including into Asia. In 1886 it started an annual subsidy of 4 million marks over fifteen years to North German Lloyd (NDL) to establish a line linking Bremen with Singapore,

Hong Kong and Shanghai, and mainlines to Japan and Australia shortly thereafter. State subsidies, mainly secured through government mail contracts, were designed 'to establish regular trade links to German colonies or to those regions where imperial Germany hoped to acquire colonies'.[72] By 1913, Hapag and NDL were the clear leaders in Germany's maritime nexus, owning an estimated 40 per cent of national shipping tonnage. The shipping needs of Germany's new industrial hinterlands also had more local effects, most notably feeding the re-emergence of Rotterdam as a major maritime logistics hub due to its direct connection to the Rhine,[73] a position that it maintains in the twenty-first century as the EU's leading port.

We noted earlier that in the 1870s the United States closely followed Britain in terms of the number of registered merchant vessels, but that it was dwarfed in terms of tonnage. It is striking that despite becoming the global hegemon, the USA never quite emerged from being a secondary player in maritime shipping. But this was not for want of trying on the part of the US state. Like Britain's merchant navy, the US merchant marine received considerable state support from the outset of Independence. The first ever session of the US Congress in 1789 legislated that US-flagged vessels must be built and owned by US citizens. And in 1817 foreign flags were banned from the cabotage trade – a common state practice of reserving coastal trade to 'national' ships. This policy was reinforced through the 1920 Merchant Marine Act (or Jones Act), which remains in place today in the USA and in similar form in many other countries.[74] In terms of transatlantic commerce, enormous congressional subsidies were provided to the Collins Line, a passenger and mail service set up to challenge the supremacy of the British Cunard Line, including an annual subvention of US$385,000 from 1846 to build and operate a transatlantic fleet of paddle steamers – subject to their quick convertibility to warships. But the British subsequently doubled the subsidy to the Cunard Line and it offered twice as many transatlantic trips. The Collins

Line was expected to step up its service, but its shares had dropped below the initial offering price and it was yet to make any dividend payments. In this context, in 1852 Collins successfully sought an uplift in subsidy to $858,000 per year. Congressmen supporting the increase laid great emphasis on national pride and 'American greatness' in the transatlantic 'boat race'. Not inaccurately, Congressman Joseph R. Chandler attacked Britain's dominance of the maritime world:

> having eaten the life out of India, Ireland, and Portugal, [it] comes now with vampire appetite to fasten upon our limbs and glut itself upon the life-blood of our commerce . . . [S]tep by step that great, that artful and specious Government is gaining upon our country.[75]

Yet one of the Collins Line ships – the *Arctic* – sank in 1854, taking 300 lives. (Infamously, an insufficient number of lifeboats meant that all children and women on board died while a high proportion of crew survived. It was the nineteenth-century equivalent to the *Titanic*.)[76] Two years later another Collins Line ship simply disappeared without trace in the Atlantic. Combined with a severe depression in 1857 and a reduction in government subsidies, the Collins Line was bankrupt a year later.[77]

By the 1920s the US state had hardened its particular brand of economic nationalism – at least with regard to labour, if not capital. Racist restrictions on shore leave for South Asian crew required shipowners to pay a US$500 deposit for each 'lascar' on board, which was forfeited should the crew member abscond. This was raised to US$1,000 in the 1930s when the US Senate passed new legislation 'authorising officials to board ships entering the United States' ports and remove or deport seamen of races ineligible for United States citizenship'.[78] This ratcheting up of right-wing populist nationalism had a specific economic goal. Given that in the summer of 1937, 85 per cent of the 7,000 South Asian crew entering East Coast ports did so on British merchant vessels, the

regulation had a disproportionately negative impact on transatlantic British shipping capital, and, by extension, on the quality of
life of the South Asian crew denied leave by captains.

Inter-imperialist political and commercial competition in the
Pacific Ocean underpinned the rise of Japanese shipping from
the 1870s onwards.[79] The pioneer was Mitsubishi. It was a
direct beneficiary both of the Meiji Restoration's nationalist
(Listian) economic policy and of the invasion of Taiwan (then
Formosa) in 1874 when thirteen troop-carrying steamships
were gifted to this *zaibatsu*.[80] It quickly ran into commercial
conflict, such as over freight rates with P&O in 1876, when the
British behemoth vainly tried to elbow its way in on the route
from Japan to Shanghai. The Japanese state concentrated on
supporting two *shasen* (regular lines), including direct financial
and shipbuilding subsidies and mail contracts: Nippon Yusen
Kaisha (NYK), the product of an 1885 merger led by Mitsubishi,
and Osaka Shosen Kaisha (OSK), an 1884 amalgam of dozens
of smaller companies.[81] Emboldened, in the 1890s NYK broke
into British spheres of geopolitical economic influence by creating lines to (then) Bombay in collaboration with Tata to supply
raw cotton to Japan's booming spinning industry, to Seattle for
the mass transit of Japanese migrant labour, and eventually to
London.[82] Tracing the trajectory of the European liners, Japan's
shipping firms were beneficiaries of, and agents in, the opening
of new commercial networks with imperial Japan's expansion
in East and South East Asia.

NYK and OSK were the only non-Western liners to break
into international shipping, which had been set out and often
monopolised by British shipping capital along latitudinal routes.
As part of the Japanese state's attempt to reduce competition
between its two major liners, NYK and OSK operated on non-
competing routes and became members of competing shipping
cartels ('conferences'). This set these two firms on a path of
direct commercial collaboration with the very European firms
they were established to counter. The integrated nature of

Japan's pre-Second World War model of capitalism meant that Mitsubishi was also among the country's leading shipbuilders, unsurprisingly supplying NYK with most of its ships.[83]

Smaller tramp shipping firms were considered *shagaisen* (outsiders) and received far fewer subsidies, but still appeared to be profitable. The *zaibatsu* Mitsui chartered these vessels to carry its own bulk trade, eventually emerging as a major shipowner and operator. The *shagaisen* had the advantage of being exempt from the government cap on freight rates as a condition of subsidy provision, which meant that they were able to make super-profits during the First World War with the growing attrition of European tonnage.[84] In the interwar period, Japanese liners and trampers such as Mitsui began to develop longitudinal routes, in part with their pioneering fleets of diesel-powered ships.

The development of Japan's liner companies, like the earlier US examples, makes plain that narratives of competition along international axes elide a more complicated history of transnational maritime networks and strategies of accumulation.[85] With the rapid growth of vast overlapping networks of oceanic transport capacity, shipping line owners colluded to dull the sharpening of international competition – a relationship that was enabled by the confluence of shipping mobility, the 'free seas' and the direct interaction (and often interpenetration) of 'national' capital. Despite the international character of this form of capitalist association, it is unlikely that it could have been maintained without the complicity of British-owned liner firms because of their ongoing global dominance. The conference system involved representatives of shipowners meeting to 'decide tactics ... designed to protect the interests of members through price-fixing and market-sharing techniques and to exclude competitors'.[86] In practice, this meant that freight was charged according to fixed schedules, agreed in advance.

Rooted in Britain in the 1850s, the conference system became firmly established in the 1870s when overcapacity on major routes induced a fall in freight rates and profitability. Conferences were organised on a regional basis, sharing lines and pooling capacity, dividing up routes through the global ocean among shipping capital from Britain, France, Germany, Italy, Japan, the Netherlands and Russia. Collusion was maintained even when rates recovered, allowing industrial shipping capital to capture a portion of the surplus value produced in the global South through the overpriced shipping of primary commodities. This was well recognised by the governments of Brazil, Chile and Peru when, in the early 1900s, they each launched national bulk steamer companies to carry raw material exports and bring back coal, albeit with varying success.[87] Despite these efforts, maritime logistics remained largely governed by the conference system.

There is some debate over the effectiveness of the conference system. Like all capitalist cartels, it was plagued by competitive strategies to gain short- and long-term commercial advantage, including cheating on rates and building more productive ships. Further, in the context of the free seas (and ports), maintaining a watertight monopoly was a fraught affair. Tramp shipowners and other 'outsiders' would sell freight below conference rates. Despite these dynamics, it is likely that the conferences resulted in European cargo owners paying liners more to transport their commodities. But because the system was ubiquitous, we cannot know the counterfactual. In general, cargo owners seem to have accepted the system. The United States was the only major complainant – although the enactment of anti-trust legislation in 1890 and 1914 was ineffectual in practice. This acceptance seemed to stem in large part from the relative stability, regularity and reliability of liner shipments, and the fact that advanced publishing of rates meant that competitors largely paid the same price and reduced the costs of bargaining. The system was probably also tolerated by states because the bigger, more powerful capitalists received preferential rates on large-scale contracts (as they continue to do today). For example, Manchester exporters combined to negotiate cheaper freight rates, while big raw material importers of coffee and iron ore in Britain and the USA respectively played lines off against each other.[88] The system also provided the conditions for another response: commercial and industrial capital squeezed by a conference could vertically integrate and operate their own shipping capacity, especially in specialised shipping segments such as refrigerated cargo where oligopoly among shipping firms was tighter.

Tramping and the deepening of specialisation in oceanic shipping

Steamships moving commodities in the world's first capitalist empire should not be characterised by the iconic liner fleet alone, important though it was. Even in 1910, the total tonnage of Britain's liners was smaller than that of its tramp fleet, although tramps carried less valuable or time-sensitive cargos, such as grain, jute, ore, phosphates or timber on their return trips and coal on their outward ones.[89] Until sail's eventual retreat into obscurity by 1930, steam tramps competed directly with sailships for cargo, especially on the movement of bulk commodities. There was no equivalent to the conference system in tramp shipping and as such profitability of individual enterprises was ruled by relative bargaining power and opportunism, with captains, supercargos or shipowners shifting ports according to a matrix of market dynamics such as selling price, estimated turnover time in port, and the local availability of profitable cargo. The combined cheapening effect of cheap energy, labour exploitation and capitalist competition was significant: between 1870 and 1914, the average freight price for grain and coal on medium to long voyages (c.5,000 nautical miles) dropped by around 45 per cent.[90]

Specialisation in steam shipping began with oil tankers from the 1870s and ore carriers from the 1890s. Innovation here was often introduced by shippers (cargo owners) rather than independent shipowners. Before the Second World War, around 60 per cent of the tonnage of the world's oil tanker fleet was owned by the 'Seven Sisters': oil corporations and governments who controlled the global oil economy.[91] Specialisation also developed after trial and error with refrigeration technology saw reefers open new commodity frontiers, especially in white settler colonies in Latin America, Australia and New Zealand, from where meat, apples and butter could now be profitably shipped to feed the growing working classes of Europe.[92] By the 1920s, over 50 per cent of meat consumed in Britain was imported on reefers. In this way, the cumulative development of maritime technologies in the pursuit of profit created new and unequal structures of seaborne international exchange, with the 'settler colonial' food regime generalising a wheat–livestock diet for the labouring classes, and raw materials exported from periphery to metropole in exchange for imported industrial inputs and wage goods.[93] In these ways, the maritime logistics of industrial capitalism catalysed the transformation of social relations of production, cultures of consumption and entire landscapes, both in the industrial cores of the world economy and in the global South.

While British capital dominated world shipping from the 1850s to 1913, through the interwar period it quickly declined in both absolute and relative terms in the wake of a confluence of factors.[94] The nexus of Britain's shipyards and shipowners was slow to adapt to the emergence of cheaper or more efficient oil-fuelled shipping, while rivals such as Japan in liner shipping and emerging commercial giants of tramp shipping from Greece and Norway advanced both technologically and organisationally.[95] Relatedly, the reduction in ballast cargo with the fall of Britain's coal exports from around 90 million tons a year in the 1910s to 40 million in 1935 hit a vital source of profit on outward trips for tramp ships and cleared the way for greater specialisation after the Second World War. At the same time, liners were adversely affected by the secular decline in industrial production and trade volumes during the Great Depression, as were the leisure-oriented transatlantic mass passenger trades, which had already seen the market for the movement of migrant workers erode with increasingly restrictive US immigration policies in the 1920s.[96] By the Second World War, Britain's maritime logistics industry was floundering and, while it would recover briefly after the war, this was a mere flow tide before it receded into relative insignificance. Despite this, as we shall see in the next section, the interplay of capitalist competition, inter-imperial rivalry and transnational coordination in international shipping in the late nineteenth century produced a mosaic of companies and maritime powers which continue to play a leading role in maritime logistics in the twenty-first century.

Maritime logistics in contemporary globalisation, 1950s–2010s.

It is widely recognised that we have witnessed a 'revolution' in maritime logistics since the generalisation of containerisation in the 1980s and associated emergence of port-based logistics clusters (PLCs). These are terraqueous spaces par excellence, insofar as the design and operation of PLCs seeks to integrate traditional seafaring and port-based activities such as cargo handling, basic warehousing and associated government functions (e.g. customs and port authorities) with a number of additional activities and services such as retail distribution centres and third-party logistics. But this was preceded by two prior 'shipping revolutions' in the post-war era, no less important in expanding and reproducing capitalist circuits, namely purpose-built bulk carriers and oil tankers.[97] Indeed, the post-war 'golden age' of capitalist development both incorporated, and was enabled by, a boom in oceanic shipping. While the average annual growth rate in global shipping capacity in the 150 years between 1850 and 2000 was 2.8 per cent, between 1950 and 1975 it expanded by 5.7 per cent a year – the fastest in recorded history.[98]

The container ship typically comes to mind when picturing the movement of commodities across the oceans. And when thinking about (and with) logistics the centrepiece is the process of containerisation – the intermodal movement of commodities between trucks, trains and ships in metal twenty-foot equivalent-unit (TEU) containers, feeding from and into ports, PLCs and hinterlands. Much has been written about containerisation, including from technical, economic and political perspectives, spanning popular non-fiction to the latest fashion in social theory. The container unquestionably carries significant analytical weight in writing on logistics and supply chain capitalism. Yet most of this work on logistics papers over segmentation in the shipping industry. For example, combined bulk shipping (dry and oil) dominates the *tonnage* of the world merchant fleet at three-quarters of the total (see Figure 5.1). Indeed, over 60 per cent of global tonnage shifted by sea in the twenty-first century is associated with two sectors alone – energy and metals.[99] We think even less about the variety of ships specialised in moving particular cargos, the main ones being

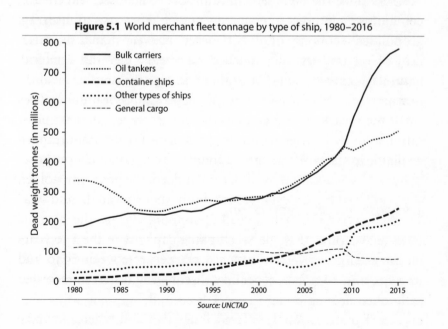

Figure 5.1 World merchant fleet tonnage by type of ship, 1980–2016

Source: UNCTAD

chemicals, liquefied gases, vehicles, forest products and refrigerated and frozen food – each integrated into discrete global production networks, which are in turn dominated by a small number of giant multinational corporations.

Contemporary shipping is differentiated materially, both in terms of what ships carry and in terms of the specifications of the vessels designed to carry it; organisationally by the length and frequency of trips, time spent in port, sailing without freight (deadheading) and the number of onshore staff necessary to manage them; and economically in relation to profit rates and how this drives investment, the typical number of transactions and the dynamics of business 'cycles'. It is thus unsurprising, as we shall shortly illustrate, that there exists a wide variety of accumulation strategies both between and within shipping industry segments. Yet there are also important direct and indirect interactions between segments. Direct interactions include between reefers and container ships, with the latter competing for the former's business since the commercialisation of refrigerated and freezer containers.[100] Indirect interactions include the ways in which the geopolitical economy of global energy markets shapes the business of oil tankers and liquefied petroleum gas and liquefied natural gas carriers, which are otherwise entirely separate production networks.[101] In what follows, then, we underline the complexity of these various interactions, thereby interpreting containerisation as one of a wide repertoire of modes of seaborne transport available in the world economy today.

The post-war shipping boom

Industrial capital after the Second World War was deeply reliant on the oceanic movement of 'natural' resources – especially oil, iron ore and coking coal – and subsequently began to strategically outsource shipping to specialised bulk shipping firms. Oil and steel multinationals offered long-term contracts and time charters to shipowners, giving them the security needed to leverage the enormous loans required to build larger fleets of bigger ships. The improved turnaround and industrial scale achieved meant that rail transport *within* a country such as the USA was often eclipsed in cost terms by inter-oceanic movement *between* countries, undermining the prior advantage of national coal and iron mines.[102] Despite initial close ties to their multinational backers, oil and bulk shipowners were (and are) set against each other by shippers (cargo owners) in intense competitive struggles for cargo contracts. Between the 1950s and mid-1970s, world merchant shipping had transformed, with specialised ships carrying all of the major commodities.

Onshore, these multinationals invested with states in both deep-water port terminals and the speed up of (un)loading systems. In the USA alone, diverse port authorities forged earlier in the twentieth century to manage commercial hubs like those of New York or Oakland were reinvented in the 1960s as container ports.[103] Indeed, the state-of the-art wharfs at Port Elizabeth, New Jersey, which launched the career of the modern container, were built by the Port Authority of New York and New Jersey in large measure to reinvigorate that bi-state metropolitan region through a political act of displacement: from the breakbulk wharfs of lower Manhattan and Brooklyn to the mechanised container ports of New Jersey.[104] Very similar stories could be told of most other contemporary container ports from Los Angeles–Long Beach to Busan. Whether reinventions of historical harbours like Rotterdam or Singapore, or entirely new creations like Shenzhen or Dubai, ports have been relocated from urban waterfronts into what Allan Sekula and Noël Burch labelled the 'forgotten space': vast 'port-based logistics clusters' in metropolitan hinterlands, managed by public–private partnerships and operated by a dwindling workforce that has been dwarfed by the automation of cargo handling.[105] Deborah Cowen has more recently examined the geographical reconfiguration of such spaces through transnational logistics 'gateways' and 'corridors', which usually have a container port as a terminus.[106] Consortia such as the Asia-Pacific Gateway and Corridor Initiative, or the Maputo Corridor Logistics Initiative, combine the public legislative and fiscal authority of states with the private capital and resources of corporations to generate intermodal 'freeways' aimed at lubricating and accelerating the flow of goods across borders.

The shipping boom in the 1950s and 1960s was first and foremost a product of cheap oil, fuelled by and fuelling the automobile age. Europe's growing addiction to oil was, as Timothy Mitchell shows, externally elevated by the 1948 European Recovery Programme (or Marshall Plan), designed in part to encourage industrial uses of oil as an alternative to coal in France and West Germany in order to further prop up the US dollar as the world-money and oil currency, as well as to weaken the structural power of European miners by substituting coal with a more easily transported energy, in the case of industrial action, for example. The terraqueous infrastructure of international shipping is central here:

> whereas the movement of coal tended to follow dendritic networks, with branches at each end but a single main channel, creating potential choke points at several junctures, oil flowed along networks that often had the properties of a grid, like an electricity network, where there is more than one possible path and the flow of energy can switch to avoid blockages or overcome breakdowns.[107]

Between 1950 and 1980, oil tanker capacity grew tenfold (in gross registered tonnage and deadweight tonnage), surpassing the capacity of all dry cargo combined as early as 1960.[108] As with bulk shipping, a prominent competitive strategy in the tanker industry in this period was to launch ever bigger ships.

Braided through, and shaping, these dynamics of competitive accumulation in the tanker shipping business were political

crises, nationalisations and war. Triggered by the 1951 nation-
alisation of a British Petroleum (BP) refinery in Iran, the integrated oil corporations (the then 'Seven Sisters') began to shift
their refineries from the Middle East to their principal markets
in Western Europe and Japan. Although the conflict between
Iran and BP was (temporarily) resolved by 1954, the technical
design and spatial organisation of the Middle East-centred oil
production network was reconfigured, with crude oil tankers
replacing the products carriers which had transported highly
refined petrol, kerosene and lubricating oils, or dirtier fuel oils,
the latter including the 'bunker fuels' used by ships.[109] In parallel, the Korean War sparked a 1951 boom in the shipping of
natural resource commodities, including oil, as Western companies stockpiled materials, boosting speculative shipbuilding. But
this quickly resulted in overcapacity. The subsequent cheapening of freight rates was interrupted by the Franco-British occupation of Suez and the canal closure in 1956, pushing ships
around the Cape where the longer voyage absorbed shipping
capacity and boosted profit, triggering another building boom
of larger ships. Profitability was compromised through a combination of shipping overcapacity and the broader late 1950s
recession in the world economy. The 1967 Six Day War reversed
this downturn when the Suez Canal was closed once again,
ushering in a new boom in shipbuilding and cementing the era
of the supertanker. Increasingly built in Japan for financiers in
Greece and Hong Kong, the very large crude carrier (VLCC) of
between 200,000 and 299,000 deadweight tonnage began to
dominate long-haul routes from the 1960s.[110] This sequential
story is a simplification, but it indicates the ways in which
Western colonialism, Cold War proxy wars and national independence movements contributed to revolutionising maritime
transport and made (and unmade) fortunes among shipping
corporations and magnates (most famously Aristotle Onassis).

The Cold War geopolitical economy also inflected the technical design and spatial organisation of deep-sea cable

networks. As in the late nineteenth century, marine cables play a pivotal role in communications among the cities and regions that combine to make the world economy. But in the 1950s technical innovations in analogue coaxial cables using submerged repeaters to amplify signals allowed the transmission of voice, telex and low-resolution television. The oceanic geography of laying submarine cable was now shaped by the threat of nuclear war, which motivated a more decentralised approach to this infrastructure. Landing stations were both diversified and located away from major coastal cities, and marine cable took precedence over exposed terrestrial routes, even if the former were considerably longer. Finally, American firms such as AT&T emerged as world leaders in undersea cable systems – like British telecommunications before them, these systems were shaped by both commercial and geopolitical considerations.[111]

Iron ore was the leading dry bulk shipping commodity in the post-war era. Prominent here was Japan. In addition to the vast volumes of freight produced by its rapidly growing export-oriented economy, Japan's demand for raw materials drove the vast majority of *global* growth in dry cargo shipping.[112] Japan's Ministry of International Trade and Industry and Export–Import Bank had identified steel, shipping and shipbuilding as priority post-war generative industries and 'took the lead in the creation of the most tightly coupled relationship between capital and the state in history'.[113] This included construction of new maritime industrial development areas using land expropriated by the state.

As early as 1956, Japan was the world's largest builder of merchant ships. It overtook the combined might of Western Europe's shipyards in 1966, and by the 1970s Japanese shipyards constructed around 50 per cent of the world's merchant fleet (Figure 5.2). As with much of the rest of Japan's post-war industry, its shipyards were characterised by highly segmented labour regimes, with long-term casual labour supplementing the permanent workforce. This provided capital with the flexibility to restructure and divest from this infamously undulating, terraqueous industry with less resistance from organised labour.[114] Japan's maritime industries were in turn fuelled by the vast volumes of freight produced by the country's rapidly growing export-oriented economy, and, as noted, its raw material imports drove the post-war boom in dry cargo shipping.

Figure 5.2 World merchant ship building by leading countries and regions, 1964–2014

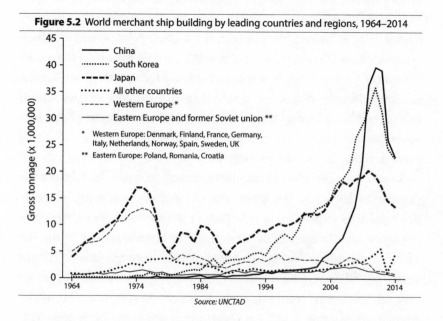

Source: UNCTAD

Many of the top twenty liner firms in the 2010s were already leading shipping liners before the 1970s. But with the exception of Japanese firms, very few had existed before the 1950s. Japan was a world leader in merchant shipping throughout the twentieth century, and in 2017 held the second-largest tonnage by beneficial ownership of the world fleet.[115] MOL (Mitsui), NYK and K Line were the world's eleventh-, thirteenth- and fifteenth-largest container liner companies in 2016. However, this underplays their real industrial weight because each are involved, to varying degrees, in tankers, bulk, ro-ro, LNG and cruise ships. This was not the outcome of a post-war 'miracle' because, as we have seen, each shipping firm can trace its origins to the late nineteenth century, including access to low-cost loans both from the state and from within the parent *zaibatsu*.[116] After the war, Mitsui transformed itself from a *shagaisen* (outsider) when it merged in 1964 with OSK, one of the *shasen* (regular lines). Mitsui OSK also continued to be a leader in bulk shipping, leveraging long-term cargo contracts with Japan's major steel corporations to build new vessels, so that by the 1980s it was shifting around 20 per cent of Japan's imports of iron ore.[117] The other *shasen*, NYK, continued to benefit from close ties to Mitsubishi, itself 'reformed' by the post-war Occupying Authority into a *sōgō shōsha*, but maintaining diverse holdings, including shipbuilding and cargo contracts. Kawasaki Kisen Kaisha Ltd – today's K Line – emerged from a 1919 merger and was the thirteenth-largest liner firm in the world in 1926.

South Korea and Taiwan followed Japan's emphasis on maritime logistics as part of an integrated and planned approach to export-oriented industrialisation – both embarking on programmes of heavy industry development from the 1970s that relied on highly oppressive labour regimes.[118] Both states simultaneously supported the development of privately owned national merchant fleets such as Hanjin, Hyundai Merchant Marine and Evergreen Line, while South Korea also became a world-leading shipbuilder (Figure 5.2). The Cold War again provides the crucial context to understanding the emergence of these newly industrialised countries as maritime powers. The networks of oceanic trade on which South Korea and Taiwan depended – in relation to securing both raw materials from the global South and preferential access to the American consumer goods market – were ordered by US hegemony, including overseas development aid, US military contracts (especially for Korea) and the nuclear 'umbrella'.[119] Simultaneously, the dynamics of North East Asia's geopolitical economy allowed these states to frame their repressive labour regimes in relation to the imminent 'threats' of Communist China and North Korea. This was the context that pushed these regionally isolated Western allies to look seawards and reintegrate with Japanese capital in regional production networks that were held together by the sinews of their respective maritime logistics industries.

From the 1955 Bandung Conference onwards, a rapidly growing number of independent states of the global South challenged the structure of the Western-dominated world economy – culminating in the 1970s call for a New International Economic Order.[120] As we have seen, since the seventeenth century, international shipping had been structured around European mercantilism and slavery, the triangular trades, and by the late nineteenth century had internationalised the world market in large part around colonial production and trade regimes based upon the latitudinal movement of commodities. Highly uneven concentrations of global production excluded vast swathes of the South from major liner routes (i.e. globally competitive movement) because of low freight volumes. This reinforced dependence on often irregular and more expensive feeder routes, which further undermined possibilities of competitive accumulation, especially for import-substituting and export-oriented manufacturing where much post-colonial statist development policy had focused attention.[121]

Over time, the attention of elites in the global South began shifting to 'invisible transactions, where shipping accounts for a major portion of income transfers', but even where developing states created national shipping firms, they were excluded by the conference system, which was 'not seen merely as exploitative in nature but as a very important aspect of neocolonialism'.[122] Various Group of 77 pronouncements in the 1970s sought to redress the polarising tendencies of international shipping through calls for promotional freight rates for the poorest and most vulnerable developing countries.[123] The 1974 United Nations Code of Conduct on Liner Conferences demanded the opening up of the conference system to new entrants; to fix freight rates 'at as low a level as is feasible ... [to] permit a reasonable profit for shipowners', to take special account of developing and landlocked countries; and to offer promotional freight rates for 'non-traditional exports' as well as providing a dispute settlement process to enforce provisions.[124] Despite eventually coming into force in 1983, the Code of Conduct faced a new world-historical context characterised by the debt crisis and neoliberal counterrevolution, the fragmentation of always fragile South–South cooperation, and the rise of liner firms working outside the conference system.[125] Further, bulk shipping was always excluded from the 1974 Code of Conduct, despite its importance to primary commodity exporters. Meanwhile, low-cost liner shipping continued to marginalise entire swathes of developing countries because of the lack of freight volumes, contributing to the reproduction of uneven development.[126]

The Great Shipping Crisis and the neoliberalisation of maritime logistics

Crisis plagued the shipping industry from the late 1970s to 1985. It was marked by a construction slowdown and, at points, decline in world tonnage, with only container shipping steaming against the tide.[127] The lead-up, and capital's response, to this crisis would transform the industrial organisation and financing of the shipping industry. In this context, international shipping played a central part in the emergence of global neoliberalism, even if this was neither inevitable nor all by design. State policies on shipping continue to compromise any notion of a 'pristine market', despite the claim common among mainstream economists that shipping is the closest we have come to a free market, assuming as they do that freight rate price is determined purely by the laws of supply and demand. In this sense, the global shipping industry encapsulates a 'neoliberal paradox', articulated around six axes.[128]

First, the legal 'denationalisation' of shipping capital with the generalised shift to flags of convenience simultaneously undermined the capacity for self-organisation among seafarers from 'embedded' maritime states in the capitalist core and opened up maritime labour markets to crew from developing countries (Chapter 3). This process saw a radical cheapening of wage costs per trip. Second, a variety of forms of state intervention contributed to overcapacity in global shipping. In the stagflationary West and in the Soviet bloc, shipyards were propped up to counter growing unemployment in often politically militant industrial hinterlands. In East Asia, as noted, the promotion of maritime industries as part of broader state-managed industrialisation strategies witnessed the rise of new giant shipyards and internationally competitive shipping companies, while other countries of the global South engaged in Third Worldist responses to the continued Western dominance of the world economy, leading to state investments in maritime industries. Third, intensified competition among merchant shipping capitals and the associated erosion of profitability drove investment into new technologies. Principal among these was the gradual emergence of a global fleet of specialised container vessels, designed to carry more of the manufactured and intermediate goods generated by the new international division of labour. This pushed outmoded general-cargo ships (also able to shift containers) to feeder routes, resulting in a widening of global maritime trade and an attendant increase in volume and competitive intensity. Fourth, the neoliberal counterrevolutionary attack on dock workers in North America and Western Europe that accompanied, and to a large extent drove, containerisation undermined, but did not nullify, solidarities among maritime workers, enhancing the capacity of capitalists to plan

regional networks of production and global commodity circulation. Fifth, the prior four elements combined and coevolved in
a radical cheapening of maritime logistics, enabling the emergence of highly calibrated networks of global production, characterised by global labour arbitrage and just-in-time supply
chains. This allowed simultaneous competition between regional
and national labour regimes in a system of global production
that is coordinated and controlled by a small minority of multinational corporations. Finally, the legal 'offshore' innovation of
the FOC – which allows capital to choose the laws that bind it
– was mimicked onshore in the emergence of the new terraqueous space of the export processing zone or special economic
zone (see Chapter 6).

The fourfold increase in oil prices in 1973 and again in 1979
hit the oil tanker industry hard. The age of the ever-expanding
supertanker came to an end in the early 1980s and vessel size
subsequently stabilised when the limits of the advantages of
scaling up were reached and the environmental devastation of
accidents became all too apparent with the 1967 *Torrey Canyon*
oil tanker disaster – 'the greatest shipwreck ever to have
afflicted the British coast' – which, for some, spurred the 'new'
environmental movement and prompted coverage of marine
pollution in several subsequent international conventions.[129]
The ultra-large crude carrier of 300,000 deadweight tonnage
and above never really took off commercially – the largest-ever
oil tanker was built in 1979 – and was mainly used for at-sea
storage; indeed, many were scrapped early in their commercial
lifespan.[130]

Other industry-specific components of the Great Shipping
Crisis can be traced to debt-fuelled, speculative shipbuilding
with the post-1973 flooding of capital markets with Eurodollars,
the connected global overcapacity in shipyards, and the process
of the growing concentration of *control* of shipping capital
combined with the fragmentation and specialisation of shipping
services.[131] Specialised bulk ships got bigger between the 1980s

and the 2000s, pushing down the profitability of smaller ships.[132] These were in turn pushed into lower-volume routes where new shipping capacity and the associated cheapening of freight contributed to the opening of new labour regimes, commodity frontiers and markets. The bulk carrier industry boomed on the back of the early twenty-first-century commodity supercycle (Figure 5.1). Indeed, it is the bulk trades that best highlight the container-centrism of much thinking on contemporary logistics; instead of making Africa and even Latin America invisible because of their relatively smaller share in the global movement of container ships, these regions are in fact tightly integrated into the flows of global capitalism most visibly in bulk carrier and tanker movements.

We saw in Chapter 3 that Japanese shipping capital effectively sidestepped national regulation of crew and taxation to become a leading user of flags of convenience, especially from the 1980s, and by 2016 less than 13 per cent of Japan's merchant vessels used the national flag.[133] In this way, the shipping industry can be seen as a vanguard sector of neoliberalism. The international mobility of the means of producing movement combined with the regulatory innovation of the FOC to produce a situation where, in the 1980s, even social-democratic states such as Denmark and Norway capitulated to a tiered approach to the social regulation of shipping, with international shipping registries coexisting alongside their national ones.[134] While there is debate over the extent to which all second registries are as regulatory lax as the 'traditional' FOC, the fundamental outcome is the same: capital is 'freed' from the obligation to pay as much (if any) tax and can intensify the rate of exploitation of labour through lower wages and working conditions for ratings and junior officers, although senior officers and captains on FOC ships remain disproportionately represented by the global North. Further, by the late 1970s, shipbuilding in the former European centres of maritime logistics had embarked on a trajectory of absolute decline, albeit with important national and sub-regional differences (Figure 5.2).[135]

The TEU is perhaps the most emblematic symbol of the neoliberalisation of maritime logistics.[136] The steel or aluminium box is not only responsible for transporting the vast majority of the world's non-bulk goods, it is also an intermodal freight technology premised on three distinctive properties: it is universal, it is standardised and it needs to be moved mechanically. The pioneering intermodal transport firm which launched the first transatlantic crossing of a container ship in 1966 was appropriately called Sea-Land Services. Founded by Malcom McLean, a trucking company owner from North Carolina frustrated by the increasing congestion and social conflict on post-war US highways and waterfronts, Sea-Land Services commissioned the design of a container that could be detached from trucks and directly stacked onto seagoing vessels. This led McLean reportedly to boast, 'I don't have vessels, I have seagoing trucks!'[137]

Performing this geographical conjuring trick, so obviously reminiscent of the 'annihilation of space by time' discussed earlier, was premised on extra-economic processes and institutions. Chief among these were the combination of a revolution in military logistics occasioned by the Vietnam War, the New Right's recalibration of public and private power (through states and markets), the repression of organised labour in ports the world over, including through legislative restrictions on the resort to solidarity strikes, and the process of standardisation of international economic regimes through technical bodies like the International Standards Organisation.

But the uptake of the container in reconfiguring the movement of cargo from factory to factory and to end-consumer markets was not as frictionless or as automatic as is often assumed. Container ships began to criss-cross the Atlantic and the Pacific Oceans in the late 1960s and ply the trans-oceanic trade between Asia and Europe from 1972. Yet specialised container shipping tonnage continued to be dwarfed by general-cargo ships shifting a combination of break-bulk and increasing loads of containers carried on deck and in converted holds. Even in 1990 the global fleet of general-cargo ships was double the tonnage of container vessels.[138] The relative cost of specialised container shipping compared to general-cargo vessels had never been in doubt. By 1985, the reduced port time of container ships meant that 'a string of nine container-ships could do the work of 74 cargo-liners'.[139] Yet a combination of class politics in ports and the often related slow-moving infrastructure investment by port authorities necessary to shift containers all contributed to delaying the generalisation of containerisation in maritime logistics. Only in 2004 did the registered tonnage of container ships overtake that of general cargo, yet by 2015 container ship tonnage was over three times that of general-cargo ships (Figure 5.1). Container shipping tonnage grew by 7.4 per cent annually through the 1980s and by over 9 per cent in the 1990s. But in terms of *volume*, the rise of the container ship was more rapid and dramatic: it was equal to the three major bulk cargos by 1990 and on a par with the global tanker fleet by 2000.[140]

The driving logics of containerisation were twofold. First was the widely recognised ambition to minimise labour costs and the turnover time of capital. Second, and often downplayed in the theorisation of logistics, was the objective of introducing greater *regularity* into shipping patterns – enhancing the ability of capitalists to *plan* increasingly fragmented networks of global production. What is interesting for our purposes is how the attributes of the shipping container just identified – its universality, standard features and automobility – convey a particular disposition, expressing the 'ambivalent' (as opposed to 'neutral') nature of technology, whereby certain socially and politically determined technical codes 'invisibly sediment values and interests in rules and procedures, devices and artefacts that routinize the pursuit of power and advantage by a dominant hegemony'.[141]

A further dimension in the neoliberalisation of – and through – the global ocean, albeit on the seabed as opposed to the ships plying its surfaces, is the laying of fibre optic cable systems from the mid-1980s. The spatial organisation of this technical development was shaped profoundly by the denationalisation and deregulation of telecommunications industries. Like their analogue-only equivalent, the laying of fibre optic cables was again centred on the oceans to reduce the risk of accidental damage and sabotage. But deregulation meant that this was no longer part-coordinated by governments through national champions – whether privately or publicly owned – and was instead a purely profit-centred activity by transnational consortia of investors. This resulted in something of a bonanza in the 1990s as cables 'crossed paths and overlaid one another' or 'companies extended cables into more risky areas and put less preparation into securing routes, which led to an increase in faults'.[142] By the 2010s, submarine cables carried over 97 per cent of all intercontinental data flows.[143] Unlike the analogue era, communications satellites do not have the capacity to absorb contemporary capacity should fibre optic cables be cut, as they were during the 2011 Tōhoku earthquake and tsunami, or when an entire country was taken offline such as Mauritania during the severing of the submarine cable from the African coast to Europe by a trawler in the spring of 2018. This maritime infrastructure of networks of cables reminds us of the materiality of the Internet – much of the information we receive and send from our screens is carried among continents in packets of information across the floor of the deep-sea world.

Accumulation, control and crisis in maritime logistics

The beginning of the new millennium witnessed a further crisis in world shipping. A combination of unpredictable factors – cheap oil, axes of inter-capitalist competition such as vessel specialisation, growing global fleet capacities – combined with the attack on organised port workers (with the mix of repression, technological fixes and geographical sidestepping via new port complexes), delivered an economic climate where, in real terms, dry-bulk freight costs were around one-fifth in the year 2000 of what they had been 150 years before.[144] Growing shipping capacity and shrinking profits encouraged cargo owners to further divest from shipownership. For instance, while the integrated oil corporations continue to manage a degree of backward integration in tanker shipping in the early twenty-first century (at around 7 per cent of the total tanker fleet), this is to maintain only minor strategic shipping capacity alongside another portion of shipping that is under long-term control with ten- to fifteen-year charters.[145] Yet at the same time, and unlike the era of the transatlantic liners' leverage in the late nineteenth century, even when the oil and mining majors outsource, they maintain levels of oversight unthinkable in the trade for containerised goods

Merchant shipping had a turnover of around US$426 billion in 2004. Over half of all the world's merchant vessels were owned by around 360 companies, the remainder being held by over 5,200 firms, competing fiercely for a share of an annual global freight expenditure of around US$270 billion.[146] As in the nineteenth century, shipping firms continue to seek to stabilise accumulation through inter-capitalist cooperation. While the liner conference system stumbled along in fits and starts in the post-war era, the great shipping crisis meant that the estimated 350 shipping conferences operating in the 1980s lost any effectiveness. The major liner firms – now increasingly specialised in container shipping – responded by establishing new, global alliances in an attempt at maintaining competitive advantage through improved utilisation of ever-bigger ships, via slot sharing, and by portioning routes and vessels – in other words, capitalist planning of maritime movement on a global scale.

Association among the few was made possible by increasing corporate centralisation with a marked geographical dimension: four of the top five carriers in 2016 were European, with the majority of the remaining top twenty based in East Asia, and none in Africa or the Americas.[147] By 2017, the top liners had joined forces in three global alliances, reduced from four in 2016. The 2M Alliance combines Maersk (with Hamburg Süd) and the Mediterranean Shipping Company (MSC); the Ocean Alliance groups CMA CGM, Evergreen, the China Ocean Shipping Company and the Orient Overseas Container Line; and THE Alliance links Hapag-Lloyd (recently merged with United Arab Shipping Company), Ocean Network Express (itself an alliance of Japanese liners K Line, NYK, MOL (Mitsui) and OSK) and Yang Ming. Hidden behind many of these often well-known corporations are ship and crew management companies such as Anglo-Eastern and V. Group. The three global alliances include the top ten container shipping lines (plus K Line – the fourteenth-largest) and collectively control 77 per cent of global container shipping capacity and over 90 per cent of the traffic on the east–west superhighway, leaving less than a quarter of market share available to the world's other container shipping lines.[148]

Bulk shipping remains very different to the container liner business, with distinct types of operation, levels of bureaucratic infrastructure and forms of vessel ownership and financing. A useful illustrative example is the number of interactions with cargo owners: a typical bulk ship will undertake six voyages a year, carrying a single cargo each time, while a container ship will engage in between 10,000 and 50,000 transactions to fill its holds, each with particular service requirements. Specialised shipping sits somewhere between these two. Bulk shipping thus only requires a small onshore staff; in contrast, container shipping demands a multinational army of white collar workers.[149] Ever-bigger ships fill the headlines in industry press, and the scale that they command shifts thinking on the maximum rate of profit achievable in the sector. But the headlines obscure the long life of older 'sub-optimal' ships which continue to ply the oceans, selling movement. The many small capitals owning five or fewer ships in non-liner segments organise in revenue-sharing 'pools' where vessels of the same specialisation combine to sell the movement of cargo. While bigger new-built liners, bulks or tankers take over from relatively smaller ones on longer-distance high-volume routes, the smaller ships often switch to sell transport on lower-volume routes. This has contributed to the formation of finer-grained differentiation *within* shipping industry segments, such as the distinction between VLCCs, Capesize, Suezmax, Panamax and Handy vessels in the oil and bulk fleets. Suezmax and Panamax are designed to comply with the size regulations of the Suez and (thinner) Panama canals when traversing between oceans, while Capesize are too large to transit either and so have to pass either the Cape of Good Hope or Cape Horn.

The general narrative of overcapacity and squeezed profit rates in merchant shipping masks important fluctuations and potential for accumulation. For example, the commodity super-cycle of the early twenty-first century saw the Baltic Dry Index (an average of around fifty routes for commodities such as coal, iron ore, cement and grains) peak at its highest level of the past sixty-five years in 2008.[150] The super-profits captured by ship operators in the early years of the commodity super-cycle were chased in a flurry of vessel construction so that, by the end of the cycle, chronic overcapacity once again haunted world shipping and in 2016 the Baltic Dry Index had dropped to its lowest point in over thirty years. The container shipping segment saw a parallel shipbuilding boom, despite the global economic slump, with tonnage increasing by almost three times between 2005 and 2016 (Figure 5.1), so that 'while the cost to carry a container from Shanghai to the US East Coast in March 2015 was $2,500, that price fell to US$1,500 by June and less than US$400 by January 2016'.[151] This culminated (so far) in the 2016 collapse of Hanjin, then the world's eighth-biggest container shipping firm, under the weight of US$4.5 billion in debt.[152]

Hanjin's collapse in the summer of 2016 was just one manifestation of undulating crises in the shipping business, illustrating the underlying problem of overcapacity generated by capitals-in-competition: what makes sense to an individual enterprise such as Maersk ordering a fleet of Triple-E class container ships can have a deleterious effect on the industry as a whole.[153] At the same time, precisely because of this overcapacity, Hanjin's competitors quickly filled the gap left by its collapse. The Hanjin case also shone light on the centrality of leasing arrangements, with around 60 per cent of its fleet being owned by others. Given that shipping companies had been transporting cargo at a loss for some years, the crisis raised the question of how many other liner firms are 'zombie carriers . . . those shipping companies who stand only because the banks decided not to let them fail'.[154] The state is once again shown to be crucial to accumulation strategies in maritime logistics, with, for example, Hyundai Merchant Marine's debt being bought by the Korea Development Bank, which, combined with the propping up of Korea's two shipbuilders that had been left with abruptly cancelled orders, meant that it was unwilling or unable to bail out Hanjin too.

Integral to the geography of merchant shipping and port-based logistics is the (re-)emergence and relentless, albeit uneven, growth of East Asia as the leading export-oriented pole of global manufacturing. The east–west superhighway (or historical 'westline') connecting the global triad of North America, Europe and East and South East Asia is characterised by enormous scale. Yet, contrary to contemporary populist narratives of China's export-oriented economy, the vast majority of its manufacturing exports are owned or controlled by foreign capital, including from within the East Asian region.[155] The centrality of the maritime factor in East Asian networks of production, which increasingly incorporated swathes of South

East Asia from the 1970s onwards, is indicated by the importance that leading regional states and multinational capital place on maritime logistics; for example, East Asian shipyards accounted for over 90 per cent of global merchant vessel production in the 2010s (Figure 5.2).

Table 5.1. World top twenty container ports by TEU throughput in 1997 and 2016

		1997		2016
Rank	Port	TEU	Port	TEU
1	Hong Kong, China/UK	14,567,000	Shanghai, China	37,135,000
2	Singapore	14,135,000	Singapore	30,930,000
3	Kaohsiung, Taiwan	5,693,340	Shenzhen, China	23,980,000
4	Rotterdam, Netherlands	5,445,000	Ningbo, China	21,565,000
5	Busan, South Korea	5,233,880	Hong Kong, China	19,580,000
6	Long Beach, USA	3,504,600	Busan, South Korea	19,378,000
7	Hamburg, Germany	3,337,480	Guangzhou, China	18,859,000
8	Antwerp, Belgium	2,969,200	Qingdao, China	18,050,000
9	Los Angeles, USA	2,959,710	Dubai, UAE	14,772,000
10	Dubai, UAE	2,600,100	Tianjin, China	14,523,000
11	Shanghai, China	2,530,000	Port Kelang, Malaysia	13,167,000
12	New York, USA	2,456,890	Rotterdam, Netherlands	12,385,000
13	Tokyo, Japan	2,382,630	Kaohsiung, Taiwan	10,460,000
14	Yokohama, Japan	2,328,000	Antwerp, Belgium	10,037,000
15	Felixstowe, UK	2,251,380	Xiamen, China	9,614,000
16	Kobe, Japan	2,056,750	Dalian, China	9,584,000
17	Tanjung Priok, Indonesia	1,898,000	Hamburg, Germany	8,900,000
18	Bremerhaven, Germany	1,703,000	Los Angeles, USA,	8,857,000
19	Algeciras, Spain	1,537,630	Tanjung Pelepas, Malaysia	8,029,000
20	Gioai Tauro, Italy	1,448,400	Cat Lai, Vietnam	7,547,000
	Top 20 ports' share of world TEU throughout (~170,000,000):	47%	Top 20 ports' share of world TEU throughout (701,420,047):	45%

Source: UNCTAD, *Review of Maritime Transport*, various years.

The locations of the world's leading container ports high-light, once again, the relevance of the maritime factor in the shifting contours of global production. The TEU throughput of the top twenty container ports was 47 per cent of the world total in 1997 (across ~3,000 ports); while this share dropped slightly to 45 per cent in 2016 it was of a *fourfold* increase in total volume – indicating both the absolute growth and the sheer geographical concentration of global manufacturing production and trade volumes (Table 5.1). TEU throughput is far from a rigorous measure of the ocean-facing export manu-facturing trade, not least because of double counting (exports that use imported intermediate goods) and the statistical distortion of trading hubs such as the PLCs in Dubai, Hong Kong and Singapore where containers are offloaded and sorted for consolidation on different vessels. It is, nonetheless, a useful description of global shifts in the centres of manufac-turing and assembly. In 1997 East and South East Asia accounted for nine of the top twenty ports, three of which were in Japan, and Shanghai was China's only top twenty port alongside Hong Kong after the mid-year 'handover' by the UK. Yet in 2016, nine of the top twenty container ports were located in China alone, and fifteen of the top twenty were in East and South East Asia (none of which were in Japan). The silences in the data also indicate ongoing processes of exclu-sion and uneven development in global manufacturing – ports in Africa, Latin America, Oceania and South Asia are not included in the top twenty throughout the twenty-year period, despite accounting for over half of the global population.[156] The structural problem for seaward-facing capital accumula-tion in these regions is that, given the often low rates of profit in the global competition to articulate with manufacturing supply chains, relative freight costs can undermine manufac-turing in entire regions, contributing, along with a variety of other factors, to ongoing processes of economic exclusion. To this extent, the contemporary structure of maritime logistics is reminiscent of the hierarchies of global development produced by steam shipping in the late nineteenth century, as outlined above.

Continuity and change in maritime logistics

The capitalist transformation of maritime logistics, we have argued, is characterised by two overarching dynamics: the disaggregation of ownership in retail, shipping and shipbuilding, and the resulting organised coordination of these distinct sectors for the purposes of constantly shifting commodities across the seas in the most profitable way. These properly capitalist features of logistics have in turn been powerfully shaped by developments in the maritime sector, with shipping, shipbuilding, flagging and many of their associated services (including ports) playing a critical role in the successive industrialisation of capitalist economies since the nineteenth century. State subsidies and contracts, inter-firm competition and collaboration, labour disputes and technological innovations (the latter in many respects facilitated by the preceding factors) have conditioned the specific articulation of maritime logistics across different spatio-temporal contexts. But the common denominator in these experiences is the *planned movement* of commodities across otherwise fragmented points of production and consumption. Capitalist logistics thus articulate money, commercial and productive capital without conflating them. The capital-intensive nature of the maritime sector has made it especially sensitive to profitable coordination between production (shipbuilding) and circulation (shipping), in large measure explaining the extraordinary eastward pivot of maritime economics during the twentieth century.

We have set out three broad periods in the development of capitalist shipping. The last two were the focus of this chapter and were periods of maritime logistics – understood as the capitalist planning of production and the circuit of capital on

263

a global scale. The first, discussed at various points in the first three chapters, was the era of commercial capitalism which saw Dutch, then English (and British) merchant fleets dominating the global ocean based on investment in vessel productivity and imperial ordering. Shipping in this era continued to be tied to, and *driven* by, the logic of commercial capital: ships were generally used to carry a merchant's own merchandise for the purposes of 'buying cheap and selling dear', leasing cargo space to others only where available. Shipping, ports, communications and other forms of transport were not yet fully integrated according to the imperatives of capitalist logistics – a system of planning oriented toward increasing labour productivity (generating relative surplus value), maximising returns from the means of production (ships) in the race against depreciation, and minimising the turnover time of capital in the realisation of the circuit of capital (moving cargos of commodities for sale).

The second period took us from the 1860s to the interwar era and was largely dominated by Britain's capitalist empire and steam shipping. For the first time, capitalists could plan trans-oceanic networks of production and distribution without being so deeply subject to the vagaries of the wind. This saw 'a revolution in ownership' of increasingly capitalised giant shipping lines and the generalisation of the sale by shipowners of transport to other capitalists, a process facilitated by the creation of marine telegram cable networks. Maritime logistics in this period were supported by states engaged in inter-imperialist rivalries seeking to develop trans-oceanic, deep-sea steam shipping routes which were shaped profoundly by colonial production and trade regimes (within which we include the white settler colonies). But while inter-imperialist rivalry was rife, it coexisted with a more complicated history of transnational maritime networks and strategies of accumulation reliant on capitalist association (e.g. the shipping conferences) and inter-penetration of capital.

The third period from the post-war era to the 2010s is one of continuity and change compared to the prior period. The nineteenth-century division between the liner and tramp industries saw an ever-greater degree of specialisation and a number of 'shipping revolutions' – the oil tankers, the bulk trades and containerisation – each of which, in different ways, acted as a vanguard in the emergence and evolution of neoliberal capitalism, revolutionising, expanding and reconfiguring the world economy and its associated geographies. State power continued to reproduce maritime logistics – such as the repositioning of Japan's post-war seaward focus on maritime industries, quickly followed by other major East Asian states. The centralisation of shipping tightened through this period, with a rapidly diminishing number of firms controlling a greater proportion of shipping capacity. Despite these moves toward concentration, shipping capital has been unable to contain the crisis tendencies within the industry. Unlike the period of global dominance by the giant liner companies in the late nineteenth century, liners today are not able to shape freight rates vis-à-vis shippers, despite their attempts to stabilise the system by organising in only three global alliances by the late 2010s (and their near universal exemption from competition law in doing so).

Britain and Japan were singled out in this chapter as two leading illustrations of developments in maritime logistics between the 1860s and the 2010s. These case studies provide important insights into the development of industrial powers, and the global maritime logistics complex in general. Both demonstrate the crucial role of maritime logistics in capitalist planning, and each also makes clear the centrality of the state to the formation and reproduction of this system. From this perspective, capitals-in-competition in the shipping industry certainly generated technological and organisational change, but they did so because of political interventions by states. We also saw a degree of continuity in Japan's leading position in shipping and shipbuilding between the 1870s and the twenty-first century, albeit augmented by the system of 'flagging out', while Britain, the previous world hegemon, gradually dropped altogether off the maritime map in the post-war era. Only the City of London retained an integral role in marine insurance, reinventing itself as a global financial and commercial hub by weaving together a web of overseas territories into an offshore world, to which we now turn.

6

Offshore

At a London Superyacht Investor conference in 2017, one of the most popular sessions is reported to have been on cyber-crime.[1] IT expert Campbell Murray demonstrated at the exclusive event, held in a private members' club, how control of a nearby superyacht's navigation, Wi-Fi and communications systems could be hijacked in the space of a few hours by dedicated hackers. The promise of exclusive superyacht mobility and connectivity detached from the mainland entanglements of state regulation and public scrutiny has been compromised by new technologies, so the IT specialist appeared to be warning. As the world's super-rich transform their luxury vessels into offshore spaces not just of leisure, ostentation and elite networking, but also as mobile business centres, it is data and communications as well as the passengers on board the ship that have become targets of cybertheft, blackmail and extortion. Where they prove successful, the proceeds of such criminality by transnational mafias are likely to end up on the ledger of a shell bank account, trust fund or dummy corporation registered in one of the sixty estimated tax havens or 'secrecy jurisdictions' across the world.[2]

Many of these tax havens also offer the flag-of-convenience services we encountered in previous chapters, as in the case of Bermuda, where agrochemical mogul Andrey Melnichenko's £360 million *Sailing Yacht A* is registered.[3] Melnichenko's marine interests are not, however, merely recreational. One of his EuroChem Group factories near Kingisepp, in north-west Russia, has been associated with toxic phosphorus discharges into the river Luga, which flows into the Baltic Sea, thus prompting several international investigations into the source of the spillage and the subsequent construction of a surface water collection and treatment system to address the pollution.[4] This is one of countless illustrations of how the sea acts as a locus for the deep interconnection between luxury and waste, big business and organised crime, open registries and secret jurisdictions. Like thousands of other superyacht billionaires, Melnichenko displays part of his accumulated capital in one sea, but overlooks the contamination created by his agrochemical company (incidentally, headquartered in the Swiss tax haven of Zug) in another sea. All the while, fellow tax haven clients could – in the form of transnational criminal syndicates – also be the main threat to his maritime assets.

Linking and facilitating these global interactions is the concept and institution of the 'offshore'. At once an actual place and a legal fiction, the offshore world is characterised by exception and exemption: from the laws, regulations and oversight that obtain 'onshore' (be that a geographical mainland or a legal body of norms and conventions). This emphatically does not mean that offshore spaces are lawless or unregulated; nor does it mean that they are exclusively maritime. Secrecy jurisdictions stipulate severe penalties for any bank employee who discloses financial information, and tax havens jealously guard their juridical sovereignty – arguably their most lucrative asset. More precisely, perhaps, the offshore world is about legal differentiation: being connected to, but distinguished from, the onshore world. 'The "offshore"', political economist Ronen Palan notes, 'refers not to the geographical location of economic activities, but to the juridical status of a vast and expanding array of specialized realms.'[5] Many offshore centres – including landlocked flag-of-convenience states like Luxembourg, Mongolia or Bolivia – are firmly ensconced inland, and the offshore world covers a multitude of sins: money laundering, trafficking, tax avoidance and evasion, gambling and gaming, illicit Internet domains, waste dumping and penal colonies. Offshoring is also a process – 'a strategy of class warfare', as John Urry (echoing Warren Buffet) has argued.[6] But in this chapter we are interested less in the jurid-ico-political role of offshore as financial secrecy and its politi-cal economy, and more in the offshore as a general historical–sociological practice, concept and phenomenon in capitalist development, and the specific ways in which this interplays with the 'maritime factor'.[7]

At different junctures in the development of capitalism – especially since the mid-nineteenth century – offshoring has emerged as a device in furthering particular class and state interests, offering a mechanism for the unfettered concentration of wealth, the conduct of opaque political and commercial transactions, the practices of labour arbitrage explored in Chapter 2 on exploitation, and the disposal of unwanted excess, be it in the form of convicts or of contaminants. In all this, the sea and its islands have acted as a critical venue, both literally and figuratively, in the unfolding of these various capitalist pathologies: simultaneously a conduit for what in the Romance languages is rendered as offshore 'fiscal paradises', and a living hell for those entombed in slave ships or sentenced to hard labour in penal colonies; a utopian playground for capitalist libertarian advocates of deregulated 'free' markets, as well as a dump site for various toxins and forms of waste emitted by global capitalism (including those responsible for global envi-ronmental change today).

The offshore world often appears as a realm of exceptional freedom and experimentation, suspending all sorts of laws and regulations. It can be many of these things but also a domain anchored in, and authored by, the most political and territorial expressions of modern power: state sovereignty. That is, the offshore world is the product of (and is sustained by) onshore authority. Moreover, despite the sea not always being the only or principal locale for offshore practices, it does act as a physical repository for much of the surplus, excess and waste generated by capitalist accumulation. Here the *oceanic* offshore world is conceived, perceived and produced as a place where capitalist 'externalities' are absorbed in their environmental expression (acidification, dead zones, coral bleaching, carbon sinks and plastic garbage patches), in their sociopolitical forms (depredation, people trafficking, 'surplus' populations and 'dangerous' classes), or in the economic shape of tax evasion and avoidance. To that extent, the oceans are often presented as an 'outlaw' space, a domain for discarding and forgetting. Yet as we'll endeavour to show, such notions of the sea as an abject zone underplay the very terrestrial sources of marine alienation. Neoliberal capitalism in particular projects a conflictive and contradictory relationship with the sea: at times a new frontier of enterprise, efficiency and (upward) mobility; on other occasions, the ungoverned site of 'freedom, chaos, and criminality'.[8] There is, in our view, no easy reconciliation or resolution of such tensions and contradictions between (neoliberal) capitalism and the sea. Instead the offshore world reflects back onto the rest of the planet the intractability of our predicament, exposing the gross inequalities in wealth and power, and the potentially ruinous consequences of global warming.

Maritime utopias and insular infernos

An offshore sublime

Approximately 60 per cent of the world's tax havens are located in geographical islands, and only about a handful (including the admittedly powerful exceptions of Switzerland, Liechtenstein and Andorra) are not in coastal states. The English word 'haven' is derived from Old English (and apparently Old Icelandic too) for 'port' or 'harbour'.[9] Moreover, most secrecy jurisdictions – again measured both in numbers and in estimated value transferred – are former colonies, overseas dependencies of one sort or another, or reinvented medieval polities like the City of London, the Principality of Monaco or the Duchy of Luxembourg.[10] There is also an odd temporality involved, with the unsimultaneous historical overlap between today's rebranded offshore islands like Bermuda or Singapore, which not long ago acted as imperial outposts of slavery, indentured labour and convict transportation. What is it about islands that makes them a preferred location for 'fiscal paradises'? And what explains the historical continuity between the late twentieth-century financial innovation of the tax haven, and the juridico-political authority of past feudal and colonial institutions?

Our answer to these questions is twofold. One explanation is that small-island developing states (SIDS) often have few exports available to them economically beyond tourism and fish. Offshore banking allows SIDS to use sovereignty as a going concern – as with FOCs, their jurisdictions are for sale, and many SIDS have since the 1970s opted for this route to develop-ment.[11] For some, this means that '"offshore" centres such as the Cayman Islands and Jersey indicate how money and other flows are challenging our state centred conception of property rights and capital accumulation'.[12] But seen through a class-analytic lens, 'offshore' island jurisdictions in fact assume a form of *state property* – coordinating with finance capital and its advisers to capture a portion of surplus value from global capital flows by allowing for the maximisation of that capital's post-tax profitability.

While recognising that offshore financial centres, including SIDS, are the product of a specific legal feint conceived sometime in the late 1950s,[13] this chapter aims to provoke fresh conceptu-alisations of the 'offshore' as a more capacious category encom-passing both the social processes that are physically discharged at sea, or displaced overseas, and the particular maritime and island imaginaries that accompany such practices. We want, in other words, to insist that thinking of 'offshore' as a larger domain than just secrecy jurisdictions – one that combines both distinctive physical and imaginary attributes – can add to our understanding of the relationship between capitalism and the sea, and indeed of their own independent dynamics.

The second part of the answer to the questions just posed therefore focuses on the fantasy of maritime evasion from the bonds of terrestrial hierarchies; the offshore disdain for the crowded, demotic and conflictive mainland life which, like Verne's Captain Nemo (Nobody) finds its corollary in the Utopia (non-place) of the remote, pacified and private isolation on offer in the superyacht, residential cruise or secrecy jurisdiction. The offshore world displays a recurrent aspiration to simultaneously be everywhere and nowhere: to transcend geography by accessing all the global connectivity necessary to conduct business transactions, while also remaining hidden from the gaze of the general public, and the fiscal or law enforcement agencies of the state. As such, offshore centres adopt some of the qualities that Marc Augé identified with the 'non-places' of 'supermodernity' where the past is reduced to an exotic spectacle (former colonial infrastructure, from police stations to docks, are redeveloped as heritage trails and cruise ship stopovers), and what remains is an 'immense parenthesis' of a location dedicated to the incessant and anonymous transit and transfer of people, commodities, money and wealth.[14] There is no question, as dedicated students of the issue have shown, that an early twentieth-century emergence of tax havens across (often landlocked) jurisdictions, and the subsequent distinctive post-war global political economy, provided the conditions for the proliferation of today's offshore world – sometimes involving the accidental or opportunistic invention of instruments like the 'Eurodollar' market. Yet this universe of corporate transfer pricing, discretionary offshore trusts and absolute privacy is also animated by a utopian vision of the oceans as a space beyond the interference of politics and the nuisance of class antagonism. 'No taxes of any

kind in Cayman', the island's International Monetary Bank
has sloganeered. 'No reports to any government. Confidential
accounts with complete privacy'.[15]

In the West, islands have since the European Renaissance
served as the privileged geographical location for Utopia.
The late medieval and early modern insular utopias were inex-
tricably tied to the European 'discovery of the sea' and its
accompanying primitive accumulation of capital, to the extent
that, as John Gillis argues, the very conceptual separation
of sea islands from continental land masses was the product of
this period of overseas expansion.[16] Islands like the Canaries or
Madeira were 'a vital part of the symbolic discourse of early
colonialism, albeit an ambiguous part', in their combination of
eschatological, political, economic, geographical and environmental qualities central to the enterprise of conquest.[17] Such
islands came to represent earthly paradises, with their Edenic
abundance (not least of fresh water and timber), 'primitive'
natives requiring salvation and enslavement, a natural sea moat
that facilitated defence and control, and a strategic location en
route to El Dorado. Imperial needs were thus married to expansionist desires.

Among the many possible typologies, Enrico Nuzzo has
suggested that modern island utopias involve either a concrete
projection ('the construction of a new, cultural, artificial
world'), or a discovery ('an escape marked by the dream of a
naturally egalitarian reality').[18] More's *Utopia* belongs to the
former as, subsequent to their pacification by philosopher-king
Utopos, the indigenous population is put to work in building
the fifteen-mile canal separating the territory from its fictional
mainland, thereby creating the island idyll. However, even after
this foundational act of secession, household slavery continues
to feature in More's paradise – every Prospero has a Caliban,
every Robinson Crusoe a Man Friday. Like most modern insular utopias, the eminently violent political act of discovering,
conquering or creating treasure islands is consigned to an

accidental moment in the distant past: the existence of these polities is dependent on (financial) futures that erase histories of plunder, predation and enslavement.

The connection between the sea, overseas territories and the offshore world crystallised during the modern period in the intimate association between maritime imaginaries (most notably represented in the birth of the English novel) and the burgeoning institutions of credit explored in Chapter 1. The risks to, and opportunities for, enrichment afforded by the ocean vastness required leaps of faith on the part of entrepreneurs and the investing public which were in many important ways bridged by the 'dark arts of projectors' – men like Daniel Defoe or Jonathan Swift who 'engaged in fantastic speculation in order to convince others to invest in their imaginings, to give them credit and therefore substance'.[19] Fiction, credit, adventure, enterprise and wealth thus combined to produce by the start of the eighteenth century a social and political environment in England (and London in particular) conducive to the valorisation of activities and social relations at sea, its islands, and what lay beyond in the colonies. On this account, the English mercantile imagination of the sea at the time (in novels, ballads, maps and paintings) complements its physical control (in the shape of 'freedom of the seas') and the resource appropriation of islands and coastlines (through conquest, displacement and colonisation). Today's seemingly rhetorical description of offshore financial centres as fiscal *paradises* constructed on a legal *fiction* is in fact related to the very concrete mobilisation in previous centuries of collective imaginaries in the building of actual overseas colonial outposts, separate but connected to the metropolitan mainland, for the purposes of capital circulation and accumulation. Although, formally, the juridical entity of the offshore centre would not come into its own until the universalisation of sovereign territorial states in the course of the twentieth century, the imaginary of an offshore world was being carved out from the overseas territory long before then.

The infamous case of the South Sea Bubble neatly captures the activation of a distinctive offshore imagination in the 1700s through the interlacing of maritime trade, state formation, the City of London's financial revolution, and Britain's efforts at ruling the seas. Like scores of other joint-stock companies that had mushroomed in the City of London during the 1690s, the South Sea Company was launched in 1711 to an investing public increasingly familiarised with the risk, volatility and potential reward of speculating on a stock market built on trans-oceanic trade. Much like its predecessors – most notably the Bank of England – the company emerged from a City milieu characterised by the maritime networks of émigré traders, merchant subscribers and overseas investors, and was founded in response to a war-induced crisis in government debt (in this case, the War of Spanish Succession from 1701 to 1714). The new scheme's unique selling point, however, was the promise of monopolising the lucrative seaborne commerce across the South Atlantic shores (most significantly, appropriating from the Spanish the *Asiento* privileges over the import of slaves into South America), thus opening a new maritime frontier – which reportedly had, since the times of Francis Drake, played a signal role in the English popular imaginary – to the City of London.[20] 'An Establishment of a South-Sea Trade', a pamphlet attributed to Daniel Defoe proclaimed the day after the South Sea Company was presented to Parliament, 'must tend exceedingly to the good of all Degrees and Ranks of Men amongst us: the Poor will be more employ'd in manufactures, the Product of the Estates of our landed Men will become more valuable, and the Trading part of the Nation will be greatly encouraged'.[21]

Assisted by a flood of similar pamphlets, satirical ballads and topographical accounts, the South Sea Company did for many years capture the speculating public's imagination, together fostering, as one literary critic suggests, a set of linked figures and narratives that reflect the particular qualities of fluidity and energy that characterize this experience [of the seas] and to shape from a material encounter with the river of English commerce – the Thames – and the oceans of the world to which it reaches, a cultural fable, a composite story that gives meaning to a complex historical moment.[22]

In this way, a profound connection was established between the onshore liquidity of stocks and money on the banks of the Thames and the offshore flow of wealth from across distant seas into the City of London. Although the company's profitability has been the subject of much specialist debate, there appears to be no controversy over its creditworthiness among investors given the steady appreciation of company stock, from an initial £90 to a maximum of £120 in 1717. Nor was the South Sea Company's role in the Atlantic slave trade negligible, as it accounted for about a fifth of England's total traffic of enslaved Africans during those years. The notoriety of the South Sea Bubble thus rests mainly on its spectacular demise following the debt-for-equity swap conjured up by the seasoned financial speculator John Law and his broker sidekick John Blunt, which witnessed the wild inflation of company shares from £128 to £1,050 in the space of a year and their proverbial blowout in 1721 as the investing public finally

> stood blinking and disbelieving at what they saw before them: a company whose trading prospects had been non-existent in the past, and would be non-existent in the future . . . a company that was, quite nakedly, a machine for making profit out of debt reclamation, and not a trading enterprise at all.[23]

A fictional entity, in short, built on the promise of hegemony over distant seas.

Contemporary offshore treasure islands are in many respects an unintended legacy of this combination of conquest and artifice; the conditions of political marginalisation and economic underdevelopment which in the 1960s and 1970s encouraged many SIDS to rent out their sovereignty were in most cases facilitated by a history of colonial domination, appropriation and exploitation. At once exotic, exclusive, expensive and remote, the archetypal small-island secrecy jurisdiction today also offers the safety, stability and connectivity necessary for the discrete conduct of major international business transactions. The attraction of sociopolitical separation in the physical form of insularity is accompanied by the security of being firmly plugged into the legal, financial and communication networks of global capital, while retaining political control within a given jurisdiction. Smooth flows are guaranteed by solid infrastructures and sovereign authority. In their ethnography of the Caribbean luxury island resort of St Barts, Bruno Cousin and Sébastien Chauvin encounter all the tropes of an offshore sublime among the billionaire residents and aspiring visitors of this French overseas collectivity: 'today "St Barts" simultaneously connotes insular exclusiveness, tropical exoticism, French refinement and Euro-American cosmopolitanism, while evoking the transatlantic mobility inherent to luxury yachting'.[24] Like other elite yachting destinations across the world, St Barts was initially rediscovered and revalorised by tycoons such as David Rockefeller Sr, Edmond de Rothschild and Francis Goelet in the 1960s and 1970s. Although St Barts is now principally a high-end tourist destination, it is plainly integrated into the wider offshore world through both material legal–financial services and symbolic markers such as the omnipresence of premium brands or (over the Christmas period in particular) the latest gaggle of metropolitan celebrities. As in other comparable offshore spaces, unwanted traces of colonialism, slavery or oppression are erased through the imposition of new, invented 'cosmo-tropical' culinary, musical and architectural vernaculars built on an amalgam of other, distant but equally exotic locations in Africa, Asia and the Americas: the 'world cuisine' on offer in St Barts is devoid of Creole dishes, the playlists on the VIP dancefloors largely beat to a foreign rhythm, and the architectural designs conform to international styles recognisable in similar exclusive offshore locations.[25] Indeed, the confluence of on- and offshore jet-set lifestyles also finds its way into interior design, where top-end studios aim for a seamless continuity between private residence, automobile, aircraft and yacht: 'The key point of difference', says designer Francesca Muzio, whose work straddles the ship industry and super-luxe hotels like the London Shard's Shangri-La,

> is that the superyacht is more like a floating boutique hotel; you can change the panoramic every day if you wish – it is all about capturing the essence of the journey. We took the same philosophy for The Shard where we wanted to optimise the 180-degree views, so we chose clean, smooth lines and contoured furniture shapes . . . that allow us to achieve the stroboscopic effect, giving the impression of floating over the city, just like you float in water.[26]

While there is no disputing the performative dimensions of superyacht ownership (there to be admired by peers and plebeians alike), it is equally important to recognise these vessels as an investment and a means of travel.[27] The superyacht is certainly a status symbol given the stratospheric barriers to entry in acquiring and running one, but membership of this exclusive club also opens all manner of fresh business opportunities for proprietors and their associates. More significantly, the superyacht combines the mobility of the private jet and SUV with the home comforts of a private residence. It allows not just static segregation from the general public in the shape of the gated mansion or hypersecuritised apartment, but also mobile suspension from the ordinariness of the onshore world via the constant maritime circulation from one offshore haven to the next – a neoliberal version of Captain Nemo's *Nautilus, mobilis in mobile.*

If the superyacht has realised the utopia of 'floating boutique hotel' for the super-rich, residential cruise liners like *The World* have extended the privilege to the merely very wealthy.[28] Consisting of 165 apartments available for purchase (only those with a minimum net worth of US$10 million need apply), *The World* is marketed as 'the largest residential ship on the planet', since its launch in 2002, 'continuously circumnavigating the globe, spending extensive time in the most exotic and well-traveled ports, allowing Residents to wake up to a new destination every few days'.[29] The ship's name declares a cosmopolitan intent, as does the promise of a unique onboard 'Enrichment Program', including lectures on 'world cultures'. It is, moreover, a Norwegian-built, Bahamas-registered and American-operated ship. Intriguingly, the extensive online promotional gallery only shows white people (a dark-skinned cook can just about be discerned in the background picture for the vessel's Asian restaurant 'East'), and 130 resident families stem from a curiously selective geography: only nineteen countries in North America, Europe, Australia, South America, Asia and South Africa. An even more extreme version of the neoliberal 'floating island' fantasy is the Seasteading Institute, a think tank aiming to 'bring a start-up sensibility to the problem of government monopolies that don't innovate sufficiently' by constructing seasteading communities or floating cities at sea.[30] Co-founded, appropriately, by Milton Freedman's grandson Patri Friedman and 'technology entrepreneur, investor and philanthropist' Peter Thiel, the institute has recently revised its ambition to found a new city on the high seas, and is seeking instead to establish a seazone with a 'unique governing framework' within the territorial waters of French Polynesia.

However illusory, the prospect of 'social secession' from the mainland admixture of peoples and government rule reflected in these ventures suggests a continuity between the early modern

Figure 6.1. 'Aerial view of the island Utopia;
surrounded by waters with two sailing vessels,
standing in left foreground Morus and Hythlodaeus,
on right Petrus Aegidius' (top) and 'Floating
City, Seasteading Institute' (bottom)
Sources: British Museum (top) and Gabriel Scheare, Luke
Crowley, Lourdes Crowley, and Patrick White (bottom).

insular utopias and today's offshore world. There is certainly a direct comparison to be made with terrestrial gated communities, start-up cities and exclusive penthouses – plainly, many of the spatial strategies of segregation characteristic of these marine experiments are also present on land. Yet the permanent, seamless mobility and juridical autonomy afforded by the high seas, coupled with the possibility of only landing onshore in offshore locations, gives the oceans a special value for the world's super-rich and affluent seeking to distinguish themselves from the rest of society. What we have been calling the 'offshore sublime' – the awesome sense of floating above and beyond society – conjures up both the real and the imaginary power of the sea and its islands as places where dreams of exclusive luxury, detachment, discretion and freedom can come true.

Prisoners of paradise

The spatial dimensions of social inequality are starkly represented in the contrasting experiences of offshore mobility and confinement during the modern period. While propertied elites have over the past century or so sought anonymous retreat and liberty at sea, the very same islands and oceans have long before then acted as spaces of enslavement, transportation and retribution for subaltern classes and peoples. The former aim to elude wider society in secluded archipelagos and floating utopias; the latter think only of escaping from ships and islands where the most brutal forms of government deprive them of freedom. These dialectics of offshore autonomy and coercion are not purely contingent, as the infrastructures of global banishment – to penal colonies, or as bonded and indentured labour – are intimately connected to capitalist development, both during episodes of primitive accumulation and in the reproduction of global capitalism thereafter. Clearly, not all contemporary offshore centres have a past as convict settlements or slave plantations. But many do, and a consideration of the historical continuities sheds light on the otherwise forgotten links between accumulation and unfreedom in the offshore world.

Overseas transportation has been a constant means of punishment and exploitation across different societies since antiquity. From the galley slaves of successive Mediterranean empires to Japan's early modern island exile (*ontō*) of vagrants, gamblers and petty criminals, offshore banishment long pre-dates capitalism.[31] (In the Communist form of the Gulag 'archipelago' and Chinese re-education camps, it also clearly transcends capitalism). Yet the extensive and systematic re-mobilisation of overseas transportation during the long sixteenth century as a mechanism of both sentencing and settlement was in many ways tied to the development of capitalism in England and, later, the colonial world. Leaving aside the African slave trade proper (which belongs to a different scale of magnitude and had distinct socio-economic dynamics and cultural-political consequences), the drivers of, and destinations for, Euro-Asian and Pacific convict, indentured and bonded labour varied considerably through time and place. One common denominator, however, was the imperative of dealing with 'surplus' populations and 'dangerous' classes by redeploying them as forced labour in overseas colonial outposts. Initially targeted at vagabonds, outlaws, offenders and ethnic or religious minorities, banishment and transportation were subsequently extended to include political prisoners, debtors, paupers, and displaced or vanquished populations from both colony and metropole.[32] Again, though punishment (or profit) of some kind was the main impetus, the outcome was offshore relocation for the purposes of hard labour and colonisation.

Richard Hakluyt is often cited as a notable contemporaneous advocate of the colonial absorption of metropolitan expulsions. In his 'Discourse Concerning Western Planting', aimed at persuading notables and merchants, as well English monarch Elizabeth I, to invest in American and Caribbean colonies,

Hakluyt argues, 'The frye [children] of the wandering beggars of England that grow up idly, and hurteful and burdenous to this Realm may there be unladen, better bred up, and may people waste countries to the home and foreign benefit'.[33] Historians suggest Hakluyt's pleas were largely ignored initially, but that by the start of the seventeenth century courts in port cities like London and Bristol began to routinely banish both alleged minor offenders (before they were tried) and those sentenced to death (and then reprieved) to Barbados, Bermuda, St Christopher's (today's St Kitts) or Virginia.[34] Soon the English language acquired the term 'Barbadosed' to describe shipment under duress to the West Indies, which as a destination until the 1660s received more Britons than did the American colonies.[35] Civil war, Cromwell's colonisation of Ireland, the Highland clearances and the persecution and repression of rebels and ethnic and religious minorities all swelled the ranks of those forcibly dispatched across the Atlantic from the British Isles. Many contemporaries challenged the benefits of transportation, with one visitor to the island infamously claiming that Barbados had become 'the dunghill whereon England doth cast forth its rubbish'.[36]

By the end of the eighteenth century, the transatlantic population transfer had become unstoppable, with hundreds of thousands of English, Scots, Welsh and Irish men, women and children – about three-quarters of whom are estimated to have been bonded in some form or other – arriving on American and Caribbean shores as indentured servants, banished felons, persecuted Nonconformists, convict rebels or simple kidnap victims. Although unquestionably the outcome of diverse, often conflicting, logics of punishment, repression, social regulation and profit seeking, overseas transportation from Britain during the seventeenth and eighteenth centuries was closely intertwined with processes of enclosure, dispossession, appropriation, repression and state formation which accompanied the birth of the world's first capitalist nation. 'Crime,' Gwenda Morgan and

Peter Rushton have written of this period of primitive accumulation across both sides of the Atlantic, 'was therefore one of the links that bound colonies to the "mother country" . . . far from being invisible, punishment of criminals by transportation stimulated cultural and political exchanges between Britain and its colonies.'[37] The sea here becomes a unique geographical marker of both separation and connection: it generates a form of distancing that allows state authorities to outcast whole populations in the name of 'cleansing' the metropole, while at the same time projecting demographic power onto colonised overseas territories. The dual role of the ocean-space thus involves acting as an unfathomable void separating 'home' from 'overseas' (and by extension 'offshore' from 'onshore'), while simultaneously allowing the appropriation and exploitation of faraway lands, peoples and resources through the infrastructure of an integrated overseas empire.

Two world-historical processes – the Atlantic revolutions and the abolition of the African slave trade – transformed the nature and geography of marine transportation in the nineteenth century. Following the American proclamation of independence, Britain's remaining Atlantic colonies acquired even greater economic and strategic relevance. Bermuda – the island said to have inspired Shakespeare's 'brave new world' in *The Tempest* – received over 9,000 British and Irish transportees in the four decades between the 1823 Act of Parliament authorising the shipment of convicts to the colonies and its closure in 1863 as a penal station. Their forced labour was dedicated to building breakwater defences and a Royal Naval dockyard in this crucial staging post between loyalist Canada and the motherland.[38] Thus Bermuda extended its function as a major commercial entrepôt, shipping centre and sometime smuggling hub in the offshore Atlantic.

The protracted and uneven replacement of slavery with other labour regimes in the Americas and West Indies, coupled with the eastwards turn in Britain's 'second empire' after the loss of its thirteen American colonies, made the southern hemisphere the new focus of transportation. Here the Straits Settlements and Singapore in particular became paradigmatic of the mid-nineteenth century mobilisation of convict labour for the purposes of empire-building. The estimated 20,000 South Asian felons transported between 1790 and 1857 by the East India Company to the Straits Settlements (Penang, Malacca and Singapore) were put to work on draining marshlands; fortifying shorelines; and building roads, piers, embankments, bridges, lighthouses and squares, and subsequently were tasked with maintaining this public infrastructure (including the culling of stray dogs).[39] Recidivist offenders, radical insurgents, mutineers, murderers, robbers and thieves were also offshored to the plantation colonies of Mauritius, Seychelles, Burma and eventually beyond, to Natal, Fiji or the West Indies. Transportation and re-transportation across the oceans – whether as a malfeasant or an indentured worker – thus became an integral part of imperial circulation, physically connecting disparate outposts of empire not just via administrative coordination and communication networks but also, and crucially, through the forced transfer of colonial subjects in the population of overseas territories with exceptional juridical status. 'Its widespread appeal as a penal sanction,' Clare Anderson says of transportation, 'was also closely associated to the display of colonial strength that the permanent removal of social undesirables surely represented.'[40]

In the course of the nineteenth century, mass migrations of peoples across continents made the distinction between transportation, banishment, indentured labour and voluntary emigration ever more fluid, with many convicts using their 'ticket of leave' to relocate in different colonies, while nominally consensual and waged 'coolie' or 'lascar' labour was often 'Shanghai'ed' (impressed or abducted) to work in the mines, docks, plantations or ships that characterised the globalisation of industrial capitalism. The offshore world was therefore always a part of an overseas colonial complex, but the two were plainly not coterminous. Countries like Japan, China or the lands of the Ottoman Empire that had not been subject to formal European colonisation exported millions of workers (both free and indentured) to the Americas and the Caribbean, as well as anglophone colonies like Hawaii, Guam and Fiji (albeit in far smaller numbers). Meanwhile, European imperial powers old and new dotted parts of their colonial possessions with recently inaugurated or revitalised penal stations like those in islands off New Caledonia or French Guiana, where the state hoped to cast out and contain the 'criminal classes' which they claimed were degenerating the republic.

The French experience is especially instructive when exploring the contradictory mobilities of the offshore world as it evolved in tandem with capitalist industrialisation. Much in the same way that vagrancy, crimes against property and threats to public order had exercised authorities governing the unfolding of agrarian capitalism in Stuart England, a moral panic over the mobility, dissoluteness and insubordination of a growing nineteenth-century urban proletariat led the French government to seek a solution in overseas imprisonment. Established in 1852 and 1863 respectively, the offshore penal stations (*bagnes*) in French Guiana and New Caledonia at their height held just over 17 per cent of France's total prison population.[41] Among the *bagnards* were common law criminals and repeat offenders, but also political prisoners like Alfred Dreyfus (who spent four years of his life sentence on Devil's Island in French Guiana) and thousands of *communards* exiled to New Caledonia after the 1870–1871 insurrection. Thus the figure of the vagabond – incorrigibly idle, unproductive yet also dangerous in his/her deracination – was combined by the forces of order with that of the revolutionary – subversive, unpatriotic and morally devious – to generate a fear of mobility and mobilisation within French society. This generalised anxiety around the seemingly uncontrollable alliance between crime, unemployment, movement and insurrection, Stephen Toth suggests, 'was rooted in a profound demographic shift that swept poor and uneducated workers out of the rural countryside and into the streets of Paris and other urban areas in search of employment and a better life'.[42] Such a social malaise was often represented by reformers and reactionaries alike as urban France's problem with 'refuse and dead weight' populations polluting and degrading the country's moral order. The answer was to transport these undesirable Frenchmen and -women to overseas colonies – as one contemporary put it – 'to purify Paris by removing those perverted beings teeming its gutters ... who pose a permanent danger for public security'.[43]

The offshore confinement of France's criminal classes in response to the social maladies of industrial mobility during the belle époque represents the flip side of the freedom of the seas we have explored in this and other chapters. The offshore sublime which from the beginning of the twentieth century has drawn the world's super-rich to remote islands and exclusive harbours is, as we have seen, literally founded on the environmental, cultural and socio-economic infrastructure built, exploited and maintained by convicts, slaves, servants and 'coolies' displaced during previous centuries of capitalist development, first in the Atlantic world and thereafter across other oceans. The historical causality is, to be sure, by no means linear: the dialectic of offshore freedom and captivity played itself out discontinuously (with new penal colonies opening as others closed, one overseas migration route replacing another) and unevenly (indentured and bonded labour substituting slavery in plantation colonies). Nor is the geographical definition of the offshore world always clear and settled – though in many cases overlapping, the terms 'colony', 'overseas' and 'offshore' were combined and differentiated in diverse spatio-temporal settings by state authorities, merchants, human traffickers and financiers. These caveats notwithstanding, it is difficult to make full sense of today's offshore world without incorporating the history of prior accumulation in both the colonies and the metropole. Secrecy jurisdictions and penal stations have been legally differentiated, but never politically detached, from onshore authority. Far from being a historical anomaly or socio-political irregularity, the offshore islands explored above have constituted an integral component of capitalist development, acting as a destination for the excess (profits, populations, pollutants) generated in the process. The key social characteristic of the oceanic offshore world – its juridical distinction from the mainland – has combined with the geographical features of remoteness and isolation to deliver a crucial outlet for all manner of market surpluses and externalities.

Remnants of empire

With anything between a quarter and a third of the globe's total wealth registered in secrecy jurisdictions, their place in the world economy is in no way marginal. Tax havens and offshore financial centres are important, even if not indispensable, to the reproduction of contemporary capitalism because they allow the rich (both individuals and corporations) to get richer, as well as providing a significant source of revenue and economic activity for host governments and fees for the Big Four and other accounting firms.[44] On some mainstream accounts, the mushrooming of fiscal paradises in the 1960s and 1970s was the opportunistic response to the liberalisation of international financial markets that accompanied the internationalisation of capital during the long post-war boom.[45] The erosion and eventual collapse of the Bretton Woods system, coupled with the flood of petrodollars into the world economy after 1973, accelerated the process of neoliberal deregulation, conventional wisdom suggests. The so-called Eurodollar market, managed from the City of London but trading in international deposits that lie outside the jurisdiction of any particular state, is generally seen as the origin of what subsequently became offshore financial centres.

288

However, despite offshore financial centres also often acting as tax havens, the two have not always historically coincided. Any sovereign jurisdiction can theoretically act as a 'tax haven' for non-resident asset holders given the difference in tax regimes across countries. Toward the end of the nineteenth century, an 'incorporation game' developed – initially on the eastern American seaboard and subsequently in the European heartlands – whereby rival states (or cantons in the Swiss case) competed for outside investment, 'not necessarily in lowering corporate taxation – which in any case was quite low – but in offering a more permissive environment for corporations'.[46] As the twentieth century progressed, the incorporation in different jurisdictions of private multinational firms like William and Edward Vestey's food transport and retail emporium enabled the development of an international network of subsidiary companies linked to a holding parent company in a low-tax jurisdiction, thus spreading liabilities in such a way as to avoid taxation. Speaking of early attempts by the League of Nations to regulate international taxation during the interwar period, Nicholas Shaxson wryly observes, 'The multinationals had turned a system designed to avoid double taxation into one of double *non*-taxation.'[47]

Today's offshore financial centres are therefore a circuitous and, in many respects, inadvertent outcome of legal reforms, corporate legislation and competing jurisdictions which accompanied the globalisation of capitalism at the end of the nineteenth century. They are, however, inconceivable without the practice of territorial sovereignty, which, as a 'legal fiction', establishes discrete jurisdictions, guarantees property rights, regulates differentiated financial and tax regimes, and enables the distinction between beneficial ownership and legal registration, all of which are then exploited by capitalist firms and individuals. Physical location plays more than a circumstantial role in this equation in the double sense that offshore centres have a peculiar historical geography, and insofar as offshore asset holders need to define their residency. In the end, offshoring is an exercise in creative dislocation, most cynically displayed in the so-called 'Sark Lark', where 'City of London directors would sail in [to the Channel Island of Sark], eat lunch, pretend to have a directors' meeting to tick the British regulators' boxes, then return, inebriated, to London.'[48]

Venerable state institutions like the Bank of England or the UK Treasury were, and continue to be, protagonists in the reproduction of the Anglosphere's global offshore network centred in the City of London. Gary Burn's path-breaking study of the origins of the Euromarkets makes a persuasive case for the centrality of the newly nationalised Bank of England in facilitating the rise of this offshore money market during the late 1950s and early 1960s.[49] Acting as an institutional conduit between the City's private financiers and the Treasury's public servants, the Bank of England allowed some of its leading officials at the time – Sir George Bolton is one, Lord Cromer another – to build a case for a parallel, unregulated market in US dollars operating from the City of London, but outside any national jurisdiction. 'The Eurodollar market,' Burn indicates, 'evolved . . . out of a non-regulatory vacuum in the City.'[50] The poster child of post-war financial neoliberalism was thus the offspring of a relationship between the City and the British state, with the latter acting as the absent parent.

In a partial inversion of the centre–periphery relationship, overseas variants of Euromarkets quickly established themselves first in the Channel Islands, then in Britain's Caribbean overseas territories, and eventually in its (now former) colonies of Hong Kong and Singapore. Indeed, Sir George Bolton himself lost no time, on leaving his post at the Bank of England, in setting up the Bank of London and Latin America in 1957, soon expanding its operations to the Bahamas, Cayman Islands and Antigua. Together with other outlying anglophone offshore centres, this global matrix of secrecy jurisdictions forms a 'spider's web' of banking, insurance, money laundering, shipping and trust management services which together act as the chief overseas lenders to UK-based banks.[51] For those plugged into the City network, they offer access to services across all the major financial time zones and to the world's strategic economic gateways.

From the perspective of institutional or global political economy, the causal connections between offshore development and neoliberalism are fairly uncontroversial. But a focus on the historical geography of offshore centres also sheds light on the imperial, mercantilist continuities in today's fiscal paradises. For a start, the transactional benefits accrued from a shared language and legal system (English and common law in the British case) are hardly natural. As we saw earlier, several centuries of colonial domination underpin the acculturation of Europe's treasure islands (including relative latecomers such as Singapore and Hong Kong) to the norms, customs, values and institutions prevailing onshore. Tellingly, all the major anglophone Caribbean offshore centres bar the Bahamas have retained their status as British overseas territories, replicating the arrangements characteristic of 'informal empire' where foreign affairs, defence and policing are the preserve of the motherland, while the law, economic policy and provision of public services are devolved to local authorities. Indirect rule is represented in the figure of a London-appointed governor (true of Singapore and Hong Kong too, until independence) who shares governance responsibilities with a local cabinet and small legislative assemblies (once more, until recently only partially elected through direct and universal suffrage). Closer to home, the peculiar status of the Isle of Man and the Channel Islands as Crown dependencies also licenses unrepresentative forms of 'self-government' that mirror the Corporation of London's own opaque governance structures. It is precisely their heteronomous character that grants these archipelagic remnants of empire a unique jurisdictional power. The possibility of exploiting regulative loopholes or fiscal incentives is accentuated by the differentiated, yet interconnected, sovereignty of London-centred island havens.

Language, law, governance and time zone are, therefore, some of the principal advantages of the Anglosphere's global tax haven complex. But it is a material infrastructure of communications that literally connects these assets, and here imperial traces are also readily identifiable. As discussed in the preceding chapter, the laying of submarine transatlantic telegraph cables at the end of the nineteenth century by British-subsidised companies linked the metropole to its Caribbean colonies and beyond to Cuba, Panama, Florida and Nova Scotia. Bermuda and the Turks and Caicos Islands became critical nodal points in this newly consolidated imperial communications network, thereby not just facilitating inter-colonial rule and commerce, but also connecting Britain and its empire to the emerging American markets.[52] Such enterprises entailed the mobilisation and coordination of engineers, technicians, construction workers and operatives, which in turn fostered an inter-colonial and circum-Caribbean migration that integrated otherwise small, outlying and sparsely populated islands into a wider political, economic and cultural universe. By the time Cayman, Bermuda, Turks and Caicos and the British Virgin Islands had become the focus of attention for offshore pioneers in the 1960s and 1970s, these places and their populations already had a history of exposure to, and incorporation into, the metropolitan onshore world.

It is certainly essential, as Bill Maurer insists, not to read back into these histories some inevitable, direct and cumulative progression from colonial outpost to offshore tax haven – there are very contingent political and economic reasons why the Cayman Islands is today the fifth-largest offshore centre and Jamaica is not; or why Singapore was transformed into a world city and Aden has not. But plainly any account of the proliferation in offshore secrecy jurisdictions that begins with the rise of the Euromarkets after 1957 misses the essential role of a pre-existing material and sociocultural infrastructure that underpinned the reinvention of these British colonies as global financial centres. Contrary to a vision of the offshore world that transcends geography and floats, ether-like, above and beyond the terrestrial moorings of the onshore world, fiscal paradises must be seen as residues of a vanished maritime empire which have repurposed much of their colonial heritage – language, law, governance systems and communications infrastructure – to service global finance in a post-colonial setting. They are therefore neither an aberration nor anachronistic – some purely accidental outcome of market imperfection – but rather the result of deliberate, if opportunistic, strategies to exploit the geographical distance and juridical differentiation afforded by the sea. Physical location may today appear incidental to their success as financial hubs, but the history of these treasure islands reveals a much longer, and deeper, interpenetration with imperial geographies which established the foundations for the City of London's contemporary 'spider's web' of tax havens.

For all the technological developments, financial innovations, market competition and transnational integration associated with globalisation, physical location continues to play a crucial part in the configuration of the offshore world. In a purely material sense, the combination of easy and reliable access to the world's major financial centres (principally the City of London) and the provision of distinctive, specialist services (captive insurance in Bermuda, trust funds in Cayman, private banking in Jersey, and so forth) under an autonomous, common law and British-oriented jurisdiction are all products of a unique historical geography that has the sea at its core. The Anglosphere's treasure islands replicate across different time zones the 'confluence of services' pioneered in London during England's 'first' maritime empire at the end of the sixteenth century. (City of London firms continue today to play a critical role not just in shipping, maritime insurance and finance, but also in managing ransom payments for clients whose employees have been held hostage by sea pirates.) Although offshore financial centres as we know them today are more recent inventions, the product of a specific post-war global economic conjuncture, they are functionally rooted in previous centuries of overseas colonial administration, and in the Caribbean case retain their formally dependent association with the mother country. Equally important, we have argued, is the utopian imagination that has accompanied offshore development. For these treasure islands also actualise the ambition of an enclosed space, separate but connected to the rest of the world, where free market principles can be enforced by a stable authority with minimum fuss and maximum privacy. They act, in fact, as concrete utopias.

A forgotten space?

The offshore practices and institutions we have thus far explored aim to hide or erase any record of their activities, unless it is to remind unruly peoples of the perils of banishment. Casting off undesirable populations, evading prying revenue authorities, suppressing painful memories of servitude and violence are all part of the offshore project. This process of disposal and neglect is especially true of the contamination of the sea. Since the ocean surface occludes physical traces of that which has passed through it, the sea becomes a favoured depository of much which the terrestrial world wishes to discard and conceal – a forgotten space, as Sekula and Burch would have it, which is out of sight and therefore out of mind, submerged under the waves. The sea's liquid properties dilute the effluents of modern society, and its vast mass is used to soak up atmospheric heat, carbon emissions, nuclear detonations, oil slicks and leakages, among other human-induced toxins. And yet a growing realisation that the sea is a vital organ of our biosphere has resulted in various initiatives to conserve, protect and revive precarious marine habitats.[53] The oceans have thus also become a place for experimentation with zoning and governance systems aimed at guaranteeing the sustainable reproduction of marine life in all its precious diversity. Global warming has added to this focus on the sea as a barometer of climate change, with the oceans themselves being transformed through their role as a carbon sink and heat absorber. As rising sea levels threaten not just the survival of millions living in coastal areas but also the very existence of low-lying island states, the welfare of the ocean world clamours for our attention. The offshore world seems to be washing back onshore.

Midway Atoll offers a good vantage point for considering this contradictory confluence of waste and accumulation. Annexed by America in the late nineteenth century as part of its imperial expansion into the Pacific, by the early twentieth century Midway Atoll had become a strategic communications station and military base for the USA. After the Japanese attacks on Pearl Harbour and Midway in 1941, the decisive naval battle near the atoll in the summer of 1942 (where the Japanese fleet suffered severe losses at the hands of the US Navy) secured its place as a critical offshore resource for Washington's war efforts in Korea and later Vietnam. With the end of the Cold War, the territory was declared a National Wildlife Refuge administered by the US Department of the Interior. 'Midway Atoll's three small islands,' an official website today states, 'provide a virtually predator-free safe haven for the world's largest albatross colony encircled by a ring of coral reef that hosts an amazing variety of unique wildlife including green sea turtles, spinner dolphins, and endangered Hawaiian monk seals among an unprecedented rate of endemic fish.'[54] The fairy tale transition from war theatre to bird sanctuary thus appears to be complete. Visitors to this website will, however, search in vain for any information on the estimated twenty tons of man-made debris (a quarter of which is fed to the nesting chicks of the atoll) that washes up on Midway shores, or is ensnared on the island's coral reef. Overwhelmingly composed of plastics, the rubbish landing on this exceptional wildlife refuge is drift material separated from a 3.5 million-square-kilometre 'garbage patch' driven by the North Pacific gyre – one of five permanently circulating across the Pacific, Atlantic and Indian Oceans. Experts find it difficult to establish exact quantities, but it has been estimated that anything between 4.8 to 12.7 million metric tons of plastic waste finds its way *every year* from land to sea, and that a minimum of 5.25 trillion pieces of plastic, weighing over 250,000 tons, float on the ocean's surface.[55] The highest figures in these admittedly conservative calculations barely reach 5 per cent of the estimated plastic waste produced annually by coastal states, but they do nonetheless highlight the pervasiveness of plastic's presence at sea, with deleterious effects on both marine wildlife and the microorganisms that reproduce unique coastal and deep-sea ecosystems.[56]

In the whirl of media clamour and public outrage at the offshore impacts of our use of plastics, many of us now carry tote bags and reusable coffee cups and water bottles, and mainstream policy attention has been (temporarily) captured, such as the EU advancing an insipidly narrow Single Use Plastics Directive. But this emphasis on plastics pollution is disproportionate as it remains a minor concern compared to ocean acidification, warming and overfishing. Perhaps this is explained in part because this offshore waste washes very visibly back onshore – over 80 per cent of 'marine litter' in the EU is plastic, which is measured as counts of *beach* litter[57] – and also in part because consumer-centred 'solutions' and quick technological 'fixes' readily present themselves in this case – individualised shopping choices among the world's privileged minority are, once again, able to Save the World, but without, of course, interfering with the lifestyles that underpin capitalist accumulation. Meanwhile, bottled water sales topped US beverage sales for the second year running in 2017 and boomed in the UK's equal-hottest summer on record in 2018, and, globally, bottled water offers capital a '$334 Billion Opportunity' by 2023, compared to 2015 global sales of US$185 billion.[58]

That plastic is a derivative of the oil industry underscores the positive feedback loops involved in making the sea a dump site for onshore waste. Petroleum itself flows to sea principally as river run-off, from tankers and refineries, and only in smaller measure as a result of accidental spills or offshore oil production. It combines with other contaminants (chemicals, sewage, metals) dredged, discharged or extracted from coastal areas and beyond to produce a poisonous cocktail of societal waste that has entered the marine food chain and contributes to various visible and invisible forms of pollution, ranging from eutrophication to microplastics in fish. But it is the combustion of oil, with the accompanying release of greenhouse gases (GHGs), which is most accentuating the interaction between climate change and the oceans. The global ocean can store fifty times more carbon, and has a thousandfold greater heat capacity, than the atmosphere.[59] And so it is that the world's oceans are acting as the primary heat sink in our biosphere – like a cooling agent for accelerating global production. Around 90 per cent of the Earth's excess energy – anthropogenic heating – since the 1950s has been absorbed by the world's oceans.[60] As Andreas Malm has so powerfully shown, this outcome has its roots in the class antagonism of capital seeking to wield greater power over labour through the control of mobile energy (coal) in industrialising Britain.[61] Put directly, the underlying social relations producing 1,500 billion tons of carbon by the twenty-first century from the burning of fossil fuel were always socially and spatially unequal, as will be the consequences.[62] As such, the current geological Age of Humans – the Anthropocene – may well be more accurately couched as the Age of Capital – the Capitalocene.[63] Prominent earth systems scientists have taken on board this point and now differentiate among 'humanity as a whole', both between countries and within them, and stress that 'most of the human imprint on the Earth System is coming from the OECD world'.[64] They also underline that while the origins of the Anthropocene lie in the nineteenth century, the Great Acceleration of this imprint can be dated to the post-war era. Indeed, of all the heat taken in by the oceans between 1865 and 2015 almost half was imbibed in the last two decades *alone*.[65] To put this in perspective, each year the oceans absorb an equivalent in heat energy to '150 times the energy humans produce as electricity annually'.[66] As might be expected, the majority is accumulated in the upper layers – the epipelagic and mesopelagic zones to 700 metres in depth. But over a third is stored in the deep waters below this and the heat here is 'steadily rising'.[67] This means that the oceans will continue to heat the atmosphere even if GHG emissions were to end tomorrow.

Marine microorganisms like phytoplankton have proved critical in sequestrating the carbon dioxide captured in the seas, while ocean circulation redistributes atmospheric heat horizontally across latitudes and vertically from the surface to the seabed, thus securing some equilibrium in global temperatures above and below sea level. The problem is that such capabilities have natural limitations, and their long-term consequences are by definition not immediately discernible. The more carbon is incorporated into the ocean, the more pH is reduced to levels that compromise the marine ecosystem's capacity to calcify carbohydrates. The warmer saltwater becomes, the greater its expansion and the lighter its volume, thus reducing the sea's overturning circulation (i.e. encouraging a noxious stratification of ocean layers).[68] This in turn has the effect of drastically altering the distribution of oxygen, nutrients and biodiversity in the global ocean, as well as potentially changing major currents, precipitation patterns, seasonal winds and cloud cover – all of which reinforces existing marine pollution, overfishing and proliferation of invasive species caused by the 'deadly trio' of warming, acidification and deoxygenation present in previous global mass extinction events.[69] The deadly trio combined with overfishing threatens in particular large-bodied animals living at the top of trophic levels in the oceans' ecosystems. Their removal 'from the modern oceans, unprecedented in the history of animal life, may disrupt ecosystems for millions of years even at levels of taxonomic loss far below those of previous mass extinctions'.[70] This is a *likely* oceanic outcome of 'business as usual' for global capitalism.

The Atlantic Meridional Overturning Circulation (AMOC) – aka the Gulf Stream – is weakening. As we learned at school, warm water from the Gulf of Mexico is carried towards the North Pole, where it cools down and sinks, returning south. Anthropogenic global warming has been weakening this natural ocean system, especially since the mid-1970s, and has been identified as 'an unprecedented event in the past millennium'.[71] The AMOC reached a new low in the 2010s, having weakened by 15 per cent since the mid-1950s.[72] Greater volumes of fresh meltwater in the northern Atlantic from the Greenland Ice Sheet will accelerate this process in a positive feedback loop. The rapid Greenland Ice Sheet melt during the extreme heat of the summer of 2012 grabbed headlines as it threatened to intensify this feedback loop as well as rapidly raise sea levels – Greenland's ice holds over seven metres of sea-level-equivalent mass. North of Greenland, temperature peaks in February 2018 resulted in the breaking up for the first time of sea ice in the Last Ice Area – old, four-metre-thick ice that was expected to act as a bastion against the Great Melt.[73]

As on the land, heatwaves in the oceans can be a natural, cyclical phenomenon such as the El Niño southern oscillation, but they are intensifying in frequency and length with anthropogenic climate change. Global average annual marine heatwave days increased by 54 per cent between 1925 to 2016.[74] Marine heatwaves are regionalised and varied. Certain regions of the Atlantic, Indian and Pacific Oceans are especially vulnerable and the extreme heat can cause widespread mortality, undermining biodiversity and even entire ecosystems, including critical species in the lower trophic levels such as corals, kelps and seagrasses which underpin the marine food pyramid.[75] The most vulnerable species are living near the edge of their biological warm limits and there has been an observed push polewards by over 100 kilometres following marine heatwaves. The implications for non-human life and its appropriation, especially by small-scale fishers in the global South, are profound.

While it is important to emphasise that global oceanic warming and the ice sheet melt is not just about sea level rise, this remains an existential threat and the most literal example of the sea biting us back. The oceans are already rising, in part because of the Great Melt, in part through connected ocean heating, as water expands when it warms. Between 1901 and 2010, the global mean sea level increased by nineteen centimetres, which the Intergovernmental Panel on Climate Change's 2014 consensus science exercise pointed out, with 'high confidence', is 'larger than the mean rate during the previous two millennia'.[76] Projections by the IPCC based on an ensemble of models in 2014 compare 2081–2100 sea level rise to that of 1986–2005 and range from twenty-six centimetres to fifty-five centimetres for the best-case scenario, and between forty-five and eighty-two centimetres for the worst case. While sea level rise will always be uneven within and across oceanic regions, it *will* impact 95 per cent of the global ocean area.

But given the fast-moving nature of advances in scientific modelling and the emergence of new observed data, the IPCC's 2014 probabilistic estimates are even more conservative than was originally assumed.[77] The systemic effects of tipping points are notoriously difficult to factor in to models because of the no-analogue state and the sheer complexity of interactions – the surprising acceleration of the Great Melt noted above is one. Another actually existing global environmental change discovered since the IPCC's Fifth Assessment Report in 2014 draws on twenty-five years of satellite altimeter measurements. It shows that sea level rise is not increasing at a steady rate, as was previously assumed and modelled, but is *accelerating incrementally*.

These *observed* data double prior best-case projections for total global sea level rise to around sixty-five centimetres by 2100.[78] Further, the most commonly used climate simulations – including those that informed the 2015 Paris Agreement – do not examine the *feedbacks* between cryosphere, ocean and atmosphere as a consequence of ice sheet melting. In the context of growing evidence that we have passed the tipping points for certain ice sheets, a new simulation of their melting shows that warm water will be trapped below the ocean surface by meltwater from Antarctica, creating a feedback loop that *increases* the decline of Antarctic ice; at the same time, meltwater from Greenland will substantially slow down the AMOC.[79] In this context, the National Oceanic and Atmospheric Administration, a far from alarmist organisation, project a new 'scientifically plausible' worst case of sea level rise of up to 250 centimetres by 2100.[80]

Sea level rise will continue well after global warming has stopped. The IPCC is *virtually certain* that it will continue to rise for centuries beyond the entirely arbitrary 2100 cut-off point. Even if GHG emissions peak in 2035 and reach net zero in the second half of the twenty-first century – and there is no evidence to suggest that it will be without revolutionary social change – the median global sea level will continue to rise until at least 2300.[81] Gravitational effects, subsidence and the rebound effect of ice sheet melting mean that any rise will be experienced unevenly. The most vulnerable are people living in the global South in low-elevation coastal zones and in areas exposed to storm surges, especially in China, India, Bangladesh, Indonesia and Vietnam, as well as projected populations living on West and East African coasts.[82]

Oceanographers and other marine scientists have over the past few decades alerted the wider public to the tight and potentially destabilising interconnections between climate crisis and our aquatic world. The sea is no longer a forgotten space for those concerned with global warming. Yet the inherent contradiction between the daily reproduction of a global fossil economy and the multilateral attempts at combating climate change is particularly salient in the experience of a shrinking cryosphere. As global warming accelerates the contraction of planetary ice sheets, ice caps, glaciers and sea ice, all kinds of catastrophic environmental changes, ranging from ocean expansion to the intensification of extreme weather patterns, appear on the horizon.

The maritime transport sector is acutely aware of these hazards, as storm surges, increased precipitation, sea level rise and more intense and frequent tropical cyclones all combine to raise the risk and cost of seaborne trade.[83] At the same time, however, thinning ice cover opens up the possibility in coming decades of seasonal navigation across the Arctic Northwest and Northern Passages. This is one important reason why China, India, Japan, Singapore and South Korea – alongside other decidedly non-polar European states – have been granted observer status in the Arctic Council. Even though the economic viability of these northern sea routes has been questioned on account of the limited port infrastructure and market calculations relating to bunker fuel prices, insurance premiums or global economic demand, the fact remains that such channels would shorten the transit time of goods from East Asia to Europe by anything between 35 and 60 per cent compared to the conventional southern route through the Malacca Straits and the Suez Canal.[84] For economies reliant on overseas trade there are therefore some perverse benefits attached to global warming.

Another reason for resource-hungry states' interest in the Arctic region is the possibility of bioprospecting, mineral extraction and hydrocarbon exploitation facilitated by the receding ice. The estimates vary considerably, but a 2008 analysis by the US Geological Survey suggested that 'the total mean undiscovered conventional oil and gas resources of the Arctic are estimated to be approximately 90 billion barrels of oil, 1,669 trillion cubic feet of natural gas, and 44 billion barrels of natural gas liquids' – about 22 per cent of the global undiscovered conventional oil and gas resources.[85] *None* of which can be burned if humanity wishes to stay within global warming of more than 2 °C.[86] The four major oil- and gas-producing Arctic states (Russia, the USA, Canada and Norway) have increased their output exponentially since the 1970s and have recently been joined by small producers Greenland and Faroe Islands, opening some 20 per cent of the land area and 17 per cent of the marine area north of 60° to oil and gas fields.[87] Regardless of the enduring technical and logistical challenges of operating in extreme climatic conditions, the Arctic region continues to attract major energy investment. A warming world has paradoxically also intensified research into unique polar habitats and their biodiverse organisms, making the Arctic the latest frontier in commercial bioprospecting for food technologies, cosmetics, enzymes with industrial and life science applications and nutritional supplements, as well as medicine and pharmaceuticals.[88] As the world's polar ice caps melt, companies like Unilever have genetically modified antifreeze proteins present in Arctic eels for the commercialisation of low-fat ice cream. However much global temperatures rise, we will at least be able to cool down enjoying a cone of Wall's Soft Scoop Vanilla Light.

Reference to biotechnological and energy frontiers is entirely apposite in this context since, beyond the perception of a scramble for resources, the governance of these new spaces of appropriation remains complex and contested. Earlier chapters have shown how the 'Area' and the high seas beyond EEZs are only partially regulated by the International Seabed Authority for mining concerns, and by regional fisheries management organisations for highly migratory species. The principles of conservation and sustainability nonetheless permeate the conception of these offshore spaces, once again reflecting experimentation at sea with models of governance and regulation which adopt some of the onshore practices of land management. In the face of global climate change, the 'zoning' of marine reserves and protected areas has emerged as an alternative mode of territorialising the sea. Marked by the shift from a purely 'species' approach to marine management to one that incorporates 'spaces' (particularly coastal zones), marine spatial planning, according to UNESCO, is 'a public process of analysing and allocating the spatial and temporal distribution of human activities in marine areas to achieve ecological, economic, and social objectives that are usually specified through a political process', with marine protected areas (MPAs) as the specific delineation of zones of permitted and non-permitted uses of marine resources.[89] The Aichi Biodiversity Targets set out in 2010 under the Convention on Biological Diversity included a commitment to designate at least 10 per cent of coastal and marine waters as MPAs by 2020. In 2019 there were almost 15,000 MPAs covering 23 million square kilometres, or about 18 per cent of national waters, and just over 1 per cent of the high seas.[90] This has been driven by very large MPAs (VLMPAs) of over 100,000 square kilometres, which are principally in the overseas countries and territories of France, the UK and the USA – reiterating the imperialist and Cold War geopolitical legacies of contemporary ocean ordering discussed in Chapters 2 and 4. Indeed, the waters of these three countries constitute over half of the world's total area of MPAs – with those of Australia, Cook Islands, Mexico and New Zealand another 30 per cent. This flurry of VLMPAs means that on a quantitative measure the Aichi targets will be more than adequately met, but it masks the qualitative dimensions of the commitment to target 'ecologically representative' waters of 'particular importance for biodiversity and ecosystem services', which are to be 'effectively and equitably managed'.[91] In this way, once again, waters distant from the capitalist metropoles are being appropriated – this time to meet national conservation 'targets' – but in doing so the biodiversity being protected is far from 'ecologically representative'. Instead, state mediation of the inevitable social conflict involved in ocean zoning is being pushed offshore to the waters of overseas island territories and their small, politically marginal and economically vulnerable populations, who are dependent on marine resources.[92]

While such zoning does not always preclude commercial exploitation, its chief function is to allow the relatively undisturbed recovery and reproduction of marine environments. To that extent, ocean zoning is less about keeping market forces at bay, and more about facilitating a 'green' or sustainable valorisation of the sea. As one notable advocate of ocean zoning has indicated, this form of marine management creates 'a better climate for private sector investment in both ocean industries and marine conservation, since zoning brings both clarity on rights and some guarantee that rights will be honoured'.[93] In this way, having had their waters ravaged by industrial fishing nations through the twentieth century (as discussed in Chapter 4), SIDS like Nauru, Kiribati and Seychelles are now using their sovereign rights to create VLMPAs and 'debt for nature swaps' in their EEZs under the 'guidance and seeming control of US-based environmental foundations' such as Conservation International, Pew and the Nature Conservancy, who in turn are seeking to use private financial instruments to produce an offshore technical fix to the global environmental crisis produced by the capitalist core.[94] Yet at the same time, the financial resources at the heart of such projects in private oceanic ordering are woefully inadequate to sustain their reproduction in the face of more lucrative forms of ground rent captured through state landed property, such as fisheries access and seabed mining. In short, '"blue growth solutions" … have profound impact through their '"antipolitical" framing of climate and environmental change that precludes radical agendas' necessary to the social transformation of the ways in which humans interact with the global ocean.[95]

There is, then, a nagging paradox in contemporary initiatives aimed at saving the oceans from the devastation wrought by global warming: the more terrestrial mechanisms of zoning are brought to the sea, the greater the risk of underplaying the onshore sources of the climate crisis. The symptoms are in danger of being confused with the causes, as no amount of marine conservation can do away with the biospheric interaction between air, land and water. Some of the ocean's unique properties – its circulation, vastness, remoteness, invisibility and solvent qualities – have turned this space into a favoured destination for industrial society's residues and a new site of financial accumulation. The growing recognition that such practices of offshore disposal are surfacing back ashore has highlighted the integrated nature of planetary life. Healthier seas can no doubt mitigate catastrophic climate change, as well as addressing some of challenges – from food security to coastal urbanisation – faced by a growing yet deeply unequal world population. The protection and revitalisation of the ocean does not, however, go to the root causes of global warming, which remain firmly grounded on land. Bringing to the surface the marine detritus generated by continental activity has the virtue of rendering visible what is often submerged, but it also runs the danger of naturalising the sea as the life force that will rescue our planet from irreversible climate change.

The offshore presence

We began this chapter with a consideration of the utopian dimensions of the offshore world, noting the foundational act of secession from a mainland which characterised King Utopos's island paradise. This association ceases to be purely figurative and acquires a distinctively material quality when attention is drawn to the role of convict labour in building, maintaining and repairing the defensive, transport and communications infrastructure which allowed erstwhile overseas colonies like Bermuda or Singapore to become today's offshore centres. We have therefore adopted an elastic understanding of the offshore world in order to fix attention on the continuities and complicities between overseas expulsion, enslavement, contamination and confinement on the one hand, and maritime mobility, exclusivity, exemption and connectivity on the other. The offshore world is a real and powerful realm of contemporary politics and society and, as we have sought to demonstrate here, has a long and violent history associated with both capitalist development and modern state formation. It plainly cannot be simplistically reduced to a coherent whole, with some teleological destination automatically linking penal colonies to contemporary tax havens, or marine waste discharge to lawlessness and criminality. Rather, the chapter has argued, banishment, secrecy, toxicity, laundering and evasion interconnect the sea, overseas territories and offshore practices in ways that underscore the symbiosis between public authority and private gain, waste and surplus, distance and mobility, detachment and connectivity, visibility and concealment in the reproduction of an offshore world.

In this effort to remain separate from but connected to any given mainland, the offshore world necessarily implies a living contradiction: between the past and the present, freedom and oppression, ostentation and obfuscation, purity and pollution, utopian paradise and sealed-off social pressure cooker. The configuration of the offshore has since the advent of capitalism been imbued both with the promise of prosperity, progress and privacy, and with exclusion, domination and crisis. A peculiar geographical imagination has fuelled this condition whereby the offshore world is both an idea or aspiration and a very concrete place and political jurisdiction. Such imaginings conjure up conflicting but related ideas of the sublime, the spectral, the abject and the uncanny, where the sea and its islands induce feelings, memories and associations – depending on one's standpoint – of luxury and loss, attraction and repulsion, inheritance and forgetting, or shimmering clarity and silent torment. We cannot do justice here to these complex cultural tropes and expressions, although other parts of the book address the implications of thinking of the sea as history, and the ocean floor as a cemetery of human life. Instead we close this chapter with some brief considerations of the place of offshoring in the reproduction of global capitalism.

The offshore world, we have insisted, is always present in onshore life, even if it claims a distant, hidden and reclusive existence. The terraqueous territoriality we have been exploring throughout the book, where land and sea are engaged in a constant dance of different but connected materialities, generates distinctive spatial forms, which in the case of the offshore world include tax havens, penal colonies and marine protected areas, among others. These places and spaces are unquestionably sociohistorical constructs, but they are built on certain natural attributes of the sea – remoteness, immensity, seclusion and fluidity – engineered by those in and with power to differentiate the onshore from the offshore. Offshoring is not a functional requirement for capitalist reproduction – the surpluses accumulated and discharged offshore are significant, but in no way critical: capitalism would survive the closure of all the world's tax havens; most of the waste that finds its way into the sea originates onshore. Rather, offshoring in its manifold expressions is a product of political strategies aimed at variously upholding or reinforcing the dominant social order, be it to facilitate financial flows, pacify unruly populations or test the nuclear weapons that will secure such order. It is an instrument of power that moulds the terraqueous features of our planet, generally to the benefit of the already rich and powerful. The proliferation of secrecy jurisdictions since the 1960s in particular must be explained with reference to the rise and consolidation of neoliberal modes of governance and exploitation. As we have seen, the bountiful legacy of overseas colonial outposts has been revalorised economically and recharged politically over the last half-century by diverse state institutions. The neoliberal celebration of private wealth accumulation unencumbered by public scrutiny and devoid of social responsibility yet reliant on state authority, found in the treasure islands of various far-flung oceans, offers the idyllic model of society: Bermuda, Cayman, Singapore represent such concrete utopias, seasteading its most exuberant fantasy. The sea and its islands thus hold a central place in the neoliberal imaginary, itself sedimented upon centuries of imperial dreams of island paradise.

If the utopian reverie of a private, fertile and pacified island is the prevalent motif of neoliberal visions of the sea, the figure of the shipwreck is perhaps most evocative of a dystopian future where nature strikes back against the invasive technologies and infrastructures of modern society. Here the warming, expanding and acidified oceans come to represent a vengeful nature which, in its untamed and unfathomable vastness, has been persistently dumped on and neglected, only to return as a destructive force wreaking global havoc through storm surges, coastal flooding, marine degradation and species extinction. Such simplistic and static contrasts between land and sea risk overlooking ways in which the oceans have also been nurtured and protected by land-based management systems. Human activity on the continents is plainly changing the saltwater world in visible but unpredictable ways that are potentially disastrous for the whole of the biosphere. The offshore thus understood can no longer be perceived and conceived as some thing or some place outside the onshore world, extraneous and residual to human activity on land. The terraqueous nature of the planet has always involved a complex biophysical interaction between land and sea, but over the past century – and the last fifty years in particular – global warming has intensified and accelerated such interdependence in ways that seriously compromise the distinction between offshore and onshore. Carbon emissions respect no jurisdiction, and to that extent the environmental effects of a global carbon economy have integrated oceans and continents, throwing up a conundrum about how to address catastrophic climate change on a planetary scale. Unlike convicts, money, ship registrations or beneficial ownership, greenhouse gases cannot be offshored in any material sense (except perhaps in the abstract, commodified form of carbon trading). The neoliberal strategy of offshoring land-side surplus and excess thus encounters intractable obstacles in the natural properties of an ocean world that constantly feeds back in biophysical form the effects of global warming. As a consequence, capitalist states and enterprises are having to climate-proof their onshore investments and infrastructure. Crises, let us remember, always present a business opportunity for different sectors of capital, and the shipwreck, in all its cataclysmic, irreparable material destruction, has, through insurance, trade and finance in particular, been at the heart of capitalist value creation from the beginning.

Conclusion

Terraqueous horizons

There is a particular variant of liberal thought, stretching back to at least the nineteenth century, which traces a continuous thread of seafaring freedom, peace and prosperity across maritime states from Athens, Venice, the Dutch Republic and Great Britain, culminating in the USA. The conjunction of the ocean's natural flows and the ever-accelerating transnational circulation of capital, so the story goes, points to a world of spatial transgression and political transformation. The interaction between our ocean world and market societies demonstrates that wealth, liberty and the pursuit of happiness are to be found by reaching for the offshore horizon beyond our own parochial terrestrial limits. This line of thinking, which finds expression in authors as diverse as Hegel and Mahan[1] (although Marx wasn't entirely immune to its charms), contrasts the enterprise, openness and democracy of (generally) Western, ocean-going polities to the stagnant, hierarchical despotism of (mostly) Eastern land-based empires (Athens versus Sparta; Britain versus India; America versus the USSR). For one recent exponent of such liberal ideology,

It is a natural process: seafaring and trade beget merchants; merchants accumulate wealth and bring the pressure of money to bear on hereditary monarchies and landowning aristocracies ... and sooner or later merchant values prevail in government. Chief of these are dispersed power and open, consultative rule, since concentrated power and the arbitrary rule of closed cabals are unresponsive to the needs of trade and fatal to sound finance.[2]

A central aim of this book has been to debunk such liberal fantasies by constantly reading the progressive features of the 'maritime factor' against the current, thereby bringing to the surface the many ways in which the sea is also a domain of intense exploitation, brutality, war, conquest, oppression, degradation and obfuscation. In opposition to the crude dichotomisation of land and sea, we have argued throughout the book that capitalism adopts specific forms of terraqueous territoriality which both shape and are shaped by the natural forces of the global ocean. The critique of terracentrism is a necessary response to the 'unspoken proposition that the seas of the world are unreal spaces, voids between the real places, which are landed and national'.[3] But it should not be replaced with 'an equally problematic focus on "aquamobility" in isolation'.[4] The interface between capitalism and the sea is objectively mediated by all sorts of socio-economic, political and ecological structures that are relatively fixed and static, but which nonetheless outline the subjective potential of this interaction for a politics of liberation. We invoke in this conclusion the notion of 'horizons' by way of probing the political lessons that might emerge from studying capitalism and the sea, in particular for democratic projects seeking to transcend capitalist social relations.

The first of these horizons is the global climate emergency created by fossil capital. The sea and its islands, we have seen, are a repository for all kinds of waste, excess and surplus, the most threatening of which is the amount of carbon and heat absorbed by the oceans. Nowhere is the presence of historical capitalism's production of CO_2 and other greenhouse gases (GHG) more apparent than in the warming and acidification of the oceans. The blue-water part of our planet 'contains 15 times more carbon than the atmosphere and all living and dead (soil) organic matter on the planet combined', while 'the so-called heat capacity of the world ocean is over 1000 times greater than that of the atmosphere'.[5] If, as Andreas Malm so eloquently puts it, the compound accumulation of past GHG emissions today means that 'the air is heavy with time',[6] even more so is the sea. Indeed, the widely contrasting temporalities at play here – the saltwater world has been slowly changing over millions of years only to be rapidly transformed in the space of a few decades by a social system barely a few centuries old – already tell a powerful story about the disjointed timescales of the crisis we are facing. To make matters worse, the centrality of the oceans to the reproduction of our biosphere – its critical role in regulating atmospheric temperatures and humidity, and thereby extreme weather events; its significance in the global food chain; its part in sustaining both marine and terrestrial ecosystems – accentuates the risks of seaborne climate change. The full implications of warmer, anoxic and acidified oceans today may not become entirely apparent until a more distant future, since the sea's heat and carbon release are a more protracted process than, say, that produced through deforestation. But that means that the consequences are likely to be even more devastating than the climate change we are witnessing at present, thus making plausible the prospect in coming generations of a mass extinction event comparable to that which took place some 250 million years ago at the end of the Permian geologic era.[7]

In the meantime, because climate change acts as a 'force multiplier' of existing social injustices and inequalities across the world, the poorer, darker-skinned, more vulnerable coastal populations of the world – many of them concentrated in delta and lagoon cities like Dhaka, New Orleans or Lagos – will continue bearing the disproportionate burden of risk accompanying sea-level rise, more frequent and intense cyclones, and the consequent extreme flooding.[8] This is also true of the billions whose livelihoods and sources of protein and nutrients come from the sea: the further disruption to marine habitats and the continued stratification of the oceans caused by climate change, as we discussed at length in Chapter 6, is drastically reducing marine biodiversity and altering the geographical distribution of fish populations.

The sea thus tells us a great deal about the limits to life on Earth under capitalism. This does not, however, mean that we should restrict our focus to the sea. The global success of consciousness-raising television programmes like Sir David Attenborough's BBC *Blue Planet* has certainly drawn attention to the oceans. But the sources of the climate crisis lie firmly on land. For all the attempts at mitigating the effects of global warming by protecting marine ecologies and regulating the exploitation of our oceans, it is only by radically decarbonising our societies that we might contain average global temperature increases below the 1.5 °C target identified by the 2015 Paris Agreement. Here – perhaps unsurprisingly – the relationship between capitalism and the sea throws up contradictory results which point to a second set of horizons. On the one hand, the capitalist valorisation of the sea produced some of the early expressions of global governance, going back as far as the 1856 Paris Declaration Respecting Maritime Law which abolished privateering, and then followed by the first international organisations such as the 1865 International Telegraphic Union. On the other hand, the globally dominant model of export-oriented capitalist development has over the past fifty years accelerated GHG emissions. The sea as a space has thus been both victim and vehicle of global warming since the advent of industrial capitalism.

There is little doubt that – in addition to slavery, appropriation, war and exploitation – the oceans have been the locus of progressive forms of internationalism. In all manner of direct and more circuitous ways, international cooperation at sea, or relating to the sea, has inspired a cosmopolitan imagination that conceives of global warming as a planetary crisis which, like the high seas and the Area, requires multilateral governance. The sea has been a key component in the development of international public and commercial law, both conceptually (in principles of free trade or common heritage of humankind) and practically (in institutions like the diplomatic consulate or chambers of commerce). We saw in Chapter 2 how the ocean floor beyond extended continental shelves (the 'Area') is administered by the International Seabed Authority on behalf of humanity, and in Chapter 4 how regional fisheries management organisations foster multilateral cooperation in international waters, albeit woefully weakly. Efforts at stemming marine pollution in the Mediterranean, or monitoring circumpolar biodiversity, have produced transnational 'epistemic communities' of scientific experts, and intergovernmental organisations like the Arctic Council. Ships themselves have become icons of internationalism, from the USS *Augusta*, where Churchill and Roosevelt signed the 1941 Atlantic Charter, to Greenpeace's ill-fated *Rainbow Warrior*, bombed in 1984 while docked in Auckland, New Zealand, by French intelligence services seeking to undermine environmentalist campaigns against nuclear testing in the Southern Pacific. More anecdotally, in 1926 a New York University psychology professor inspired by pragmatist philosophers John Dewey and William James took fellow faculty and 504 fortunate students on an 'eight-month "educational cruise around the world" . . . Promising a "college year of educational travel and systematic study to develop an interest in foreign affairs, to train students to think in world terms, and to strengthen international understanding and good will"'.[9] Such maritime cosmopolitanism flourished during the early twentieth-century gilded age of ocean liners – 'Life aboard a ship is a little world between two worlds,' a 1929 Cunard brochure declared, neatly capturing the prospect of elite emancipation from onshore ordinariness.[10]

However, it is precisely this ruling-class-driven, (neo)liberal cosmopolitanism of the 'frequent-flier lounge' (or upper deck) that has overseen the intensification of capitalist globalisation responsible for global warming.[11] Looking at international cooperation through a maritime lens shows up the limitations of a nautical internationalism that simply mediates, and doesn't seek to radically transform, existing property and inter-state relations (the compatibility of MPAs with capitalist appropriation through 'debt for nature' swaps, noted in Chapter 6, is a case in point). The central contradiction, then, of existing multilateral efforts at combating climate change – whether of maritime inspiration or otherwise – is that they are unable, or at least unwilling, to think of a world beyond market-dependence.

This conflicted legacy of maritime cosmopolitanism is powerfully conveyed in the form of the shipping container, which, far more than a mere freight technology, is a political artefact that facilitated a new international division of labour in the course of the 1970s, where global commodity chains deliver just-in-time production and assembly of goods across different low-cost geographical locations, today concentrated in the coastal export-processing zones of East, South East and South Asia.[12] In universalising 'seagoing trucks' mentioned in Chapter 5, the first major container firm, Sea-Land Service, created a terraqueous infrastructure for a twenty-foot equivalent unit 'that made the world smaller and the world economy bigger'.[13] Although obviously not itself solely responsible for climate change, the development model inherent to the shipping container is based upon the carbon-fuelled production of goods and services for a global market addicted to what Jason Moore and Raj Patel call the 'seven cheaps': nature, money, work, care, food, energy and lives.[14] Radically decarbonising the planet will require a fundamental revalorisation of the seven cheaps – not only properly rewarding and redistributing care and work, or renewing energy and repairing lives, but also recalibrating the social power and significance of technologies like the shipping container when catering for a society organised around the provision of democratically agreed human needs. This would likely involve descaling international trade, reorienting production from consumer to social goods, and rebalancing domestic markets against export-oriented growth strategies, all administered through socialised property and collectivised government.

The big challenge for a twenty-first-century revolutionary politics is reconciling such profound rebalancing of our relation to nature with the internationalist commitment to doing so in a way that transcends the narrow confines of community, nation or region. Here ocean life also serves as a source of inspiration. An internationalist politics of liberation requires harnessing the best of the innovation, imagination and enterprise that seafaring has provided through the centuries, with the sense of belonging, stability and continuity that life on land has conventionally afforded. It is about bringing the offshore ashore, subjecting socio-economic flows to democratic control without falling into the reactionary insularity of 'socialism in one country' or nativist tropes about 'rootless cosmopolitans'. How such programmatic ambitions are concretised remains an open question, subject to different sociopolitical contexts and balances of forces. But the experiences of maritime exploitation and appropriation analysed in these pages hopefully offer a glimpse into the possibilities (and indeed limitations) of worker organisation on ships, internationalist solidarity at sea, the decommodification of fisheries or the retreat from marine and coastal habitats that might contribute toward the strategic aims of decarbonising and democratising the global 'blue economy'.

Against the business class cosmopolitanism of frequent fliers we reclaim a saltwater cosmopolitanism of motley crews, thereby pushing the boundaries of our contemporary political imagination. Shipping was the first capitalist sector to employ wage earners as part of a genuinely multi-ethnic, polyglot, syncretic and pluri-national workforce which, through cooperation in labour process and shared lifeworlds, developed its own distinctive creole cultures of work and leisure that straddled and transgressed the division between land and sea. Port towns across the world are dotted with neighbourhoods built on the admixture of ocean-faring, or at least sea-dependent, peoples of the globe – be it in Cardiff's Tiger Bay or San Telmo in Buenos Aires – which undermine essentialist conceptions of ethnic identity or national homogeneity. Similarly, the diasporic interconnections fostered by transnational seaborne movement, be it forced or voluntary, have generated a rich variety of internationalisms, ranging from Marcus Garvey's pan-Africanism to Ho Chi Minh's communist anti-colonialism. The sea, and in particular the promise it has offered for both physical movement and political mobilisation, is integral to emancipatory politics, both personal and collective. We must celebrate the mobility – of people, ideas, goods and cultures – induced by the oceans while all the time recognising that such movement needs to be democratically channelled in the pursuit of more just and equal societies, generally grounded on more static institutions of public representation and rule. Here the history of the 'maritime factor' in labour internationalism (touched upon especially in Chapter 3) offers some sobering lessons for today's struggles. Motley crews can be deeply hierarchical and racist, navalism has been central to modern imperialism, closed shops in some sea-facing trades have spawned reactionary labour aristocracies. As we saw in Chapter 3, class-based solidarities are often disarticulated by other relations of domination and subordination such as race and nationality, and the precarity of ratings' employment contracts undermines the scope for labour organising, with crew instead often cooperating with management in an effort to secure future employment. There is, therefore, nothing inherently progressive about the sea, or maritime movement; only a distinctive *potential* for a saltwater cosmopolitanism which needs to be constantly realised, nurtured and sustained by actual organisations, concerted campaigns and concrete actions.

In this regard, another important structural feature of our terraqueous predicament, which has otherwise been muted in this book, comes to the fore: namely the profoundly gendered separation of land and sea. As discussed in Chapter 3 with reference to seafarer's 'family allotments', or in Chapter 4 in relation to women cannery workers, the highly (and generally toxically) masculinised lives at sea have always relied on female labour on land. Noteworthy here is how the innovative, pioneering dimensions of the maritime factor in the modern world also reproduce the most patriarchal sexual divisions of labour, and the most reactionary of social categorisations. The liminal spaces where land meets sea (including the ship itself) have, to be sure, generated multiple and diverse queer identities, practices and imaginaries.[15] But these have rubbed against the violently heteronormative strictures that govern life at sea to this day. There is much research still to be done on the masculinist, productive (versus reproductive) bias of the maritime world, and clearly there are political implications to this when it comes to celebrating the histories of resistance and rebellion among seafaring peoples. At this juncture, all we can offer is a further reclaiming not only of the political subjectivities offered by motley crews, but also of the social practices of solidarity, subversion, pleasure and excess characteristic of the best harbour-side neighbourhoods.

If adopting a maritime viewpoint gives us a sense of the opportunities and limitations accompanying struggles for democratic emancipation – from the decarbonisation of the world economy to multilateral cooperation, gender equality to different forms of internationalism – it also opens a final, related, debate around the strategic value of stoppage and disruption in democratic politics. The addition of the English word 'strike' to the lexicon of class struggle in 1768 was famously the outcome of London sailors and coal heavers 'striking the sails' (removing the topsail) of their ships in a collective act of sabotage aimed at halting the transfer of goods until they received a pay rise.[16] This political exercise in the interruption of commercial circulation has since been a central plank in the repertoire of industrial action, focused during the twentieth century on the coordinated withdrawal of labour, but, in the case of general strikes, requiring the paralysis or disruption of major transport and communication networks (not least to dissuade strike breakers from crossing picket lines). The power of logistics in the reproduction of global capitalism today, and the key role of shipping in this process (explored in Chapter 5), has put the notion of 'hydraulic' or 'supply chain' capitalism and the accompanying potential of land-side blockages at the centre of discussions about global anti-capitalist strategies.[17] More recently, scholar–activists have continued to chart the past militancy of seamen and dockworkers in both local and international struggles for liberation, while also mapping the contemporary trajectories of different global commodity chains, thus embedding them in the concrete social relations between living human beings who actually shift commodities. This opens up further possibilities of countering the logistical suppleness of capital with a working-class agility of organisation.[18]

In principle, seafarers, dockers and other trans-oceanic labour employed at the major choke points of global capitalism have the capacity to orchestrate international stoppages and boycotts. It would only take a small number of militant workers, organised in transnational alliances, to slow down or even block the arteries of maritime logistics. The maritime sections of the International Transport Workers' Federation and the International Dockworkers Council are the organisations that offer (often competing) views on how to do this. Yet as we considered in Chapter 3, the segmented, regimented and isolated nature of seafaring labour in particular, together with the history of racism and national chauvinism among some seafarers' and dockers' unions, makes the organisation and effectiveness of the maritime blockade a much more complicated proposition than is often recognised – including among scholars in the sub-field of labour geographies, where there is a 'tendency to amplify (if not exaggerate) the highpoints of workers' triumphs ... disabling a more sober but realistic assessment of labour's weaknesses'.[19] As Jeremy Anderson has argued, the notion of 'choke point' in such debates is often overstretched to include any location along the supply chain, thus begging a question over its strategic usefulness given that 'building alliances across the supply chain' as a whole would 'seem the more ambitious aim.[20] Objectively, too, it is worth noting that, compared to other transport and communication sectors, shippers have relatively greater scope to deploy what Bernes calls the qualitative 'agility' of logistics: 'that is, the power to change, as quickly as possible, the speed, location, origin and destination of products, as well as product type, in order to meet volatile market conditions'.[21] For all its geographical mobility, maritime labour faces the additional challenge of working and living within a confined space with only occasional and often weak access to wider support networks among families, neighbourhoods, associations or community spaces so important to industrial action, and which have historically been more readily available to land-based labour.

The continuities between today's highly financialised, centrally controlled global commodity chains and the commercial capitalism of the seventeenth and eighteenth centuries explored in Chapter 1 underline the centrality of circulation to capitalist development. Moreover, the past and present class struggles involving capitalism and the sea show unambiguously the distinctive political power of maritime labour in disrupting circulation. What has also been made apparent throughout this book is the centrality of the state to the reproduction of the ocean world – be it in logistics, shipbuilding, war making, fishing, offshore oil and mineral extraction, or the trade in drugs and humans. Direct and indirect state subsidies are central to the accumulation strategies of the shipping industry, whether in terms of lax safety regulations or generous public contracts for mail services and military transport, or as bankroller and operator of new and existing ports.[22] Similarly, as discussed earlier (and in greater depth in Chapter 2), intergovernmental institutions and maritime conventions – many of them the brainchild of naval empires like Great Britain or the USA – have with different levels of success since the seventeenth century upheld world orders through a combination of war and law.

It is in this context that our study underlines the importance not only of linking circulation to production (significant as that is), but also of bringing the state and political mobilisation into the calculation of how, and in what ways, capitalism and the sea interact. One aspect of the debates around the role of interruption and circulation in counterhegemonic politics today involves the promises and pitfalls of 'repurposing' or 'reconfiguring' logistics and other capitalist infrastructures for a post-capitalist world.[23] Some are adamant that, under the present conditions of a just-in-time supply chain capitalism, 'the creation of communism will require a massive process of delinking from the planetary factory as a matter of survival'.[24] Our gambit, in contrast, has been to underline the imperative for anti-capitalist politics of embracing the flows, connections and universalisation that issue from the relationship between capitalism and the sea, and to channel and harness them into more settled, enduring structures of collective distribution and democratic rule – including those of the state. Democratic emancipation must be terraqueous in its ambition to combine freedom and stability, mobility and permanence, innovation and regulation. This applies to the urgent strategies of decarbonisation as much as to the seemingly distant aspirations to a more just and equal organisation of social life beyond the value form. If there is one thing an investigation of the relationship between capitalism and the sea affords us, it is the possibility of rendering visible and intelligible that which is often hidden, forgotten or merely obscured by the powerful. Whether it is the submerged histories of the Atlantic and other seaborne slave trades or the illicit surplus deposited in offshore financial centres, the human costs accompanying the insatiable consumption of dwindling fish populations or the catastrophic accumulation of heat and carbon in the oceans. Looking at the sea reminds us that capitalism is only a very recent historical arrival on our shores, and that humanity deserves much more to outlive this upstart social force we ourselves have created than the other way around. The best prospect of a revolutionary horizon is gazing at the sea from land.

Notes

Introduction: A Terraqueous Predicament

1. We are grateful to James Dunkerley for noting the word 'terraqueous' in response to a presentation on piracy some years ago, at Queen Mary University of London. In Chapter 14 of Melville's *Moby-Dick* we are told that 'two-thirds of this terraqueous globe are the Nantucketer's'. Good overviews of the historical-geographical relationship between land and sea can be found in John R. Gillis, *The Human Shore: Seacoasts in History*, Chicago and London: The University of Chicago Press, 2012; and Lincoln Paine, *The Sea and Civilization: A Maritime History of the World*, London: Atlantic Books, 2014. The present book would also have been unthinkable without the long tradition of 'thalassology', old and new, including foundational works by Fernand Braudel, *The Mediterranean and the Mediterranean World in the Age of Philip II*, 2 vols., Berkeley: University of California Press, 1996; K. N. Chaudhuri, *Trade and Civilisation in the Indian Ocean: An Economic History from the Rise of Islam to 1750*, Cambridge: Cambridge University Press, 1985; Marcus Rediker, *Between the Devil and the Deep Blue Sea: Merchant Seamen, Pirates, and the Anglo-American Maritime World, 1700–1750*, Cambridge: Cambridge University Press, 1987; and Paul Gilroy, *The Black Atlantic: Modernity and Double Consciousness*, London and New York: Verso, 1993. For a critical appraisal of these classic and newer writings on the sea, see Peregrine Horden and Nicholas Purcel, 'The Mediterranean and "the New Thalassology"', *American Historical Review*, Vol. 111, No. 3, 2006, pp. 722–740; and for a useful historical-geographical overview,

see David Lambert, Luciana Martins and Miles Ogborn, 'Currents, Visions and Voyages: Historical Geographies of the Sea', *Journal of Historical Geography*, Vol. 32, No. 3, 2006, pp. 479–493.

2. Phil Steinberg's *The Social Construction of the Ocean*, Cambridge: Cambridge University Press, 2001, remains an indispensable reference point in our understanding of terraqueous territoriality.

3. This stretches back to the early writings of Karl Wittfogel and his Marxist contemporaries and, via David Harvey's work, to Henri Lefebvre. The approach of Eric R. Wolf, Sidney W. Mintz, Michael Watts, Nancy Peluso, Mike Davis and – with a strong Foucauldian flavour – Timothy Mitchell is also informed by this transaction. Outside the Marxist tradition, but very much concerned with the same problematic of the spatio-temporal relationship between society and nature, is the *Annales* school and, in relation to capitalism and the sea in particular, the work of its leading light, Fernand Braudel. See the useful overview by Peter Burke, *The French Historical Revolution: The Annales School 1929–2014*, 2nd edn, Cambridge: Polity, 2014. Although only intermittently concerned with the land–sea distinction, several environmental histories also broach this subject. See, inter alia, John F. Richards, *The Unending Frontier: An Environmental History of the Early Modern World*, Berkeley: California University Press, 2006; Alfred W. Crosby, *Ecological Imperialism: The Biological Expansion of Europe, 900–1900*, Cambridge: Cambridge University Press, 2004; William Beinart and Lotte Hughes, *Environment and Empire*, Oxford: Oxford University Press, 2009; Richard H. Grove, *Green Imperialism: Colonial Expansion, Tropical Island Edens and the Origins of Environmentalism, 1600–1860*, Cambridge: Cambridge University Press, 2010.

4. Derek Walcott, 'The Sea Is History' in *Collected Poems, 1948-1984*, London: Faber and Faber, 1986, p. 365.

5. Édouard Glissant, *Poetics of Relation*, Ann Arbor: University of Michigan Press, 1997, p. 6.

6. Elizabeth Deloughrey, 'Heavy Waters: Waste and the Atlantic Modernity', *PLMA*, Vol. 251, No. 3, 2010, p. 705.

7. Kamau Brathwaite, *Contradictory Omens: Cultural Diversity and Integration in the Caribbean*, Mona: Savacou Publications, 1974, p. 64.

8. Robert Macfarlane, *The Old Ways: A Journey on Foot*, London: Hamish Hamilton, 2011, p. 91.

9. On the Pacific see, inter alia, Eric Waddell, Vijay Naidu and Epeli Hau'ofa (eds.), *A New Oceania: Rediscovering Our Sea of Islands*, Suva, Fiji: The University of the South Pacific School of Social and Economic Development, 1993; and David Lewis, *We, the Navigators: The Ancient Art of Landfinding in the Pacific*, Honolulu: University of Hawaii Press, 1994. For the Norse experience, see B. Ambrosiani and H. Clarke (eds.), *The Twelfth Viking Congress: Development around the Baltic and the North Sea in the Viking Age*, Stockholm: Birka Studies, 1994; J. Geipel, *The Viking Legacy: The Scandinavian Influence on the English Language*, Newton Abbott: David and Charles Ltd, 1971; R. M. Karras, *Slavery and Society in Medieval Scandinavia*, New Haven: Yale University Press, 1988; and E. Roesdahl, *The Vikings*, London: Penguin, 1992.

10. Robin Blackburn, *The Making of New World Slavery: From the Baroque to the Modern, 1492–1800*, London and New York: Verso, 1997. p. 10.

11. Stephanie E. Smallwood, *Saltwater Slavery: The Middle Passage from Africa to American Diaspora*, Cambridge, MA and London: Harvard University Press, 2007.

12. For the classic discussion of 'social death', see Orlando Patterson, *Slavery and Social Death: A Comparative Study*, Cambridge, MA and London: Harvard University Press, 1982.

13. Sowande' M. Mustakeem, *Slavery at Sea: Terror, Sex, and Sickness in the Middle Passage*, Urbana, Chicago and Springfield: University of Illinois Press, 2016, p. 7.

14. Mustakeem, *Slavery at Sea*, p. 43.

15. The painful irony of slave-ship sailors being at the forefront of free workingmen's claims for liberty and just pay (indeed introducing the term 'strike' to modern industrial relations) is expertly considered in Emma Christopher, *Slave Ship Sailors and Their Captive Cargoes, 1730–1807*, Cambridge: Cambridge University Press, 2006; and in Marcus Rediker's *Between the Devil and the Deep Blue Sea*.

16. Gilroy, *The Black Atlantic*; Ian Baucom, *Specters of the Atlantic: Finance Capital, Slavery, and the Philosophy of History*, Durham, NC: Duke University Press, 2005; Marcus Rediker, *The Slave Ship: A Human History*, London: John Murray, 2008.

17. Patterson, *Slavery and Social Death*.

18. Wolf, *Europe*, p. 298.

19. Nicky Gregson, Mike Crang, and C. N. Antonopoulos, 'Holding Together Logistical Worlds: Friction, Seams and Circulation in the Emerging "Global Warehouse"', *Environment and Planning D*, Vol. 35, No. 3, 2017, pp. 381–398.

20. 'Materiality' is a fiendishly polysemic term, conveying all sorts of often compatible meanings. For a good discussion of its geographical uses, see Karen Bakker and Gavin Bridge, 'Material Worlds? Resource Geographies and the "Matter of Nature"', *Progress in Human Geography*, Vol. 30, No. 1, 2006, pp. 5–27.

21. Andreas Malm, *The Progress of This Storm: Nature and Society in a Warming World*, New York and London: Verso, 2018. Malm in turn borrows and develops this formulation from both Antonio Negri, *Marx beyond Marx: Lessons on the Grundrisse*, New York: Autonomedia, 1991; and Carolyn Merchant, *Autonomous Nature: Problems of Prediction and Control*, New York: Routledge, 2016.

22. Neil Smith, *Uneven Development: Nature, Capital and the Production of Space*, 3rd edn, New York and London: Verso, 2010, p. 68.

23. Jason W. Moore, *Capitalism and the Web of Life: Ecology and the Accumulation of Capital*, London: Verso, 2015.

24. Philip Steinberg and Kim Peters' call for a 'wet ontology', where 'the ocean – through its material reformation, mobile churning and nonlinear temporality – creates the need for new understandings of mapping and representing, living and knowing; governing and resisting', is an attractive proposition for those of us wishing to denaturalise the separation between land and sea, while all the time recognising their material particularities. But we part ways with these formulations when they ascribe to heterogeneous, non- and more-than-human 'actants' agentic powers 'that may provisionally

exhibit internally coherent, efficacious organizations; objects forming and emerging within relational fields, bodies composing their natural environment in ways that are corporeally meaningful for them, and subjectivities being as open series of capacities or potencies that emerge hazardously and ambiguously within a multitude of organic and social processes'. Philip Steinberg and Kimberley Peters, 'Wet Ontologies, Fluid Spaces: Giving Depth to Volume through Oceanic Thinking', *Environment and Planning D*, Vol. 33, No. 2, 2015, p. 258. Diana Cole and Samantha Frost (eds.), *New Materialisms: Ontology, Agency, and Politics*, Durham, NC and London: Duke University Press, 2010, p. 10.

25. Steinberg and Peters, 'Wet Ontologies', p. 258.

26. Marcus Rediker, 'Toward a People's History of the Sea', in David Killingray, Margarette Lincoln and Nigel Rigby (eds.), *Maritime Empires: British Imperial Maritime Trade in the Nineteenth Century*, Woodbridge: Boydell Press, 2004, p. 198, italics in original.

27. Amitav Ghosh, *Sea of Poppies*, London: Picador, 2008; *River of Smoke*, London: Picador, 2011; *Flood of Fire*, London: Picador, 2015. See the round table discussion 'History Meets Fiction in the Indian Ocean: On Amitav Ghosh's Ibis Trilogy', *American Historical Review*, Vol. 121, no. 5, 2016, pp. 1521–1565.

28. This and other internationalist lives are recounted in Gopal Balachandran, *Globalizing Labour? Indian Seafarers and World Shipping, c.1870–1945*, New Delhi: Oxford University Press, 2012. See also David Featherstone, 'Maritime Labour and Subaltern Geographies of Internationalism: Black Internationalist Seafarers' Organising in the Interwar Period', *Political Geography*, Vol. 49, November 2015, pp. 7–16.

29. Margaret S. Creighton and Lisa Norling (eds.), *Iron Men, Wooden Women: Gender and Seafaring in the Atlantic World, 1700–1920*, Baltimore, MD: Johns Hopkins University Press, 1996. See also Heide Gerstenberger's study of German seamen during the age of sail, where she underlines how the onshore lifeworld affected workplace relations and vice versa: 'social connection between the different circles of relatives, friends and acquaintances [of sailors] was

close enough for anyone who behaved deviantly to understand that relatives, friends, the girl he hoped to marry – in short, everybody in his world – would sooner or later be informed'. Heide Gerstenberger, 'Men Apart: The Concept of "Total Institution" and the Analysis of Seafaring', *International Journal of Maritime History*, Vol. 8, No. 1, 1996, p. 177.

30. See James Kneale, 'Islands: Literary Geographies of Isolation and Transformation', in Robert Tally (ed.), *Routledge Handbook of Literature and Space*, London and New York: Routledge, 2017, pp. 204–213.

31. Carl Wennerlind, *Casualties of Credit: The English Financial Revolution, 1620–1720*, Cambridge, MA: Harvard University Press, 2011.

32. See Valerie Hamilton and Martin Parker, *Daniel Defoe and the Bank of England: The Dark Arts of Projectors*, Winchester and Washington, DC: Zero Books, 2016.

33. See China Miéville, 'Floating Utopias', *In These Times*, 28 September 2007, inthesetimes.com, accessed 1 December 2017.

34. Alain Corbin, *The Lure of the Sea: The Discovery of the Seaside in the Western World 1750–1840*, trans. Jocelyn Phelps, Cambridge: Polity Press, 1994, p. 33. See also Christopher Connery, 'There Was No More Sea: The Supersession of the Ocean, from the Bible to Cyberspace', *Journal of Historical Geography*, Vol. 32, No. 3, 2006, pp. 494–511.

35. For anglophone literature, see Margaret Cohen, *The Novel and the Sea*, Princeton: Princeton University Press, 2012; John Peck, *Maritime Fiction: Sailors and the Sea in British and American Novels, 1719–1917*, London: Palgrave, 2001; and Cesare Casarino, *Modernity at Sea: Melville, Marx, Conrad in Crisis*, Minneapolis: Minnesota University Press, 2002.

1. Circulation

1. Karl Marx, *Capital: A Critique of Political Economy*, Volume 1, London: Penguin, 1990, p. 915.
2. Ibid., p. 874.
3. Ibid., p. 875.

4. J. H. Parry, *The Discovery of the Sea*, Berkeley: University of California Press, 1982.
5. Paul R. Pinet, *An Invitation to Oceanography*, 7th edn, Burlington, MA: Jones & Bartlett Learning, 2014.
6. John Mack, *The Sea: A Cultural History*, London: Reaktion Books, 2011, p. 57.
7. Paine, *The Sea and Civilization*, pp. 366–371.
8. Nancy Um, *The Merchant Houses of Mocha: Trade & Architecture in an Indian Ocean Port*, Seattle and London: University of Washington Press, 2009, p. 21.
9. Laleh Khalili, *Sinews of War and Trade: Shipping and Capitalism in the Arabian Peninsula*, London and New York: Verso, 2020, p. 83.
10. Fernand Braudel, *The Perspective of the World: Civilization and Capitalism 15th–18th Century*, Volume 3, London: Phoenix Press, 2002, p. 620, italics in the original.
11. Donatella Calabi does this for several early modern European marketplaces in her *The Market and the City: Square, Street and Architecture in Early Modern Europe*, Aldershot and Burlington, VT: Ashgate, 2004. See also Um, *The Merchant Houses*.
12. Perry Gauci, *Emporium of the World: The Merchants of London 1660–1800*, London: Hambledon Continuum, 2007, p. 39.
13. Robert Lopez, *The Commercial Revolution of the Middle Ages*, New York: Cambridge University Press, 1976.
14. Janet Abu-Lughod, *Before European Hegemony: The World System A.D. 1250–1350*, New York and Oxford: Oxford University Press, 1989, p. 8.
15. Markman Ellis, *The Coffee House: A Cultural History*, London: Weidenfeld and Nicolson, 2004. This account is disputed by others, who suggest that Oxford was the home of the first coffee house in England and Vienna that in Europe. See Brian William Cowan, *The Social Life of Coffee: The Emergence of the British Coffeehouse* New Haven, CT: Yale University Press, 2011.
16. Ellis, *The Coffee House* p. 26.
17. Andre Gunder Frank, *ReOrient: Global Economy in the Asian Age*, Berkeley, Los Angeles and London: University of California Press, 1998; Eric Wolf, *Europe and the Peoples*

without History, Berkeley: University of California Press, 1998; Ronald Findlay and Kevin H. O'Rourke, *Power and Plenty: Trade, War, and the World Economy in the Second Millennium*, Princeton, NJ: Princeton University Press, 2009.

18. Wolf, *Europe and the Peoples without History*, p. 32.

19. Alfred E. Lieber, 'Eastern Business Practices and Medieval European Commerce', *Economic History Review*, Vol. 21, No. 2, 1968, pp. 230–243. See also Edwin S. Hunt, *The Medieval Super-companies: A Study of the Peruzzi Company of Florence*, Cambridge: Cambridge University Press, 1994.

20. See Findlay and O'Rourke, *Power and Plenty*, pp. 95–98, for a helpful summary. S. D. Goitein's meticulous study of the priceless Geniza papers is the main source of this debate. See his *A Mediterranean Society: The Jewish Communities of the Arab World as Portrayed in the Documents of Cairo Geniza*, Berkeley: University of California Press, 1978.

21. A classic case study of early modern Andalusia can be found in Ruth Pike, *Enterprise and Adventure: The Genoese in Seville and the Opening of the New World*, Ithaca, NY: Cornell University Press, 1966.

22. Philip D. Curtin, *Trade Diasporas and Cross-cultural Trade*, Cambridge: Cambridge University Press, 1984. See also Irfan Habib, 'Merchant Communities in Pre-colonial India', in James D. Tracy (ed.), *The Rise of Merchant Empires: Long-Distance Trade in the Early Modern World, 1350–1750*, Cambridge: Cambridge University Press, 1990, pp. 371–99; and Olivia Remie Constable, *Housing the Stranger in the Mediterranean World: Lodging, Trade, and Travel in Late Antiquity and the Middle Ages*, Cambridge: Cambridge University Press, 2009.

23. Curtin, *Trade Diasporas*, p. 113.

24. Ibid., p. 114.

25. Michael N. Pearson, *The Indian Ocean*, London and New York: Routledge, 2003. Abdul Sheriff, *Dhow Cultures of the Indian Ocean: Cosmopolitanism, Commerce and Islam*, London: Hurst & Company, 2010.

26. Pedro Machado, *Ocean of Trade: South Asian Merchants, Africa and the Indian Ocean, c.1750–1850*, Cambridge: Cambridge University Press, 2014, p. 90.

27. Ibid., p. 91.

28. See Lakshmi Subramanian, *Medieval Seafarers*, New Delhi: The Lotus Collection, 1999; Patricia Risso, *Merchants and Faith: Muslim Commerce and Culture in the Indian Ocean*, Boulder, CO: Westview Press, 1995; Sebastian R. Prange, *Monsoon Islam: Trade and Faith in the Medieval Malabar Coast*, Cambridge: Cambridge University Press, 2018; Gagan D. S. Sood, *India and the Islamic Heartlands: An Eighteenth-Century World of Circulation and Exchange*, Cambridge: Cambridge University Press, 2016.

29. Machado, *Ocean of Trade*, p. 91.

30. Felipe Fernández-Armesto, *Before Columbus: Exploration and Colonisation from the Mediterranean to the Atlantic 1229–1492*, London: Macmillan, 1987, p. 96.

31. See Alex Anievas and Kerem Niçancloğlu, *How the West Came to Rule: The Geopolitical Origins of Capitalism*, London: Pluto, 2015.

32. The best descriptive overview of both companies remains G. V. Scammell, *The World Encompassed: The First European Maritime Empires, c.800–1650*, London and New York: Methuen, 1981. See also P. Lawson, *The East India Company: A History*, London and New York: Longman, 1993; Braudel, *The Perspective of the World*, Chapter 3; Jonathan I. Israel, *Dutch Primacy in International Trade, 1585–1740*, Oxford: Clarendon Press, 1990; and C. R. Boxer, *The Dutch Seaborne Empire 1600–1800*, London: Hutchinson and Co., 1965. More recent accounts can be found in Julia Adams, *The Familial State: Ruling Families and Merchant Capitalism in Early Modern Europe*, Ithaca, NY: Cornell University Press, 2004; and Matthew David Mitchell, 'British Joint-Stock Companies and Atlantic Trading', in D'Maris Coffman, Adrian Leonard and William O'Reilly (eds.), *The Atlantic World*, London and New York: Routledge, 2015, pp. 441–456.

33. For a detailed account of these class interactions in the English case, see Robert Brenner, *Merchants and Revolution: Commercial Change, Political Conflict, and London's Overseas Traders, 1550–1653*, London and New York: Verso, 2003.

34. The centrality of labour and merchant migration to the urban Netherlands in the hegemonic rise of the Dutch republic is documented in Jan Lucassen, 'Labour and Early Modern

Economic Development', in Karel Davids and Jan Lucassen (eds.), *A Miracle Mirrored: The Dutch Republic in European Perspective*, Cambridge: Cambridge University Press, 1995, pp. 367–409.

35. Ricardo Padrón, 'Mapping Plus Ultra: Cartography, Space and Hispanic Modernity', *Representations*, Vol. 79, No. 1, 2002, pp. 28–60; Daviken Studnicki-Gizbert, *A Nation upon the Ocean Sea: Portugal's Atlantic Diaspora and the Crisis of the Spanish Empire, 1492–1640*, Oxford and New York: Oxford University Press, 2007.

36. In Chapter 2 of his *Matters of Exchange: Commerce, Medicine, and Science in the Dutch Golden Age*, New Haven, CT and London: Yale University Press, 2007, Harold John Cook offers an illuminating account of how changing associations between credit, credibility and trust among these merchant communities were institutionalised, codified and indeed performed and displayed through rituals of modesty, decorum, honesty and linguistic clarity.

37. See the description reported in Frank C. Spooner, *Risks at Sea: Amsterdam Insurance and Maritime Europe, 1766–1780*, Cambridge: Cambridge University Press, 1983, p. 19.

38. Gauci, *Emporium of the World*, p. 142.

39. 'A bill of exchange was an offer of a certain amount of credit to a borrower – usually a merchant – who would then take the bill to where he was trading and, once his business was finished, redeem it with the local currency. Because currencies fluctuated in value against each other, the bank made sure that the borrower paid back more than he received; this was a form of interest, disguised by currency exchange rates'. James Cimet, 'Finance and Credit', in C. Clark Northrup (ed.), *Encyclopaedia of World Trade: From Ancient Times to the Present*, London: Routledge, 2013, pp. 357–362. See also Larry Neal, *The Rise of Financial Capitalism: International Capital Markets in the Age of Reason*, Cambridge: Cambridge University Press, 1991, pp. 5–6.

40. Abu-Lughod, *Before European Hegemony*, p. 223; and Lieber, 'Eastern Business Practices'.

41. Fernand Braudel, *The Structures of Everyday Life: Civilization & Capitalism 15th–18th Century*, Volume 1, London: Phoenix Press, 1981, p. 472.

42. Jan de Vries and Adrian van der Woude, *The First Modern Economy: Success, Failure, and Perseverance of the Dutch Economy, 1500–1815*, Cambridge: Cambridge University Press, 1997, p. 136. See also Violet Barbour's classic account in her *Capitalism in Amsterdam in the Seventeenth Century*, Ann Arbor: University of Michigan Press, 1963.

43. Neal, *The Rise of Financial Capitalism*, p. 46. See also Anne L. Murphy, *The Origins of English Financial Markets: Investment and Speculation before the South Sea Bubble*, Cambridge: Cambridge University Press, 2009.

44. De Vries and Van der Woude, *The First Modern Economy*, pp. 385, 118.

45. R. C. Nash, 'The Organization of Trade and Finance in the British Atlantic Economy, 1600–1830', in Peter A. Coclanis (ed.), *The Atlantic Economy during the Seventeenth and Eighteenth Centuries: Organization, Operation, Practice, and Personnel*, Columbia: University of South Carolina Press, 2005, pp. 95–151.

46. Jacob M. Price, *Perry of London: A Family and a Firm on the Seaborne Frontier, 1615–1753*, Cambridge, MA and London: Cambridge University Press, 1992, p. 2.

47. See Adrian B. Leonard (ed.), *Marine Insurance: Origins and Institutions, 1300–1850*, London: Palgrave, 2016; and Christopher Ebert, 'Early Modern Atlantic Trade and the Development of Maritime Insurance to 1630', *Past and Present*, Vol. 213, No. 1, 2011, pp. 87–114.

48. J. H. Parry, *The Discovery of the Sea*, Berkeley: University of California Press, 1982.

49. Studnicki-Gizbert, *A Nation upon the Ocean Sea*, p. 7.

50. Spooner, *Amsterdam Insurance*, Chapter 1.

51. Ibid., p. 12.

52. Ibid.

53. Nuala Zahedieh, *The Capital and the Colonies: London and the Atlantic Economy, 1660–1700*, Cambridge: Cambridge University Press, 2010, pp. 85–86.

54. See Chapter 1 of Tim Armstrong, *The Logic of Slavery: Debt, Technology, and Pain in American Literature*, Cambridge: Cambridge University Press, 2012.

55. Geoffrey Clark, *Betting on Lives: The Culture of Life Insurance in England, 1695–1775*, Manchester and New York: Manchester University Press, 1999.

56. Quoted in James Oldham, 'Insurance Litigation Involving the Zong and Other British Slave Ships, 1780–1807', *Journal of Legal History*, Vol. 28, No. 3, 2007, p. 308, italics in the original. See also Anita Rupprecht, '"Inherent Vice": Marine Insurance, Slave Ship Rebellion and the Law', *Race & Class*, Vol. 57, No. 3, 2016, pp. 31–44.

57. Simon Schama, *The Embarrassment of Riches: An Interpretation of Dutch Culture in the Golden Age*, London: Random House, 1997.

58. Robert C. Davis, *Shipbuilders of the Venetian Arsenal: Workers and Workplace in the Pre-industrial City*, Baltimore, MD: Johns Hopkins University Press, 2007.

59. De Vries and Van der Woude, *The First Modern Economy*, p. 297; and Pepijn Brandon, *War, Capital, and the Dutch State (1588–1795)*, Leiden: Brill, 2015, p. 166.

60. Van der Woude, *The First Modern Economy* p. 297.

61. Richard W. Unger, 'Technology and Industrial Organization: Dutch Shipbuilding to 1800', *Business History*, Vol. 17, No. 1, 1975, pp. 56–72.

62. Braudel, *The Perspective of the World*, p. 190.

63. Michael Berlin, 'Experimentation in Shipbuilding in Jacobean London: The English East India Company', *Journal de la Renaissance*, Vol. 2, 2004, pp. 31–40.

64. Ibid., p. 34.

65. Renisa Mawani, 'Archival Legal History: Towards the Ocean as Archive', in Markus D. Dubber and Christopher Tomlins (eds.), *The Oxford Handbook of Legal History*, Oxford: Oxford University Press, 2018, p. 306.

66. 'October 1651: An Act for increase of Shipping, and Encouragement of the Navigation of this Nation', in *Acts and Ordinances of the Interregnum, 1642–1660*, ed. C. H. Firth and R. S. Rait, London, 1911, pp. 559–562. *British History Online*, british-history.ac.uk, accessed 23 April 2019. Also Fernand Braudel, *The Perspective of the World: Civilization & Capitalism, 15th–18th Century*, Volume 3, trans. Sian Reynolds, London: Collins, 1984, p. 260; Lincoln Paine, *The Sea and Civilization: A Maritime History of the World*, London: Atlantic Books, 2014, p. 486.

67. Braudel, *The Perspective of the World*, 1984, p. 355.

68. From 115,000 tons to 340,000 tons. Peter Linebaugh and

Marcus Rediker, *The Many-Headed Hydra: The Hidden History of the Revolutionary Atlantic*, London: Verso, 2000, p. 146.

69. See the classic account in Ralph Davis, *The Rise of the English Shipping Industry in the Seventeenth and Eighteenth Centuries*, Newton Abbott: David & Charles, 1962.

70. Mawani, 'Archival Legal History', p. 306, emphasis added. Mawani goes on to argue that entry into ship ledgers and manifests further transformed captive Africans into property: 'As practices of enumeration, lists also classify, categorize, and abstract, often forcefully and violently . . . Manifests were required for all ships that entered foreign ports of call. These "lists" did not simply catalogue persons and commodities. They determined their status as animate/inanimate, legal/illegal, and free/unfree'. Ibid., p. 307.

71. Davis, *The Rise of the English Shipping Industry*, p. 70; Arthur Herman, *To Rule the Waves: How the British Navy Shaped the Modern World*, New York: Harper Perennial, 2005, p. 244. See also Philip Banbury, *Shipbuilders of the Thames and Medway*, Newton Abbott: David & Charles, 1971.

72. Davis, *The Rise of the English Shipping Industry*, p. 62.

73. Ibid., p. 390.

74. Rediker, *Between the Devil and the Deep Blue Sea*, pp. 28–29.

75. As discussed in John Merrington, 'Town and Country in the Transition to Capitalism', *New Left Review*, Vol. 1, No. 93, September–October 1975, p. 80.

76. Even within ship construction itself, see Eyûp Özveren, 'The Ship Building Commodity Chain, 1590–1790', in Gary Gereffi and Miguel Korzeniewicz (eds), *Commodity Chains and Global Capitalism*, Westport, CT: Praeger, 1994.

77. This summary is derived from De Vries and Van der Woude, *The First Modern Economy*, pp. 243–255.

78. Ibid., p. 243.

79. Ibid., p. 246.

80. Marx, *Capital*, Volume 3, London: Lawrence and Wishart, 1974, p. 325.

81. Wolf, *Europe*, p. 298.

82. Here we take our cue from Jason W. Moore's claim that human societies are always already inserted into a 'web of life' which acquires historically specific properties: 'how the mosaic of relations that we call capitalism work *through*

nature; and how nature works *through* that more limited zone, capitalism'. *Capitalism in the Web of Life: Ecology and the Accumulation of Capital*, London and New York: Verso, 2015, p. 1, italics in the original.

83. Karl Marx, *Grundrisse: Foundations of the Critique of Political Economy*, London: Penguin, 1993, p. 107.

84. Maxime Rodinson, *Islam and Capitalism*, trans. Brian Pearce, London: Allen Lane, 1974, pp. 6–8.

85. Louis Althusser and Étienne Balibar, *Reading Marx*, London and New York: Verso, 2016.

86. Aidan Foster-Carter, 'The Modes of Production Controversy', *New Left Review*, Vol. 1, No. 71, 1978, pp. 28–43.

87. Jairus Banaji, *Theory as History: Essays on Modes of Production and Exploitation*, Leiden and Boston, MA: Brill, 2010.

88. Ellen Meiksins Wood, *The Origin of Capitalism: A Longer View*, London and New York: Verso, 1999.

89. Robert Brenner, 'The Low Countries in the Transition to Capitalism', *Journal of Agrarian Change*, Vol. 1, No. 2, 2001, pp. 169–241; and Ellen Meiksins Wood, 'The Question of Market Dependence', *Journal of Agrarian Change*, Vol. 2, No. 1, 2002, pp. 50–87.

90. Immanuel Wallerstein, *The Modern World-System I: Capitalist Agriculture and the Origins of the European World-Economy in the Sixteenth Century*, New York: Academic Press, 1974, p. 91.

91. Giovanni Arrighi, *The Long Twentieth Century: Money, Power and the Origins of Our Time*, London and New York: Verso, 1994, p. 39.

92. Immanuel Wallerstein, *Historical Capitalism*, London and New York: Verso, 1983, p. 30.

93. Arrighi, *The Long Twentieth Century*, p. 11.

94. Robert Brenner, 'The Origins of Capitalist Development: A Critique of Neo-Smithian Marxism', *New Left Review*, Vol. 1, No. 104, 1977, p. 76.

95. Wood, *The Origin of Capitalism*, Chapter 4.

96. As demonstrated by Karl Polanyi in *The Great Transformation: The Political and Economic Origins of Our Time* (1944), New York: Beacon Press, 2002.

97. Wood, *The Origin of Capitalism*, p. 64.

98. Ibid., p. 84. See also Lauro Martines, *Power and Imagination: City-States in Renaissance Italy*, Baltimore, MD: Johns Hopkins University Press, 1988.

99. Wood, *The Origin of Capitalism*, pp. 85–86. On the tributary mode of production, see John Haldon, *The State and the Tributary Mode of Production*, London: Verso, 1993.

100. As Henry Bernstein asks rightly, albeit rhetorically, are these competing approaches not simply 'holding up a mirror to each other's strengths and weaknesses?', in 'Historical Materialism and Agrarian History', *Journal of Agrarian Change*, Vol. 1, No. 2, 2013, p. 325. Giovanni Arrighi also called the dispute between Brenner and Wallerstein one of the 'non-debates of the 1970s', arguing that 'class relations and conflicts are not reducible to core–periphery relations, just as the latter are not reducible to class relations and conflicts'. See his 'Capitalism and the Modern World-System: Rethinking the Non-debates of the 1970s', *Review (Fernand Braudel Center)*, Vol. 21, No. 1, 1998, pp. 113–129.

101. Marx, *Capital*, Volume 3, p. 332.

102. As Marx himself did across Volumes 1 and 2 of *Capital* and then developed in a more concrete synthesis in his notes for Volume 3.

103. See Jairus Banaji, *A Brief History of Commercial Capitalism*, Chicago: Haymarket Books, forthcoming.

104. Marx, *Capital*, Volume 3, pp. 309, 310.

105. Sidney Mintz, *Sweetness and Power: The Place of Sugar in Modern History*, London: Penguin, 1986, pp. 51–52.

106. Philip E. Steinberg, *The Social Construction of the Ocean*, Cambridge: Cambridge University Press, 2001. For the notion of 'ecological regime' see Moore, *Capitalism*, p. 158.

2. Order

1. See Gerrit W. Gong, *The Standard of 'Civilization' in International Society*, Oxford: Oxford University Press, 1984.

2. Carl Schmitt, *Land and Sea*, Washington, DC: Plutarch Press, 1997, p. 1.

3. *A Discourse of the Invention of Ships, Anchors, Compass, &c* (1650), quoted in Susan Ratcliffe, *Oxford Treasury of Sayings and Quotations*, Oxford: Oxford University Press, 2011, p. 403.

4. Ken Booth, *Law, Force & Diplomacy at Sea*, London: Allen & Unwin, 1985, p. 6.

5. Philip E. Steinberg offers a good summary of this 'battle of the books' in his *The Social Construction of the Ocean*, Cambridge: Cambridge University Press, 2001. See also Tullio Treves, 'Historical Development of the Law of the Sea', in Donald Rothwell, Alex G. Oude Elferink, Karen N. Scott and Tim Stephens (eds.), *The Oxford Handbook of the Law of the Sea*, Oxford: Oxford University Press, 2015.

6. Hugo Grotius, *The Free Sea*, Indianapolis: Liberty Fund, 2004, p. 37.

7. This statement appears in the title page of Selden's *Mare Clausum* (1635).

8. For a more detailed account, see Peter Borschberg, *Hugo Grotius, the Portuguese and Free Trade in the East Indies*, Singapore: National University of Singapore Press, 2011.

9. Grotius, *The Free Sea*, p. 30.

10. Steinberg, *The Social Construction of the Ocean*, Chapter 3.

11. Ibid., p. 98.

12. For an illuminating discussion of the distinction, see Lauren Benton, *A Search for Sovereignty: Law and Geography in European Empires 1400–1900*, Cambridge: Cambridge University Press, 2010, Chapter 3.

13. See the informative introduction by David Armitage to the Richard Haklyut translation *The Free Sea* (2004).

14. A thorough and historically contextualised reading can be found in Martine Julia van Ittersum, *Profit and Principle: Hugo Grotius, Natural Rights Theories and the Rise of Dutch Power in the East Indies (1595–1615)*, Leiden and Boston, MA: Brill, 2006.

15. Cited in Borschberg, *Hugo Grotius*, p. 50.

16. On this 'heteronomous' diversity of polities in the Indian Ocean, see Andrew Phillips and J. C. Sharman, *International Order in Diversity: War, Trade and Rule in the Indian Ocean*, Cambridge: Cambridge University Press, 2015.

17. See Borschberg, *Hugo Grotius*, Chapter 1.

18. Paul M. Kennedy, *The Rise and Fall of British Naval Mastery*, London and Basingstoke: Macmillan, 1983, p. 48.

19. Cited in ibid., p. 59.

20. Jaap R. Bruijn, *The Dutch Navy of the Seventeenth and Eighteenth Centuries*, Columbia: University of South Carolina Press, 1992.

21. Andrew Lambert, *War at Sea in the Age of Sail 1650–1850*, London: Cassell, 2000, p. 61. See also Michael A. Palmer, *Command at Sea: Naval Command and Control since the Sixteenth Century*, Cambridge, MA and London: Harvard University Press, 2005; and David Davies, 'The Birth of the Imperial Navy? Aspects of English Naval Strategy *c.*1659–90' in Michael Duffy (ed.), *Parameters of British Naval Power 1650–1850*, Exeter: Exeter University Press, 1995, pp. 14–38.

22. Richard Harding, *Seapower and Naval Warfare 1650–1830*, London: UCL Press, 1999, p. 41.

23. Ibid.

24. Ibid., p. 48.

25. See Rediker, *Between the Devil and the Deep Blue Sea*; and Margarette Lincoln, *British Pirates and Society, 1680–1730*, Farnham and Arlington, VT: Ashgate, 2014.

26. Benton, *A Search for Sovereignty*, p. 161.

27. Harding, *Seapower*, p. 185; and Lambert, *War at Sea*, p. 89.

28. Lambert, *War at Sea*, p. 25.

29. Daniel A. Baugh, 'Great Britain's "Blue-Water" Policy, 1689–1815', *International History Review*, Vol. 10, No. 1, 1988, p. 41. See also BennoTeschke, 'The Social Origins of 18th Century British Grand Strategy: a Historical Sociology of the Peace of Utrecht', in Alfred H.A. Soons (ed.), *The 1713 Peace of Utrecht and its Enduring Effects*, Leiden: Brill, forthcoming, pp. 120–55.

30. Eric Hobsbawm, *The Age of Revolution 1789–1848*, London: Abacus, 1997, p. 130.

31. Kennedy, *The Rise and Fall of British Naval Mastery*, p. 173; and Paine, *The Sea and Civilization*, p. 528.

32. Jan Martin Lemnitzer, *Power, Law and the End of Privateering*, Houndmills and New York: Palgrave Macmillan, 2014.

33. Andrew Lambert, 'The Pax Britannica and the Advent of Globalization', in Daniel Moran and James A. Russell (eds.),

Maritime Strategy and Global Order: Markets, Resources, Security, Washington, DC: Georgetown University Press, 2016, pp. 3–31, 20.

34. See Pat O'Malley, 'The Discipline of Violence: State, Capital and the Regulation of Warfare', *Sociology*, Vol. 22, No. 2, 1988, pp. 253–270.

35. Craig N. Murphy, *International Organization and Industrial Change: Global Governance since 1850*, Cambridge: Polity Press, 1994, p. 57.

36. Lambert, 'The Pax Britannica and the Advent of Globalization', p. 11.

37. Paine, *The Sea and Civilization*, p. 527.

38. Ibid., p. 560.

39. For a comparative overview, see Lisle A. Rose, *Power at Sea: The Age of Navalism, 1890–1918*, Columbia and London: University of Missouri Press, 2007. See also Mark Shulman, *Navalism and the Emergence of American Sea Power, 1882–1893*, Annapolis, MD: Naval Institute Press, 1996; David C. Evans and Mark R. Peattie, *Kaigun: Strategy, Tactics, and Technology in the Imperial Japanese Navy, 1887–1941*, Annapolis, MD: Naval Institute Press, 1997.

40. For a detailed account, see Bernard Semmel, *Liberalism and Naval Strategy: Ideology, Interest and Sea Power during the Pax Britannica*, London: Allen & Unwin, 1986.

41. For an overview see Chapter 2 of Geoffrey Till, *Seapower: A Guide for the Twenty-First Century*, London and Portland, OR: Frank Cass, 2004.

42. Alfred T. Mahan, *The Influence of Sea Power upon History, 1660–1783*, Boston, MA: Little, Brown, 1890, p. 138.

43. Ibid., p. 439.

44. Mark Shulman, 'Institutionalizing a Political Idea: Navalism and the Emergence of American Sea Power', in Peter Trubowitz, Emily O. Goldman and Edward Rhodes (eds.), *The Politics of Strategic Adjustment: Ideas, Institutions, and Interests*, New York: Columbia University Press, 1999, p. 82.

45. Rose, *Power at Sea*, p. 129.

46. Cited in Sadao Asada, *From Mahan to Pearl Harbor: The Imperial Japanese Navy and the United States*, Annapolis, MD: Naval Institute Press, 2006, p. 22.

47. Ibid., Chapter 2.

48. See John W. Coogan, *The End of Neutrality: The United States, Britain, and Maritime Rights 1899–1915*, Ithaca, NY and London: Cornell University Press, 1981; Andrew Lambert, 'Great Britain and Maritime Law from the Declaration of Paris to the Era of Total War', in R. Hobson and T. Kristiansen (eds.), *Navies in Northern Waters 1721–2000*, London and Portland, OR: Frank Cass, 2004, pp. 11–38; and Semmel, *Liberalism and Naval Strategy*.

49. Julian Stafford Corbett, *Some Principles of Maritime Strategy*, New York: Pantianos Classics, 1911, p. 44.

50. Jon Tetsuro Sumida, 'Reimagining the History of Twentieth-Century Navies', in Daniel Finamore (ed.), *Maritime History as World History*, Gainesville: University Press of Florida, 2004, pp. 167–182.

51. Lawrence Freedman and Ephraim Karsh, *The Gulf Conflict*, London and Boston: Faber & Faber, 1993, p. 85.

52. Naval History and Heritage Command, history.navy.mil, downloaded on 9 April 2017.

53. Stephen P. Dodd, 'Desert Shield/Desert Storm Employment of the Maritime Prepositioned Force: Triumph Or Mixed Success?' (1991), www.globalsecurity.org, downloaded on 9 April 2017.

54. C. T. Sandars, *America's Overseas Garrisons: The Leasehold Empire*, Oxford: Oxford University Press, 2000, p. 42.

55. Ibid., p. 70.

56. Ibid., p. 4.

57. James Blaker, *United States Overseas Basing*, New York: Praeger, 1990.

58. James Kraska, *Maritime Power and the Law of the Sea: Expeditionary Operations in World Politics*, Cambridge: Cambridge University Press, 2011, p. 83.

59. The Atlantic Charter, 14 August 1941, avalon.law.yale.edu.

60. NSC 68: United States Objectives and Programs for National Security, 14 April 1950, mtholyoke.edu.

61. See Alejandro Colás, 'Open Doors and Closed Frontiers: The Limits of American Empire', *European Journal of International Relations*, Vol. 14, No. 4, 2008, pp. 619–643.

62. Leo Panitch and Sam Gindin, *The Making of Global Capitalism: The Political Economy of American Empire*, London and New York: Verso, 2013.

63. The Atlantic Charter, 14 August 1941, avalon.law.yale.edu.
64. Barry R. Posen, 'Command of the Commons: The Military Foundation of U.S. Hegemony', *International Security*, Vol. 28, No. 1, 2003, p. 8.
65. 'Declaration of Panama', October 1939, www.loc.gov, accessed 17 April 2017. See also Clyde Sanger, *Ordering the Seas: The Making of the Law of the Sea*, London: Zed Books, 1986, p. 56.
66. Treves, 'Historical Development of the Law of the Sea', p. 10.
67. Proclamation 2667: Policy of the United States with Respect to the Natural Resources of the Subsoil and Sea Bed of the Continental Shelf, 28 September 1945, gc.noaa.gov/documents/gcil_proc_2667.pdf, accessed 2 May 2020.
68. John Hannigan, *The Geopolitics of Deep Oceans*, Cambridge: Polity Press, 2016.
69. Steinberg, *Social Construction*.
70. Proclamation 2667.
71. David Vine, *Island of Shame: The Secret History of the US Military Base in Diego Garcia*, Princeton, NJ and Oxford: Princeton University Press, 2011, p. 41.
72. Quoted in Ibid., p. 42.
73. Ibid., p. 8; and Sandars, *America's Overseas Garrisons*, pp. 55 ff.
74. Till, *Seapower*, p. 215.
75. Philip Windsor, *Strategic Thinking: An Introduction and Farewell*, London and Boulder, CO: Lynne Rienner, 2002.
76. Till, *Seapower*, p. 215.
77. Posen, 'Command of the Commons', p. 8.
78. 'Somalia Piracy: How Foreign Powers Are Tackling It', *BBC News*, 11 December 2018, bbc.co.uk.
79. Available, inter alia, on the Nato Shipping Centre website, shipping.nato.int.
80. MSCHOA, 'Safeguarding Trade through the Horn of Africa', mschoa.org.
81. IMO, 'Piracy and Armed Robbery against Ships off the Coast of Somalia', 29 November 2007, imo.org.
82. 'Pirate activity generally reduces in areas affected by the South West monsoon, and increases in the period following the monsoon. The onset of the North East monsoon generally has a lesser effect on piracy activity than the South West

monsoon'. Best Management Practices for Protection against Somalia Based Piracy 4, August 2011, p. 3, eunavfor.eu.

83. 'The Economic Cost of Maritime Piracy', Oceans Beyond Piracy, One Earth Future working paper, December 2010, oceansbeyondpiracy.org.

84. For an excellent overview and discussion, see Katherine Morton, 'China's Ambition in the South China Sea: Is a Legitimate Maritime Order Possible?', *International Affairs*, Vol. 92, No. 4, 2016, pp. 909–940.

85. Ibid.; Bill Hayton, *The South China Sea: The Struggle for Power in Asia*, New Haven, CT and London: Yale University Press, 2014; Leszek Buszynski, 'The South China Sea: Oil, Maritime Claims, and US–China Strategic Rivalry', *Washington Quarterly*, Vol. 35, No. 2, 2012, pp. 139–156.

86. Hayton, *The South China Sea*, pp. 212–213.

87. Kraska, *Maritime Power*, p. 167.

88. Buszynski, 'The South China Sea', 2012.

89. See, for instance, Bernard D. Cole, *China's Quest for Great Power: Ships, Oil, and Foreign Policy*, Annapolis, MD: Naval Institute Press, 2016.

90. David Shambaugh, *China Goes Global: The Partial Power*, Oxford: Oxford University Press, 2013.

91. Richard Ghiasy, Fei Su and Lora Saalman, *The 21st Century Maritime Silk Road: Security Implications and Ways Forward for the European Union*, SIPRI, September 2018. See also Thomas J. Bickford, Heidi A. Holz and Frederic Vellucci Jr, *Uncertain Waters: Thinking about China's Emergence as a Maritime Power*, Alexandria, VA: CAN China Studies, 2011.

3. Exploitation

1. Joseph Conrad, *The Shadow-Line* (1917), Oxford: Oxford University Press, 2003, p. 54.

2. *Final Report of the Royal Commission on Loss of Life at Sea*, 1887, London: Printed for HMSO by Eyre & Spottiswoode.

3. Ibid., pp. 14, 13.

4. Conrad, *The Shadow-Line*, p. 54.

5. *Final Report of the Royal Commission*, 1887.

6. Ibid., pp. 14, 13.
7. Heide Gerstenberger, 'Men Apart: The Concept of "Total Institution" and the Analysis of Seafaring', *International Journal of Maritime History*, Vol. 8, No. 1, 1996, p. 175.
8. Kobayashi Takiji, *The Crab Cannery Ship and Other Novels of Struggle* (1929), trans. Zeljko Cipris, Honolulu: University of Hawaii Press, 2013, p. 84.
9. W. G. Beasley, *The Rise of Modern Japan: Political, Economic, and Social Change since 1850*, Basingstoke and New York: Palgrave Macmillan, 2000, p. 184.
10. Leon Fink, *Sweatshops at Sea: Merchant Seamen in the World's First Globalized Industry, from 1812 to the Present*, Chapel Hill: University of North Carolina Press, 2014, p. 94.
11. Robin McDowell, Margie Mason and Martha Mendoza, 'AP Investigation: Are Slaves Catching the Fish You Buy?', 25 March 2015: https://www.ap.org/explore/seafood-from-slaves/ap-investigation-slaves-may-have-caught-the-fish-you-bought.html; Peter Vandergeest, Olivia Tran and Melissa Marschke, 'Modern Day Slavery in Thai Fisheries: Academic Critique, Practical Action', *Critical Asian Studies*, Vol. 49, No. 3, 2017, pp. 461–464; Christina Stringer, D. Hugh Whittaker and Glenn Simmons, 'New Zealand's Turbulent Waters: the Use of Forced Labour in the Fishing Industry', *Global Networks*, Vol. 16, No. 1, 2015, pp. 3–24.
12. S. E. Roberts, D. Nielsen, A. Kotłowski and B. Jaremin, 'Fatal Accidents and Injuries among Merchant Seafarers Worldwide', *Occupational Medicine*, Vol. 64, 2014, pp. 259–266.
13. David Walters and Nick Bailey, *Lives in Peril: Profit or Safety in the Global Maritime Industry*, Basingstoke: Palgrave Macmillan, 2013, pp. 2, 9.
14. ILO, *Seamen's Code*, p. 33.
15. Maritime Labour Convention, 2006, Article II (4).
16. Within the broad category of seafarers there are considerable contemporary dividing lines, such as by subsector (dry bulk, container vessels, specialised cargo; see Chapter 5); by different flags and/or firms within a subsector; and between crew in the same boat, such as by rank, perceived skill and technical division of labour, nationality, race, gender, conditions of work and pay.

17. 'Normal' in the sense of excluding both general capitalist crises of the system as a whole and industry-specific crises (e.g. of seafreight overcapacity where cost-price squeezes such as high gasoil price and low demand for freight might make journey *slowdowns* more profitable, as occurred in the 2000s). Chapter 5 develops this further.

18. See Stuart Hall, 'Race, Articulation and Societies Structured in Dominance', in UNESCO (ed.), *Sociological Theories: Race and Colonialism*, UNESCO: Poole, 1980, pp. 305–345; Jonathan Pattenden, *Labour, State and Society in Rural India: A Class-Relational Approach*, Manchester: Manchester University Press, 2016; and Liam Campling, Satoshi Miyamura, Jonathan Pattenden and Benjamin Selwyn, 'Class Dynamics of Development: A Methodological Note', *Third World Quarterly*, Vol. 37, No. 10, 2016, pp. 1745–1767.

19. Jairus Banaji, *Theory as History: Essays on Modes of Production and Exploitation*, Leiden: Brill, 2010, p. 145, emphasis added. Here, wage labour is not a simple, descriptive term, but a concrete category of 'capital-positing, capital-creating labour'. Karl Marx, *Grundrisse: Foundations of the Critique of Political Economy*, trans. Martin Nicolaus, Harmondsworth: Penguin, 1993, p. 463.

20. Compare Gerard Hanlon, *Dark Side of Management: A Secret History of Management Theory*, London: Routledge, 2015; with Alessandra Mezzadri, *The Sweatshop Regime: Labouring Bodies, Exploitation, and Garments Made in India*, Cambridge: Cambridge University Press, 2017.

21. Christian Parenti, 'The Environment Making State: Territory, Nature, and Value', *Antipode*, Vol. 47, No. 4, 2015, pp. 829–848; Alessandra Mezzadri, 'On the Value of Social Reproduction: Informal Labour, the Majority World and the Need for Inclusive Theories and Politics', *Radical Philosophy*, Vol. 2, No. 4, 2019, pp. 33–41.

22. See Suzanne J. Stark, *Female Tars: Women Aboard Ship in the Age of Sail*, Annapolis: Naval Institute Press, 1996. We do not claim to explore relations of gender or sexuality at sea, important though they are to the history of capitalism and the sea. For a collection of essays that break down the barrier of land and sea in the framing of gendered roles and

whose editors, in their introduction, 'argue that sailors' masculinity has been varied in form and meaning, that women have played active and important roles in maritime enterprise, and that the shore has been vital in shaping seafaring experience', see Creighton and Norling, *Iron Men, Wooden Women*, p. vii. For an exploration of maritime gender relationships between men and women – including the interpenetration of labour – told through diaries and letters, see Lisa Norling, *Captain Ahab Had a Wife: New England Women and the Whalefishery, 1720–1870*, Chapel Hill: University of North Carolina Press, 2000. For a careful study based on interviews with gay men on their experiences in the merchant navy from the 1950s to the 1980s, see Paul Baker and Jo Stanley, *Hello Sailor! The Hidden History of Gay Life at Sea*, London: Routledge, 2003.

23. The circuit of capital highlights the sequence of relations wherein people and things (variable and constant capital) are brought together by capitalists; value is produced by labour and realised through exchange; and the circuit returns to 'its original qualitative starting form', but with a quantitative augmentation of value now the property of capitalists ('surplus value'). Ray Hudson, 'Cultural Political Economy Meets Global Production Networks', *Journal of Economic Geography*, Vol. 8, No. 3, 2008, p. 423.

24. Jonathan Pattenden, 'Working at the Margins of Global Production Networks: Local Labour Control Regimes and Rural-Based Labourers in South India', *Third World Quarterly*, Vol. 37, No. 10, 2016, pp. 1809–1833; and Elena Baglioni, Liam Campling, Alessandra Mezzadri, Satoshi Miyamura, Jonathan Pattenden and Benjamin Selwyn, 'Exploitation and Labour Regimes: Production, Circulation, Social Reproduction, Ecology', unpublished paper, 2019.

25. A labour regime cannot be understood in isolation but is defined relationally, vis-à-vis other regimes in an industry or sector, and even within the same workplace. See Steffen Fischer, 'Labour Regimes, Embeddedness and Commodity Chains: Liberia's Iron Ore and Rubber Industries', PhD thesis, Queen Mary University of London, 2016.

26. The physical and geographical containment of seafarers bears some equivalence with onshore dormitory labour regimes,

such as in factories in China, two major differences being that ships move among jurisdictions and national regulation can shift overnight with flags of convenience. See, for example, Pun Ngai, 'Gendering the Dormitory Labor System: Production, Reproduction, and Migrant Labor in South China', *Feminist Economics*, Vol. 13, Nos. 3–4, 2007, pp. 239–258.

27. L. Cope Cornford, *The Merchant Seaman in War*, London: Hodder and Stoughton, 1918, p. xiii; Yrjö Kaukiainen, 'Growth, Diversification and Globalization: Main Trends in International Shipping since 1850', in Lewis R. Fischer and Even Lange (eds.), *International Merchant Shipping in the Nineteenth and Twentieth Centuries: The Comparative Dimension*, St John's, NF: International Maritime Economic History Association, 2008.

28. Peter Linebaugh, *The London Hanged: Crime and Civil Society in the Eighteenth Century*, 2nd edn, London: Verso, 2003, pp. 123, 125 – the 'deep-sea proletariat' is Linebaugh's term.

29. These data do not include those receiving wages from the Royal Navy, whose ranks swelled during Britain's many wars. See Roger Morriss, *The Foundations of British Maritime Ascendancy: Resources, Logistics and the State, 1755–1815*, Cambridge: Cambridge University Press, 2011, pp. 226–7, Table 6.1; and N. A. M. Rodger, *The Command of the Ocean: A Naval History of Britain 1649–1815*, London: Penguin, 2005, p. 396.

30. Morriss, *The Foundations of British Maritime Ascendancy*, p. 230.

31. Ibid., pp. 244–246; Rodger, *Command of the Ocean*, p. 404.

32. Rediker, *Between the Devil and the Deep Blue Sea*.

33. W. Jeffrey Bolster, *Black Jacks: African American Seamen in the Age of Sail*, Cambridge, MA: Harvard University Press, 1997, p. 78.

34. Paine, *The Sea and Civilization*, 2014, pp. 426–427.

35. Morriss, *British Maritime Ascendancy*, p. 247; Linebaugh, *London Hanged*, p. 127; Brian Lavery, *The Conquest of the Ocean: The Illustrated History of Seafaring*, London: Dorling Kindersley, 2013, p. 134.

36. See Elizabeth A. Sibilia on the distinction between progressive depreciation (the sense used here) and periodic depreciation in

shipping: 'Oceanic Accumulation: Geographies of Speculation, Overproduction, and Crisis in the Global Shipping Economy', *Environment and Planning A*, Vol. 51, No. 2, 2019, pp. 467–486. Also Stephen Graham and Nigel Thrift, 'Out of Order: Understanding Repair and Maintenance', *Theory, Culture & Society*, Vol. 24, No. 3, 2007, pp. 1–25.

37. Braudel, *The Perspective of the World*, 1984, p. 506.

38. Respectively, fourteen and seventeen tons per crew member and 4.5 tons per crew. Matthias van Rossum, Lex Heerma van Voss, Jelle van Lottum and Jan Lucassen, 'National and International Labour Markets for Sailors in European, Atlantic and Asian Waters, 1600–1850', in Maria Fusaro and Amélia Polónia (eds.), *Maritime History as Global History* (Research in Maritime History No. 43), Liverpool: Liverpool University Press, 2017, p. 65.

39. For a comparative sketch of the commodity chains enabled by the merchant navy in the era of commercial capitalism, see Jairus Banaji, 'Merchant Capitalism, Peasant Households, and Industrial Accumulation: Integration of a Model', in Liam Campling and Jens Lerche (eds.), *The Political Economy of Agrarian Change: Essays in Appreciation of Henry Bernstein, Journal of Agrarian Change*, Vol. 16, No. 3, 2016, pp. 410–431.

40. In intra-Asian shipping between 1778 and 1783, the sluggish development of capitalism in France is reflected in an average 5.9 tons per crew member compared to boats from the Dutch Republic at 10.2 tons. See Van Rossum et al., 'National and International Labour', p. 66.

41. Linebaugh, *London Hanged*, p. 133.

42. Braudel, *The Perspective of the World*, p. 504.

43. Bolster, *Black Jacks*, p. 76.

44. Ibid., p. 194.

45. Van Rossum et al., 'National and International Labour Markets', p. 67.

46. In the case of the British Admiralty, a detailed list of questions were asked of captains and crew members to discern whether the vessel and its cargo were legitimate enemies. Ibid., pp. 48–49.

47. Gonçal López Nadal, 'Mediterranean Privateering between the Treaties of Utrecht and Paris, 1715–1856: First

Reflections', in David J. Starkey, E. S. van Eyck van Heslinga and J. A. de Moor (eds.), *Pirates and Privateers: New Perspectives on the War on Trade in the Eighteenth and Nineteenth Centuries*, Exeter: Exeter University Press, 1997.

48. Van Rossum et al., 'National and International Labour', pp. 55–56.

49. Frank Broeze, 'The Muscles of Empire: Indian Seamen and the Raj, 1919–1939', *Indian Economic and Social History Review*, Vol. 1, 1981, pp. 43–67.

50. Van Rossum et al., 'National and International Labour', pp. 62–63, 66. One of the few records where 'lascars' were interrogated – the assessment of an Armenian-owned prize – indicates that the South Asian crew had a better knowledge of crew and passenger numbers and their composition than did their French captain.

51. The term 'lascar' (generally translated as 'soldier') is of Persian/Urdu origin but has multiple meanings and a complex etymology. It is generally used to refer to people from South Asia (the sense used here), but this spills over to include seafarers from the Indian Ocean region, such as those of African, Arab and South East Asian origin. Part of the complication stems from its fluid use by people from various places to try to work within British labour regulations. See the discussions in Balachandran, *Globalizing Labour?*, pp. 28–34; Amitav Ghosh, 'Of Fanas and Forecastles: The Indian Ocean and Some Lost Languages of the Age of Sail', *Economic and Political Weekly*, Vol. 43, No. 25, 2008, pp. 56–62; and David A. Chappell, 'Ahab's Boat: Non-European Seamen in Western Ships of Exploration and Commerce', in Bernhard Klein and Gesa Mackenthun (eds.), *Sea Changes: Historicizing the Ocean*, London: Routledge, 2004, pp. 75–89.

52. While 'lascars' are generally thought to have entered employment as crew 'freely', there is evidence to show some occasional overlap with slavery. See Anna Winterbottom, 'From Hold to Foredeck: Slave Professions in the Maritime World of the East India Company, c.1660–1720', in Fusaro and Polónia, *Maritime History as Global History*.

53. Van Rossum et al., 'National and International Labour', pp. 52–53, 56.

54. Ibid., pp. 68–69.
55. Ibid., p. 72.
56. Morriss, *British Maritime Ascendancy*, p. 230. Van Rossum et al., 'National and International Labour', do not consider Irish to be foreigners on British boats, but we expect that, as a subjugated people, Irish sailors would largely have considered the English to be 'foreign'.
57. For example, the banning of foreigners on local ships was one of the grievances of the seafarers' strike in 1815 in North East England. Norman McCord, 'The Seamen's Strike of 1815 in North-East England', *Economic History Review*, Vol. 21, No. 1, 1968, pp. 127–143.
58. Isaac Land, 'Customs of the Sea: Flogging, Empire, and the "True British Seaman" 1770 to 1870', *Interventions*, Vol. 3, No. 2, 2001, pp. 174, 171, 181.
59. Seltzer, 'Sailors Tavern'.
60. Morriss, *British Maritime Ascendancy*, p. 229.
61. Fink, *Sweatshops at Sea*, p. 11 and p. 204.
62. Ibid., p. 17.
63. Ibid., pp. 19, 22–23. British shipping dominated the Atlantic maritime economy throughout the nineteenth century; see Chapter 5, 'Logistics'.
64. Gopal Balachandran, 'South Asian Seafarers and Their Worlds, *c.*1870–1930s', in Jerry H. Bentley, Renate Brindenthal and Karen Wigen (eds.), *Seascapes: Maritime Histories, Littoral Cultures and Trans-oceanic Exchanges*, Honolulu: University of Hawaii Press, 2007, pp. 187–188.
65. Laura Tabili, '"A Maritime Race": Masculinity and the Racial Division of Labor in British Merchant Ships, 1900–1939', in Creighton and Norling, *Iron Men, Wooden Women*, p. 177.
66. Jonathan Hyslop, 'Steamship Empire: Asian, African and British Sailors in the Merchant Marine *c.*1880–1945', *Journal of Asian and African Studies*, Vol. 44, No. 1, 2009, p. 57.
67. Van Rossum et al., 'National and International Labour', pp. 71, 58–62.
68. Rediker, *Between the Devil and the Deep Blue Sea*.
69. Ravi Ahuja, 'Mobility and Containment: The Voyages of South Asian Seamen, *c.*1900–1960', *International Review of*

Social History, Vol. 51, 2006, pp. 111–141; Balachandran, 'South Asian Seafarers'.

70. Ahuja, 'Mobility and Containment', p. 111. Balachandran, 'South Asian Seafarers', p. 188.

71. Balachandran, *Globalizing Labour*, p. 27.

72. Ahuja, 'Mobility and Containment', p. 112.

73. M. H. Fisher, 'Indian *Ghat Sarangs* as Maritime Labour Recruiting Intermediaries during the Age of Sail', *Journal for Maritime Research*, Vol. 16, No. 2, 2014, pp. 153–166.

74. Ibid., p. 155.

75. Balachandran, *Globalizing Labour?*, p. 62.

76. Ibid., p. 63.

77. Ibid., p. 72.

78. Janet J. Ewald, 'Bondsmen, Freedmen, and Maritime Industrial Transportation, c.1840–1900', *Slavery & Abolition*, Vol. 31, No. 3, 2010, pp. 451–466.

79. Ibid., p. 453.

80. Morriss, *British Maritime Ascendancy*, p. 234.

81. Davis, *The Rise of the English Shipping Industry*, pp. 146, 171, 153.

82. Morriss, *British Maritime Ascendancy*, pp. 234, 232; Linebaugh, *London Hanged*, p. 128.

83. Linebaugh, *London Hanged*, p. 127; Rediker, *Between the Devil and the Deep Blue Sea*, pp. 130–132. On Britain's slave ships, this practice appears to have been reserved exclusively for captains and senior officers, wherein a pre-specified number of slaves or (later) a proportion of the monetary value from the eventual sale of slaves was allocated as their 'privilege'. Marcus Rediker, *The Slave Ship: A Human History*, London: John Murray, 2007, pp. 194, 389 fn. 17.

84. This practice is traced variously to ancient Byzantine maritime law – when Rhodes was a maritime power in the third century BCE – and to the medieval Laws of Oleron (1194 CE), where crew took a share of the profits of a voyage or a portion of the cargo space. Paine, *The Sea and Civilization*, pp. 224–225; Rediker, *Between the Devil and the Deep Blue Sea*, p. 130.

85. Linebaugh and Rediker, *The Many-Headed Hydra*, pp. 162–167, 328–333.

86. Linebaugh, *London Hanged*, p. 130.

87. Morriss, *British Maritime Ascendancy*, pp. 249, 258–259.
88. Land, 'Customs of the Sea', pp. 174–175.
89. For example, Burkard Sievers, 'Before the Surrogate of Motivation: Motivation and the Meaning of Work in the Golden Age of the American Whaling Industry. Part 1', *Critique*, Vol. 37, No. 3, 2009, pp. 391–431.
90. Niklas Frykman, Clare Anderson, Lex Heerma van Voss and Marcus Rediker, 'Mutiny and Maritime Radicalism in the Age of Revolution: An Introduction', *International Review of Social History*, Vol. 58, No. S21, 2013, p. 3.
91. 'Royal Navy Articles of War 1757', Naval Marine Archive, The Canadian Collection, navalmarinearchive.com, last accessed 23 April 2019.
92. Morriss, *Foundations*, p. 267; Land, 'Customs of the Sea'. Flogging was phased out in the Royal Navy by the 1870s, but American captains were permitted to beat and imprison sailors under US law until 1898.
93. Peter Earle, *Sailors: English Merchant Seamen 1650–1775*, London; Methuen, 2007, pp. 147–148.
94. Ibid., p. 147.
95. Bolster, *Black Jacks*, p. 72. See also Chapter 3 of Emma Christopher's *Slave Ship Sailors and Their Captive Cargoes, 1730–1807*, Cambridge: Cambridge University Press, 2006.
96. N. A. M. Rogers, 'Shipboard Life in the Georgian Navy, 1750–1800: The Decline of the Old Order', in Lewis R. Fischer, Harald Hamre, Poul Holm and Jaap R. Bruijn (eds.), *The North Sea: Twelve Essays on Social History of Maritime Labour*, Stravanger: Stavanger Maritime Museum/The Association of North Sea Societies, 1992, pp. 29–39.
97. Morriss, *British Maritime Ascendancy*, p. 265, Table 6.10.
98. As cited by Land, 'Customs of the Sea', p. 174.
99. Conrad Dixon, 'The Rise and Fall of the Crimp, 1840–1914', in Stephen Fisher (ed.), *British Shipping and Seamen, 1650–1960*, Exeter: University of Exeter Press, 1984, pp. 49–67; Seltzer, 'Haven and a Heartless Sea'.
100. Winterbottom, 'From Hold to Foredeck', p. 116; Rediker, *The Slave Ship*, pp. 268–270.
101. Clive Emsley, 'The Recruitment of Petty Offenders during the French Wars 1793–1815', *Mariner's Mirror*, Vol. 66, No. 3, 1980, p. 199.

102. Morriss, *British Maritime Ascendancy*, pp. 236–238 (Table 6.2), 242. Also Rodger, *Command of Ocean*, pp. 397–398. It is worth noting that even the well-paid and protected craft work in the shipyards of the 1700s had been subject to forced labour in the 1500s and 1600s. Linebaugh, *London Hanged*, p. 392.

103. Morriss, *British Maritime Ascendancy*, pp. 241, 243–244.

104. Marine Society 'History', marine-society.org; Linebaugh, *London Hanged*, p. 129.

105. Morriss, *British Maritime Ascendancy*, p. 228.

106. Frank Broeze, 'Militancy and Pragmatism: An International Perspective on Maritime Labour, 1870–1914', *International Review of Social History*, Vol. 36, No. 2, 1991, pp. 165–200.

107. E. P. Thompson, *The Making of the English Working Class*, New York: Vintage Books, 1966, pp. 604 fn. 2, 62–63, also 81; Land, 'Customs of the Sea', p. 171.

108. Linebaugh, *London Hanged*, p. 335.

109. Morriss, *British Maritime Ascendancy*, pp. 242–243.

110. McCord, 'The Seamen's Strike of 1815'.

111. On shore, some out-of-work sailors would resort to petty crime to survive and here, as at sea, their transgressions were met with extreme consequences. Linebaugh details the stories of sailors 'hanged as examples to other sailors whose lives were valuable precisely to the extent that their labours brought to England the wealth of nations'. Linebaugh, *London Hanged*, p. 126.

112. Morriss, *British Maritime Ascendancy*, pp. 261–262; Frykman et al., 'Mutiny and Maritime Radicalism', p. 4.

113. D. J. Rowe, 'A Trade Union of the North-East Coast Seamen in 1825', *Economic History Review*, Vol. 25, No. 1, 1972, pp. 81–98; John Flanagan, '"A Gigantic Scheme of Co-operation": The Miners' and Seamen's United Association in the North-East, 1851–1854', *Labour History Review*, Vol. 74, No. 2, 2009, pp. 143–159.

114. Luke Trainor, 'The Historians and Maritime Labour, c.1850–1930', in Frank Broeze (ed.), *Maritime History at the Crossroads: A Critical Review of Recent Historiography* (Research in Maritime History No. 9), Liverpool: Liverpool University Press, 2017.

115. Flanagan, 'A Gigantic Scheme', pp. 144–145.

116. Such as the blockade of the Tyne and the Wear in 1815 in North East England by sailors over pay and a minimum (safe) number of crew per tonnage. McCord, 'The Seamen's Strike of 1815'; see also Walters and Bailey, *Lives in Peril*, pp. 174–176.

117. Nicolette Jones, *The Plimsoll Sensation: The Great Campaign to Save Lives at Sea*, London: Little, Brown, 2006.

118. Broeze, 'Militancy and Pragmatism, pp. 172–173.

119. Originally an organisation of exclusively maritime labour, the International Federation of Ship, Dock and River Workers changed its name to the ITF in 1898 when other transport workers joined.

120. 1897 poster, *The International Movement, What It Is, Its Programme and Policy*, document reference MSS.159/3/C/A/14/31, University of Warwick Library, Modern Records Centre, The International Transport Workers' Federation online exhibition, warwick.ac.uk, last accessed 23 April 2019.

121. Broeze, 'Militancy and Pragmatism'.

122. Which, incidentally, was where Ernest Bevin cut his political teeth. Trainor, 'The Historians and Maritime Labour', p. 287.

123. Ibid., pp. 280–281.

124. For Broeze, 'Militancy and Pragmatism', p. 172, 'maritime labour contained within itself a fundamental and never-ending dialectic conflict between militancy and pragmatism'.

125. G. Atchkanov 192–, *Havelock Wilson Exposed*, Seaman's Section of Transport Workers' Minority Movement, London, p. 8.

126. L. H. Powell, *The Shipping Federation: A History of the First Sixty Years, 1890–1950*, London: Shipping Federation, 1950 pp. 1–2. Today it is called the Chamber of Shipping.

127. Broeze, 'Militancy and Pragmatism'; Trainor, 'The Historians and Maritime Labour',

128. Edna Bonacich and Jake B. Wilson, *Getting the Goods: Ports, Labor, and the Logistics Revolution*, Ithaca, NY: Cornell University Press, 2008.

129. Fink, *Sweatshops at Sea*.

130. Cope Cornford, *The Merchant Seaman in War*, p. xiii.

131. Dik Gregory and Paul Shanahan, *The Human Element: A Guide to Human Behaviour in the Shipping Industry*, UK Maritime and Coastguard Agency, 2010, p. 10.
132. Seltzer, 'The Sailors' Tavern', p. 65. Also Walters and Bailey, *Lives in Peril*, p. 95.
133. See for example, the 2017 collection of research edited by Malcolm MacLachlan, *Maritime Psychology: Research in Organizational & Health Behavior at Sea*, Cham: Springer.
134. See the excellent book by Penny McCall Howard, *Environment, Labour and Capitalism at Sea: 'Working the Ground' in Scotland*, Manchester: Manchester University Press, 2016; Alastair Couper, Hance D. Smith and Bruno Ciceri, *Fishers and Plunderers: Theft, Slavery and Violence at Sea*, London: Pluto, 2015. On wage forms, see Penny McCall Howard, 'Sharing or Appropriation? Share Systems, Class and Commodity Relations in Scottish Fisheries', *Journal of Agrarian Change*, Vol. 12, Nos. 2–3, 2012, pp. 316–343.
135. Rogers, 'Shipboard Life'.
136. Sampson, *International Seafarers*, p. 77; Walters and Bailey, *Lives in Peril*, p. 73.
137. The basic requirements were set out from 1978 with the International Convention on Standards of Training, Certification and Watchkeeping for Seafarers (or STCW).
138. Walters and Bailey, *Lives in Peril*, p. 75.
139. Margareta Lützhöft, Erik Styhr Petersen and Apsara Abeysiriwardhane, 'The Psychology of Ship Architecture and Design', in Malcolm MacLachlan (ed.), *Maritime Psychology: Research in Organizational & Health Behavior at Sea*, Cham: Springer, 2017, pp. 69–98; and H. Sampson, N. Ellis, I. Acejo, N. Turgo and L. Tang, *The Working and Living Conditions of Seafarers on Cargo Ships in the Period 2011–2016*, Cardiff: Seafarers International Research Centre, 2018.
140. Crewing costs are proportionally lower across different types of modern ships, e.g. 'when the capacity of a containership increases by 340%, the labor costs rise by 40%'. Corinne Bagoulla and Patrice Guillotreau, 'Shortage and Labor Productivity on the Global Seafaring Market', in Patrick Chaumette (ed.), *Seafarers: An International Labour Market in Perspective*, Bilbao: Gomylex, 2016, p. 25; see also J. M. Silos, F. Piniella, J. Monedero, J. Walliser, 'Trends in the

Global Market for Crews: A Case Study', *Marine Policy*, Vol. 36, No. 4, 2012, pp. 845–858, Table 1.

141. Although there is evidence that this has improved on bigger, newer ships in the 2010s. See Sampson et al., *The Working and Living Conditions of Seafarers*. A small number of cargo ships were designed in the early 1970s as experiments with practices of industrial democracy. See Javier Lezaun, 'Offshore Democracy: Launch and Landfall of a Socio-technical Experiment', *Economy and Society*, Vol. 40, No. 4, 2009, pp. 553–581.

142. Sampson, *International Seafarers*; Walters and Bailey, *Lives in Peril*.

143. Sampson, *International Seafarers*, pp. 79–90.

144. A. D. Couper, with C. J. Walsh, B. A. Stranberry and G. L. Boerne, *Voyages of Abuse: Seafarers, Human Rights and International Shipping*, London: Pluto, 1999, pp. 11–12; Walters and Bailey, *Lives in Peril*, p. 74; Sampson, *International Seafarers*, p. 8.

145. Malcolm MacLachlan, 'Maritime Psychology: Definition, Scope and Conceptualization', in MacLachlan, *Maritime Psychology*, pp. 1–17; Walters and Bailey, *Lives in Peril*, pp. 77–78.

146. UNCTAD, *Review of Maritime Transport 2013*, Geneva: UNCTAD, 2014, p. 55.

147. See Chapter 5 for further discussion of crises and business cycles in the shipping industry.

148. John Urry, *Offshoring*, Cambridge: Polity, 2014, p. 159.

149. All industries rely on migrant labour in varied forms, and export processing zones sometimes allow for the employment of people from anywhere, but there are often conditions attached (e.g. work permits), and no other industry has the globally generalised labour market conditions that characterise international shipping.

150. Francisco Piniella, Juan Ignacio Alcaide and Emilio Rodríguez-Díaz, 'The Panama Ship Registry: 1917–2017', *Marine Policy*, Vol. 77, March 2017, pp. 13–22; North Atlantic Fisheries Intelligence Group and Interpol, *Chasing Red Herrings: Flags of Convenience and the Impact on Fisheries Crime Law Enforcement*. Oslo: NA-FIG, 2017.

151. WTO, *Trade Policy Review – Vanuatu*, Geneva: WTO Secretariat, 2018.

152. Fink, *Sweatshops at Sea*, p. 178.
153. Jane Joshua, 'Gov't Nets Vt1.9 Billion Revenue from Vanuatu Shipping Registry', *Vanuatu Daily Post*, 5 October, 2014; and International Monetary Fund, Government Finance Statistics Yearbook and data files, last accessed 18 February 2019.
154. Rodney Carlisle, 'Second Registers: Maritime Nations Respond to Flags of Convenience, 1984–1998', *Northern Mariner/le marin du nord*, Vol. 19, No. 3, 2009, pp. 319–340.
155. ITF Seafarers, 'Defining FOCs and the Problems They Pose', www.itfseafarers.org, last accessed 24 April 2019.
156. See the extensive discussion of new entrant FOC states in Tony Alderton and Nik Winchester, 'Regulation, Representation and the Flag Market', *Journal for Maritime Research*, Vol. 4, No. 1, 2002, pp. 89–105.
157. DeSombre does not reach this conclusion herself, but it is apparent from a comparison of the data in her Appendix C. Elizabeth DeSombre, *Flagging Standards: Globalization and Environmental, Safety and Labor Regulations at Sea*, Cambridge, MA: MIT Press, 2006, pp. 260–263.
158. Walters and Bailey, *Lives in Peril*.
159. Stephen E. Roberts and Tim Carter, 'Causes and Circumstances of Maritime Casualties and Crew Fatalities in British Merchant Shipping since 1925', *International Maritime Health*, Vol. 69, No. 2, 2018, p. 108.
160. Tony Alderton and Nik Winchester, 'Globalisation and De-regulation in the Maritime Industry', *Marine Policy*, Vol. 26, 2002, pp. 35–43; Couper et al., *Voyages of Abuse*.
161. Sampson, *International Seafarers*, pp. 40–41: Couper et al., *Voyages of Abuse*.
162. Shin Goto, 'Globalization and International Competitiveness: The Experience of the Japanese Shipping Industry since the 1960s', in David J. Starkey and Gelina Harlaftis (eds.), *Global Markets: The Internationalization of the Sea Transport Industries since 1850*, St. John's, NF: International Maritime Economic History Association, 1998.
163. Interviews, Japanese industry representatives, 2006.
164. Goto, 'Japanese Shipping', pp. 363–364.
165. Ibid., pp. 373–77.
166. Silos et al., 'Trends in the Global Market', p. 851.
167. Beneficial ownership of the merchant fleet in the early

twenty-first century sees capital headquartered in Western Europe and, increasingly, East Asia (see Chapter 5).

168. Martin Stopford, *Maritime Economics*, 3rd edn, London: Routledge, 2008, p. 225.

169. BIMCO/ISF, *Manpower 2015 Update: The Worldwide Demand for and Supply of Seafarers*, Bagsværd and London: Baltic and International Maritime Council and International Shipping Federation, 2015.

170. *Drewry*, 'Shipping's Recovery Insufficient to Lift Seafarer Wage Costs', 4 September 2017; Silos et al., 'Trends in the Global Market', p. 851.

171. Bagoulla and Guillotreau, 'Shortage and Labor', pp. 17, 27.

172. For officers it was China, Philippines, India, Indonesia and Russia. BIMCO/ISF, *Manpower 2015*, p. 11. But these data collapse junior and senior officers and thus tell us little about the relationship between nationality and social hierarchy on boats. Among capital-supplying countries where vessel ownership lies, the ratio of officers to ratings is a lot higher than in Labour supply countries. N. Ellis and H. Sampson, 'The Global Labour Market for Seafarers Working Aboard Merchant Cargo Ships 2003', Cardiff: Seafarers International Research Centre, 2008; Bagoulla and Guillotreau, 'Shortage and Labor'; Nathan Lillie, 'Global Collective Bargaining on Flag of Convenience Shipping', *British Journal of Industrial Relations*, Vol. 42, No. 1, 2004, p. 59 Table 2.

173. Alastair Couper, 'Implications of Maritime Globalization for the Crews of Merchant Ships', *Journal for Maritime Research*, Vol. 2, No. 1, 2000, pp. 1–8.

174. Sampson, *International Seafarers*, p. 38.

175. Liam Campling, 'The Tuna "Commodity Frontier": Business Strategies and Environment in the Industrial Tuna Fisheries of the Western Indian Ocean', *Journal of Agrarian Change*, Vol. 12, Nos. 2–3, 2012, pp. 252–278.

176. Multiple interviews, representatives of French and Spanish boat owners, and Malagasy and Seychellois crew, Antsiranana, Madagascar, December 2013, and Port Victoria, Seychelles, January 2014.

177. Kate Barclay, *A Japanese Joint Venture in the Pacific: Foreign Bodies in Tinned Tuna*, London: Routledge, 2008, p. 60. See Chapter 4 below for more on Japan's distant-water fishing.

178. Personal communication, EU distant-water fleet representative, January 2014; multiple interviews, labour representatives in Madagascar and Seychelles, 2013 and 2014.
179. ILO, *The International Seamen's Code*, p. 38.
180. Participating in an international meeting of fishers' trade unions in 2014, one of the authors was struck by the similarities in the types of lines being taken in inter-*state* negotiations at the WTO on issues related to the fisheries trade that he had also attended. Several of the fishers' unions took explicit 'national interest' lines which were often defensive in relation to national industry (and thus 'national' jobs).
181. Robyn Magalit Rodriguez, *Migrants for Export: How the Philippine State Brokers Labor to the World*, Minneapolis: University of Minnesota Press, 2010.
182. Maragtas S. V. Amante, *Philippine Global Seafarers: A Profile*, Cardiff: Seafarers International Research Centre, 2003; Philippine Overseas Employment Administration, 'Overseas Employment Statistics: Deployed Overseas Filipino Workers 2016 vs 2015', poea.gov.ph, last accessed 26 April 2019.
183. Maragtas S. V. Amante, 'Industrial Democracy in the Rough Seas: The Case of Philippine Seafarers', US Industrial Relations Research Association, 56th Annual Proceedings, 2004.
184. Sampson, *International Seafarers*, p. 75; Walters and Bailey, *Lives in Peril*, pp. 92–94.
185. Sampson, *International Seafarers*; Walters and Bailey, *Lives in Peril*, p. 93; interview, fishing crew representative, Antsiranana, Madagascar, December 2013.
186. Interviews, union representatives, Antsiranana, Madagascar, December 2013.
187. Interview, crew agency representative, Antsiranana, Madagascar, December 2013. Similar sentiments were shared by another two crew agencies in Madagascar interviewed at the same time and two in Seychelles interviewed a month afterwards.
188. Sampson, *International Seafarers*, p. 45.
189. William Gorham Rice and W. Ellison Chalmers, 'Improvement of Labor Conditions on Ships by International Action', *Monthly Labor Review*, Vol. 42, No. 5, 1936, p. 1181.

190. Couper et al., *Voyages of Abuse*, p. 142.

191. Trainor, 'The Historians and Maritime Labour', pp. 284–5, 287.

192. Michael B. Miller, *Europe and the Maritime World: A Twentieth-Century History*, Cambridge: Cambridge University Press, 2012.

193. Gary M. Fink (ed.), *The Greenwood Encyclopaedia of American Institutions: Labor Unions*, Westport, CT: Greenwood Press, 1977, pp. 214–215. The Spring Strike of 1936 against poor working conditions at sea was the spark in the creation of the National Maritime Union – the main American union of 'unlicensed' seafarers.

194. Balachandran, *Globalizing Labour?*, pp. 192–193.

195. Featherstone, 'Maritime Labour and Subaltern Geographies of Internationalism', p. 9.

196. M. Sherwood, 'Strikes! African Seamen, Elder Dempster and the Government, 1940–42'. *Immigrants and Minorities*, Vol. 13, Nos. 2–3, 1994, pp. 130–145.

197. David Featherstone, 'Maritime Labour', p. 12.

198. Amante, 'Industrial Democracy'; Walters and Bailey, *Lives in Peril*, p. 178.

199. Sampson, *International Seafarers*, p. 45.

200. ITF, *Seafarers' Bulletin*, 2019.

201. For a descriptive history, see Chapter 14 of ITF, *Solidarity: The first 100 Years of the International Transport Workers' Federation*, London: Pluto, 1996.

202. UNCLOS (1982), Article 91(1), and the prior Convention on the High Seas (1958), Article 5(1), each specify, 'There must exist a genuine link between the State and the ship'. But there is no consensus on what this link means or, in turn, its consequences in law. See Robin R. Churchill with Christopher Hedley (2000), 'The Meaning of the "Genuine Link" Requirement in Relation to the Nationality of Ships', study prepared for the International Transport Workers' Federation. The political/industrial distinction draws from Heather Leggate McLaughlin, 'Seafarers and Seafaring', in Wayne K. Talley and Wayne K. Talley (eds.), *The Blackwell Companion to Maritime Economics*, John Wiley & Sons, 2012, pp.321–332.

203. Lillie, 'Global Collective Bargaining'.

204. Nathan Lillie, 'Union Networks and Global Unionism in Maritime Shipping', *Industrial Relations*, Vol. 60, No. 1, 2005, pp. 88–109.

205. Lillie, 'Global Collective Bargaining', pp. 63–64.

206. 'ITF Uniform Total Crew Cost Collective Bargaining Agreement for Crews on Flag of Convenience Ships, 1 January 2019–2020'. This is the most numerous of the various types of ITF agreement. For examples see itfseafarers. org, last accessed 26 April 2019.

207. *ITF Seafarers Bulletin*, 2017, p. 4; 2018, p. 4; 2019, p. 5.

208. For example, some open registries *reduced* the number of ITF agreements between 2000 and 2001, e.g. Panama from 34 per cent to 27.6 per cent, Liberia from 54 per cent to 40.7 per cent, and Vanuatu from 15 per cent to 10.5 per cent. DeSombre, *Flagging Standards*, Appendix F.

209. Personal communication, ITF representative, December 2014; Peter Turnbull, 'The War on Europe's Waterfront: Repertoires of Power in the Port Transport Industry', *British Journal of Industrial Relations*, Vol. 44, No. 2, 2006, pp. 305–326; Katy Fox-Hodess, '(Re-)Locating the Local and National in the Global: Multi-scalar Political Alignment in Transnational European Dockworker Union Campaigns', *British Journal of Industrial Relations*, Vol. 55, No. 3, 2017, pp. 626–647.

210. This discussion of the MLC benefited from a collective reading by the London Sea Reading group, particularly the legal interpretations of Stephanie Jones and Stewart Motha.

211. Sampson, *International Seafarers*.

212. It also prohibits the practice noted above of negative listing of seafarers by crew agents.

213. For example, some seek to explain the internationalisation of the firm as a divide-and-rule strategy vis-à-vis labour: James Peoples and Roger Sugden, 'Divide and Rule by Transnational Corporations', in Christos N. Pitelis and Roger Sugden (eds.), *The Nature of the Transnational Firm*, 2nd edn, London: Routledge, 2001, pp. 174–192.

214. ILO, 'Database on Reported Incidents of Abandonment of Seafarers', ilo.org, last updated 26 April 2019.

215. Fischer, 'Labour Regimes', drawing on Cindi Katz, *Growing*

Up Global: Economic Restructuring and Children's Everyday Lives, Minneapolis: University of Minnesota Press, 2004.
216. Sampson, *International Seafarers*, p. 79.

4. Appropriation

1. There is, of course, huge geographical variation in consumption patterns: on the one hand, in 2015 China accounted for 38 per cent of the total (at around forty-one kilogrammes per capita) and some Pacific islands were at over fifty kilogrammes per capita, while on the other hand, some landlocked countries in Africa and Central Asia were just above two kilogrammes per capita. FAO, *The State of World Fisheries and Aquaculture 2018*, Rome: Food and Agriculture Organization of the United Nations, 2018.
2. FAO, *The State of World Fisheries and Aquaculture 2010*, Rome: Food and Agricultural Organization, 2010; World Bank, *The Hidden Harvests: The Global Contribution of Capture Fisheries*, Washington, DC: World Bank, 2010, p. 4. This number rises to around 260 million when including small-scale fishers and indirect jobs. Lydia C. L. Teh and U. R. Sumaila, 'Contribution of Marine Fisheries to Worldwide Employment', *Fish and Fisheries*, Vol. 14, No. 1, 2013, pp. 77–88.
3. Ben Fine, *Marx's Capital*, London: Macmillan, 1984, p. 36.
4. The four firms are Bolton Foods, Dongwon Industries, Princes (Mitsubishi) and Thai Union, which between them dominate European and North American retail markets through the control of multiple canned seafood brands: Calvo, Chicken of the Sea, Rio Mare, Isabel, John West, King Oscar, Mareblu, Nostromo, Palmera, Parmentier, Petit Navire, Princes, Saupiquet, Starkist and Vier Diamanten. See Elizabeth Havice and Liam Campling, *Corporate Dynamics in the Shelf-Stable Tuna Industry*, Honiara: Pacific Islands Forum Fisheries Agency, 2018.
5. IntraFish Business Intelligence, *The World's Top Seafood Companies*, Bergen: IntraFish, 2019.
6. FAO, *State of World Fisheries 2018*.

7. Stefano B. Longo, Rebecca Clausen and Brett Clark, *The Tragedy of the Commodity: Oceans, Fisheries, and Aquaculture*, New Brunswick, NJ: Rutgers University Press, 2015, p. 164.
8. Marx, *Capital*, Volume 1, p. 133. See also Malm, *The Progress of This Storm*, Chapter 5. This is *not* to argue that humans cannot so profoundly affect nature as to transform biological or physical systems. See Chapter 6, 'Offshore', for discussion of the oceanic dimensions of contemporary climate change.
9. This draws on a neat turn of phrase coined by William M. Tsutsui, 'The Pelagic Empire: Reconsidering Japanese Expansion', in Ian Jared Miller, Julia Adeney Thomas and Brett L. Walker (eds.), *Japan at Nature's Edge: The Environmental Context of a Global Power*, Honolulu: University of Hawaii Press, 2013. On marine epistemic communities, see Peter M. Haas, *Saving the Mediterranean: The Politics of International Environmental Cooperation*, Political Economy of International Change, New York: Columbia University Press, 1990.
10. Jason W. Moore, 'Nature in the Limits to Capital (and Vice Versa)', *Radical Philosophy*, Vol. 193, 2015, p. 13.
11. Elena Baglioni and Liam Campling, 'Natural Resource Industries as Global Value Chains: Frontiers, Fetishism, Labour and the State', *Environment and Planning A*, Vol. 49, No. 11, 2017, pp. 2437–2456; Noel Castree, 'Commodifying What Nature?', *Progress in Human Geography*, Vol. 27, No. 3, 2003, pp. 273–297.
12. Teh and Sumaila, 'Contribution of Marine Fisheries'.
13. The following draws from multiple observations in tuna canneries in Papua New Guinea, Japan, Thailand and the USA in 2006 and Seychelles in 2014.
14. Sidney Mintz, *Sweetness and Power: The Place of Sugar in Modern History*, London: Penguin, 1986. The early impetus for commercial processing was contracts from the French Navy supplied by a small factory attached to Appert's house, but because he used glass containers there were limits to their durability during rough periods at sea.
15. Darian Warne, *Manual on Fish Canning* (FAO Fisheries Technical Paper 285), Rome: FAO, 1988, Section 1.1; Sue

Shephard, *Pickled, Potted and Canned: How the Art and Science of Food Preserving Changed the World*, London: Simon & Schuster, 2000, p. 231; N. D. Jarvis, 'Curing and Canning of Fishery Products: A History', *Marine Fisheries Review*, Vol. 50, No. 4, 1988, pp. 180–185.

16. Shephard, *Pickled, Potted and Canned*, pp. 233, 236, 241–242, 243.

17. João Ferreira Dias and Patrice Guillotreau, 'Fish Canning Industries of France and Portugal: Life Histories', *Economia Global e Gestão*, Vol. X, No. 2, 2005, pp. 65–66.

18. Richard White, *The Organic Machine: The Remaking of the Columbia River*, New York: Hill and Wang, 1995.

19. Alicja Muszynski, *Cheap Wage Labour: Race and Gender in the Fisheries of British Columbia*, London: McGill-Queen's University Press, 1996, p. 13.

20. Susanne Freidberg, *Fresh: A Perishable History*, Cambridge, MA: Harvard University Press, 2009, p. 243.

21. Muszynski, *Cheap Wage Labour*, p. 14.

22. White, *The Organic Machine*; Freidberg, *Fresh*.

23. Multiple interviews, industry representatives, 2006, 2007 and 2014. See also Adrian Carril Diaz, 'Technological Developments in Tuna Canning and Processing', in S. Subasinghe and Sudari Pawiro (eds.), *Global Tuna Industry Situation and Outlook: Resources, Production & Marketing Trends and Technological Issues*, Kuala Lumpur: INFOFISH, 2002, p. 143.

24. Havice and Campling, *Corporate Dynamics*, pp. 14–15.

25. Paul K. Gellert, 'Renegotiating a Timber Commodity Chain: Lessons from Indonesia on the Political Construction of Global Commodity Chains', *Sociological Forum*, Vol. 18, No. 1, 2003, pp. 53–84; Gavin Bridge, 'Global Production Networks and the Extractive Sector: Governing Resource-Based Development', *Journal of Economic Geography*, Vol. 8, No. 3, 2008, pp. 389–419; and Liam Campling, 'The Tuna "Commodity Frontier": Business Strategies and Environment in the Industrial Tuna Fisheries of the Western Indian Ocean', *Journal of Agrarian Change*, Vol. 12, Nos. 2–3, 2012, pp. 252–278.

26. FAO, *State of World Fisheries 2018*, pp. 10, 41.

27. IOTC, *Report of the Sixth Session of the Indian Ocean Tuna*

Commission Victoria, Seychelles, 10–14 December 2001, Victoria: IOTC, 2002, p. 62; John Hampton and Peter Williams, *The Western and Central Pacific Tuna Fishery: 2001 Overview and Status of Stocks* (Tuna Fisheries Assessment Report No. 4), Oceanic Fisheries Programme, Noumea: Secretariat of the Pacific Community, 2003, p. 35; Stefano Longo and Brett Clark, 'The Commodification of Bluefin Tuna: The Historical Transformation of the Mediterranean Fishery', *Journal of Agrarian Change*, Vol. 12, Nos. 2–3, 2012, pp. 204–226; Department of the Environment, '*Thunnus maccoyii*', in *Species Profile and Threats Database*, Canberra: Department of the Environment, 2019.

28. Edward C. Gallick, *Exclusive Dealing and Vertical Integration: The Efficiency of Contracts in the Tuna Industry* (Bureau of Economics Staff Report to the Federal Trade Commission), Washington, DC: Federal Trade Commission, 1984.

29. Simon Jennings, Michael J. Kaiser and John D. Reynolds, *Marine Fisheries Ecology*, Oxford: Blackwell, 2001.

30. Based on multiple interviews, industry representatives and fisheries specialists, 2005–2007.

31. Elizabeth Havice and Liam Campling, 'Where Chain Governance and Environmental Governance Meet: Inter-firm Strategies in the Canned Tuna Global Value Chain', *Economic Geography*, Vol. 93, No. 3, 2017, pp. 292–313.

32. In interviews, US tuna industry executives themselves routinely refer to the 'mom and pop' lines (i.e. low-quality for working-class consumers) of their own product as 'tuna soup' (multiple interviews, 2006). The product also contains hydrolysed protein to 'pack out' the tuna meat, a practice banned in the EU since 2003. Liam Campling, Elizabeth Havice and Vina Ram-Bidesi, *Pacific Island Countries, the Global Tuna Industry and the International Trade Regime*, Honiara: Pacific Islands Forum Fisheries Agency, 2007; and Elizabeth Havice, 'Price-Fixing Saga Nears Conclusion: Bumble Bee Files for Bankruptcy', *FFA Trade and Industry News*, Vol. 12, No. 6 (November–December 2019), p. 6.

33. Theodore Bestor, *Tsukiji: The Fish Market at the Center of the World*, Berkeley, CA: University of California Press, 2004.

34. In 2016, around 60 per cent of all fishery workers in Japan were aged fifty-five and over. MAFF, *The 92nd Statistical Yearbook of [the] Ministry of Agriculture, Forestry and Fisheries*, Tokyo, 2018.

35. Tadashi Yamamoto, 'Current Status of Japan's Tuna Market', in Henri de Saram and N. Krishnasamy (eds.), *Tuna 93 Bangkok: Papers of the 3rd INFOFISH Tuna Trade Conference, 26–28 October, 1993, Bangkok, Thailand,* Kuala Lumpur: INFOFISH, 1993.

36. FAO, *FAO Yearbook: Fishery and Aquaculture Statistics 2016*, Rome: FAO, 2018.

37. Data for 2003. Kazuo Shima and Taro Kawamoto, 'Japanese Market for Sashimi and Non-sashimi Tuna: New Trends and Issues', paper presented at the INFOFISH Tuna conference 2006.

38. Anthony Bergin and Marcus Haward, Japan's *Tuna Fishing Industry: A Setting Sun or a New Dawn?*, New York: Nova Science, 1996 p. 12; Bestor, *Tsukiji*, p. 142.

39. Steve Williams, 'Understanding Japanese Seafood Markets: History and Tradition', *Australian Fisheries*, 1992, p. 35.

40. Liam Campling, Antony Lewis and Mike McCoy, *The Tuna Longline Industry in the Western and Central Pacific Ocean and Its Market Dynamics*, Honiara: Pacific Islands Forum Fisheries Agency, 2017.

41. Peter Makoto Miyake, 'A Brief History of Tuna Fisheries of the World', in William H. Bayliff, Juan Ignacio de Leiva Moreno and Jacek Majkowski (eds.), 'Second Meeting of the Technical Advisory Committee of the FAO Project "Management of Tuna Fishing Capacity: Conservation and Socio-economics"', Madrid, Spain, 15–18 March 2004, *FAO Fisheries Proceedings, No. 2*, Rome: FAO, 2005, pp. 23–50. For example, pre-Second World War annual longline tuna catch was estimated at 4,500 tonnes in the years 1936–1940. See Sidney Shapiro, *The Japanese Long-Line Fishery for Tunas*, Fishery Leaflet 317, Fish and Wildlife Service, United States Department of the Interior, 1950.

42. Miyake, 'A Brief History of Tuna Fisheries'.

43. This discussion draws on A. Domingo, R. Forselledo, P. Miller, S. Jiménez, F. Mas and M. Pons, 'Chapter 3.1.2: Longline', in ICCAT 2006–2016, *ICCAT Manual,*

International Commission for the Conservation of Atlantic Tuna, 2014. FAO, *Research Implications of Adopting the Precautionary Approach to Management of Tuna Fisheries* (FAO Fisheries Circular No. 963), Rome: FAO, 2001; James Joseph, 'The World Tuna Fishery: Status of the Stocks, Management Issues and Outlook for the Future', in S. Subasinghe, S. Pawiro and S. M. Anthonysamy (eds.), *Tuna 2004 Bangkok: 8th INFOFISH World Tuna Trade Conference and Exhibition*, Bangkok: INFOFISH, 2004.

44. In January 2019, the record was broken yet again when a bluefin was auctioned at Tsukiji for US$3 million. For example, Megan Specia, 'Japan's "King of Tuna" Pays Record $3 Million for Bluefin at New Tokyo Fish Market', *New York Times*, 2 January 2019.

45. Statistics Japan, *National Survey of Family Income and Expenditure*, Tokyo: Ministry of Internal Affairs and Communications, 2017. On supermarket power in seafood, see Havice and Campling, 'Where Chain Governance and Environmental Governance Meet'.

46. Campling, Lewis and McCoy, *The Tuna Longline Industry*.

47. Huxley was chair of Britain's Sea Fisheries Commission (1863–1866) and inspector of fisheries (1881–85). T. H. Huxley, Inaugural Address: Fisheries Exhibition, London (1883), available at mathcs.clarku.edu.

48. Jennifer Hubbard, 'In the Wake of Politics: The Political and Economic Construction of Fisheries Biology, 1860–1970', *Isis*, Vol. 105, No. 2, 2014, pp. 367–368. See also Madhuri Ramesh and Naveen Namboothri, 'A Myth and Its Manifold Effects: Maximum Sustainable Yield', *Economic and Political Weekly*, Vol. 53, No. 41, 2018, pp. 58–63.

49. As cited by August Felando, 'U.S. Tuna Fleet Ventures in the Pacific Islands', in David Doulman (ed.), *Tuna Issues and Perspectives in the Pacific Islands Region*, Honolulu: East–West Center, 1987, pp. 103–104, 95–96.

50. Jennifer Hubbard, 'Mediating the North Atlantic Environment: Fisheries Biologists, Technology, and Marine Spaces', *Environmental History*, Vol. 18, No. 1, 2013, p. 90.

51. Jennifer Hubbard, 'Fisheries Biology and the Dismal Science: Economists and the Rational Exploitation of Fisheries for

Social Progress', in Gordon M. Winder (ed.), *Fisheries, Quota Management and Quota Transfer*, Cham: Springer, 2018, pp. 31–61; Liam Campling, Elizabeth Havice and Penny Howard, 'The Political Economy and Ecology of Capture Fisheries: Market Dynamics, Resource Access and Relations of Exploitation and Resistance', *Journal of Agrarian Change*, Vol. 12, Nos. 2–3, 2012, pp. 177–203.

52. The FAO defines 'biological sustainable levels' as 'abundance at or above the level associated with maximum sustainable yield (MSY)' – see below on MSY. FAO, *State of World Fisheries 2018*, pp. 39–40.

53. Half of all primary production is marine, and over 99 per cent of this is already metabolised when it reaches the higher trophic species. Jeppe Kolding, Alida Bundy, Paul A. M. van Zwieten and Michael J. Plank, 'Fisheries: The Inverted Food Pyramid', *ICES Journal of Marine Science*, Vol. 73, No. 6, 2015, pp. 1697–1713.

54. H. Scott Gordon, 'The Economic Theory of a Common Property Resource: The Fishery', *Journal of Political Economy*, Vol. 62, No. 2, 1954, pp. 124–142; Anthony Scott, 'The Fishery: The Objectives of Sole Ownership', *Journal of Political Economy*, Vol. 63, No. 2, 1955, pp. 116–154; and Garrett Hardin, 'The Tragedy of the Commons', *Science*, Vol. 162, No. 3859, 1968, pp. 1243–1248.

55. Hardin, 'The Tragedy of the Commons', p. 1248. For a useful discussion of the contrast between the natural rights and 'conventional' (commons) schools of thought on property, see Franklin Obeng-Odoom, 'Property in the Commons: Origins and Paradigms', *Review of Radical Political Economics*, Vol. 48, No. 1, 2016, pp. 9–19.

56. Bonnie McCay, 'Development Issues in Fisheries as Agrarian Systems', *Culture and Agriculture*, Vol. 11, 1981, pp. 1–8; Daniel W. Bromley, 'The Crisis in Ocean Governance: Conceptual Confusion, Spurious Economics, Political Indifference', *Maritime Studies*, Vol. 6, No. 2, 2008, pp. 7–22; Liam Campling and Elizabeth Havice, 'The Problem of Property in Industrial Fisheries', *Journal of Peasant Studies*, Vol. 41, No. 5, 2014, pp. 707–727.

57. Contrast the powerful arguments of Becky Mansfield, 'Neoliberalism in the Oceans: "Rationalization", Property

Rights, and the Commons Question', *Geoforum*, Vol. 35, No. 3, 2004, pp. 313–326, with the recourse to polemic by Rögnvaldur Hannesson, *The Privatization of the Oceans*, Cambridge, MA: MIT Press, 2004.

58. H. Österblom, J-B. Jouffray, C. Folke, B. Crona, M. Troell, A. Merrie, et al., 'Transnational Corporations as "Keystone Actors" in Marine Ecosystems', *PLoS ONE*, Vol. 10, No. 5, 2015, pp. 1–15.

59. Longo, Clausen and Clark, *The Tragedy of the Commodity*.

60. As are chickens. The question of the sustainability and (il) logics of aquaculture feeding cycles depends entirely upon the species of fish and the use to which it is being put. See, for example, Jillian P. Fry, Nicholas A. Mailloux, David C. Love, Michael C. Milli and Ling Cao, 'Feed Conversion Efficiency in Aquaculture: Do We Measure It Correctly?', *Environmental Research Letters*, Vol. 13, No. 2, 2018, pp. 1–8.

61. Moore, *Capitalism*.

62. Jason W. Moore, '"Amsterdam Is Standing on Norway": Part II. The Global North Atlantic in the Ecological Revolution of the Long Seventeenth Century', *Journal of Agrarian Change*, Vol. 10, No. 2, 2010, p. 219; Moore's framework has some parallels with Ben Fine's work on 'extensive and intensive development', which draws a distinction between 'the extension of existing methods of production on to new lands and the intensive application of capital to land already in use'. Ben Fine, 'Coal, Diamonds and Oil: Toward a Comparative Theory of Mining?', *Review of Political Economy*, Vol. 6, No. 3, 1994, p. 283.

63. Moore, 'Cheap Food & Bad Money', p. 228.

64. Christian Parenti, 'The Environment Making State: Territory, Nature, and Value', *Antipode*, Vol. 47, No. 4, 2015, pp. 829–848.

65. Liam Campling, 'Trade Politics and the Global Production of Canned Tuna', *Marine Policy*, Vol. 69, 2016, pp. 220–228; U. Rashid Sumaila, Vicky Lamb, Frédéric Le Manach, Wilf Swartz and Daniel Pauly, 'Global Fisheries Subsidies: An Updated Estimate', *Marine Policy*, Vol. 69, 2016, pp. 189–193.

66. 'National production system' is used here as a proximate conceptualisation of the inextricable articulations of

'national' industrial fishing and processing capital and European, Japanese and US states; but as we go on to show, each 'system' also contained several commercial tensions and competitive contradictions.

67. See, for example, Shapiro, *The Japanese Long-Line Fishery*.
68. This argument draws on Gary Fields, *Territories of Profit: Communications, Capitalist Development, and the Innovative Enterprises of G. F. Swift and Dell Computer*, Stanford,CA: Stanford University Press, 2004.
69. Fiona McCormack, *Private Oceans: The Enclosure and Marketisation of the Seas*, London: Pluto Press, 2017; Hannesson, *The Privatization of the Oceans*.
70. Gísli Pálsson and Agnar Helgason, 'Figuring Fish and Measuring Men: The Individual Transferable Quota System in the Icelandic Cod Fishery', *Ocean & Coastal Management*, Vol. 28, Nos. 1–3, 1995, p. 120.
71. McCormack, *Private Oceans*, Chapter 1; and M. De Alessi, 'The Political Economy of Fishing Rights and Claims: The Maori Experience in New Zealand', *Journal of Agrarian Change*, Vol. 12, Nos. 2–3, 2012, pp. 390–412.
72. Mansfield, 'Neoliberalism in the Oceans', p. 321.
73. Karl Marx, *Capital: A Critique of Political Economy*, Volume 3 (1894), trans. David Fernbach, New York: Penguin, 1981.
74. What Marx called, respectively, differential rent I and II. For more, see Campling and Havice, 'The Problem of Property'; and Gavin Capps, 'Tribal-Landed Property: The Political Economy of the Bafokeng Chieftaincy, South Africa, 1837–1994', PhD thesis, London School of Economics, 2010. As Romain Felli has shown, ground rent – and its class relation – also has analytical purchase when considering climate change in terms of the partial valuation of 'waste' carbon. See 'On Climate Rent', *Historical Materialism*, Vol. 22, Nos. 3–4, 2014, pp. 251–280.
75. Elizabeth Havice, 'Unsettled Sovereignty and the Sea: Mobilities and More-Than-Territorial Configurations of State Power', *Annals of the American Association of Geographers*, Vol. 108, No. 5, 2018, pp. 1280–1297.
76. 'Efficient' in terms of narrow capitalist logics of producing surplus value, but inefficient in terms of reproducing the life upon which that production is dependent.

77. John F. Richards, *The Unending Frontier: An Environmental History of the Early Modern World*, Berkeley, CA: University of California Press, 2005, p. 591.

78. Callum Roberts, *The Unnatural History of the Sea: The Past and Future of Humanity and Fishing*, London: Gaia, 2007, pp. 108–109.

79. Noel Castree, 'Nature, Economy and the Cultural Politics of Theory: The "War against the Seals" in the Bering Sea, 1870–1911', *Geoforum*, Vol. 28, No. 1, 1997, pp. 1–20.

80. Roberts, *The Unnatural History of the Sea*, p. 97.

81. Richards, *Unending Frontier*, pp. 592–593.

82. Roberts, *The Unnatural History of the Sea*, p. 94; Richards, *Unending Frontier*, pp. 594, 604, 612.

83. Burkard Sievers, 'Before the Surrogate of Motivation: Motivation and the Meaning of Work in the Golden Age of the American Whaling Industry. Part 1', *Critique*, Vol. 37, No. 3, 2009, p. 394.

84. Ibid., p. 398. The harpoon grenades used today by Norwegian and Icelandic whalers reportedly kill the animals instantly, at least 87 per cent (!) of the time. The Japanese equivalent is less efficient. See Egil Ole Øen, 'Killing Efficiency in the Icelandic Fin Whalehunt', report to the Directorate of Fisheries in Iceland, 2015.

85. For an illuminating history of early capitalism through cod, see Mark Kurlansky, *Cod: A Biography of the Fish That Changed the World*, London: Vintage, 1997. See also Roberts, *The Unnatural History of the Sea*, and Richards, *The Unending Frontier*.

86. Dietrich Sahrhage and Johannes Lundbeck, *A History of Fishing*, Berlin and Heidelberg: Springer-Verlag, 1992.

87. This last phrase is from Fields, *Territories of Profit*. Parts of the following discussion were published in Liam Campling and Elizabeth Havice, 'The Global Environmental Politics and Political Economy of Seafood Systems', *Global Environmental Politics*, Vol. 18, No. 2, 2018, pp. 72–92.

88. Kate Barclay, 'Ocean, Empire and Nation: Japanese Fisheries Politics', in Devleena Ghish, Heather Goodall and Stephanie Hemelryk Donald (eds.), *Water, Sovereignty and Borders in Asia and Oceania*, London: Routledge, 2009; Tsutsui, 'The

Pelagic Empire'; Albert W. C. T. Herre, 'Japanese Fisheries and Fish Supplies', *Far Eastern Survey*, Vol. 12, No. 10, 1943, pp. 99–101.

89. Herre, 'Japanese Fisheries'; William G. Beasley, *Japanese Imperialism, 1894–1945*, Oxford: Oxford University Press, 1987.

90. Sozui Sen'ichi writing in the pro-government, English-language quarterly *Contemporary Japan*, as cited by Tsutsui, 'The Pelagic Empire', p. 25.

91. Yoshiaki Matsuda, 'History of Fish Marketing and Trade with Particular Reference to Japan', paper prepared for Tenth Biennial Conference of the International Institute of Fisheries Economics and Trade, 10–14 July 2000, Oregon, USA.

92. John G. Butcher, *The Closing of the Frontier: A History of the Marine Fisheries of Southeast Asia c.1850–2000*, Singapore: Institute of Southeast Asian Studies, 2004, pp. 67–68.

93. Herre, 'Japanese Fisheries'.

94. Matsuda, 'History of Fish Marketing'.

95. David L. Howell, *Capitalism from Within: Economy, Society, and the State in a Japanese Fishery*, Berkeley: University of California Press, 1995.

96. Until their forced break-up under post-war American occupation, the *zaibatsu* dominated Japan's political economy.

97. R. S. Mathieson, 'The Japanese Salmon Fisheries: A Geographic Appraisal', *Economic Geography*, Vol. 34, No. 4, 1958, pp. 352–353.

98. From a select committee's list of fourteen 'Advantages of Consolidation', cited in Howell, *Capitalism from Within*, p. 169.

99. Mathieson, 'Japanese Salmon Fisheries'; Howell, *Capitalism from Within*.

100. Migrant Chinese and Indian workers were in need of a stable supply of protein to feed their bodies labouring to extract tin for European factories, which were in turn producing, among other things, cans for food. Butcher, *The Closing of the Frontier*, pp. 61–63; Corey Ross, 'The Tin Frontier: Mining, Empire, and Environment in Southeast Asia, 1870s–1930s', *Environmental History*, Vol. 19, No. 3, 2014, pp. 454–479.

101. Butcher, *The Closing of the Frontier*, p. 71.
102. Marcus Haward and Anthony Bergin, 'Taiwan's Distant Water Tuna Fisheries', *Marine Policy*, Vol. 24, No. 1, 2000, pp. 33–43; Henry Chen, 'Japan and the Birth of Takao's Fisheries in Nanyo, 1895–1945', *International Journal of Maritime History*, Vol. 20, No. 1, 2008, pp. 133–152; Yun-Hu Yeh, Huan-Sheng Tseng, Dong-Taur Suc and Ching-Hsiewn Ou, 'Taiwan and Japan: A Complex Fisheries Relationship', *Marine Policy*, Vol. 51, January 2015, pp. 293–301.
103. Barclay, 'Ocean, Empire and Nation'.
104. Herre, 'Japanese Fisheries'.
105. David Doulman, 'Distant-Water Fishing Operations and Regional Fisheries Cooperation', in David Doulman (ed.), *The Development of the Tuna Industry in the Pacific Islands Region: An Analysis of Options*, Honolulu: East–West Center, 1987, p. 36.
106. Barclay, *A Japanese Joint Venture*, pp. 144–145.
107. Fred C. Cleaver and Bell M. Shimada, 'Japanese Skipjack Fishing Methods', *Commercial Fisheries Review*, Vol. 12, No. 11, 1950, pp. 1–27.
108. Butcher, *The Closing of the Frontier*, p. 71.
109. N. Fujinami, 'Development of Japan's Tuna Fisheries', in Doulman, *Tuna Issues and Perspectives*, pp. 57–70; Shapiro, 'The Japanese Long-line Fishery'.
110. Santiago Gorostiza and Miquel Ortega Cerdà, '"The Unclaimed Latifundium": The Configuration of the Spanish Fishing Sector under Francoist Autarky, 1939–1951', *Journal of Historical Geography*, Vol. 52, 2016, pp. 26–35.
111. Ana I. Sinde Cantorna, Isabel Diéguez Castillón and Ana Gueimode Canto, 'Spain's Fisheries Sector: From the Birth of Modern Fishing through to the Decade of the Seventies', *Ocean Development & International Law*, Vol. 35, No. 4, 2007, p. 364.
112. The Great Depression and the Second World War also contributed to the dramatic decline of the French sardine and tuna canning industry. See J. Ferreira-Dias and P. Guillotreau, 'Fish Canning Industries of France and Portugal: Life Histories', *Economia Global e Gestão*, Vol. 10, No. 2, 2005, pp. 61–79.
113. Gorostiza, 'The Unclaimed Latifundium'.

114. Roberts, *The Unnatural History of the Sea*, p. 219.

115. Liam Campling and Elizabeth Havice, 'Industrial Development in an Island Economy: US Trade Policy and Canned Tuna Production in American Samoa', *Island Studies Journal*, Vol. 2, No. 2, 2007, pp. 209–228.

116. Paul Antonietti, 'The Tuna Industry in West Africa: Situation and Prospects', in Henri de Saram and N. Krishnasamy (eds.), *Tuna 93 Bangkok: Papers of the 3rd INFOFISH Tuna Trade Conference, 26–28 October, 1993, Bangkok, Thailand*, Kuala Lumpur: INFOFISH, 1993.

117. Steven Rockland, 'The San Diego Tuna Industry and Its Employment Impact on the Local Economy', *Marine Fisheries Review*, Vol. 40, No. 7, 1978, pp. 5–11.

118. Gallick, *Exclusive Dealing*, pp. 7, 103, 107, 126–7 and 117.

119. Jacek Majkowski, 'Precautionary Approach and Tuna Research: Perspective from the 1995 UN Agreement', in P. Cayre and J-Y. Le Gall (eds.), *Tuna Prospects and Strategies for the Indian Ocean*, Paris: Éditions de l'Orstom, 1998, pp. 433–460.

120. For example, in 1981 Heinz bought France's largest canned seafood brand and its factories in France and Africa. For periodisation and detailed discussion, see Liam Campling, 'The EU-Centred Commodity Chain in Canned Tuna and Upgrading in Seychelles', PhD thesis, School of Oriental and African Studies, University of London, 2012.

121. Multiple interviews, Japanese industry representatives, 2006; Salvatore Comitini, 'Japanese Trading Companies: Their Possible Role in Pacific Tuna Fisheries Development', in Doulman, *The Development of the Tuna Industry in the Pacific Islands Region*, p. 265; Marcus Haward and Anthony Bergin, 'The Political Economy of Japanese Distant Water Tuna Fisheries', *Marine Policy*, Vol. 25, No. 2, 2001, pp. 91–101; Shui-Kai Chang, Kun-Yu Liu and Yann-Huei Song, 'Distant Water Fisheries Development and Vessel Monitoring System Implementation in Taiwan: History and Driving Forces', *Marine Policy*, Vol. 34, No. 3, 2010, pp. 541–548.

122. Taiwan Fisheries Agency, *Fisheries of the Republic of China (Taiwan)*, Kaohsiung City, 2015; Fisheries Agency, Council of Agriculture and Overseas Fisheries Development Council, 'Tuna Fisheries Status Report of Chinese Taipei in the

Western and Central Pacific Region', 12th meeting of the WCPFC Scientific Committee, 2016.

123. For example, the USA import price for canned lightmeat tuna dropped from US$30.38 per case in 1981 to US$19.06 in 1985. Robert T. B. Iverson, 'U.S. Tuna Processors', in Doulman, *The Development of the Tuna Industry in the Pacific Islands Region*, p. 282.

124. Jesse M. Floyd, 'U.S. Tuna Import Regulations', in Doulman, *The Development of the Tuna Industry in the Pacific Islands Region*, p. 86.

125. Cantorna, Castillón and Canto, 'Spain's Fisheries Sector'; Liam Campling, 'Stratégies d'accumulation impérialiste de la pêche européenne du thon', *Alternatives sud*, Vol. 24, No. 1, 2017, pp. 133–157.

126. As cited by Felando, 'U.S. Tuna Fleet', p. 96.

127. The shift from icing fish to using frozen brine was a major turning point in extending the commodity frontier as boats could stay at sea for longer. See 'Pole Fishing for Tuna, 1937–1941: An Interview with Edward S. Soltesz', *Journal of San Diego History*, Vol. 37, No. 3, 1991: sandiegohistory.org.

128. As a crew member working US tuna boats in the late 1930s pointed out, this fishing capital quickly used up a central basis of the ecological surplus – the bait fish. 'At that time fishing was becoming scarce. Bait had disappeared from almost everywhere [1940–1941]. We [the tuna fleet] had fished out all the bait and sardines and the anchovies down in Mexico and it was very hard to find bait'. 'Pole Fishing for Tuna'.

129. Carmel Finley, *All the Fish in the Sea: Maximum Sustainable Yield and the Failure of Fisheries Management*, Chicago: The University of Chicago Press, 2011.

130. Proclamation 2667 of 28 September 1946. Truman had reportedly been pushed by Interior Secretary Harold Ickes, who as early as 1943 had suggested to President Roosevelt the possibility of 'availing ourselves fully of the riches of this submerged land'. Cited by Ann L. Hollick, 'Managing the Oceans', *Wilson Quarterly*, Summer 1984, p. 79.

131. Ann L. Hollick, 'U.S. Oceans Policy: The Truman Proclamations', *Virginia Journal of International Law*, Vol. 17, No. 1, 1976, pp. 23–55.

132. Satya Nandan, *The Exclusive Economic Zone: A Historical Perspective*, Rome: FAO, 1987. For a detailed account from a pro-US perspective, see Ann L. Hollick, 'The Roots of U.S. Fisheries Policy', *Ocean Development & International Law*, Vol. 5, No. 1, 1978, pp. 61–105; and Hollick, 'U.S. Oceans Policy'.

133. Proclamation 2668 of 28 September 1946.

134. Finley, *All the Fish in the Sea*.

135. An alternative to MSY is maximum economic yield (MEY), which is generally a more conservative conservation measure as it requires a fishery to 'yield' profit, which requires a heathier population. But both measures are contested because they focus on single stocks (i.e. those of commercial interest), ignoring a population's embeddedness and interactions within an ecosystem.

136. Timothy Cooper, 'Peter Lund Simmonds and the Political Ecology of Waste Utilization in Victorian Britain', *Technology and Culture*, Vol. 52, No. 1, 2011, pp. 21–44.

137. See, for example, P. A. Larkin, 'An Epitaph for the Concept of Maximum Sustainable Yield', *Transactions of the American Fisheries Society*, Vol. 106, No. 1, 1977, pp. 1–11.

138. See, for example, anonymous, *Report of the IOTC Performance Review Panel: January 2009*, Mahé: Indian Ocean Tuna Commission, 2009, p. 24.

139. Imperialism, of course, continued on land, such as when the Cold War got 'hot', most often through proxy wars in decolonisation struggles and post-colonial wars.

140. Vina Ram-Bidesi, 'Domestication of the Tuna Industry in the Pacific Islands: An Analysis of National and Regional Strategies', PhD thesis, Centre for Maritime Policy, University of Wollongong, 2003; Barclay, *A Japanese Joint Venture*, pp. 178–179.

141. C. De Fontaubert and I. Lutchman, *Achieving Sustainable Fisheries: Implementing the New International Legal Regime*, Geneva: IUCN, 2003.

142. Peter Nolan, 'Imperial Archipelagos: China, Western Colonialism and the Law of the Sea', *New Left Review*, Vol. 2, No. 80, 2013, pp. 77–95.

143. Hollick, 'Managing the Oceans'.

144. France's principal OCT EEZs are based in (sub)tropical islands, mainly French Polynesia and New Caledonia in the

376

Pacific; Mayotte and Réunion in the Indian Ocean; and French Guiana, Guadeloupe and Martinique in the Caribbean.

145. Nolan, 'Imperial Archipelagos'.

146. Rachel A. Schurman, 'Tuna Dreams: Resource Nationalism and the Pacific Islands' Tuna Industry', *Development and Change*, Vol. 29, No. 1, 1998, pp. 107–136.

147. Arvid Pardo and Elisabeth Mann Borgese, *The New International Economic Order and the Law of the Sea*, Msida: International Ocean Institute, Royal University of Malta, 1976; Hollick, 'Managing the Oceans'; James Joseph, 'The Management of Highly Migratory Species: Some Important Concepts', *Marine Policy*, Vol. 1, No. 4, 1977, p. 280.

148. Giulio Pontecorvo, 'The Enclosure of the Marine Commons: Adjustment and Redistribution in World Fisheries', *Marine Policy*, Vol. 12, No. 4, 1988, pp. 361–372; Tony Loftas, 'FAO's EEZ Programme: Assisting a New Era in Fisheries', *Marine Policy*, Vol. 5, No. 3, 1981, pp. 229–239.

149. Campling and Havice, 'The Problem of Property'.

150. Ifremer, *Evaluation of the Fisheries Agreements Concluded by the European Community: Summary Report*, Community Contract No 97/S 240-152919, 1999; Michael Earle, 'Paying for Unsustainable Fisheries: Where the European Union Spends Its Money', in D. M. Lavigne (ed.), *Gaining Ground: In Pursuit of Ecological Sustainability*, International Fund for Animal Welfare and University of Limerick, 2006, pp. 227–242; S. F. Walmsley, C. Barnes, I. Payne and C. Howard, *Comparative Study of the Impact of Fisheries Partnership Agreements: Technical Report*, London: MRAG, CRE and NRI, 2007.

151. Vlad M. Kaczynski and David L. Fluharty, 'European Policies in West Africa: Who Benefits from Fisheries Agreements?', *Marine Policy*, Vol. 26, No. 2, 2002, pp. 75–93; Campling, 'EU-Centred Commodity Chain'; Frédéric Le Manach, Mialy Andriamahefazafy, Sarah Harper, Alasdair Harris, Gilles Hosch, Glenn-Mariee Lange, Dirk Zeller and Ussif Rashid Sumaila, 'Who Gets What? Developing a More Equitable Framework for EU Fishing Agreements', *Marine Policy*, Vol. 38, March 2013, pp. 257–266.

152. Japan and Kiribati in 1978; Korea and Kiribati in 1979.
153. Sandra Tarte, *Diplomatic Strategies: The Pacific Islands and Japan* (Pacific Economic Papers No. 269), Canberra: Australia–Japan Research Center, 1997; see Elizabeth Havice and Liam Campling, 'Shifting Tides in the Western Central Pacific Ocean Tuna Fishery: The Political Economy of Regulation and Industry Responses', *Global Environmental Politics*, Vol. 10, No. 1, 2010, pp. 89–114.
154. Roniti Teiwaki, 'Access Agreements in the South Pacific: Kiribati and the Distant Water Fishing Nations 1979–1986', *Marine Policy*, Vol. 11, No. 4, 1987, p. 279; Alessandro Bonanno and Douglas Constance, *Caught in the Net: The Global Tuna Industry, Environmentalism and the State*, Lawrence: University Press of Kansas, 1996, p. 132.
155. Elizabeth Havice, 'The Structure of Tuna Access Agreements in the Western and Central Pacific Ocean: Lessons for Vessel Day Scheme Planning', *Marine Policy*, Vol. 34, No. 5, 2010, pp. 979–987.
156. In practice, if not quite in international law, as the USA remains one of the few non-signatories of UNCLOS.
157. Gavin Capps, 'Tribal-Landed Property: The Value of the Chieftaincy in Contemporary Africa', *Journal of Agrarian Change*, Vol. 16, No. 3, 2016, pp. 452–477.
158. Mansfield, 'Neoliberalism in the Oceans', p. 322; Henning Melber, 'Of Big Fish & Small Fry: The Fishing Industry in Namibia', *Review of African Political Economy*, Vol. 30, No. 95, 2003, pp. 142–149; Elizabeth Havice and Kristin Reed, 'Fishing for Development? Tuna Resource Access and Industrial Change in Papua New Guinea', *Journal of Agrarian Change*, Vol. 12, Nos. 2–3, 2012, pp. 413–435.
159. This argument draws on Gavin Capps, 'A Bourgeois Reform with Social Justice? The Contradictions of the Minerals Development Bill and Black Economic Empowerment in the South African Platinum Mining Industry', *Review of African Political Economy*, Vol. 39, No. 132, 2012, pp. 315–333.
160. Ibid., p. 318. See also Fernando Coronil's seminal theorisation in his *The Magical State: Nature, Money and Modernity in Venezuela*, Chicago and London: The University of Chicago Press, 1997.
161. Nolan, 'Imperial Archipelagos'.

162. Opinions of [China's] Ministry of Agriculture Regarding the Promotion of the Sustainable and Healthy Development of the Distant Water Fishing Industry (Nongyufa [2012] No. 30), 11 July 2012. Reproduced and translated in Delegation of the United States to the WTO, 'Request from the United States to China Pursuant to Article 25.10 of the Agreement' [on Subsidies and Countervailing Measures], 15 April 2016.

163. Marine-capture fisheries statistics are generally very poor, and China's in particular, which for reasons of domestic politics and secrecy overinflate catch in its EEZ and underreport outside it. See D. Pauly, D. Belhabib, R. Blomeyer, W. W. W. L. Cheung, A. M. Cisneros-Montemayor, D. Copeland, S. Harper, V. W. Y. Lam, Y. Mai, F. Le Manach, H. Österblom, K. M. Mok, L. van der Meer, A. Sanz, S. Shon, U. R. Sumaila, W. Swartz, R. Watson, Y. Zhai and D. Zeller, 'China's Distant-Water Fisheries in the 21st century', *Fish and Fisheries*, Vol. 15, No. 3, 2014, pp. 474–488.

164. Ibid.; FAO Fisheries and Aquaculture Information and Statistics Branch online query, accessed 31 January 2019.

165. Central Committee of the Communist Party of China, *The 13th Five-Year Plan for Economic and Social Development of the People's Republic of China (2016–2020)*, Beijing: Compilation and Translation Bureau, 2016.

166. Liam Campling and Elizabeth Havice, 'Mainstreaming Environment and Development at the WTO? Fisheries Subsidies, the Politics of Rule-Making and the Elusive "Triple Win"', *Environment and Planning A*, Vol. 45, No. 4, 2013, pp. 835–852.

167. Author observations of fisheries subsidies negotiations at the WTO, Geneva, 2018 and 2019.

168. Enric Sala, Juan Mayorga, Christopher Costello, David Kroodsma, Maria L. D. Palomares, Daniel Pauly, U. Rashid Sumaila and Dirk Zeller, 'The Economics of Fishing the High Seas', *Science Advances*, Vol. 4, No. 6, 2018, pp. 1–13.

169. China's Ministry of Agriculture 2012; Tabitha Grace Mallory, 'China in Distant Water Fisheries: Evolving Policies and Implications', *Marine Policy*, Vol. 38, 2013, pp. 99–108.

170. Mark Godfrey, 'China Increasingly Dominating Fishing Rule-Making', *SeafoodSource*, 13 December 2018.

5. Logistics

1. Frank Broeze, 'Underdevelopment and Dependency: Maritime India during the Raj', *Modern Asian Studies*, Vol. 18, No. 3, 1984, p. 429.

2. UNCTAD, *Review of Maritime Transport 2016*, Geneva: UNCTAD, 2016; UNCTAD, *Review of Maritime Transport 2017*, Geneva: UNCTAD, 2017.

3. Karl Marx, *Grundrisse*, trans. Martin Nicolaus, Harmondsworth: Penguin, 1973, pp. 536, 538.

4. Karl Marx, *Capital: A Critique of Political Economy*, Volume 1, trans. Ben Fowkes, London: Penguin, 1976, pp. 198–208; Karl Marx, *Capital: A Critique of Political Economy*, Volume 2, trans. David Fernbach, London: Penguin, 1992, pp. 123–124.

5. Niccolò Cuppini and Mattia Frapporti, 'Logistics Genealogies: A Dialogue with Stefano Harney', *Social Text*, Vol. 36, No. 3, 2018, p. 95.

6. This does not mean that capital will always accumulate at a greater rate as a result of mergers and acquisitions (M & As) as the process is often speculative and can lead to the destruction of value by (and to) the supposed expropriator. Over 70 per cent of M & As fail on these terms. Robert F. Bruner, 'Does M & A Pay? A Survey of Evidence for the Decision-Maker', *Journal of Applied Finance*, Vol. 12, No. 1, 2002, pp. 48–68.

7. Marx *Capital*, Volume 1, pp. 777, 780.

8. UNCTAD, *Trade and Development Report 2018*, Geneva: UNCTAD, 2018, Chapter 2; Sean Starrs, 'American Economic Power Hasn't Declined – It Globalized! Summoning the Data and Taking Globalization Seriously', *International Studies Quarterly*, Vol. 57, No. 4, 2013, pp. 817–830.

9. Karl Marx, *Capital: A Critique of Political Economy*, Volume 3 (1894), trans. David Fernbach. New York: Penguin, 1981; Brett Christophers, *The Great Leveller: Capitalism and Competition in the Court of Law*, Cambridge, MA: Harvard University Press, 2016.

10. Michael A. Lebowitz, *Beyond Capital: Marx's Political Economy of the Working Class*, Basingstoke: Palgrave Macmillan, 2003; James Peoples and Roger Sugden, 'Divide

and Rule by Transnational Corporations', in C. N. Pitelis and R. Sugden (eds.), *The Nature of the Transnational Firm*, 2nd edn, London: Routledge, 2001.

11. And, as such, shipping was a prominent indicator that the 2007 crisis was becoming a global economic one when in 2008 ocean-going freight rates had dropped, sharply. For example, see Izabella Kaminska, 'Who's in the Wake for Shipping Losses?', *Financial Times*, 4 November, 2008.

12. The thorny question of measure makes it difficult to compare across the different segments of contemporary shipping. Tonnage is used to measure cargo that has a mass equivalent to or higher than seawater, *and* that can be packed, lifted or pumped into a hold with relative ease and efficiency. Here, the *deadweight tonnage* of the vessel is the principal measure of capacity, e.g. tankers and dry-bulk carriers. For lighter goods such as cotton or timber, volume is imperative, and thus *cargo-hold volume* is the principal measure. More awkward cargos such as vehicles are best measured on a per-unit basis, but often volume is used; and, of course, the mass passenger trades cannot usefully be measured by ton or volume. The twenty-foot equivalent-unit (TEU) container introduces a particularly tricky element: the *average* net weight of the cargo carried in containers is around nine tons per TEU, but because they have a volume of around thirty-three cubic metres, TEU containers can hold up to twenty-five tons of grain or thirty-three tons of coal or iron ore. Given that such a wide range of goods are carried now in containers because of the ease of loading/unloading relatively small volumes at a wider variety of ports, weight-based estimates of the container trade grossly underestimate the productivity of the industry. See Yrjö Kaukiainen, 'Growth, Diversification and Globalization: Main Trends in International Shipping since 1850', in Fischer and Lange, *International Merchant Shipping in the Nineteenth and Twentieth Centuries*, p. 8.

13. This is also the case in the Fordist labour process – regularity and reliability are the premium, not strength or speed. See Paul Meadows, 'The Leadership of an Industrial Society', *American Journal of Economics and Sociology*, Vol. 7, No. 2, 1948, pp. 205–214.

14. See, for example, Stopford, *Maritime Economics*, p. 54.
15. Kaukiainen, 'International Shipping since 1850', p. 55; Neil M. Coe, 'Missing Links: Logistics, Governance and Upgrading in a Shifting Global Economy', *Review of International Political Economy*, Vol. 21, No. 1, 2014, pp. 224–256.
16. Marx, *Capital*, Volume 1, pp. 135, 226–227, emphasis added.
17. As Neil Coe has pointed out, there is a 'lack of studies that focus upon the logistics *industry*, that is, as a complex of profit-seeking, strategic actors, rather than as simple providers of an important production function'. Coe, 'Missing Links', p. 235 (original emphasis).
18. Lewis R. Fischer and Even Lange, 'Introduction', in Fischer and Lange, *International Merchant Shipping in the Nineteenth and Twentieth Centuries*, p. viii.
19. Stopford, *Maritime Economics*, pp. 22, 107, and others make clear that while independent shipowners existed in the late 1700s, selling transport to cargo owners, this was not yet the dominant tendency.
20. Luigi Pascali, 'The Wind of Change: Maritime Technology, Trade, and Economic Development', *American Economic Review*, Vol. 107, No. 9, 2017, pp. 2821–2854.
21. Stopford, *Maritime Economics*, p. 23 and Table 1.2.
22. Deborah Cowen, *The Deadly Life of Logistics: Mapping Violence in Global Trade*, Minneapolis: University of Minnesota Press, 2014.
23. See Morriss, *The Foundations of British Maritime Ascendancy*.
24. There were (and are) important links between the military, the merchant navy and the configurations of the world economy. From merchant mariners and boats acting as reserve crew and infrastructure for bolstering national naval forces in times of war, to the centrality of state naval power in the regional and global ordering of capitalist empires.
25. Yrjö Kaukiainen, 'International Freight Markets in the 1830s and 1840s: The Experience of a Major Finnish Shipowner' in Starkey and Harlaftis, *Global Markets*, pp. 6–7; William D. Wray, 'National Alliances and Global Webs: The Internationalization of Japanese Shipping', in ibid., p. 100.
26. Edna Bonancich and Jake B. Wilson, *Getting the Goods:*

Ports, Labor, and the Logistics Revolution, Ithaca, NY and London: Cornell University Press, 2008.

27. Stopford, *Maritime Economics*.

28. Jochen Bläsing and Ton Langenhuyzen, 'Dutch Sea Transport in Transition: The German Hinterland as Catalyst, 1850–1914', in Starkey and Harlaftis, *Global Markets*, p. 103; A. D. Couper, *Geography of Sea Transport*, London: Hutchinson & Co., 1972, p. 45.

29. Although not without technical teething troubles and resistance from port workers. See Adrian Jarvis, 'The Nineteenth-Century Roots of Globalization: Some Technological Considerations', in Starkey and Harlaftis, *Global Markets*, pp. 217–237.

30. John Armstrong, 'The Crewing of British Coastal Colliers, 1870–1914', *Great Circle*, Vol. 20, No. 2, 1998, pp. 73–89.

31. William J. Hausman, 'The English Coastal Coal Trade, 1691–1910: How Rapid Was Productivity Growth?', *Economic History Review*, Vol. 40, No. 4, 1987, pp. 588–596; John Armstrong, 'The English Coastal Coal Trade, 1890–1910: Why Calculate Figures When You Can Collect Them?', *Economic History Review*, Vol. 46, No. 3, 1993, pp. 607–609.

32. Roy Fenton, 'The Introduction of Steam to UK Coastal Bulk Trades: A Technological and Commercial Assessment', *International Journal of Maritime History*, Vol. 22, No. 2, 2008, pp. 175–200.

33. Edward W. Sloan, 'The First (and Very Secret) International Steamship Cartel, 1850–1856', in Starkey and Harlaftis, *Global Markets*, p. 35.

34. Bläsing and Langenhuyzen, 'Dutch Sea Transport'; Stopford, *Maritime Economics*, p. 25.

35. Malm, *The Progress of This Storm*, p. 20. See also Andreas Malm, 'Who Lit This Fire? Approaching the History of the Fossil Economy', *Critical Historical Studies*, Vol. 3, No. 2, 2016, pp. 215–248.

36. Fink, *Sweatshops at Sea*, p. 32; Paine, *The Sea and Civilization*, 2014, p. 528. In terms of the number of vessels, in the 1870s Britain and the USA's combined merchant fleets constituted 82 per cent of the world total, with 580 and 530 boats respectively.

37. Stopford, *Maritime Economics*, p. 112.

38. Kaukiainen, 'International Shipping since 1850', p. 31.
39. Jarvis, 'The Nineteenth-Century Roots of Globalization', pp. 218–219.
40. Bläsing and Langenhuyzen, 'Dutch Sea Transport', p. 108.
41. Nicole Starosielski, *The Undersea Network*, Durham, NC: Duke University Press, 2015; John Tully, 'A Victorian Ecological Disaster: Imperialism, the Telegraph, and Gutta-Percha', *Journal of World History*, Vol. 20, No. 4, 2009, pp. 559–579.
42. Paine, *The Sea and Civilization*, 2014, p. 527; Stopford, *Maritime Economics*, p. 27.
43. Gary Field, *Territories of Profit: Communications, Capitalist Development, and the Innovative Enterprises of G. F. Swift and Dell Computer*, Stanford, CA: Stanford University Press, 2004.
44. Anna Tsing, 'Supply Chains and the Human Condition', *Rethinking Marxism*, Vol. 21, No. 2, 2009, pp. 148–176.
45. Simone M. Müller and Heidi J. S. Tworek, '"The Telegraph and the Bank": On the Interdependence of Global Communications and Capitalism, 1866–1914', *Journal of Global History*, Vol. 10, 2015, pp. 259–283.
46. R. W. D. Boyce, 'Imperial Dreams and National Realities: Britain, Canada and the Struggle for a Pacific Telegraph Cable, 1879–1902', *English Historical Review*, Vol. 115, No. 460, 2000, p. 39.
47. For example, in Britain in 1912, an estimated 37 per cent of tramp companies only owned one or two boats. Stopford, *Maritime Economics*, p. 33.
48. Ibid., pp. 23, 27, 29. For a historical case study of a tramp shipowners' business activities, see Kaukiainen, 'International Freight Markets'.
49. Lars U. Scholl, 'The Global Communications Industry and Its Impact on International Shipping before 1914', in Starkey and Harlaftis, *Global Markets*, p. 212.
50. A history of state subsidies also contributes to explaining the global dominance of Britain's merchant navy, but we do not emphasise it here because in the period under consideration competing capitalist states were similarly lavishing their merchant marine with direct and indirect supports.
51. Sarah Palmer, 'British Shipping from the Late Nineteenth

Century to the Present', in Fischer and Lange (eds) *International Merchant Shipping in the Nineteenth and Twentieth Centuries*, pp. 129–130.

52. Ibid., pp. 129–130.

53. See, for example, Sloan, 'International Steamship Cartel'; and for a snapshot of Britain's nineteenth-century shipping magnates, see Robert Kubicek, 'The Proliferation and Diffusion of Steamship Technology and the Beginnings of "New Imperialism", in Killingray, Lincoln and Rigby, *Maritime Empires*, pp. 102–104.

54. Broeze, 'Militancy and Pragmatism', pp. 179, 175.

55. Leslie Hughes Powell, *The Shipping Federation: A History of the First Sixty Years, 1890–1950*, London: Shipping Federation, 1950, pp. 1–2. 'Enemy brothers' is the term Marx used in his discussion of capitalist association vis-à-vis labour. Marx, *Capital*, Volume 3, p. 362.

56. E. P. Thompson, 'Time, Work-Discipline, and Industrial Capitalism', *Past & Present*, Vol. 38, 1967, p. 60.

57. International Labour Office, *The International Seamen's Code*, Geneva: ILO, 1921, p. 88.

58. Stopford, *Maritime Economics*, p. 194.

59. Freda Harcourt, *Flagships of Imperialism: The P&O Company and the Politics of Empire from Its Origins to 1867*, Manchester: Manchester University Press, 2006, p. 12.

60. This estimate is from the 1960s and is drawn from a UK government commission on the shipping industry. Stopford, *Maritime Economics*, p. 65.

61. Harcourt, *Flagships of Imperialism*.

62. Freda Harcourt, 'British Oceanic Mail Contracts in the Age of Steam, 1838–1914', *Journal of Transport History*, Vol. 9, No. 1, 1988, p. 1; Paine, *The Sea and Civilization*, p. 513.

63. Bläsing and Langenhuyzen, 'Dutch Sea Transport', p. 119.

64. Broeze, 'Underdevelopment and Dependency', pp. 441–445.

65. Greenhill, 'Competition or Co-operation', p. 62.

66. Meat slaughtered in British ports commanded higher prices than imported refrigerated meat. C. Knick Harley, 'Steers Afloat: The North Atlantic Meat Trade, Liner Predominance, and Freight Rates, 1870–1913', *Journal of Economic History*, Vol. 68, No. 4, 2008, pp. 1028–1058.

67. Pascali, 'The Wind of Change', p. 2824.

68. For example, a report in 1883 to the Japanese government detailed vast subsidies to shipowners, including US$4.75 million by France, US$3 million by Britain, US$1.54 million by Italy, and US$0.8 million by Austria. Katayama Kunio, 'The Expansion of Japan's Shipping Interests before the Sino-Japanese War', in Starkey and Harlaftis, *Global Markets*, p. 151.

69. Bläsing and Langenhuyzen, 'Dutch Sea Transport', p. 117.

70. Broeze, 'Militancy and Pragmatism' p. 175.

71. Müller and Tworek, 'The Telegraph and the Bank', p. 263.

72. Kunio, 'Japan's Shipping Interests', p. 152; Jarvis, 'The Nineteenth-Century Roots of Globalization', p. 198.

73. Kaukiainen, 'International Shipping since 1850', p. 12; Bläsing and Langenhuyzen, 'Dutch Sea Transport'.

74. Fink, *Sweatshops at Sea*, p. 33.

75. As cited by Edward W. Sloan, 'The Baltic Goes to Washington: Lobbying for a Congressional Steamship Subsidy, 1852', *Northern Mariner/Le marin du nord*, Vol. V, No. 1, 1995, pp. 27, 20.

76. Paine, *The Sea and Civilization*, pp. 514–516.

77. Sloan, 'The Baltic Goes to Washington'.

78. Cited by Ravi Ahuja, 'Mobility and Containment: The Voyages of South Asian Seamen, *c.*1900–1960', *International Review of Social History*, Vol. 51, 2006, p. 124.

79. Daniel Finamore argues that, until the age of steam, intermittent imperial ambitions by Japan's elite were 'penned in or pinned down' by the difficult weather systems between Japan's islands and China and Taiwan. See his 'Introduction: (Maritime) History: Salting the Discourse', in Daniel Finamore (ed.), *Maritime History as World History*, Gainesville: University Press of Florida, 2004, p. 12.

80. An act repeated in the Sino-Japanese War (1894–1895) when the government gifted NYK fourteen steamships.

81. Davies, 'Japan's Modern Shipping', pp. 107–109. NYK was formed with the merger of Mitsubishi Shokai (founded by the Tosa clan) and Kyodo Unyu Kaisha, itself an 1882 state-funded amalgam of several smaller firms. The government forced them to combine because sharp freight competition between them was undermining both businesses.

82. Kunio, 'Japan's Shipping Interests', p. 154; Wray, 'Internationalization of Japanese Shipping', p. 90.
83. Wray, 'Internationalization of Japanese Shipping', p. 87.
84. Davies, 'Japan's Modern Shipping'; Mariko Tatsuki, 'Cooperation and Reorganization on the North–South Routes from Japan in the Interwar Period', in Starkey and Harlaftis, *Global Markets*, pp. 163–194.
85. William D. Wray, 'National Alliances and Global Webs: The Internationalization of Japanese Shipping', in Starkey and Harlaftis, *Global Markets*, pp. 81–102.
86. Robert G. Greenhill, 'Competition or Co-operation in the Global Shipping Industry: The Origins and Impact of the Conference System for British Shipowners before 1914', in Starkey and Harlaftis, *Global Markets*, p. 55.
87. Greenhill, 'Competition or Co-operation'.
88. Graeme J. Milne, 'North of England Shipowners and Their Business Connections in the Nineteenth Century', in Fischer and Lange, *International Merchant Shipping*, p. 149; Greenhill, 'Competition or Co-operation'. A similar practice exists today where large-volume shippers combine to leverage better shipping rates. Author interviews, executives from Heinz and Princes (UK), 2003 and 2007.
89. The distinction between liner and tramp shipping could be porous to the extent that they would often compete for cargo. Nonetheless, Britain's liners overtook its tramps by 1933. See Palmer, 'British Shipping', p. 129; Kaukiainen, 'International Shipping since 1850', pp. 13–14.
90. Yrjö Kaukiainen, 'Journey Costs, Terminal Costs and Ocean Tramp Freights: How the Price of Distance Declined from the 1870s to 2000s', *International Journal of Maritime History*, Vol. 18, No. 2, 2006, pp. 17–64; Saif I. Shah Mohammed and Jeffrey G. Williamson, 'Freight Rates and Productivity Gains in British Tramp Shipping, 1869–1950', *Explorations in Economic History*, Vol. 41, No. 2, 2004, pp. 172–203.
91. Kaukiainen, 'International Shipping since 1850', pp. 10–11, 14.
92. Jarvis, 'The Nineteenth-Century Roots of Globalization', pp. 222–223; Couper, *Geography of Sea Transport*, p. 55.
93. Harriet Friedmann and Philip McMichael, 'Agriculture and the State System: The Rise and Decline of National

Agricultures, 1870 to the Present', *Sociologia Ruralis*, Vol. 29, No. 2, 1989.

94. Palmer, 'British Shipping', Table 1 on p. 134.
95. Stig Tenold, 'Norwegian Shipping in the Twentieth Century', in Fischer and Lange, *International Merchant Shipping*, pp. 57–78; and Gelina Harlaftis, 'The Greek Shipping Sector, 1850–2000', in ibid, pp. 79–104.
96. Kaukiainen, 'International Shipping since 1850', p. 15.
97. Oil tankers are so significant that they are analysed separately to other bulk trades. Kaukiainen, 'International Shipping since 1850', p. 27; Stopford, *Maritime Economics*, p. 66.
98. Kaukiainen, 'International Shipping since 1850', p. 6. See also Stopford, *Maritime Economics*, p. 120.
99. Stopford, *Maritime Economics*, p. 58.
100. Multiple interviews, tuna industry representatives, Seychelles (2013) and Thailand (2015).
101. Gavin Bridge and Michael Bradshaw, 'Making a Global Gas Market: Territoriality and Production Networks in Liquefied Natural Gas', *Economic Geography*, Vol. 93, No. 3, 2017, pp. 215–240.
102. Stopford, *Maritime Economics*, p. 39; Timothy Mitchell, *Carbon Democracy: Political Power in the Age of Oil*, London: Verso, 2011.
103. Jameson W. Doig, *Empire on the Hudson: Entrepreneurial Vision and Political Power at the Port of New York Authority*, New York: Columbia University Press, 2001.
104. Marc Levinson, *The Box: How the Shipping Container Made the World Smaller and the World Economy Bigger*, Princeton, NJ and Oxford: Princeton University Press, 2006.
105. Alan Sekula and Noël Burch, 'The Forgotten Space: Notes for a Film', *New Left Review*, Vol. 69 (May–June 2011), pp. 78–80.
106. Cowen, *The Deadly Life of Logistics*. See also Xiangming Chen, *As Borders Bend: Transnational Spaces on the Pacific Rim*, Oxford: Rowman & Littlefield, 2005.
107. Mitchell, *Carbon Democracy*, pp. 38, 29–31.
108. Kaukiainen, 'International Shipping since 1850', pp. 18–19.
109. J. Strange, 'Oil Tankers, Chemical Tankers and Gas Carriers', in Robert Gardiner (ed.), *The Shipping Revolution: The*

Modern Merchant Ship, London: Conway Maritime Press, 1992, pp. 63–83.

110. For comparison, a typical products carrier leading up to and during the Second World War was only 16,000 deadweight tonnage. See ibid.

111. Starosielski, *The Undersea Network*, pp. 38–43. Starosielski also documents (ibid., pp. 42–43) an international club system of national communications monopolies in the Western world which coordinated, and occasionally blocked, each other's submarine cable networks.

112. Stopford, *Maritime Economics*, p. 38.

113. Paul S. Ciccantell and Stephen Bunker, 'International Inequality in the Age of Globalization: Japanese Economic Ascent and the Restructuring of the Capitalist World-Economy', *Journal of World-Systems Research*, Vol. 8, No. 1, 2002, p. 74; Chalmers Johnson, *MITI and the Japanese Miracle: The Growth of Industrial Policy, 1925–1975*, Stanford, CA: Stanford University Press, 1982; Paul S. Ciccantell and Stephen G. Bunker, 'Japan's Economic Ascent and Its Extraction of Wealth from Its Raw Materials Peripheries', in Paul S. Ciccantell, David A. Smith and Gay Seidman (eds), *Nature, Raw Materials, and Political Economy*, Bingley: Emerald Group, 2005, pp. 187–207.

114. Davies, 'Japan's Modern Shipping', pp. 114–116, 119.

115. UNCTAD, *Maritime Transport 2017*.

116. Davies, 'Japan's Modern Shipping', p. 116.

117. Stopford, *Maritime Economics*, p. 79.

118. Ray Kiely, *Industrialisation and Development: A Comparative Analysis*, London: UCL Press, 1998; George N. Katsiaficas, *Asia's Unknown Uprisings*, Volume 1, *South Korean Social Movements in the 20th Century*, Oakland: PM Press, 2012; Hagen Koo, *Korean Workers: The Culture and Politics of Class Formation*, Cornell: Cornell University Press, 2001.

119. Jim Glassman and Young-Jin Choi, 'The Chaebol and the US military–industrial Complex: Cold War Geopolitical Economy and South Korean Industrialization', *Environment and Planning A*, Vol. 46, 2014, pp. 1160–1180; Kevin Gray, 'The Social and Geopolitical Origins of State Transformation: The Case of South Korea', *New Political Economy*, Vol. 16, No. 3, 2011, pp. 303–322; R. A. Scalapino, 'Economics,

Security, and Northeast Asia', in S. Harris and A. Mack (eds.), *Asia-Pacific Security: The Economics–Politics Nexus*, St Leonards, NSW: Allen & Unwin, 1997; and Richard Stubbs, *Rethinking Asia's Economic Miracle: The Political Economy of War, Prosperity and Crisis*, Basingstoke: Palgrave Macmillan, 2005.

120. For an intellectual history, see Vijay Prashad, *The Darker Nations: A People's History of the Third World*, London: Zed Books, 2007; and for critical reviews of the ideologies and political economy of Third Worldism, see Robert W. Cox, 'Ideologies and the New International Economic Order', *International Organization*, Vol. 33, 1979, pp. 257–300; Andrew Nash, 'Third Worldism', *African Sociological Review*, Vol. 7, No. 1, 2003, pp. 94–116; and Ray Kiely, *The BRICs, US 'Decline' and Global Transformations*, Basingstoke and New York: Palgrave Macmillan, 2015.

121. UNCTAD, *Review of Maritime Transport, 1975*, New York: United Nations, 1977; Susan Strange and Richard Holland, 'International Shipping and the Developing Countries', *World Development*, Vol. 4, No. 3, 1976, pp. 241–251.

122. Lawrence Juda, 'World Shipping, UNCTAD, and the New International Economic Order', *International Organization*, Vol. 35, No. 3, 1981, pp. 493, 497.

123. See, for example, the 1976 Manila Declaration and Programme of Action, adapted by the third ministerial meeting of the Group of 77, cited by Ervin Laszlo, Robert Baker, Elliott Eisenberg and Venkata Raman, *The Objectives of the New International Economic Order*, Oxford: Pergamon Press, 1978; and various proceedings of the United Nations Conference on Trade and Development in the 1970s. Indeed, an ongoing activity of UNCTAD, including since it was made a permanent UN agency by the G77, is to track and analyse this structural problem; see its annual *Review of Maritime Transport*.

124. Convention on a Code of Conduct on Liner Conferences, 1974, United Nations, Articles 12 and 15.

125. John Toye, *Dilemmas of Development: Reflections on the Counter-revolution in Development Theory and Policy*, Oxford: Basil Blackwell, 1987; Lawrence Juda, 'Whither the

UNCTAD Liner Code: The Liner Code Review Conference', *Journal of Maritime Law and Commerce*, Vol. 23, No. 1, 1992, pp. 101–121.

126. Average transport costs represent between 19 and 22 per cent of the value of imports for least-developed countries, landlocked developing countries and small-island developing states, while the world average is around 15 per cent and around 11 per cent for developed countries. UNCTAD, *Maritime Transport 2017*, p. 55.

127. Kaukiainen, 'International Shipping since 1850', p. 21; Stopford, *Maritime Economics*, pp. 125–126.

128. Ray Kiely, *The Neoliberal Paradox*, Cheltenham: Edward Elgar, 2018.

129. John Sheail, 'Torrey Canyon: The Political Dimension', *Journal of Contemporary History*, Vol. 42, No. 3, 2007, pp. 485–504; and Alan E. Boyle, 'Marine Pollution under the Law of the Sea Convention', *American Journal of International Law*, Vol. 79, No. 2, 1985, pp. 347–372. But contrast Sheail's argument with Timothy Cooper and Anna Green, 'The Torrey Canyon Disaster, Everyday Life, and the "Greening" of Britain', *Environmental History*, Vol. 22, January 2017, pp. 101–126. We are not suggesting that international regulation has dealt with the problem, as the infamous 1989 *Exxon Valdez* spill made clear. While oil tankers are now safer, especially since the 2010 requirement that all have double hulls, accidents continue to pollute the seas such as the 2018 *Sanchi* oil tanker collision, where thirty-two crew members died, and which produced the largest volume of marine pollution since the *Deepwater Horizon* in 2010. See https://en.wikipedia. For technical analysis, see K. Terhune, *Tanker Technology: Limitations of Double Hulls*, Sointula, BC: Living Oceans Society, 2011.

130. Strange, 'Oil Tankers'.

131. For example, despite the principle that multipurpose boats could be more profitable given their ability to shift a variety of commodities on inward and outward trips, in practice shipping capital focused on specialised vessels, with multipurpose boats declining in absolute and relative tonnage from 1980 to 2000. Kaukiainen, 'International Shipping since 1850', p. 21.

132. Stopford, *Maritime Economics*, p. 154.
133. UNCTAD, *Maritime Transport*, 2017.
134. Nathan Lillie, *A Global Union for Global Workers: Collective Bargaining and Regulatory Politics in Maritime Shipping*, Abingdon-on-Thames: Routledge, 2006; and DeSombre, *Flagging Standards*.
135. One of the many important details papered over in our account is the relative importance of Scandinavia to the European maritime logistics industries, and for Maersk and Norwegian tankers, to the world. For example, Scandinavian (Denmark, Finland, Norway, Sweden) shipyards built an annual average of around 30 per cent of total ship production in Western Europe through the fifty-one-year period from 1964 to 2014 (Figure 5.2).
136. We emphasise *symbol*. There is nothing automatically neoliberal about the technology of the container; it is more of a question of how it has been used.
137. Alexander Klose, *The Container Principle: How a Box Changes the Way We Think*, Cambridge, MA: MIT Press, 2015, p. 3.
138. In 1986, around 50 per cent of the global movement of TEU was on 'general-cargo' ships. Kaukiainen, 'International Shipping since 1850', pp. 25–26.
139. Stopford, *Maritime Economics*, p. 511.
140. Kaukiainen, 'International Shipping since 1850', p. 26.
141. Andrew Feenberg, *Transforming Technology: A Critical Theory Revisited*, Oxford: Oxford University Press, 2002, p. 15. For a discussion of material 'disposition', see Keller Easterling, *Extrastatecraft: The Power of Infrastructure Space*, London and New York: Verso, 2015.
142. Starosielski, *The Undersea Network*, pp. 54, 45.
143. APEC, *Economic Impact of Submarine Cable Disruptions*, Singapore: Asia-Pacific Economic Cooperation Policy Support Unit, 2013.
144. Kaukiainen, 'International Shipping since 1850', p. 49.
145. Benoit Doessant and Samir Saul, 'Why Are the Major Oil Companies Selling Off Their Fleets? The Case of Total', in Maria Fusaro and Amélia Polónia (eds.), *Maritime History as Global History* (Research in Maritime History No. 43), Liverpool: Liverpool University Press, 2010; Stopford, *Maritime Economics*, p. 79.

146. The freight expenditure estimate is an overestimate as it includes some inland distribution costs. Stopford, *Maritime Economics*, pp. 49 (Table 2.1), 73, 84 (Table 2.8), 80.

147. UNCTAD, *Maritime Transport 2017*.

148. Ibid.

149. Stopford, *Maritime Economics*, pp. 63, 71, 84–87.

150. Jean-Paul Rodrigue, *The Geography of Transport Systems*, 4th edn, New York: Routledge, 2017.

151. Patrick Bond, 'Durban's Contested Port-Petrochemical Complex', in Stefanie Ehmsen and Albert Scharenberg (eds.), *Take the Ports! Contesting Power in Global South Export Hubs*, New York: Rosa Luxemburg Stiftung, 2016, pp. 7–19.

152. Sergio Bologna, 'The Perfect Storm of Logistics', *The Bullet*, 3 October 2016 (originally published in *Il Manifesto*); UNCTAD, *Maritime Transport 2017*.

153. Jonny Jones, 'Hanjin and the Crisis in Shipping', unpublished paper, 2016.

154. Bologna, 'The Perfect Storm'.

155. Kevin Honglin Zhang, 'International Production Networks and Export Performance in Developing Countries: Evidence from China', *Chinese Economy*, Vol. 40, No. 6, 2007, pp. 83–96; Peter Nolan, *Is China Buying the World?*, London: Polity, 2012; Starrs, 'American Economic Power'.

156. The only exception is San Juan, Puerto Rico, which was ranked nineteenth in 2000.

6. Offshore

1. Rupert Neate, 'Cybercrime in the High Seas: The New Threat Facing Billionaire Superyacht Owners', *The Guardian*, 5 May 2017.

2. The latter term is Nicholas Shaxson's, who in his *Treasure Islands: Tax Havens and the Men Who Stole the World*, London: Bodley Head, 2011, arrives at a similar number of tax havens, as do Ronen Palan, Richard Murphy and Christian Chavagneux in their *Tax Havens: How Globalization Really Works*, Ithaca, NY and London: Cornell University Press, 2011.

3. 'The Face of Luxury: First Sneak Peek inside Russian

Oligarch's £360 Million Super Yacht A Shows Chair in the Shape of a Giant Head', *Mail Online*, 6 May 2017, downloaded 3 August 2017.

4. Eurochem Group press release, 'Independent Audit Confirms Reliability of the Surface Water Treatment System Near Phosphorit Plant in Kingisepp, Russia, and Low Phosphorus Levels in the Luga River', 1 October 2015.

5. Ronen Palan, *The Offshore World: Sovereign Markets, Virtual Places, and Nomad Millionaires*, Ithaca, NY and London: Cornell University Press, 2006, p. 2.

6. John Urry, *Offshoring*, Cambridge: Polity, 2014, p. 11.

7. In addition to Urry's layered conceptualisation of offshoring as accelerated 'movement, relocation and concealment ... across borders [in] a world of secrets and sometimes lies', ibid., p. 8, Jamie Peck's *Offshore: Exploring the Worlds of Global Outsourcing*, Oxford: Oxford University Press, 2017, considers the political economy and geography of offshoring in relation to the 1990s boom in the outsourcing of work.

8. As conveyed in William Langewiesche, *The Outlaw Sea: A World of Freedom, Chaos, and Criminality*, New York: North Point Press, 2005.

9. Robert K. Barnhardt, *Chambers Dictionary of Etymology*, Edinburgh and New York: Chambers, 2002.

10. Their secrecy makes the valuation and ranking of offshore financial centres (OFCs) a complicated matter. Multiple international and non-governmental organisations, ranging from the IMF and OECD to Oxfam and the Tax Justice Network, have compiled OFC lists (see the European Parliament Briefing from May 2018, at europarl.europa. eu). We have drawn on the very useful consolidated list offered in Palan, Murphy and Chavagneux, *Tax Havens*. One alternative method has focused on 'offshore-intensity ratio', contrasting *sink-OFCs* such as Cayman, Virgin Islands and Bermuda with 'small domestic economies and large values of foreign assets', and *conduit-OFCs* such as the Netherlands, Ireland and the UK that 'typically have low or zero taxes imposed on the transfer of capital to other countries ... [and] highly developed legal systems that are able to cater to the needs of multinational corporations'. Javier Garcia-Bernardo, Jan Fichtner, Frank W.

394

Takes and Eelke M. Heemskerk, 'Uncovering Offshore Financial Centers: Conduits and Sinks in the Global Corporate Ownership Network', *Scientific Reports*, Vol. 7, July 2017, pp. 1–10.

11. G. Baldacchino, 'Innovative Development Strategies from Non-sovereign Island Jurisdictions? A Global Review of Economic Policy and Governance Practices', *World Development*, Vol. 34, No. 5, 2006, pp. 852–867.

12. K. Dodds and S. A. Royle, 'The Historical Geography of Islands – Introduction: Rethinking Islands', *Journal of Historical Geography*, Vol. 29, No. 4, 2003, pp. 487–498.

13. Gary Burn, *The Re-emergence of Global Finance*, Basingstoke and New York: Palgrave Macmillan, 2006.

14. Marc Augé, *Non-places: An Introduction to Supermodernity*, trans. John Howe, London: Verso, 1995, pp. 110–111.

15. Quoted in William Brittain-Catlin, *Offshore: The Dark Side of the Global Economy*, New York: Farrar, Strauss and Giroux, 2005, p. 24.

16. John R. Gillis, *Islands of the Mind: How the Human Imagination Created the Atlantic World*, Basingstoke: Palgrave Macmillan, 2009.

17. Richard H. Grove, *Green Imperialism: Colonial Expansion, Tropical Island Edens and the Origins of Environmentalism 1600–1860*, Cambridge: Cambridge University Press, 1995.

18. Enrico Nuzzo, 'Le double statut de l'insularité: l'île entre imaginaire et réalité dans la littérature d l'utopie anglaise du XVIIème siècle', in Jean-Claude Marimoutou and Jean-Michel Racault (eds.), *Insularité thématique et représentations*, Saint-Denis: Université de la Réunion, 1992, p. 129.

19. Valerie Hamilton and Martin Parker, *Daniel Defoe and the Bank of England: The Dark Arts of Projectors*, Alresford: Zero Books, 2016, p. 1.

20. Carl Wennerlind, *Casualties of Credit: The English Financial Revolution 1620–1720*, London and Cambridge, MA: Harvard University Press, 2011, p. 198.

21. Cited in ibid., p. 203.

22. Laura Brown, *Fables of Modernity: Literature and Culture in the English Eighteenth Century*, Ithaca, NY and London: Cornell University Press, 2001, p. 63.

23. Malcolm Balen, *A Very English Deceit: The South Sea Bubble*

and the World's First Great Financial Scandal, London: Fourth Estate, 2002, p. 147.

24. Bruno Cousin and Sébastien Chauvin, 'Islanders, Immigrants and Millionaires: The Dynamics of Upper-Class Segregation in St Barts, French West Indies', in Ian Hay (ed.), *Geographies of the Super-rich*, Cheltenham and Northampton, MA: Edward Elgar, 2013.

25. See in particular Mimi Sheller's account of how superstar architect Zaha Hadid's celebration of fluidity, mobility and undulation has been incorporated into the architectural branding of luxury hospitality in the contemporary Caribbean: Mimi Sheller, 'Infrastructures of the Imagined Island: Software, Mobilities and the Architecture of the Caribbean Paradise', *Environment and Planning A*, Vol. 41, No. 6, 2009, pp. 1386–1403.

26. Helen Chislett, 'Just Add Water', in *How to Spend It*, supplement to the *Financial Times*, 17 June 2017.

27. Emma Spence, 'Performing Wealth and Status: Observing Super-yachts and the Super-rich in Monaco', in Iain Hay and Jonathan V. Beaverstock (eds.), *Handbook on Wealth and the Super-rich*, London: Edward Elgar, 2016, pp. 287–301.

28. Rowland Atkinson and Sarah Blandy, 'A Picture of the Floating World: Grounding the Secessionary Affluence of the Residential Cruise Liner', *Antipode: A Radical Journal of Geography*, Vol. 41, No. 1, 2009, pp. 92–110.

29. 'The World: Residences at Sea', aboardtheworld.com, downloaded 23 April 2019.

30. 'The Seasteading Institute: Opening Humanity's Next Frontier', seasteading.org.

31. For a succinct and informative overview, see Christian G. De Vito and Alex Lichtenstein, 'Writing a Global History of Convict Labour', *International Review of Social History*, Vol. 58, No. 2, 2013, pp. 285–325; and also the excellent online resource *Convict Voyages*, convictvoyages.org, directed by Professor Clare Anderson. Technically, transportation is different from banishment, the latter simply involving expulsion overseas, the former incarceration.

32. This strategy could, of course, backfire as island prisons such as the Seychelles would bring together anti-colonial agitators from across the British empire to create a new network of

transnational resistance. See Uma Kothari, 'Contesting Colonial Rule: Politics of Exile in the Indian Ocean', *Geoforum*, Vol. 43, No. 4, 2012, pp. 697–706.

33. 'Discourse Concerning Western Planting', available at nationalhumanitiescenter.org.

34. Peter Rushton, 'Caribbean: Barbadose'd – The Transportation of Convicts', at convictvoyages.org. See also Cynthia Herrup, 'Punishing Pardon: Some Thoughts on the Origins of Penal Transportation', in Simon Devereaux and Paul Griffiths (eds.), *Penal Practice and Culture, 1500–1900*, Basingstoke and New York: Palgrave Macmillan, 2004, pp. 121–137.

35. D. Jordan and M. Walsh, *White Cargo: The Forgotten History of Britain's White Slaves in America*, London: Mainstream Publishing, 2008.

36. Henry Whistler quoted in John Wareing, *Indentured Migration and the Servant Trade from London to America, 1618–1718*, Oxford: Oxford University Press, 2017, p. 29.

37. Gwenda Morgan and Peter Rushton, *Eighteenth-Century Criminal Transportation: The Formation of the Criminal Atlantic*, Basingstoke and New York: Palgrave Macmillan, 2004, p. 4.

38. Clare Anderson, 'Bermuda, 1823–1863', at convictvoyages.org.

39. Anoma Pieris, *Hidden Hands and Divided Landscapes: A Penal History of Singapore's Plural Society*, Honolulu: University of Hawaii Press, 2009.

40. Clare Anderson, 'Sepoys, Servants and Settlers: Convict Transportation in the Indian Ocean, 1787–1945', in Frank Dikötter and Ian Brown (eds.), *Cultures of Confinement*, Ithaca, NY: Cornell University Press, 2007, p. 189.

41. Stephen A. Toth, *Beyond Papillon: French Overseas Penal Colonies, 1854–1952*, Lincoln and London: University of Nebraska Press, 2006, p. 12.

42. Ibid., p. 3.

43. H. Le Chartier quoted in ibid., p. 35.

44. Gerard Hanlon, *The Commercialisation of Accountancy: Flexible Accumulation and the Transformation of the Service Class*, Basingstoke: Palgrave Macmillan, 1994; Chris Jones, Yama Temouria and Alex Cobham, 'Tax Haven Networks and the Role of the Big 4 Accountancy Firms', *Journal of World Business*, Vol. 53, No. 2, 2018, pp. 177–193.

45. See, for instance, Peter Dicken, *Global Shift: Mapping the Changing Contours of the World Economy*, 7th edn, London: Sage, 2014, p. 520.

46. Palan, Murphy and Chavagneux, *Tax Havens*, p. 110.

47. Shaxson, *Treasure Islands*, p. 40.

48. Ibid., p. 16.

49. G. Burn, 'The State, the City and the Euromarkets', *Review of International Political Economy*, Vol. 6, No. 2, 1999, pp. 225–261. See also Chapter 5 of Shaxson, *Treasure Islands*.

50. Burn, 'The State, the City and the Euromarkets', p. 236.

51. Tony Norfield, *The City: London and the Global Power of Finance*, London and New York: Verso, 2016, p. 208.

52. Bill Maurer, 'Islands in the Net: Rewiring Technological and Financial Circuits of the "Offshore" Caribbean', *Studies in Comparative Society and History*, Vol. 43, No. 3, 2001, pp. 467–501.

53. See, for example, J. Rockström et al., 'Planetary Boundaries: Exploring the Safe Operating Space for Humanity', *Ecology and Society*, Vol. 14, No. 2, 2009, p. 32.

54. US Fish & Wildlife Service, Midway Atoll National Wildlife Refuge and Battle of Midway National Memorial, 'Wildlife & Habitat', fws.gov, last accessed 17 April 2019.

55. See respectively Jenna R. Jambeck, Roland Geyer, Chris Wilcox, Theodore R. Siegler, Miriam Perryman, Anthony Andrady, Ramani Narayan and Kara Lavender Law, 'Plastic Waste Inputs from Land into the Ocean', *Science*, Vol. 347, 2015, pp. 768–771; and Marcus Eriksen, Laurent C. M. Lebreton, Henry S. Carson, Martin Thiel, Charles J. Moore, Jose C. Borerro, Francois Galgani, Peter G. Ryan and Julia Reisser, 'Plastic Pollution in the World's Oceans: More than 5 Trillion Plastic Pieces Weighing over 250,000 Tons Afloat at Sea', *PLOS One*, 10 December 2014.

56. Nicola J. Beaumont, Margrethe Aanesen, Melanie C. Austen, Tobias Börger, James R. Clark, Matthew Cole, Tara Hooper, Penelope K. Lindeque, Christine Pascoe, and Kayleigh J. Wyles, 'Global Ecological, Social and Economic Impacts of marine plastic', *Marine Pollution Bulletin*, Vol. 142, 2019, pp. 189–195.

57. Council of the European Union, 'Proposal for a Directive of the European Parliament and of the Council on the Reduction of

the Impact of Certain Plastic Products on the Environment –
Final Compromise Text', COM (2018) 340 final + COR 1 +
ADD 1, Brussels, 18 January 2019. Richard Stafford and Peter
J. S. Jones, 'Ocean Plastic Pollution: A Convenient but
Distracting Truth?', *Marine Policy*, Vol. 103, 2019, pp. 187–191.

58. Rachel Arthur, ' "Bottled Water Is America's Favorite Drink!"
Bottled Water Takes Top Spot in US', *BeverageDaily.com*, 1
June 2018; Rachel Arthur, 'UK Bottled Water Sales Reach
4bn Liters, with "Robust Growth" to Continue',
BeverageDaily.com, 14 March 2019; Met Office, 'Chance of
Summer Heatwaves Now Thirty Times More Likely', press
release, 6 December 2018; Mordor Intelligence, *Global
Bottled Water Market: Growth, Trends, and Forecast (2018–
2023)*, Hyderabad: Gachibowli.

59. Grantly Galland, Ellycia Harrould-Kolieb and Dorothée
Herr, 'The Ocean and Climate Change Policy', *Climate
Policy*, Vol. 12, No. 6, 2012, pp. 764–771.

60. S. Levitus, J. I. Antonov, T. P. Boyer, O. K. Baranova, H. E.
Garcia, R. A. Locarnini, A. V. Mishonov, J. R. Reagan, D.
Seidov, E. S. Yarosh and M. M. Zweng, 'World Ocean Heat
Content and Thermosteric Sea Level Change (0–2000 m),
1955–2010', *Geophysical Research Letters*, Vol. 39, No. 10,
2010, n.p.

61. Andreas Malm, *Fossil Capital: The Rise of Steam Power and
the Roots of Global Warming*, London: Verso, 2016.

62. Christophe Bonneuil and Jean-Baptiste Fressoz, *The Shock
of the Anthropocene: The Earth, History and Us*, trans.
David Fernbach, London: Verso, 2017; Andreas Malm and
Alf Hornborg, 'The Geology of Mankind? A Critique of the
Anthropocene Narrative', *Anthropocene Review*, Vol. 1, No.
1, 2014, pp. 62–69.

63. Moore, *Capitalism*, p. 77.

64. Will Steffen, Wendy Broadgate, Lisa Deutsch, Owen Gaffney
and Cornelia Ludwig, 'The Trajectory of the Anthropocene:
The Great Acceleration', *Anthropocene Review*, Vol. 2, No.
1, 2015, pp. 81–98.

65. Peter J. Gleckler, Paul J. Durack, Ronald J. Stouffer, Gregory
C. Johnson and Chris E. Forest, 'Industrial-Era Global Ocean
Heat Uptake Doubles in Recent Decades', *Nature Climate
Change*, Vol. 6, 2016, p. 391.

66. Over the twenty-five years between 1991 and 2016. Scripps Institution of Oceanography, 'Study: Ocean Warming Detected from Atmospheric Gas Measurements', 1 November 2018. See L. Resplandy, R. F. Keeling, Y. Eddebbar, M. K. Brooks, R. Wang, L. Bopp, M. C. Long, J. P. Dunne, W. Koeve and A. Oschlies, 'Quantification of Ocean Heat Uptake from Changes in Atmospheric O_2 and CO_2 Composition', *Nature*, Vol. 563, October 2018, pp. 105–108.

67. Gleckler et al., 'Industrial-Era Global Ocean Heat Uptake.'

68. Geoffrey K. Vallis, *Climate and the Oceans*, Princeton, NJ and Oxford: Princeton University Press, 2012, p. 185.

69. Jelle Bijma, H. O. Pörtner, C. Yesson and A. D. Rogers, 'Climate Change and the Oceans: What Does the Future Hold?', *Marine Pollution Bulletin*, Vol. 74, No. 2, 2013, pp. 491–552.

70. Jonathan L. Payne, Andrew M. Bush, Noel A. Heim, Matthew L. Knope and Douglas J. McCauley, 'Ecological Selectivity of the Emerging Mass Extinction in the Oceans', *Science*, 16 September 2016, pp. 1284–1286.

71. Stefan Rahmstorf, Jason E. Box, Georg Feulner, Michael E. Mann, Alexander Robinson, Scott Rutherford and Erik J. Schaffernicht, 'Exceptional Twentieth-Century Slowdown in Atlantic Ocean Overturning Circulation', *Nature Climate Change*, Vol. 5, May 2015, pp. 475–480.

72. L. Caesar, S. Rahmstorf, A. Robinson, G. Feulner and V. Saba, 'Observed Fingerprint of a Weakening Atlantic Ocean Overturning Circulation', *Nature*, Vol. 556, April 2018, pp. 191–196.

73. Jonathan Watts, 'Arctic's Strongest Sea Ice Breaks Up for First Time on Record', *The Guardian*, 21 August 2018. At the same time, satellite imaging picked up a polynya – unfrozen water surrounded by sea ice – unprecedented in this region in the winter, caused by an abrupt warming event combined with a reversal of stratospheric winds. G. W. K. Moore, A. Schweiger, J. Zhang and M. Steele, 'What Caused the Remarkable February 2018 North Greenland Polynya?', *Geophysical Research Letters*, Vol. 45, No. 24, 2018, pp. 13342–13350.

74. Their incidence and duration increased by 34 per cent and 17 per cent respectively over the same period. Eric C. J. Oliver et al., 'Longer and More Frequent Marine Heatwaves

over the Past Century', *Nature Communications*, Vol. 9, 2018, p. 1324.

75. Dan A. Smale, Thomas Wernberg, Eric C. J. Oliver and Mads S Thomsen, 'Marine Heatwaves Threaten Global Biodiversity and the Provision of Ecosystem Services', *Nature Climate Change*, Vol. 9, No. 4, 2019, pp. 306–312.

76. IPCC, *Climate Change 2014: Synthesis Report. Contribution of Working Groups I, II and III to the Fifth Assessment Report of the Intergovernmental Panel on Climate Change*, Geneva: IPCC, 2014, pp. 4, 12–13, 16, 41–43.

77. H.-O. Pörtner et al. (eds.), *IPCC Special Report on the Ocean and Cryosphere in a Changing Climate*, Geneva: Intergovernmental Panel on Climate Change, 2019.

78. R. S. Nerem, B. D. Beckley, J. Fasullo, B. D. Hamlington, D. Masters and G. T. Mitchum, 'Climate-Change-Driven Accelerated Sea Level Rise Detected in the Altimeter Era', *PNAS*, Vol. 115, No. 9, 2018, pp. 2022–2025.

79. Nicholas R. Golledge, Elizabeth D. Keller, Natalya Gomez, Kaitlin A. Naughten, Jorge Bernales, Luke D. Trusel and Tamsin L. Edwards, 'Global Environmental Consequences of Twenty-First Century Ice-Sheet Melt', *Nature*, Vol. 566, February 2019, pp. 65–72.

80. NOAA, *Global and Regional Sea Level Rise Scenarios for the United States* (NOAA Technical Report NOS CO-OPS 083), Center for Operational Oceanographic Products and Services, National Ocean Service, National Oceanic and Atmospheric Administration, 2017.

81. Matthias Mengel, Alexander Nauels, Joeri Rogelj and Carl-Friedrich Schleussner, 'Committed Sea-Level Rise under the Paris Agreement and the Legacy of Delayed Mitigation Action', *Nature Communications*, Vol. 9, 2018, p. 601.

82. Barbara Neumann, Athanasios T. Vafeidis, Juliane Zimmermann and Robert J. Nicholls, 'Future Coastal Population Growth and Exposure to Sea-Level Rise and Coastal Flooding: A Global Assessment', *PLoS ONE*, Vol. 10, No. 3, 2015; Robert McLeman, 'Migration and Displacement Risks Due to Mean Sea-Level Rise', *Bulletin of the Atomic Scientists*, Vol. 74, No. 3, 2018, pp. 148–154.

83. Andreas Kopp, 'Transport Cost, Trade and Climate Change', in Regina Asariotis and Hassiba Benamara (eds.), *Maritime*

Transport and the Climate Change Challenge, Abingdon and New York: Earthscan, 2012, pp. 42–57.

84. Tim Stephens and David L. van der Zwaag, 'Polar Oceans Governance: Shifting Seascapes, Hazy Horizons', in Tim Stephens and David L. van der Zwaag (eds.), *Polar Oceans Governance in an Era of Environmental Change*, London: Edward Elgar, 2014, pp. 1–18.

85. Cited in David Leary, 'From Hydrocarbons to Psychrophiles: The "Scramble" for Antarctic and Arctic Resources', in Stephens and Van der Zwaag, *Polar Oceans Governance*, pp. 125–145.

86. Christophe McGlade and Paul Ekins, 'The Geographical Distribution of Fossil Fuels Unused When Limiting Global Warming to 2 °C', *Nature*, Vol. 517, 2015, pp. 187–190.

87. *Assessment 2007: Oil and Gas Activities in the Arctic – Effects and Potential Effects*, Volume 1, Oslo, Arctic Monitoring and Assessment Programme, 2010.

88. David Leary, *Bioprospecting in the Arctic*, Yokohama: UNU-IAS, 2008.

89. Charles Ehler and Fanny Douvere, *Marine Spatial Planning: A Step-by-Step Approach toward Ecosystem-Based Management* (Intergovernmental Oceanographic Commission and Man and the Biosphere Programme, IOC Manual and Guides No. 53, ICAM Dossier No. 6), Paris: UNESCO, 2009. See also John Roff and Mark Zacharias, *Marine Conservation Ecology*, London and Washington, DC: Earthscan, 2011.

90. United Nations Environment World Conservation Monitoring Centre, World Database on Protected Areas, protectedplanet.net, last accessed 17 April 2018.

91. Aichi Biodiversity Targets, 10th Conference of the Parties to the Convention on Biological Diversity (CBD), Aichi, Japan, 11–29 October 2010, cbd.int, last accessed 22 April 2019.

92. P. J. S. Jones and E. M. DeSanto, 'Is the Race for Remote, Very Large Marine Protected Areas (VLMPAs) Taking Us down the Wrong Track?', *Marine Policy*, Vol. 73, 2016, pp. 231–234. See also Tor A. Benjaminsen and Ian Bryceson, 'Conservation, Green/Blue Grabbing and Accumulation by Dispossession in Tanzania', *Journal of Peasant Studies*, Vol. 39, No. 2, 2012, pp. 335–355; and Michael Fabinyi, Wolfram

H. Dressler and Michael D. Pido, 'Moving beyond Financial Value in Seafood Commodity Chains', *Marine Policy*, Vol. 94, 2018, pp. 89–92.

93. Tundi Agardy, *Ocean Zoning: Making Marine Management More Effective*, London and Washington, DC: Earthscan, 2011, p. 34.

94. Marc-Andrej Felix Mallin, 'The Political Geography of Sinking Islands: Climate Change, Blue Economy and the Production of Ocean-Space in Kiribati', PhD thesis, National University of Singapore and King's College London, 2018, p. 247; Jennifer J. Silver and Lisa M. Campbell, 'Conservation, Development and the Blue Frontier: The Republic of Seychelles' Debt Restructuring for Marine Conservation and Climate Adaptation Program', *International Social Science Journal*, 2018, doi.org/10.1111/issj.12156.

95. Mads Barbesgaard, 'Blue Growth: Savior or Ocean Grabbing?', *Journal of Peasant Studies*, Vol. 45, No. 1, 2018, pp. 130–149. See also Peter J. S. Jones, L. M. Lieberknecht and W. Qiu, 'Marine Spatial Planning in Reality: Introduction to Case Studies and Discussion of Findings', *Marine Policy*, Vol. 71, 2016, pp. 256–264.

Conclusion: Terraqueous horizons

1. Principally in G. W. F. Hegel, *Philosophy of History*, trans. J. Sibree, Kitchener, ON: Batoche Books, 1900, available at marxists.org; and Alfred T. Mahan, *The Influence of Sea Power upon History, 1660–1783* (1890), Cambridge: Cambridge University Press, 2005. In the section of his *Philosophy of History* on the 'Geographical Basis of History', Hegel proclaims, 'The sea gives us the idea of the indefinite, the unlimited, and infinite; and in *feeling his own infinite* in that Infinite, man is stimulated and emboldened to stretch beyond the limited: the sea invites man to conquest, and to piratical plunder, but also to honest gain and to commerce . . . This stretching out of the sea beyond the limitations of the land, is wanting to the splendid political edifices of Asiatic States, although they themselves border on the sea – as for example, China. For them the sea

is only the limit, the ceasing of the land; they have no positive relation to it. The activity to which the sea invites, is a
quite peculiar one: thence arises the fact that the coast-
lands almost always separate themselves from the states of
the interior although they are connected with these by a
river. Thus, Holland has severed itself from Germany,
Portugal from Spain.'

2. Peter Padfield, *Maritime Supremacy and the Opening of the
   Western Mind: Naval Campaigns That Shaped the Modern
   World, 1588–1782*, London: Pimlico, 2000.
3. Marcus Rediker, *Outlaws of the Atlantic: Sailors, Pirates, and
   Motley Crews in the Age of Sail*, London: Verso, 2004, pp. 2–3.
4. A phrase attributed to Dwaipayan Bhattacharya. See
   Featherstone, 'Maritime Labour and Subaltern Geographies
   of Internationalism', pp. 11, 15.
5. Eelco J. Rohling, *The Oceans: A Deep History*, Princeton, NJ
   and Oxford: Princeton University Press, 2017, pp. 9–10.
6. Andreas Malm, *The Progress of This Storm: Nature and
   Society in a Warming World*, London: Verso, 2018, p. 5.
7. Rohling, *The Oceans*, p. 194.
8. Ashley Dawson, *Extreme Cities: The Peril and Promise of
   Urban Life in the Age of Climate Change*, London and New
   York: Verso, 2017.
9. Tamson Pietsch, 'The Floating University of 1926', paper
   presented at a workshop on International Relations, Capitalism
   and the Sea: The Historical Sociology of Oceans and
   Inner Seas, Birkbeck College, University of London, 2013.
10. Daniel Finamore and Ghislaine Wood (eds.), *Ocean Liners:
    Speed and Style*, London: V&A Publishing in Association
    with the Peabody Essex Museum, 2018. Quote from museum
    exhibit.
11. Craig J. Calhoun, 'The Class Consciousness of Frequent
    Travelers: Toward a Critique of Actually Existing
    Cosmopolitanism', *South Atlantic Quarterly*, Vol. 101, No.
    4, 2002, pp. 869–897.
12. Alejandro Colás, 'The Infrastructure of the Global Economy:
    The Shipping Container as a Political Artefact', in Daniel
    McCarthy (ed.), *Technology and World Politics: An
    Introduction*, Abingdon: Routledge, 2017, pp. 146–164.
13. Marc Levinson, *The Box: How the Shipping Container Made*

the World Smaller and the World Economy Bigger, Princeton, NJ: Princeton University Press, 2006. See also Alexander Klose, *The Container Principle: How a Box Changes the Way We Think*, Cambridge, MA: MIT Press, 2015.

14. Jason W. Moore and Raj Patel, *A History of the World in Seven Cheap Things*, London and New York: Verso, 2018.

15. As noted in Chapter 3, a great piece of research in this vein is Paul Baker and Jo Stanley, *Hello Sailor! The Hidden History of Gay Life at Sea*, London: Routledge, 2003.

16. Rediker, *Between the Devil and the Deep Blue Sea*, p. 205. See also Dermot Feenan, 'The Birth of the Strike', *Jacobin*, 23 May 2018. Although not as explicitly marine, the French word *grève*, derived etymologically from 'gravel' or 'sand', is named after the Parisian *Place de grève* where unemployed workers gathered.

17. Jasper Bernes, 'Logistics, Counterlogistics, and the Communist Prospect', *Endnotes*, Vol. 3, 2013, n.p., endnotes. org.uk, last accessed 6 May 2019; and Tsing, 'Supply Chains and the Human Condition'.

18. Jake Alimahomed-Wilson and Immanuel Ness (eds.), *Choke Points: Logistics Workers Disrupting the Global Supply Chain*, London: Pluto, 2018.

19. Phil Taylor, Kirsty Newsome, Jennifer Bair and Al Rainnie, 'Putting Labour in Its Place: Labour Process Analysis and Global Value Chains', in Kirsty Newsome, Phil Taylor, Jennifer Bair and Al Rainnie (eds.), *Putting Labour in Its Place: Labour Process Analysis and Global Value Chains*, London: Palgrave, 2015, p. 10.

20. Jeremy Anderson, 'Review of *Choke Points: Logistics Workers Disrupting the Global Supply Chain*, edited by Jake Alimhomed-Wilson and Immanuel Ness. Pluto Press, London, 2018', *British Journal of Industrial Relations*, Vol. 57, No. 2, 2019, pp. 412–414.

21. Bernes, 'Logistics', n.p.

22. Lincoln Paine, *The Sea and Civilization: A Maritime History of the World*, New York: Vintage, 2015, pp. 513, 524, 534.

23. See Alberto Toscano's riposte to Bernes in 'Lineaments of the Logistical State', *Viewpoint Magazine*, 14 September 2014, viewpointmag.com.

24. Bernes, 'Logistics', n.p.

Index

International Dockworkers' Council,
160, 320
International Federation of Ship, Dock
and River Workers, 354n119
International Labour Conference, 110,
229
International Labour Office, 153-4
International Labour Organisation
(ILO), 156-7
international labour regulation, reform
and reaction in, 156-61, 391n129
International Maritime Organisation,
71, 99
International Organization of the
Masters, Mates, and Pilots of
America, 157
International Seabed Authority, 71, 303
International Standards Organisation,
254
International Telegraphic Union, 82, 314
International Transport Workers'
Federation (ITF), 97-8, 139, 148,
158-60, 320, 354n119
In the Heart of the Sea *(film)*, 169
Irish, as foreigners, 350n56
iron ore, 246
Italy, volume of steamships from, 224

James, William, 315
Japan
dry cargo shipping in, 246
fishery workers in, 365n34
foreign crew on ships, 150-1
industrialisation of, 83
neoliberalism in, 253
post-war shipyards in, 246-7
rise of shipping in, 235, 236
rivalry between US and, 203
seafood consumption in, 177
shipbuilding programs in, 83, 246
tie-in ships, 150
trading companies in, 197-8
Tsukiji market, 176-9, 367n44
tuna fishing in, 177-9
war, food, and imperialism, 189-94
as world leader in merchant shipping,
247-8
jeune école strategy, 83
Jidda gap, 28
Johor, as a sovereign principality, 74
joint-stock companies, 33-4, 38-9, 42

Kaiserliche Marine, 83
Kanji, Kato, 86
Kaohsiung, Taiwan, 192

Kaska, James, 104
Khalil, Laleh, 28
Khan, Dada Amir Haider, 19
K Line, 258
Kobayashi Takiji
The Crab Cannery Ship, 108-9, 191
Kontor, 35
Korea Development Bank, 260
Korean War, 89, 245
Kothi, 35
Kraska, James, 89-90
Kuwait, 88
Kyodo Unyu Kaisha, 386n81

labour. *See also* maritime labour regimes
centrality of merchant migration and,
331-2n34
cosmopolitan, 115-29
multinational, 146-56
recruitment to Britain's navies, 131-2,
134-5
Lambert, Andrew, 76, 78
Lane, Thomas, 43
large-volume shippers, 387n88
'lascar articles,' 125
lascars, 126, 127f, 129f, 234, 285,
349n50, 349n51, 349n52
Latin America, 80
Law, John, 276
Law of the Sea, 199-200
Laws of Oleron, 351n84
League of Nations, 289
leasehold empire formula, 90-1
Lefebvre, Henri, 23, 324n3
Lemnitzer, Jan Martin, 81
Lend-Lease Bill (1941), 89
liberal reform, radical resistance and,
136-42
Liberia, 147-8, 150
Limited Liabilities Act (1862), 229
Linebaugh, Peter, 118, 353n111
'line of battle,' 76
liner shipping/industry, 225-6, 228-9,
231-8, 247-8, 257-8, 387n89
lives, 18-23
Lloyd's, 31, 46
Lloyd's News, 40
logistics
accumulation, control and crisis in,
256-63
capitalist competition and liner
shipping, 232-8
in contemporary globalisation
(1950s-2010s), 240-63
continuity and change in, 263-6